QUALITATIVE PSYCHOLOGY

SAGE was founded in 1965 by Sara Miller McCune to support the dissemination of usable knowledge by publishing innovative and high-quality research and teaching content. Today, we publish more than 750 journals, including those of more than 300 learned societies, more than 800 new books per year, and a growing range of library products including archives, data, case studies, reports, conference highlights, and video. SAGE remains majority-owned by our founder, and after Sara's lifetime will become owned by a charitable trust that secures our continued independence.

Los Angeles | London | Washington DC | New Delhi | Singapore

3RD EDITION

QUALITATIVE PSYCHOLOGY

A PRACTICAL GUIDE TO RESEARCH METHODS

EDITED BY

JONATHAN A. SMITH

Los Angeles | London | New Delhi
Singapore | Washington DC | Boston

Los Angeles | London | New Delhi
Singapore | Washington DC

SAGE Publications Ltd
1 Oliver's Yard
55 City Road
London EC1Y 1SP

SAGE Publications Inc.
2455 Teller Road
Thousand Oaks, California 91320

SAGE Publications India Pvt Ltd
B 1/I 1 Mohan Cooperative Industrial Area
Mathura Road
New Delhi 110 044

SAGE Publications Asia-Pacific Pte Ltd
3 Church Street
#10-04 Samsung Hub
Singapore 049483

Editor: Luke Block
Assistant editor: Keri Dickens
Production editor: Imogen Roome
Marketing manager: Alison Borg
Cover design: Wendy Scott
Typeset by: C&M Digitals (P) Ltd, Chennai, India
Printed and bound in Great Britain by Ashford
Colour Press Ltd

Editorial arrangement and Chapter 1 © Jonathan A. Smith 2015
Chapter 2 © Peter Ashworth 2015
Chapter 3 © Jonathan A. Smith and Mike Osborn 2015
Chapter 4 © Kathy Charmaz 2015
Chapter 5 © Michael Murray 2015
Chapter 6 © Paul Drew 2015
Chapter 7 © Carla Willig 2015
Chapter 8 © Sarah Riley and Peter Reason 2015
Chapter 9 © Sue Wilkinson 2015
Chapter 10 © Victoria Clarke, Virginia Braun and Nikki Hayfield 2015
Chapter 11 © Michael Larkin 2015
Chapter 12 © Lucy Yardley 2015

Third edition published 2015

First edition published 2004. Reprinted 2006, twice 2007. Second edition printed 2008. Reprinted 2008, 2009, 2011, 2013, 2014.

Library of Congress Control Number: 2014954995

British Library Cataloguing in Publication data

A catalogue record for this book is available from the British Library

ISBN 978-1-4462-9845-9
ISBN 978-1-4462-9846-6 (pbk)

At SAGE we take sustainability seriously. Most of our products are printed in the UK using FSC papers and boards. When we print overseas we ensure sustainable papers are used as measured by the Egmont grading system. We undertake an annual audit to monitor our sustainability.

Contents

Preface to Third Edition

The guiding principle in preparing this third edition of *Qualitative Psychology* has again been evolution rather than revolution. The book works well, and that is what the feedback also tells us. However, a number of improvements have been made.

This edition has a new chapter on thematic analysis and, consistent with the distinctive feature of the book, I am delighted to have recruited two of the leaders in the development of thematic analysis in psychology, Victoria Clarke and Virginia Braun, to write this chapter along with their colleague Nikki Hayfield.

There is also an additional chapter towards the end of the book, 'Choosing your approach' by ·Michael Larkin. The primary function of the book is presenting clear and accessible guides to doing the different qualitative methodologies. I felt it would be a useful addition to have a chapter which helps the reader (after learning about the different approaches) decide how to choose the right one for a research project they are about to embark on.

A structural improvement has been made to the book. As stated above, one of the book's absolutely distinctive features is that each chapter is written by leading authorities on the approach. And the reader can really gain, therefore, by hearing the voices of experts guide them through the process of using a particular approach. As a useful balance to that, to help the reader navigate the book, there is now a consistent set of headings in each chapter.

Considerable thought has gone into the design of this edition. I am really pleased with its appearance and believe it will help the reader take full advantage of the content.

Finally, all chapters have been updated to incorporate developments since the last edition. As a result, the book remains authoritative and fresh.

Notes on Contributors

Peter Ashworth is Emeritus Professor of Educational Research at Sheffield Hallam University, UK. His publications mostly focus on the phenomenological approach to psychology, e.g., *Phenomenology and Psychological Science* (edited with Man Cheung Chung, Springer). Recent studies include the phenomenology of social participation, critique of the 'approaches to study' research tradition in higher education, and the phenomenology of the gift relationship. He is currently concerned with the phenomenology of Michel Henry. Dr Ashworth is a Fellow of the British Psychological Society.

Virginia Braun is an Associate Professor in the School of Psychology at the University of Auckland, where she teaches around critical psychology, psychology and gender, and qualitative research. A feminist and critical psychologist, her research explores gender, bodies, sex/sexuality and health. She is co-author (with Victoria Clarke) of *Successful Qualitative Research* (Sage). She is interested in intersections between academia and social engagement/social change, including through an ongoing project related to pornography (see http://www.sexualpoliticsnow.org.nz/) and via twitter (@ginnybraun).

Kathy Charmaz is Professor of Sociology and Director of the Faculty Writing Program at Sonoma State University. She has written, co-authored, or co-edited 14 books including two award-winning works, *Good Days, Bad Days: The Self in Chronic Illness and Time* (Rutgers University Press) and *Constructing Grounded Theory* (Sage), which has been translated into Chinese, Japanese, Korean, Polish and Portuguese. The much-expanded second edition of *Constructing Grounded Theory* came out in 2014, as did a co-edited four-volume set, *Grounded Theory and Situational Analysis* (Sage). Professor Charmaz lectures and leads workshops around the globe on grounded theory, qualitative methods, writing for publication, medical sociology, and symbolic interactionism.

Victoria Clarke is an Associate Professor in Sexuality Studies and member of the Centre for Appearance Research in the Department of Health and Social Sciences at the University of the West of England. Her research focuses on sexualities, particularly in relation to appearance and embodiment, and relationships and families, and her books include *Out* *in Psychology* (Wiley), *LGBTQ Psychology* (Cambridge University Press), and *Successful Qualitative Research* (Sage).

Paul Drew is Professor of Conversation Analysis at Loughborough University, UK. He has published widely on the basic practices underlying ordinary social interactions, including repair, the construction of social actions, indirectness, and the use of idioms in managing topic transition. His latest book is a collection co-edited with Betty Couper-Kuhlen on *Requesting in Social Interaction* (Benjamins). He also conducts research on a range of more specialized institutional interactions, notably criminal courts, Jobcentre interviews with claimants in the UK, and particularly medical interactions in primary and secondary care, most recently between neurologists and patients in memory clinics.

Nikki Hayfield is a Senior Lecturer in Social Psychology in the Department of Health and Social Sciences at the University of the West of England (UWE), where she teaches social psychology and qualitative research methods to students at undergraduate and postgraduate levels. Her PhD focused on bisexual women's appearance and identities and she has published journal papers and book chapters on bisexual identities and bisexual marginalization. She continues to use and develop qualitative methodologies. Her main research interests are lesbian, gay, bisexual and heterosexual sexualities, appearance, relationships, and (alternative) families.

Michael Larkin is a Senior Lecturer in Psychology at the University of Birmingham, UK, where he works as part of the clinical psychology training team. His research interests include the experience and context of psychological distress, the experience of 'loss of control', and the meaning of family and peer relationships in coping with distress.

Michael Murray is Professor of Social and Health Psychology and Head of the School of Psychology at Keele University, UK. He has published extensively on a range of issues in social and health psychology including narrative and social representation theory and critical and community health psychology. He has also written theoretical and methodological chapters on narrative psychology. His edited books include *Critical Health Psychology* (Palgrave/Macmillan) and *Qualitative Health Psychology: Theories and Methods* (with Kerry Chamberlain, Sage). Much of his current research uses participatory approaches designed to encourage community transformative action to promote health and well-being.

Mike Osborn is a Consultant Macmillan Psychologist at the Royal United Hospital in Bath, UK, working in both chronic pain and palliative care. His main research interest is in the phenomenology of chronic pain and the relationship between chronic illness, the self and the social world. He has also taught and written about the practicalities of doing qualitative research in psychology.

Peter Reason is a writer, focusing in particular on nature writing for an ecology in crisis. His award-winning book *Spindrift: A Wilderness Pilgrimage at Sea* (Vala Publishing Cooperative, 2014) weaves an exploration of the human place in the ecology of the planet into the story of a sailing voyage. Prior to his retirement from academia, he made major contributions to the theory and practice of action research in writing, teaching and research in the field of sustainability. He is Professor Emeritus at the University of Bath.

Sarah Riley is a Reader in Psychology at Aberystwyth University where she teaches qualitative methods and critical social psychology. Her research is concerned with understanding how subjectivity is formed through complex cultural locations, with a particular interest in gender and embodiment and the application of discourse analysis and cooperative inquiry. She has co-edited *Critical Bodies: Representations, Practices and Identities of Weight and Body Management* (Palgrave/Macmillan, 2008) and *Doing Your Qualitative Research Project* (Sage, 2012); and written, with Adrienne Evans, *Technologies of Sexiness: Sex, Identity and Consumer Culture* (Oxford University Press, USA, 2014) and with A. Evans and M. Robson, *Postfeminism and Health* (Routledge, forthcoming).

Jonathan A. Smith is Professor of Psychology at Birkbeck University of London, UK, where he leads the interpretative phenomenological analysis (IPA) research group. He has written many articles applying IPA to a range of areas in health, clinical and social psychology. He is co-author (with Paul Flowers and Michael Larkin) of *Interpretative Phenomenological Analysis: Theory, Method and Research* (Sage, 2009). He also has a wider interest in qualitative psychology generally and has co-edited a number of books in the area.

Sue Wilkinson is Professor of Feminist and Health Studies at Loughborough University, UK. She is the founding editor of the international journal *Feminism & Psychology*, and has published widely in the areas of gender, sexuality, health and qualitative methods. Her current research interests entail using conversation analysis to study telephone helpline interaction, and she is working with a number of charities – including Compassion in Dying, Dementia UK, and Unlock – to help them evaluate their helpline services. She is also involved in research and campaigning around end-of-life issues, particularly in relation to increasing awareness and uptake of Advance Decisions.

Carla Willig is Professor of Psychology at City University London, UK. Carla has a long-standing interest in qualitative research methodology in general, and discourse analysis in particular. Her most recent book, *Qualitative Interpretation and Analysis in Psychology* (McGraw-Hill, 2012), is concerned with the practical, conceptual and ethical challenges that qualitative researchers face when embarking upon qualitative data analysis.

Lucy Yardley is Professor of Health Psychology at the University of Southampton, UK, and leads the Centre for Applications of Health Psychology. She has published studies using a wide variety of kinds of qualitative analysis, including grounded theory, thematic analysis, framework analysis and discourse analysis. She also carries out quantitative research, and has expertise in programmes of mixed methods research that combine qualitative and quantitative studies. Her current primary interest is developing and evaluating web-based health interventions.

1 Introduction

Jonathan A. Smith

We continue to witness an expansion of interest in qualitative psychology. This has marked a significant shift in a discipline which has historically emphasized the importance of quantitative methodology. This change is reflected in a range of ways: increasing numbers of undergraduate and postgraduate students in psychology conducting qualitative research projects; the growth of psychology courses teaching qualitative methodologies; the enormous increase in numbers of qualitative psychology articles appearing in peer-reviewed journals; and the development of professional sections within, for example, the American Psychological Association and the British Psychology Society to support and foster qualitative psychology.

This book aims to facilitate the further development of this active interest by offering practical guidance to those conducting qualitative research in psychology. It is written in an accessible manner and is primarily intended as a textbook for undergraduates and postgraduates, though it will also be useful to more advanced researchers. *Qualitative Psychology* includes major qualitative approaches now used in psychology, and each chapter offers the reader a step-by-step guide to carrying out research using that particular method.

What is qualitative psychology? A dictionary definition might suggest that qualitative analysis is concerned with describing the constituent properties of an entity, while quantitative analysis is involved in determining how much of the entity there is. Indeed, much psychological research reflects the essence of that distinction. A great deal of qualitative research aims to provide rich or 'thick' (Geertz, 1973) descriptive accounts of the phenomenon under investigation, while quantitative research is more generally concerned with counting occurrences, volumes, or the size of associations between entities.

Qualitative and quantitative approaches clearly differ in terms of how the data are analysed. Quantitative research requires the reduction of phenomena to numerical values in order to carry out statistical analyses. Thus, although much quantitative research begins with verbal data – for example, answers to questionnaire items – the nature of the response is prescribed by the need for quantitative analysis, and this verbal material must be transformed into numbers for that quantitative analysis to be carried out.

By contrast, qualitative research involves collecting data in the form of naturalistic verbal reports – for example, interview transcripts or written accounts – and the analysis conducted on these is textual. Thus, the concern is with interpreting what a piece of text means rather than finding the numerical properties of it. The interpretation is then conveyed through detailed narrative reports of participants' perceptions, understandings or accounts of a phenomenon. For most qualitative researchers, this approach is consonant with a theoretical commitment to the importance of language as a fundamental property of human communication, interpretation and understanding. Given that we tend to make sense of our social world and express that sense-making to ourselves and others linguistically, qualitative researchers emphasize the value of analytic strategies that remain as close as possible to the symbolic system in which that sense-making occurs.

Qualitative approaches in psychology are generally engaged with exploring, describing and interpreting the personal and social experiences of participants. An attempt is usually made to understand a relatively small number of participants' own frames of reference or view of the world rather than trying to test a preconceived hypothesis on a large sample. For some qualitative researchers, the primary emphasis lies in how meanings are constructed and shaped discursively. Of course, there is a major theoretical underpinning to qualitative research; and the historical context of, and main themes in, that theoretical nexus are covered by Peter Ashworth in Chapter 2 of this book.

While it is true that qualitative and quantitative research projects usually differ considerably in terms of research question, orientation and execution, it is actually difficult to make categorical distinctions between qualitative and quantitative methods. Thus, for example, some quantitative researchers produce descriptive statistical accounts, and some qualitative researchers seek causal relationships. Similarly, Hayes (1997) argues that the process of analysis in qualitative research often invokes quantitative properties, as researchers make judgements, implicitly or explicitly, of the strength or otherwise of a category or property being reported, and individuals are compared with each other on various dimensions. Moreover, one can argue that quantitative research always involves interpretation by the researcher and that this process is essentially a qualitative one. So, while this book is written with a recognition of and commitment to qualitative research as a distinctive approach to psychological inquiry, it recognizes that the difference is not as categorical as sometimes portrayed.

It is also the case that qualitative psychology is not a homogeneous entity. There are a number of different approaches, each with overlapping but different theoretical and/or methodological emphases. And the growth of qualitative psychology has meant that recognizing this is increasingly important. Students need to know which particular type of qualitative method they are reading or working with, what its theoretical commitments are, and how it differs from other qualitative approaches they might encounter. So, for example, interpretative phenomenological analysis is concerned with exploring the lived experience of the participant or with understanding how participants make sense of their personal and social world. On the other hand, discourse analysis and conversation analysis are concerned with describing the linguistic resources participants draw on during conversations, the patterns those conversations take, and the social interactional work being performed during them.

This book aims to help the reader navigate through these different perspectives and procedures. The intention is for the reader new to, but curious about, qualitative psychology to learn about the different qualitative approaches in terms of both their underlying theoretical assumptions and their practical procedures. Each chapter offers a short theoretical introduction to the approach and then offers a step-by-step guide to conducting psychological research by that method. The contributors are all recognized international experts; indeed, many of them are key figures in either the inception or development of their approach, and each has extensive experience using, teaching and writing about it. At the same time, the aim has been for the chapters to be written in an accessible fashion so that newcomers to the field can understand the main features of the particular method and be encouraged to try it out for themselves. Helping to set the scene for those practical chapters, the book begins with a chapter by Peter Ashworth outlining the conceptual foundations of qualitative psychology and their connection with the contemporary field. While qualitative psychology as a vibrant empirical force is relatively new, it actually has a long and distinguished intellectual history, and Peter Ashworth provides an entry to, and overview of, that history, as well as a link to the approaches offered in the rest of the book.

2 Conceptual Foundations of Qualitative Psychology

Peter Ashworth

In this chapter, I want to point to the gradual unfolding in the history of psychology of certain ways of thinking which have, relatively recently, led to the emergence of specifically qualitative approaches to psychological matters. For, behind the use of qualitative methods lies a set of distinct conceptions of the nature of human psychology, and I will outline here some of the sources of these conceptions.

There are several different approaches to qualitative psychology, as the chapters in this book testify, but underlying each approach is a concern to uncover people's grasp of their world. I use that ungainly term 'grasp of their world' to avoid terminology which would be unacceptable to one or other of the traditions within qualitative psychology. There are important differences in opinion about how the subject matter of qualitative research should be conceptualized.

First, the 'qualities' sought in elucidating a person's grasp of their world may be seen as a system of objective *variables.* For some, qualitative research aims at discovering the variables entailed in some human situation and does not dissent from the orthodox view of the person as being part of a natural system of causes and effects (in the positivist manner). Such an approach is not the focus of this book, though it is not unusual in, for example, using a qualitative investigation as part of the process of designing the questionnaire which will later be used as part of an experimental study.

Second, the person's grasp of their world may be conceptualized as a set of quasi-linguistic *propositions* (which may or may not be seen as open to personal choice) by which the person construes or constructs their world. Such qualitative psychologists often turn their attention to the range of social interpretations of events available to a person, arguing that these interpretations are what gives form and content to the individual's grasp of their world (gender, for instance, being ready-packaged for us in particular ways). These authors are likely to shy away from the use of terms like 'experience', feeling that it points too much to the individual; what should be studied, instead, is the social nature of the constructions of the world that guide thought and action.

Third, qualitative psychologists may envisage the person's grasp of their world in terms of 'perceptions' or *meanings* (whether socially shared or idiosyncratic). This is a major aspect of the phenomenological viewpoint, in which qualitative researchers often speak of the personal 'lifeworld', and try to describe an individual's experience within this particular meaningful realm.

In the latter two types of qualitative study, qualitative psychology does not make discoveries of precisely the kind experimental psychology seeks – finding new causal factors in human behaviour or refining our understanding of known effects. Instead, what we discover in qualitative psychology are the taken-for-granted meanings by which we grasp our world. Bringing these to explicit awareness can allow us to be less perplexed about ourselves (this is the primary objective). However, as the first of the approaches to qualitative research listed above indicates, qualitative methods can also provide evidence of importance to experimental psychology in helping setting up causal models which remain connected to lived experience. So quantitative and qualitative methods may be combined in various ways in 'mixed mode' research (Todd et al., 2004).

THE BIRTH OF PSYCHOLOGY AND THE QUESTION OF 'EXPERIENCE'

Within contemporary psychology, then, those who wish to investigate the person's grasp of their world in detail will tend to turn to qualitative methods. A concentration on human *experience* as the central topic of psychology or a focus on *construction* or *interpretation* seems, for us, to lead, almost inevitably to qualitative research. Yet the history of psychology does not show a necessary link between the study of experience and qualitative methodology. It is sometimes forgotten that, when experimental psychology was founded in the second half of the nineteenth century, it was *defined* as the science of experience, and – maybe surprisingly – the methodology replicated as far as was possible that of the physical sciences. The philosophers and physiologists who began to establish psychology as a discipline had seen the immensely impressive strides in understanding the nature of the external world made by the physical sciences. Psychology would complement this by developing a scientific understanding of the 'inner world' of experience, and this inner realm would be approached experimentally and quantitatively. The major interest of those early experimentalists, in fact, was in discovering what precisely the relationship was between the outer world and the inner world.

Gustav Fechner (1801–1887), for example, aimed to discover the laws relating the physical nature of an external physical stimulus to the internal experience of the sensation it produced. Fechner's *Elemente der Psychophysik* (1860/1966) could indeed be said to be the founding publication of experimental psychology. In it, Fechner reported his findings regarding such matters as the relationship between stimulus and sensation. For instance, a measured change in the intensity of light would be compared with the extent to which the person's experience of brightness altered. So variations in objective physical energy could be graphed against variations in the subjective sensation of brightness. The brightness of light is, in a certain sense, an experience.

The limitations of Fechner's psychophysics, from the point of view of contemporary qualitative psychology, are rather obvious. What was the meaning of 'experience' in experimental work such as Fechner's? It was simply the individual report of some aspect of a sensation. But we might well object that the experience of variations in brightness was within a very specific, controlled context, with a particular social meaning (the research participants lived in a culture and historical epoch in which it made sense to play the role of 'research subject' and to turn attention exclusively to the specified aspect of the sensation). We might wonder about the vocabulary available to the participants for reporting visual sensation. We might inquire about the relations of power between experimenter and subject. We might speculate about the perceived passage of time during these possibly tedious sessions. But these wider aspects of the experience in the round were of no interest to Fechner.

Right at the start, there was scientific controversy surrounding Fechner's book. Some of it was aimed at the details of the methodology. But William James was one of the distinguished psychologists who regarded the whole enterprise of 'psychophysics' as completely without value.

The human capacity to report verbally on sensations of the elementary kind investigated by Fechner ('Which light is brighter?' 'The one on the left.') could, it seems, appear unproblematic given the restricted focus of interest of the experimental investigation. When later investigators developed psychological studies which had more complex aims, the difficulties of the approach adopted by Fechner became increasingly insistent. A more elaborate attempt at the analysis of experience is found in Wundt's *Physiologische Psychologie* (1874/1904), in which various novel methods were used, but notably Wundt focused on laboratory investigation using trained and systematic *self-observation*. While systematic in the extreme and subject to careful experimental control, the method nevertheless depended on the research participants' verbal report of their (a question-begging term) *introspections*. The accounts of the structure of experience varied between laboratories as Wundt's approach began to be adopted by other workers in the new science.

It was not only because of the unreliability of the experimental self-observation method when applied to the description of the make-up of consciousness that Wundt's work on the structure of immediate experience was challenged. In particular, Franz Brentano (1838–1917) developed a quite different approach to immediate experience. He viewed conscious experience as a process; experiencing was an act, so that different kinds of experience are to be distinguished by the particular way in which we gain consciousness of the object of experience. In particular, the 'kind' of conscious act involved in relating ourselves to something so as to form a judgement about it is different from the conscious act by which we achieve a perception of something. So judgement and perception and other modes of conscious experience involve different orientations to the object.

The key feature of conscious activity, for Brentano (1874) (and this was taken up by Husserl and the phenomenologists), was its *intentionality*, a technical term pointing to the intrinsic 'relatedness' of consciousness to the object of its attention. The fact that consciousness uniquely has this attribute of intentionality was definitive, that is, *all consciousness is consciousness of something.* And psychology, for Brentano, had the task of delineating the various ways in which consciousness could relate to its objects.

Brentano's act psychology did not gain a significant hearing outside Germany, though it had an impact on Gestalt theory. The psychology of Wundt, with its technique of self-observation and focus on mental content, gave way to functionalism and especially its behaviourist form in the Anglo-American world. But in the meantime the impressive psychological descriptions by William James (1842–1910) deserve attention.

EARLY CRITIQUE: WILLIAM JAMES AND THE 'STREAM OF CONSCIOUSNESS'

In volume I of James's *Principles of Psychology* (1890), he outlines a basic psychology of experience, primarily focusing on the stream of thought but also elaborating on two meanings of 'self'. James does not give us new research evidence, but he does detail quite systematic views on psychological matters that have in some ways been more influential than the work of James's experimentalist contemporaries.

The thing which distinguished James's description of experience from that of Wundt was that James rejected atomism in favour of the attempt to describe key features of the whole field of awareness taken in its entirety. James described consciousness as an ongoing process, having its own themes within which the current foci of attention get their meaning. So the content of consciousness is, at a particular moment, a phase of a personal 'stream'. The significance of a particular object of consciousness is due not just to its reference to the external thing but also to its relationship to the ongoing themes of my awareness – its personal relevance to me, the experiencer.

James builds up a general case for the importance of what he calls the 'fringe' of the focal object of which we are conscious. An object of awareness gains its meaning in large measure from the 'halo of relations' with which it is connected – its 'psychic overtone'. Husserl later also pointed to a similar idea: the 'horizon' of a phenomenon. That is, an object of awareness is affected intrinsically by the whole web of its meaningful connections within the world of experience. Choice is also a feature of consciousness for James. Of the available objects of attention, one becomes focal at a particular time, and others are reduced to the periphery of attention. Here we have something akin to the Gestalt psychologists' distinction between the figure and ground of awareness.

James's approach to consciousness is continued in the following chapter of the *Principles*, which is devoted to the self. James regards this as a very difficult topic, but he discusses in detail the distinction between the self as an object of thought (the self-concept, let us say), and the self as that *who* is aware of that self-concept. So the self is a 'duplex' (as James puts it) – involving both (a) the self which we can conceptualize, the self as known, the me, and (b) the self as that which 'has' that knowledge, the I. The *me*, in particular, is shown to have a complex structure. So James begins to develop a phenomenology of the self, which was elaborated on by such later authors as G.H. Mead and Gordon Allport.

The basic description of awareness and self was a valuable advance. James, much later, continued the descriptive tendency of his work in a way which also employed a form of qualitative research. This was in the ground-breaking *Varieties of Religious Experience* (1902). In this book James draws on a wide range of texts and personal accounts, which are interpreted as subjective perceptions. Thus he sets aside the question of whether a person's account of their experience of God relates to any external reality and instead describes it in the terms employed by the person themselves.

James made a considerable contribution to the kind of thinking that lies behind qualitative psychology by his descriptions of the field of thought and his analysis of the notion of the self. And among the methodological strictures James made in the *Principles* was a strong warning against what he called the *psychologist's fallacy*. This is the assumption that the research participant's experience is to be understood in terms of the readily available categories of the researcher. To do so confuses the standpoints of the researcher and the researched. The 'subjective world' of the research participant must be understood in its own terms. The ramifications of this idea are very great (Ashworth, 2009), as we shall see.

THE REJECTION OF EXPERIENCE IN BEHAVIOURISM AND COGNITIVISM

In the next generation of American theorists, we find the criticisms which James made of the kind of experimental self-observation, undertaken by Wundt and his school, ripening into an alternative school of psychology, *behaviourism*. J.B. Watson (1878–1958) published a statement of position in the paper 'Psychology as a behaviorist views it' (Watson, 1913), in which he demanded a replacement of the self-observation method by the study of behaviour. It was asserted that mental processes could not be the object of scientific study because they were not open to observation. Partly, this was an impatient reaction to the irresolvably contradictory findings of earlier psychologists. 'Objectivity' was the catchword, and this meant focusing on events which both (a) could be reported reliably and were not susceptible to idiosyncrasy, and (b) were open to observation by someone other than the person undergoing the experience.

Watson recognized that this meant that psychology would no longer be the science of consciousness (which, as we have seen, had been its definitive area of investigation), but he seems merely to have regarded this as a consequence of the requirement that psychology adopt a 'scientific' methodology. The apparent problem was neither that consciousness had previously been ill-formulated, nor that consciousness could be dismissed as unreal. Consciousness was simply not amenable to objective analysis. In the United States, especially, behaviourism was the dominant form of academic psychology for 40 or 50 years.

This historical shift was unfortunate, for it took out of play several lines of investigation which, when elaborated, are conducive to the development of qualitative psychology. When the psychologist concentrates on objective stimuli and measurable responses, attention is directed away from the following:

- *The 'first-person' perspective*. Propositions about psychological events can be stated only in the third person – from the viewpoint of the observer rather than that of the actor themselves.
- *The perceptual approach*. Behaviourism could not consider the perceptions of the research participant. Likewise other modes of intentionality of consciousness – thinking, judging, paying or switching attention, etc. – could not be properly differentiated and

researched because behaviourism could not permit itself to consider the relationship between consciousness and its objects of awareness.

- *Idiography*. Behaviourist research, though allowing for 'individual differences' due to variations in individuals' histories of reinforcement, could not regard the study of people in their uniqueness as a justifiable scientific enterprise. Objectivity would be threatened.

- *Meaning*. Meaning was sacrificed by behaviourism. In the search for the objective and observable causes of behaviour, the meaning that a situation has for the person disappeared as a topic of research. Similarly, people's own accounts of their experience were regarded as *verbal behaviour* – that is, responses which needed to be explained in terms of their causes, rather than understandable and meaningful in their own terms.

- *Specificity in the use of language*. Of course language-use is observable behaviour. However, its communicative function in expressing personal experience was attenuated in behaviourism.

- *Social relatedness*. Other people are an important source of stimuli, and my responses to them are likely to have significant repercussions, but people were not seen as different in kind from the physical objects which constitute a person's environment. Behaviourists were not able to recognize the *social nature* of the human being. In particular, they were not able to recognize fully the social *construction* of human reality.

In effect, the catalogue of things which behaviourism neglected provides a valuable list of items which are, in varying degree, central to the qualitative sensibility in psychology.

However, within behaviourism, developments in a cognitive direction were made from time to time, in an attempt to re-establish psychology as, in some sense, a science of mental life. Perhaps *Plans and the Structure of Behavior* by Miller, Gallanter and Pribram (1960) is the most obvious of these attempts, in that the authors termed themselves 'cognitive behaviourists'. In time, a self-confident and autonomous cognitive psychology developed, importantly in Neisser's ground-breaking *Cognitive Psychology* (1967), effectively replacing behaviourism as the dominant tendency in experimental psychology.

Cognitive psychology can be seen as a critique of the behaviourist neglect of inner processes, in that it allows studies to be made of perception, memory, thinking and so on. The work of Miller et al. and Neisser challenged behaviourism in its American heartland. In Britain, never so much in thrall to that theory, well-respected cognitive work had been going on – witness Bartlett (1932), Broadbent (1958) and Welford (1968). But, as I have shown in detail (Ashworth, 2000), cognitive psychology in general retains a quasi-behaviourist, methodological commitment to external, measurable and observable variables. In essence, the novelty of cognitive psychology lay in developing models of inner processes on the basis of what was externally observable. Viewing 'mental activity' as a process of *information flow*, cognitive psychologists began to test models of the operation of the mental mechanism (attention, perception, thought, memory, etc.).

The methodological approach of cognitive psychology is worth pondering because it is often thought that this approach made an advance on the sterile objectivism of the behaviourists and allowed research to turn again to the scientific study of the whole breadth of the person's grasp of their world. But, if we look again at the list of matters which behaviourism refused to give place to in its research, we can see that cognitive psychology tackles only some of these directly. Additionally, both behaviourism and cognitivism share an underlying positivism (see Box 2.1).

Behaviourism's place in history lies in its paradigm-shattering critique of self-observation in psychology. Other lines of critique failed to capture the field at that time; we now turn to one alternative approach which did not reject experience but instead sought a more subtle approach to it. This viewpoint was one which immediately called for a qualitative psychology.

BOX 2.1   POSITIVISM

The methodological viewpoint generally taken for granted within the natural sciences, and dominant also in the social sciences, is positivist. The central idea is that only events which can be observed, or that only propositions which are (at least in principle) testable, have a claim to truth (unless, like logic, they are true by definition).

Among its characteristics – as seen in psychology – are the following:

- There is a single, unitary *real* world, within which the events of interest to psychology take place. This is realism.
- The individual is part of this real world, and so such processes as memory, emotion and thought are events in the real world with *definite enduring characteristics.*
- The purpose of science is to set up experimental situations in which the characteristics of these psychological processes can reveal themselves, and this will allow the processes to be modelled.
- The world can be described in terms of measurable variables which can interact with each other in determinate ways.
- The models (mathematically formulated if possible) will show how variables interrelate, especially how they relate to each other in a cause-and-effect fashion.
- The purpose of research is to test hypotheses regarding relationships between variables, and to reach, by closer and closer approximation, theories which can begin to be regarded as having the status of scientific laws. (This sense of an ongoing development gives positivism its characteristic historical optimism, and specifically the sense that each study, based on what is *known* and available in the established literature, is potentially a contribution to the 'total knowledge' of the future.)

In rejecting positivism in this sense, qualitative psychologists put on one side concern with the idea of an unequivocal real world, in favour of attending to the accounts that people formulate of *their* reality.

PHENOMENOLOGY AND EXISTENTIALISM

The founder of phenomenology as a philosophical movement, Edmund Husserl (1859–1938), had a fundamental aim which it is necessary to have clearly in mind in assessing his work and its relevance to psychology. Although he was critical of both the experimental psychology of Wundt and the subsequent behaviourist alternative, his purpose was not primarily to reform psychology. Rather, he wanted to provide a firm foundation for *all* the disciplines – sciences, arts and humanities – by establishing the meaning of their most basic concepts. For he believed that not only psychology but all the scholarly disciplines lacked a method which would establish the nature of their fundamental concepts. What typically happened, according to Husserl, was that common-sense terms were pressed into use as if they were technical terms, or other rough-and-ready ways of developing concepts were employed. So, if asked what *perception* is, psychologists would have no precise account of the notion, but would have to answer in a way which arbitrarily built on unanalysed common sense.

Husserl, then, proposed the method of *phenomenology*, which would enable basic concepts to be framed in a rigorous way that would give a firm basis to each science.

To take psychology specifically, Husserl (1925/1977, 1931/1960) regarded the discipline as flawed in its conceptual schemes by the tendency of psychologists to turn away from concrete experience and to develop prematurely abstract and unexamined concepts. Because the concepts were not grounded in experience, they were seriously lacking in clarity and appropriateness to the subject matter they were intended to reflect. What was the solution, then? In the Husserlian slogan, it was a *return to the things themselves*, as experienced.

The core philosophical basis of Husserl's programme was a rejection of the presupposition that there is something *behind* or *underlying* or *more fundamental than* experience, which should be immediately sought. No, Husserl maintained; what appears is the starting point: we should begin our investigation with what is experienced. In attaining this phenomenological approach, any assumptions, etc. which would tend to distract the researcher from a focus on the experience must be set aside, or subjected to the 'epochē' (Husserl, 1913/1983). For psychology, this can be understood as avoiding as far as is possible the psychologist's fallacy that William James warned about. So the question of correspondence of a person's experience to reality, the cause of that experience, or its motivation, and any claims made in the literature about the nature of such experiences – all must be set aside. Any assumption that one aspect of the phenomenon takes precedence over any other must also be suspended prior to experiential evidence. It needs to be stressed that setting these and other matters aside, in order to pay proper attention to the experience as such, does not at all mean that they might not reappear in the findings. But this will happen only if it is clear from the experience. It cannot be presupposed and imposed on the description of the experience.

Phenomenology is not merely a matter of going through some mechanical process of 'analysis' of the qualitative data and thereby producing a description of experience. The reading of the data is an in-depth one. For example, it is right to report (as part of the experience of research participants) unstated aspects of the person's awareness which the researcher notices they must be assuming, taking for granted, for the experience to cohere. To give one classic example, any experience involving social interaction entails one taking it for granted that the other person is a sentient being like oneself (Husserl, 1931/1960; Ashworth, 2013).

Though this gives a flavour of the work of phenomenological clarification of psychological concepts, it will be clear that a very arduous process is involved. Something akin to James's account of the web of meanings surrounding an experience must be described (Ashworth, 1996). It is important to note that, though phenomenology was initially concerned with the clarification of the basic concepts of each discipline, it is not surprising – given the way in which Husserl insisted on the importance of experience for this purpose – that the enterprise soon discovered special implications for the practice of psychological research. Husserl established that human experience in general is *not* a matter of lawful response to the 'variables' that are assumed to be in operation. Rather, experience is of a system of interrelated meanings – a Gestalt – that is bound up in a totality termed the 'lifeworld' (Husserl, 1936/1970). In other words, the human realm essentially entails embodied, conscious relatedness to a personal world of experience. The natural scientific approach is inappropriate. Human meanings are the key to the study of lived experience, not causal variables. In a nutshell, phenomenology insists that the daffodils are indeed different for a wandering poet than they are for a hard-pressed horticulturalist.

For phenomenology, then, the individual is a conscious agent, whose experience must be studied from the 'first-person' perspective. Experience is of a meaningful lifeworld. Subsequently, 'existential phenomenologists', such as the early Heidegger (1927/1962), Merleau-Ponty (1962), and Sartre (1958; see Ashworth, 2000), developed phenomenology in a way which emphasized the lifeworld. At the same time, they tended to set aside Husserl's concern to develop, for each of the scholarly disciplines, a set of phenomenologically based concepts.

Tensions and divergences can be seen in phenomenological psychology. The emphasis may be on exhaustive *description* or on the development of essential structures of experience (see Giorgi, 1970; van Manen, 1997), and the descriptive emphasis may be idiographic (Smith et al., 1995). And there is debate about whether the empathic understanding required for phenomenological work might move towards interpretation (more of this below).

Especially in the American context, phenomenology and existentialism have been linked with 'humanistic psychology' (Misiak and Sexton, 1973). The purpose of this loose group of psychologists was to develop a way of pursuing the discipline which avoided the determinism of behaviourism and (as they believed) of psychoanalysis. What 'determinism' means here is the view that human behaviour and experience are to be regarded as the inevitable outcome of the set of variables (some internal, some environmental) which are in action on the person at a given time. In determinism, strictly understood, there is no place for a contribution of the person in how they will act. A profound concern that psychology should not be determinist in this sense led a number of authors, notably Bühler (1971), Maslow (1968) and Rogers (1967) – many of whom were psychotherapists – to call for a 'third force' of psychological thinking (Bugental, 1964) to counter the antihumanistic tendencies of the psychological mainstream.

The approach which I have personally espoused over nearly 30 years is existential phenomenology, with its fundamental concept of the lifeworld. In detail, people's lived experience of their situation may be quite specific, but all lifeworlds do have universal features such as temporality, spatiality, subjective embodiment, intersubjectivity, self-hood, personal project, moodedness, and discursiveness (Ashworth, 2006; Ashworth and Chung, 2006).

For existential phenomenology, human beings are taken as free by virtue of being conscious (consciousness entailing the capacity to envisage alternatives to what currently *is*), and resources such as language are tools for thought rather than, primarily, constraints on it. This is not to say that people are fully able to exercise the liberty which consciousness provides. Several authors within the existential-phenomenological tradition, such as Hannah Arendt (1998), have stressed that social arrangements (both local intersubjective ones and large-scale political structures) are required for the practical exercise of freedom.

In its broadest meaning, then, the phenomenological approach has the task of elucidating the taken-for-granted assumptions by which people navigate their lifeworld. To describe what everyone knows may seem a pretty empty ambition! But this impression is wrong. It has been argued that: (a) people *don't* 'know' – we act according to taken-for-granted understandings about our world which are for the most part pre-reflective, so elucidating them can often be a revelation; and (b) 'everyone' may have taken-for-granted understandings which enable a roughly shared communal life to take place – but there is scope for a great deal of idiosyncrasy.

In fact, the unique in human experience has been the focus of a further source of qualitative psychology.

IDIOGRAPHIC PSYCHOLOGY – G.W. ALLPORT

Of the earlier writers to whom the humanistic psychologists look with particular admiration, Gordon Willard Allport (1897–1967), is notable for his concern that psychology should not neglect the unique in individual experience and behaviour. Allport was a member of a generation for whom behaviourism was almost definitive of, at least American, academic psychology, yet he was remarkably independent and, in contrast to anything that could be regarded as mainstream at the time, developed a theory of personality that stressed the distinct configuration of traits and tendencies which constitutes the uniqueness of each individual:

> I object strongly ... to a point of view that is current in psychology. Eysenck states it as follows: *To the scientist, the unique individual is simply the point of intersection of a number of quantitative variables.*

> What does this statement mean? It means that the scientist is not interested in the mutual interdependence of part-systems within the whole system of personality ... [and] is not interested in the manner in which your introversion interacts with your

other traits, with your values, and with your life plans. The scientist, according to this view, then, isn't interested in the personality system at all, but only in the common dimensions. The person is left as mere 'point of intersection' with no internal structure, coherence or animation. I cannot agree with this view. (Allport, 1961: 8, his italics)

In this statement, the holism of Allport's approach is plain, and his interest in the *idiographic* approach to psychological research logically follows. The individual may be studied as a unique case. The psychology of personality does not need to be exclusively *nomothetic* (that is, restricting its attention to general dimensions on which individuals vary). The nomothetic approach assumes that the behaviour of a particular person is the outcome of laws that apply to all, and the aim of science is to reveal these general laws. The idiographic approach would, in contrast, focus on the interplay of factors which may be quite specific to the individual. It may be that the factors take their specific form only in this person; certainly, they are uniquely patterned in a given person's life (Allport, 1962).

As tends to be the case with psychologists who take a humanistic line, Allport considered in some depth the meaning of the *self*. He tried to cover a very great deal of what is linked in ordinary language in some way or other to the notion of self, using the coinage 'proprium' – to include both (a) people's *conception* of the self and the aspects of their world which they may be said to identify with; and (b) the 'integrative' mental function that may be labelled 'selfhood'.

Despite his insistence on the importance of the idiographic approach, Allport did not adopt an exclusively qualitative approach to research. Rather, his recommendation would be to study an individual person by using as many and varied means as possible. But he did pioneer some interesting qualitative approaches, such as the analysis of 'personal documents' and the use of 'self-reports' as a means of understanding the individual (Allport, 1961: 401–14; 1965).

Where Gordon Allport used qualitative methods, this largely reflected his concern with the study of the individual as a totality. He himself recognized that his holistic and idiographic interest had affinities with Gestalt theory and with existentialism. But Allport does not seem to have been interested in a qualitative psychology set up from the viewpoint of persons themselves. In the end, his is a psychology which will describe the person in individual complexity, certainly, but it would be carried out from the external vantage point of a psychologist for whom personal documents and other 'subjective' material can be used as evidence.

THE WORLD AS CONSTRUCTION

What image of psychological life is suggested as a basis for qualitative research? We have seen James's description of consciousness, the focus on experience in existential phenomenology, and Allport's idiography. All these implicitly invite us to think of the person as a *perceiver*:

All other forms of conscious experience are in one way or another *founded* on perceptual, sensory consciousness. In general terms, Husserl contrasts the *self-givenness* of perception ... with that of a very large class of forms of consciousness that are 'representational' ... or work through a modification of presencing, which Husserl terms ... 'presentification', 'presentation' or 'calling to mind' (not just in memory, but in fantasy, wishing, etc.). When we remember, imagine or fantasize about an object, we do not have precisely the same sense of immediate, actual, bodily and temporal presence of the object. (Moran, 2005: 166–7)

And perception is not a construction or representation but provides direct access to the experienced object.

Of course, individuals are very active in their perceiving – they search, they pay attention selectively, they make choices, and their perception always has a meaning which is related to their lifeworld. But the approaches to be discussed in the rest of the chapter do not see the person as a perceiver so much as a *conceiver* or a *constructor*. Research focuses not so much on individuals' perception of a lifeworld as on their construction of it. The person is a sense-maker.

Two authors are indicative of the move to the idea of construction as the way many qualitative researchers approach the investigation of the individual's grasp of their world. I will deal with them in reverse historical order because the earlier, George Herbert Mead (1863–1931), has arguably a more deep-rooted ongoing influence on current qualitative research through the 'symbolic interactionist' movement than the later, George Kelly (1905–1967). Mead provides an appropriate link with later sections of this chapter.

George Kelly (1905–1967)

Kelly's (1955) approach centred on conception rather than perception. For Kelly, people act in accordance not with the way the world actually is but with their 'construction' of it. However, Kelly did not give us a detailed theory of the development in childhood of the capacity to construe the world, nor did he apparently prioritize the social basis of thought and selfhood (though he gives a great deal of attention to relations with others, and to the various ways in which an individual's way of seeing the world coincides with that of other people). So, though Kelly was undoubtedly a constructionist, it would be controversial to label him a social constructionist; and whether constructs are to be seen as falling within discursive structures or not is moot.

The 'fundamental postulate' of Kelly's theory of personal constructs expresses the constructionist outlook strongly – 'a person's processes are psychologically channellized by the way in which he [*sic*] anticipates events.' Kelly wants us to regard the person as acting as an informal scientist who views the world ('events') by way of categories of interpretation ('constructs') which are open to modification in the light of experience. Since reappraisal is thought to be possible by conscious reflection on one's construction of the world, we have here what Kelly called 'constructive alternativism'.

Kelly takes the view that we all have our own construction of events. But there are rather powerful limitations on the extent to which my construct system and yours can differ. Though each construct system is individual, Kelly speaks of the need for the contributors to a joint activity to be able to 'construe the construction processes' of the other participants. In other words, though we might not share the others' outlooks, for joint action to occur we must know what the others' outlooks *are*. So Kelly notes that individuals may include within their own system of cognition knowledge of the perspectives of others. To interact with another person, of course, requires knowledge of this sort. Many constructs *are* shared by people in common – indeed, to the extent that constructs can be communicated, they can be shared.

Essentially, Kelly views people as relating to reality (a notion which he strongly asserts) through their own developing system of constructs, and this system is materially affected by the person's coexistence and interaction with others. It is important to mention that Kelly does not dissent from the view of the self which we have noted in other authors. The *me* is a construct like any other.

Kelly provided a valuable new research technique, a logical scheme by which the researcher might specify in an organized way individuals' construct system. It was intended to facilitate assessment without sacrificing either individuality or changeability. This was the *role construct repertory grid* ('Rep Grid') in which the associations and dissociations between certain objects of experience – usually people well known to the individual – are mapped in terms of particular constructs (maybe one such construct would be kindly/cold). This exceedingly flexible tool has been used in a wide range of investigations (Bannister and Fransella, 1971). It may be used idiographically, but there are ways in which nomothetic procedures can be based on it. For instance, mathematical characteristics of grids can be derived, and the variation in such things as the complexity with which people construe a certain realm of experience can be investigated.

It is to be emphasized that Kelly saw the Rep Grid merely as a tool; he and subsequent personal construct psychologists value personal accounts as ways of eliciting personal constructs. It must also be said, in view of the fact that claims are made that Kelly represents the phenomenological position (e.g., Mischel, 1971), that Kelly dissociated personal construct theory from phenomenology (though there is evidence in his work that he did not know the phenomenological literature in any depth; see Ashworth, 1973); and phenomenologists (e.g., Bolton, 1977) similarly distance themselves from his work, arguing (among other things) that it is too cognitive and that the fundamental postulate and corollaries entail presuppositions for which the phenomenological justification is absent. We can see, in any case, in the light of the argument that is being developed in this chapter, that Kelly's emphasis is on *construing*, not *perceiving*.

George Herbert Mead (1863–1931)

G.H. Mead's work is an important source of the constructionist orientation in qualitative psychology (Mead, 1934; see Ashworth, 1979, 2000); it was absorbed during the 1950s and 1960s into the school of social research referred to as 'symbolic interactionism'.

Symbolic interactionism is radically social. Mead (1934: 186) tells us:

What I want particularly to emphasize is the temporal and logical pre-existence of the social process to the self-conscious individual that arises within it.

Mind and self are products of social interaction, then. It is almost built into the name of the discipline, 'psychology', that the focus is on the individual person. Mead, instead, argued for the priority of the *relationship of communication* between caregiver and infant as the source of the mentality of the infant. He argued (he did not base his thinking on systematic evidence) that communication of a rudimentary kind between infant and carer comes before the development of the infant's capacity for thought. Indeed, it comes before the capacity for self-reflection. So infants interact with caregivers before they 'know what they are doing' or 'who they are'. The *meaning* of the infant's action becomes 'known' by the gradual inter-nalization of expectations about how the others in the situation will react. So thought arises in a social process, and the *individualizing* of thought is a later development, which is in any case largely dependent on the use of the social tool, language.

It is important to notice how central language and other systems of symbols are to Mead. (It should be clear now why the school of thought is named 'symbolic interactionism'.) And, very importantly, linguistic symbols are a system of socially shared, not idiosyncratic, meanings.

There are two fundamental consequences of the idea that social interaction comes before thinking and selfhood, and that the latter are built from social materials. First, inner thought and external communication are basically similar. They are made of the same stuff. Mead expects no problem of translation of thought into word. Note also that, in internalizing lan-guage, the child is not just internalizing a symbol system but the system of activity. The process of conversation is being internalized; symbols are part of interaction, or discourse. Second, the self is part of this. Having acquired the capacity to reflect on one's own actions, one can build up a self-concept or identity. And the capacity for self-reflection develops through the reactions of others to the child's behaviour.

The view of Mead and the other symbolic interactionists – the term is due to Herbert Blumer (1900–1987) – contributes to qualitative psychology a highly social outlook: the person is first of all a member of society and only later (in the context of other people) becomes an individual. Hence it is appropriate for qualitative psychology to look to the symbolic systems of society – both those which are linguistic in the simple sense and those which are embedded in the forms of activity, the practices, of the culture. Mead's outlook is one important source of the approach of *discourse analysis* and *discursive psychology*. Other foundational thinkers in this area include Goffman (1959) (for the relation between Goffman and the existentialists, see Ashworth, 1985) and Garfinkel (1967). Qualitative methodol-ogy (often ethnographic, i.e., 'participant observation') is normally seen as the appropriate approach for research arising from symbolic interactionist and related theories.

One way of reading Mead, then, is as an early social constructionist theory. Individual selves and mental processes arise in a social context, and the 'content' of thought and selfhood is to be understood in the light of the meanings which are available within the cul-ture in which the person is immersed. However, there is another emphasis, equally present in Mead (Ashworth, 1979; Natanson, 1973). For, if mind and self are products of social interaction, it is equally true to say that it is individual interaction that constitutes society. Mead does not envisage a social milieu made up of roleplaying automatons – far from it. Having developed the capacity for mind and self as a result of interaction, the individual is then able, relatively autonomously – albeit in a continuing social context – to develop selfhood and personal tendencies of thought. Mead provides a social psychological theory with implications which include an element of individual agency. People are constructed *and are also* constructors.

The distinction between a *perceptual* and a *constructionist* outlook is not absolute. Berger and Luckmann (1967), in their influential book *The Social Construction of Reality*, took their theoretical direction especially from the phenomenologist Alfred Schutz (e.g., Schutz, 1972). Nevertheless, it is as well to note the different tendencies. Qualitative psychology may be more concerned with attempting to reveal the lifeworld (the perceptual tendency) or with how one's sense of reality is constructed.

INTERPRETATION THEORY: HERMENEUTICS

We have noted the distinction – rough and ready though it may be – between the forms of qualitative psychology that tend to adopt a perceptual approach and those that are constructionist in orientation. If we were to turn constructionist thinking back onto the question of the nature of qualitative research itself, we could hardly fail to find ourselves confronting the question, 'What processes of construction have the researchers themselves employed in coming up with the findings they have presented?' For a constructionist, all is construction. Both Mead and Kelly explicitly asserted that all science, including all forms of psychology, is a matter of construction. Further than this, the conclusions of a research activity have to be regarded as *interpretations*. Psychology is going to be an interpretative activity.

In his unrivalled study *Freud and Philosophy: An Essay on Interpretation* (1970), Paul Ricoeur distinguished between two kinds of interpretation (using the term 'hermeneutics' to refer to the use of a theory of interpretation):

- The *hermeneutics of meaning-recollection* aims at faithful disclosure. For instance, studies concerned with the lifeworld of people with a certain disability, intended to inform others of the nature of their experience, would be instances of interpretation aimed at 'meaning-recollection'.
- The *hermeneutics of suspicion* aims to discover, behind the thing being analysed, a further reality which allows a much deeper interpretation to be made, and which can challenge the surface account. Plainly, psychoanalysis is definitively an instance of 'suspicion'; arguably, feminism can be as well.

The hermeneutics of meaning-recollection applies to any account of psychological life, surely. It is hardly explicit interpretation at all. In fact, though qualitative research adopting the *perceptual* model of psychological life would usually reject the hermeneutic label altogether, it certainly would be included within Ricoeur's broad definition of the hermeneutics of meaning-recollection. Indeed, it could be argued that this definition is too broad. Note that it would be in accord with the hermeneutics of meaning-recollection for a psychological research methodology to involve interviewing research participants on some aspect of their experience, analysing the interview transcripts in such a way as to elicit their experience exceedingly faithfully, and then checking with the participants themselves after the analysis is done to ensure that the research account is faithful to their meaning. Of course, this is a frequent step in qualitative research.

Whether interpretation is the strong form that we see fully developed in psychoanalytic practice – the hermeneutics of suspicion – or not, Palmer (1969) usefully characterizes hermeneutics, the general theory of interpretative activity, as the method by which

> something foreign, strange, separated in time, or experience, is made familiar, present, comprehensible; something requiring representation, explanation or translation is somehow 'brought to understanding' – is 'interpreted'. (Palmer, 1969: 14)

Such interpretation may be a matter of elucidation (in the mode of 'meaning-recollection'), or radical (in the mode of suspicion).

Martin Heidegger (1889–1976) has been mentioned in earlier pages, but a recognized early discussion of the hermeneutic method is found in his early work. In *Being and Time* (1927/1962), he attempted an analysis of the everyday manner in which human beings go about their interpretative sense-making. For him, as with the constructionists, we live in an *interpreted world* and are ourselves *hermeneutic*; we are interpreters, understanders. For qualitative research, the hermeneutic approach provides a new view of the meaning of data. Interview research, for example, is the record of a process by which the researcher interprets the research participants' constructions of their world. This is reflected in Jonathan Smith's way of doing phenomenological analysis (see Chapter 3).

It was partly the divergence between Husserl and Heidegger, on the question of whether phenomenology is truly a disciplined description of experience or whether interpretation is inevitable, which led to a rift in phenomenology (similar to, but not precisely the same as, the perception/construction divide) that still affects phenomenological psychology.

THE DISCURSIVE TURN AND A TENDENCY TO POSTMODERNISM

The first half of the twentieth century saw a striking move in several very different modes of Western philosophy which began to focus on *language use* as somehow ontologically primary. The new understanding is that language does not just reflect the world of experience, but rather the world for us is constituted by our shared language. Language is in a sense the prime reality.

We have already seen one line of thought which takes this position – G.H. Mead and the symbolic interactionist tradition. A separate ancestral line also implicated in the rise of a discursive psychology is found in the ordinary language philosophy deriving from Wittgenstein's (1889–1951) later work (*Philosophical Investigations*, 1953). Wittgenstein's rejection of the idea that there can be a 'private language' (by which he criticized the view that understanding is an inner process), and his early avowal that the boundaries of my world are coextensive with the reach of my language, are plainly important to discursive psychology.

The Wittgensteinian account of the social world in terms of discrete 'language games' constituting or correlated with 'forms of life' is also important. (Austin, 1962, should be mentioned in this context.)

So, for Wittgenstein:

- A way of life and the language employed match, or are the same thing.
- We need to think of discourse use as a delimited language game appropriate to certain circumstances.
- It is in the nature of a language to be collective – there is no 'private language'.
- The idea of raw sensations on which language 'acts' to produce meaningful perceptions should be abandoned.

In a very different realm of philosophy to that of the ordinary language philosophers, we find Heidegger, dissident protégé of Husserl, putting forward the view that experience does not 'presence' the world directly, but that presencing is an act of interpretation in which language use is fundamental.

> Language was once called the 'house of Being'. It is the guardian of presencing, inasmuch as the latter's radiance remains entrusted to the propriative showing of the saying. Language is the house of Being because, as the saying, it is propriation's mode. (Heidegger, 1957/1993: 424)

This quote gives a flavour of the writing of the later Heidegger. I read him as meaning that anything that we can say 'is' has linguistic form. It is language that, in this sense, 'houses' it and 'brings' it to vivid presence. The importance for us of this is that it, too, shows the discursive turn – but now in phenomenological philosophy. Interpretativism is involved in Heidegger's stance, then, but the discursive turn, most strongly emphasized in the chapters of this book (perhaps, in Chapters 5 to 7) can also be seen in his thinking. Other sources of discourse analysis are mentioned by Willig in Chapter 7.

We can also see a link here with the constructionist turn discussed earlier. Here, however, a particularly 'strong' form of constructionism is implicated. In particular, (1) language and other cultural sign systems gain especial importance as at least the *means* by which the individual constructs reality, and maybe as the heart or foundation of that construction such that the individual's grasp of their world is *made* of the possibilities of such cultural resources; (2) the person is understood less as a unique individual, and more as a member of society, with ways of conceiving of reality that are typical of a historical epoch of a certain culture; and (3) the psychologist is very much part of this web of cultural construction. The third of these new emphases means that research has to be seen as a joint product of researcher and researched (part of what is often termed 'reflexivity'). It also means that psychology itself needs to be seen as part of cultural activity – a science which emerged from a particular period in the history of a certain society, and which cannot be detached from the interests and concerns of that society.

Social constructionism and the idea that interpretation is universal take us within a hair's breadth of *postmodern* thinking. Kenneth Gergen has summarized the constructionist stance, extending it to the entire postmodern movement, in the following statement:

> If one were to select from the substantial corpus of post modern writings a single line of argument that (a) generates broad agreement within these ranks and (b) serves as a critical divide between what we roughly distinguish as the modern versus the post modern, it would be the abandonment of the traditional commitment to representationalism. (Gergen, 1994: 412)

By representationalism, Gergen seems to be pointing to the assumption, which I have previously called the 'perceptual tendency', that we can directly describe experience. Gergen asserts that this is not possible. Siding with the constructionists, he argues that experiences cannot but be shaped by our constructions of events. Indeed, he is making an even stronger statement than this. For Gergen, qualitative psychology does not strictly reveal a lifeworld, and a person's system of personal constructs does not relate the individual to reality. Instead, all that can be discovered by qualitative psychology is a kind of network of elements (let's call them segments of discourse), each of which gains its meaning purely from its position within the total system.

Gergen points out that this radicalization of the social constructionist perspective, whereby our conceptions do not touch the world, but all is construction or *all is text* (Derrida, 1976), is a central notion of postmodernism. It has many important implications for qualitative psychology.

One inescapable epistemological consequence is that the discursive turn undermines entirely the *correspondence theory of truth* which is assumed as a fundamental by much of psychology. This is the view that the truth of a hypothesis or theory or idea is to be found in its correspondence with 'outer reality'. Experimental design, for example, hinges on this notion. But if reality is not accessible except through discursive practices, then the separateness of idea and the real is lost. (Interestingly, lack of a separateness of the idea and the real is also the case with phenomenology, despite the fact that much phenomenology does not make the discursive turn, because 'reality' is bracketed and put out of play in order to reveal the structures of consciousness and the lifeworld.)

Modernism takes it for granted that our perceptions and constructions do relate to the real world and it allows the further assumption that ongoing *progress* is possible in research. This is because modernity has the fundamental notion that there is a non-negotiable, solid truth or reality about which it is possible to attain ever more accurate knowledge. The researcher can elaborate the structure of scientific constructs in a direction which approximates more and more to the truth of actual reality.

Modernism characterizes both the world of natural science and technology and the social and political world. It assumes that there are recognized criteria of scientific research or scholarly activity by which knowledge advances. In marked contrast, postmodernity can be viewed as a cultural movement for which such strong criteria of validity no longer exist (since the connection between 'reality' and human constructions has been dismissed). The idea of progress has nothing to refer to, because there is no standard against which to judge an innovation of theory, practice, product or policy that would enable one to see that it is an improvement over what previously existed.

Plainly, most psychology is modernist in its assumptions. There is a true reality to be uncovered by the activities of its researchers, and findings at one moment in time are the stepping-stones to refined findings later on. Postmodern thinking questions this (Kvale, 1992), and an important implication is that psychology can no longer present itself as 'outside human society, looking in'. It is not detached, but one among the many discourses within the culture – a discourse-space, a particular realm of social cognition and practical activity with its own rationality. In this view, qualitative psychology should not pretend to reveal progressively true, universal human nature, but should make us aware of the implicit assumptions (about 'human nature' and kinds of human experience) that are available to the members of a social group for the time being.

A key figure in this mode of thinking was Michel Foucault (1926–1984). Like other postmodern thinkers, he asserted the primacy of social constructions, or discourse (e.g., Foucault, 1971, 1973a, 1973b). Foucault's constructionism (like that of all postmodernists) is a fully social one. The power of discourse does not come from the individual speaker-actor, but from the culture. And discourse *constitutes* the individual.

Perhaps Foucault's major contribution to postmodern social science was to emphasize the relationship between knowledge and power, or discourse and control. Foucault's last, uncompleted, work, *The History of Sexuality* (vol. 1, 1981), stresses control-through-discourse, arguing that the discourse-space of sexuality is one in which the individual defines himself or herself. Foucault finds it no accident that morality is treated most centrally as sexual morality, for, in the self-examination that awareness of sexuality entails, a process of personal self-monitoring is established.

Whereas Foucault was, at least at one stage, interested in the relationship between discourse and other features of the social world, Derrida (1981) regards all as, in the end, discourse. Such discursive sovereignty also contrasts with the hermeneutics of Freud, for whom interpretation is grounded in the primary, biological processes of libido. For Derrida, there is no hermeneutically privileged realm – there is no area of knowledge in which the certainty of absolute truth can be found.

CONCLUSION AND LINKS TO THE CHAPTERS IN THIS BOOK

This chapter has shown the slow and subterranean development of ways of thinking which, together, constitute the qualitative sensibility in psychology. I have not strayed far over the borders of the established discipline, yet our scholarly neighbours in the social sciences have in some cases been the source of ideas that have been sparingly incorporated in qualitative psychology. One tendency that is to be encouraged, then, is qualitative psychologists' growing commerce with neighbours, both methodologically and in terms of subject matter. Disciplinary divisions do not stand up to phenomenological or discursive scrutiny.

Some historical currents within the discipline have been neglected for lack of space. The impact of psychoanalysis deserves proper recognition, both because of its focus on accounts of experience and because of the dangers of the hermeneutics of suspicion to which it can succumb, which may pose dangers to qualitative psychology more broadly. Similarly, the strong relationship between phenomenology and Gestalt theory (Gurwitsch, 1964) was historically extremely important. I have neglected the impact of existential psychiatry (Binswanger, 1963; Boss, 1979; Laing, 1965). Finally, I have not discussed one of the strongest movements pressing the claims of the qualitative sensibility over the last few decades – feminism (Gergen and Davis, 1997; Tong, 1991; Ussher, 1997; Wilkinson and Kitzinger, 1995), in its seizure of the high epistemological ground, in its quest for *voice*, in its concern that psychological thought and the process of psychological research should acknowledge the centrality of *power*, and with the need for equalization of the researcher/ researched relationship.

I have used the phrase 'the qualitative sensibility' in this chapter, yet there is sufficient evidence to doubt the unity of mind of qualitative psychologists. The *perceptual* and the *discursive* tendencies seem rather distinct in their understanding of the human condition and the purpose of qualitative research. In fact, there are overlaps. Nevertheless, it would be roughly true to say that social constructionism moves in the postmodern direction, and that this leads to one form of qualitative psychology. A different form seems to originate from the Husserlian understanding of phenomenological research, which seeks universals of human experience (an undertaking which has modernist features). However, existential phenomenology, for example, is not quite characterizable in either modernist or postmodernist terms. Thus we can see a diversity of approaches, a flourishing of difference, but we can also see a unity, a qualitative sensibility.

Let me finish with a rough-and-ready mapping of the following chapters of this book in relation to the conceptual field I have laid out. Of course, this is not a definitive model and it is possible some of the authors would see some of this differently:

- Interpretative phenomenological analysis (outlined by Jonathan Smith and Mike Osborn in Chapter 3) focuses on experience, while allowing that both the research participant and the researcher are entering into interpretation. They also note the importance of attending to the idiographic.

- With Kathy Charmaz's Chapter 4 we are introduced to grounded theory – a technique of analysis emerging from the symbolic interactionist tradition in which 'what the people themselves say' is of utmost importance in founding the analysis. However, as Charmaz points out, there are different versions of grounded theory, which means the researcher can have one of a number of theoretical approaches which guide their understanding of the structures that emerge – they may be constructionist or experiential or even more positivistic in their outlook.

- Michael Murray's account of narrative psychology (Chapter 5) emphasizes the idea that it is a prime human characteristic to make sense of our circumstances by constructing stories. Narrative psychology is clearly at the intersection of the world as construction and the discursive turn.

- In his introduction to conversation analysis (Chapter 6), Paul Drew takes the observation that the outcome of qualitative psychological research is a co-constitution of the researcher and the researched as a *theme* of research, drawing on the work of the ethnomethodologists. Here, perhaps, the prime reality is the process of interaction and the process of discourse.

- Carla Willig (Chapter 7) draws attention to two particular modes of discourse analysis: the approach of discursive psychology (in which the individual is an *agent* who draws on socially available discourses), and that inspired by the work of Michel Foucault, in which the individual is *constituted* by the available discourses of the person. In the second case, we can see the influence of the later Heidegger and his notion of *enframing*, in which a culture may have a mode of life such that there is an enveloping understanding of *what reality is like*.

- In Chapter 8, Peter Reason and Sarah Riley take this question of ontology further, for cooperative inquiry goes as far as it can in eliminating the distinction of role between the researcher and researched. Cooperative inquiry is usually an intensively practical matter – where *we* experiment on our situation and consider the outcomes.

- Focus groups are considered by Sue Wilkinson (Chapter 9) as a qualitative technique and, like the technique of grounded theory discussed in Chapter 4, there is some flexibility in the theoretical approach which the researcher may use. Again, we have a key issue of qualitative research generally: where does ontological priority lie – with the individual, the group, the interaction among the members of the group, the wider society?

- Thematic analysis is introduced by Victoria Clarke, Virginia Braun and Nikki Hayfield in Chapter 10. They make the point that this diverse set of approaches can be seen as in some way foundational in so far as the use of any qualitative method must entail the establishment from the raw empirical data (whatever they are) of a structure of themes on which the researcher may then work.

- As we have seen, there is diversity in qualitative methods. The distinction is quite a profound one, for example, between an underlying view of the person as enmeshed in the language in terms of which the world is constructed, and the view of the person as a perceiver dwelling in a personal lifeworld. In Chapter 11, Michael Larkin provides practical advice on how to make the decision about what approach to use in the context of one's specific research interest.

- Finally, Lucy Yardley addresses, in Chapter 12, the question of validity as it arises anew for researchers who adopt a qualitative position.

It is worth underscoring the value of the variety of approaches within qualitative psychology. It is arguable that the richness of the human condition is such that no one tendency would encompass the whole. Allport's idiographic psychology is needed in order to approach the person's grasp of their world. Phenomenology stresses the personal lifeworld, but is also interested in attempting to uncover general structures of meaning that all share. And much of that shared meaning can be expressed in terms of the sociocentrism of some kinds of constructionism. Pluralism in qualitative psychology is to be valued. Pluralism of qualitative outlook matches awareness of human complexity. It is in this context that qualitative psychology of whatever tendency should be judged.

3 Interpretative Phenomenological Analysis

Jonathan A. Smith and Mike Osborn

Interpretative phenomenological analysis (IPA) is an approach which is dedicated to the detailed exploration of personal meaning and lived experience. More particularly, the aim of IPA is to explore in detail how participants are making sense of their personal and social world, and the main currency for an IPA study is the meanings that particular experiences, events, and states hold for participants. IPA is now used to address a wide range of experiential research issues both in psychology and in related disciplines. The aim of this chapter is to provide for the reader new to this way of working a detailed presentation of the stages involved in doing interpretative phenomenological analysis. It gives details of each stage and illustrates them with material taken from a study conducted by the authors. At the same time, it should be recognized that, as is generally the case with qualitative research, there is no single, definitive way to do IPA. We are offering suggestions, ways we have found that have worked for us. We hope these will be useful in helping the newcomer to IPA to get under way, but remember that, as you proceed and particularly as you become more experienced, you may find yourself adapting the method to your own particular way of working and the particular topic you are investigating.

HISTORY AND THEORETICAL BACKGROUND

IPA was developed as a specifically psychological experiential research methodology 20 years ago (Smith, 1996) and is part of a small family of methods informed by phenomenological philosophy. Here we will outline the theoretical underpinnings of IPA and then briefly describe its relation to other related approaches.

IPA is phenomenological in that it involves detailed examination of the participant's lived experience; it attempts to explore personal experience and is concerned with an individual's personal perception or account of an object or event, as opposed to an attempt to produce an objective statement of the object or event itself. This follows from Edmund Husserl's declaration of phenomenology as an attempt to go 'back to things themselves' (Husserl, 1900/2001: 168); that is, as far as possible, to see things as they present themselves in their own terms, rather than as defined by prior scientific hypotheses or abstract conceptualizations. At the same time, IPA also emphasizes that the research exercise is a dynamic process with an active role for the researcher in that process. One is trying to get close to the participant's personal world, to take, in Conrad's (1987) words, an 'insider's perspective', but one cannot do this directly or completely. Access depends on, and is complicated by, the researcher's own conceptions; indeed, these are required in order to make sense of that other personal world through a process of interpretative activity. This is in tune with Heidegger's (1927/1962) interpretative or hermeneutic development of phenomenology. Thus, a two-stage interpretation process, or a double hermeneutic, is involved. The participants are trying to make sense of their world; the researcher is trying to make sense of the participants trying to make sense of their world. IPA is therefore intellectually connected to hermeneutics and theories of interpretation (Packer and Addison, 1989; Smith, 2007; see also Chapter 2 this volume).

Different interpretative stances are possible, as argued by Ricoeur (1970; see also Chapter 2 in this volume), IPA combines an empathic hermeneutics with a questioning hermeneutics. Thus, consistent with its phenomenological origins, IPA is concerned with trying to understand what it is like, from the point of view of the participants. At the same time, a detailed IPA analysis can also involve asking critical questions of the texts from participants, such as the following: What is the person trying to achieve here? Is something leaking out here that wasn't intended? Do I have a sense of something going on here that maybe the participants themselves are less aware of? We would say that both styles of interpretation are part of sustained qualitative inquiry but that the degree of emphasis will depend on the particularities of the IPA study concerned. The ordinary word 'understanding' usefully captures these two aspects of interpretation–understanding in the sense of identifying or empathizing with and understanding as trying to make sense of. Allowing for both aspects in the inquiry is likely to lead to a richer analysis and to do greater justice to the totality of the person, 'warts and all'. IPA also acknowledges a debt to symbolic interactionism (Denzin, 1995) with its concern for how meanings are constructed by individuals within both a social and a personal world.

IPA has a theoretical commitment to the person as a cognitive, linguistic, affective and physical being and assumes a chain of connection between people's talk and their thinking and emotional state. At the same time, IPA researchers realize this chain of connection is complicated – people struggle to express what they are thinking and feeling; there may be reasons why they do not wish to self-disclose; and the researcher has to interpret people's mental and emotional state from what they say.

IPA's emphasis on sense-making by both participant and researcher means that it can be described as having cognition as a central analytic concern, and this suggests an interesting theoretical alliance with the cognitive paradigm that is dominant in contemporary psychology. IPA shares, with the cognitive psychology and social cognition approaches in social and clinical psychology, a concern with mental processes. However, IPA strongly diverges from mainstream psychology when it comes to deciding the appropriate methodology for such questions. While mainstream psychology is still strongly committed to quantitative and experimental methodology, IPA employs in-depth qualitative analysis. Thus, IPA and mainstream psychology converge in being interested in examining how people think about what is happening to them but diverge in deciding how this thinking can best be studied.

Indeed, we would argue that IPA's commitment to the exploration of meaning and sense-making links it quite closely to the original concerns of cognitive psychology in its rejection of the behaviourist paradigm that had thus far dominated the discipline. It is interesting to see how Bruner (1990), one of the founders of the cognitive approach, regrets how it swiftly moved from a central concern with meaning and meaning-making into the science of information processing.

The final important theoretical underpinning for IPA is idiography (Smith, Harré and Van Langenhove, 1995). IPA is interested in the detailed examination of particular cases, in understanding how particular people have experienced particular events. It does not eschew generalizations but works painstakingly from individual cases very cautiously to more general claims. In practice, an IPA study will usually present its results as a set of convergences and divergences within the accounts of participants. This idiographic mode of inquiry contrasts with the nomothetic approach which predominates in psychology. In a nomothetic study, analysis is at the level of groups and populations, and one can make only probabilistic claims about individuals: for example, there is a 70 per cent chance that person X will respond in this way. In an idiographic study, because it has been derived from the examination of individual case studies, it is also possible to make specific statements about those individuals.

IPA has now become widely established and there are many published studies in psychology and increasingly in other disciplines applying IPA to the examination of topics in the realm of lived experience. The other best-known phenomenological approach in psychology is Giorgi's descriptive phenomenology (Giorgi, 1997). Obviously the two methodologies have much in common in attempting to articulate empirical research methods to examine experiential research questions. However, there are two major differences between the two approaches. While IPA is aligned with Heidegger's articulation of a hermeneutic phenomenology, Giorgi's methodology is avowedly descriptive and is attempting a purer Husserlian phenomenology. Also, in contrast to the emphasis placed by IPA on the importance of the case and capturing particulars of the individual's experience within the analysis, Giorgi's approach is more concerned with eliciting the general structure of the experience for the group under examination. IPA is not the only methodology influenced by hermeneutic phenomenology. Van Manen (1990) eloquently outlines an interpretative phenomenological approach to education and parenting, and Benner (1994) describes a form of inquiry especially influenced by Heidegger and applied in nursing. For more on the theoretical foundations of IPA, see Smith, Flowers and Larkin (2009).

FORMULATING A RESEARCH QUESTION AND DESIGNING A STUDY

As will be apparent, IPA is a suitable approach when one is trying to find out how individuals are perceiving the particular situations they are facing – how they are making sense of their personal and social world. IPA is especially useful when one is concerned with complexity, process or novelty. Box 3.1 illustrates the type of research questions that have been addressed by IPA. Research questions in IPA projects are usually framed broadly and openly. There is no attempt to test a predetermined hypothesis of the researcher; rather, the aim is to explore, flexibly and in detail, an area of concern.

BOX 3.1   EXAMPLES OF PSYCHOLOGICAL RESEARCH QUESTIONS ADDRESSED IN IPA STUDIES

- How do people come to terms with the death of a partner? (Golsworthy and Coyle, 1999)

- What is it like to experience depression? (Smith and Rhodes, 2014)

- How do people in the early stage of Alzheimer's disease perceive and manage the impact on their sense of self? (Clare, 2003)

- How do people make sense of possible causes for their heart attack? (French et al., 2005)

IPA studies are conducted on small sample sizes. The detailed case-by-case analysis of individual transcripts takes a long time and, as indicated above, the aim of the study is to say something in detail about the perceptions and understandings of this particular group rather than prematurely make more general claims.

IPA researchers usually try to find a fairly homogeneous sample. The basic logic is that if one is interviewing, for example, six participants, it is not very helpful to think in terms of random or representative sampling. IPA therefore goes in the opposite direction and, through purposive sampling, finds a more closely defined group for whom the research question will be significant. How the specificity of a sample is defined will depend on the study; in some cases, the topic under investigation may itself be rare and define the boundaries of the relevant sample. In other cases, where a less specific issue is under investigation, the sample may be drawn from a population with similar demographic/socio-economic status profiles. The logic is similar to that employed by the social anthropologist conducting ethnographic research in one particular community. The anthropologist then reports in detail about that particular culture but does not claim to be able to say something about *all* cultures. In time, of course, it will be possible for subsequent studies to be conducted with other groups, and so, gradually, more general claims can be made, but each founded on the detailed examination of a set of case studies. It is also possible to think in terms of theoretical rather than empirical generalizability. In this case, the readers make links between the findings of an IPA study, their own personal and professional experience, and the claims in the extant literature. The power of the IPA study is judged by the light it sheds within this broader context.

A final note on sampling: it should be remembered that one always has to be pragmatic when doing research; one's sample will in part be defined by who is prepared to be included in it!

There is no right answer to the question of the sample size. It partly depends on several factors: the degree of commitment to the case study level of analysis and reporting, the richness of the individual cases, and the constraints one is operating under. For example, IPA studies have been published with samples of one, four, nine, fifteen, and more. Recently there has been a trend for some IPA studies to be conducted with a very small number of participants. A distinctive feature of IPA is its commitment to a detailed interpretative account of the cases included, and many researchers are recognizing that this can only realistically be done on a small sample – thus, in simple terms, one is sacrificing breadth for depth. How small is small? It obviously depends on what the research is being conducted for. We now routinely recommend that undergraduates have a sample size of three. Even with this number, good IPA interviews will generate a large amount of detailed data, and in our experience this is enough to produce a well-conducted IPA analysis. It allows sufficient in-depth engagement with each individual case but also allows a detailed examination of similarity and difference, convergence and divergence. For postgraduate research, the samples will normally be larger but it does depend on the particular constraints operating, as well as the quality of the data obtained. The danger for the newcomer is that if the sample size is too large they become overwhelmed by the vast amount of data generated by a qualitative study and are not able to produce a sufficiently penetrating analysis.

The research process in an IPA study can be seen as an interpretative cycle. The researcher starts at home-base, in one's office or library, on one side of the research circle, thinking and reading about the topic of investigation. One then moves around the circle and begins to enter the world of one's participant. As preparation for this, one brackets or puts to one side the knowledge and assumptions one has acquired of the phenomenon being researched. This process is enhanced in the actual encounter with the participant by intensive engagement with what the participant is saying. One becomes a curious and attentive but 'naive' listener as the participant unfolds their story in their own terms. After the interview, one moves back around the circle to one's home-base and begins the process of formally interpreting what the respondent has said. Here one tries to make sense of what the participant has experienced and this analysis must always be grounded in the actual words of the participant. However the analysis will also be informed by one's own personal interests and expertise which are brought to the reading of the text. For more on this cycle, see Smith, 2007.

COLLECTING DATA

IPA researchers wish to analyse in detail how participants perceive and make sense of things that are happening to them. It therefore requires a flexible data collection instrument. While it is possible to obtain data suitable for IPA analysis in a number of ways, such as personal accounts and diaries (see, for example, Smith, 1999), most IPA studies have been conducted through the semi-structured interview. This form of interviewing allows the researcher and participant to engage in a dialogue whereby initial questions are modified in the light of the participants' responses, and the investigator is able to probe interesting and important areas which arise. Therefore, we will discuss semi-structured interviewing in detail in this chapter. This is also necessary because high-quality interviewing is absolutely critical to high-quality IPA. Indeed, the quality of the interview conducted sets a clear cap on how good the subsequent analysis can be. Doing good interviewing is a particular skill and one which usually takes some time to develop.

It is useful first to contrast the primary features of a *semi-structured interview* with those of a *structured interview*. The structured interview shares much of the rationale of the psychological experiment. Generally, the investigator decides in advance exactly what constitutes the required data and constructs the questions in such a way as to elicit answers corresponding to, and easily contained within, predetermined categories, which can then be numerically analysed. In order to enhance reliability, the interviewer should stick very closely to the interview schedule and behave with as little variation as possible between interviews. The interviewer will aim to:

- use short, specific questions
- read the question exactly as on the schedule
- ask the questions in the identical order specified by the schedule
- ideally have pre-coded response categories, enabling the questioner to match what the respondent says against one of those categories.

Sometimes the investigator will provide the respondent with a set of possible answers to choose from. Sometimes the respondent is allowed a free response, which can then be categorized.

Thus, in many ways, the structured interview is like the questionnaire; indeed, the two overlap to the extent that often the interview is simply the investigator going through a questionnaire in the presence of a respondent, with the interviewer filling in the answers on the questionnaire sheet based on what the respondent says.

The alleged advantages of the structured interview format are control, reliability and speed. That is, the investigator has maximum control over what takes place in the interview. It is also argued that the interview will be reliable in the sense that the same format is being used with each respondent, and that the identity of the interviewer should have minimal impact on the responses obtained.

The structured interview has disadvantages which arise from the constraints put on the respondent and the situation. The structured interview deliberately limits what the respondent can talk about – this having been decided in advance by the investigator. Thus, the interview may well miss out on a novel aspect of the subject, an area considered important by the respondent but not predicted by the investigator. And the topics which are included are approached in a way which makes it unlikely that it will allow the unravelling of complexity or ambiguity in the respondent's position. The structured interview can also become stilted because of the need to ask questions in exactly the same format and sequence to each participant.

With semi-structured interviews, the investigator will have a set of questions on an interview schedule, but the interview will be guided by the schedule rather than be dictated by it. Here then:

- there is an attempt to establish rapport with the respondent
- the ordering of questions is less important
- the interviewer is freer to probe interesting areas that arise
- the interview can follow the respondent's interests or concerns.

These differences follow from the basic concerns of an approach such as IPA. The investigator has an idea of the area of interest and some questions to pursue. At the same time, there is a wish to try to enter, as far as possible, the psychological and social world of the respondent. Therefore, the respondent shares more closely in the direction the interview takes, and the respondent can introduce an issue the investigator had not thought of. In this relationship, the respondents can be perceived as the experiential expert on the subject and should therefore be allowed maximum opportunity to tell their own story.

Thus, we can summarize the advantages of the semi-structured interview: it facilitates rapport/empathy, allows a greater flexibility of coverage and allows the interview to go into novel areas, and it tends to produce richer data. On the debit side, this form of interviewing reduces the control the investigator has over the situation, takes longer to carry out, and is harder to analyse.

Constructing the interview schedule

Although an investigator conducting a semi-structured interview is likely to see it as a co-determined interaction in its own right, it is still valuable when working in this way to produce an interview schedule in advance. Indeed, for newcomers to IPA, we believe it is almost essential. Why? Producing a schedule beforehand forces us to think explicitly about

---

BOX 3.2   INTERVIEW SCHEDULE: PATIENT'S EXPERIENCE OF RENAL DIALYSIS

A. Dialysis

1. Could you give me a brief history of your kidney problem from when it started to your beginning dialysis?
2. Could you describe what happens in dialysis, in your own words?
3. What do you do when you are having dialysis?
4. How do you feel when you are dialysing?

    Prompt: physically, emotionally, mentally.

(Continued)

(Continued)

5. What do you think about?

6. How do you feel about having dialysis?

    Prompt: some people/relief from previous illness/a bind.

7. How does dialysis/kidney disease affect your everyday life?

    Prompt: work, interests, relationships.

8. If you had to describe what the dialysis machine means to you, what would you say?

    Prompt: What words come to mind, what images? Do you have a nickname for it?

B. Identity

9. How would you describe yourself as a person?

    Prompt: What sort of person are you? Most important characteristics: happy, moody, nervy.

10. Has having kidney disease and starting dialysis made a difference to how you see yourself?

    Prompt: If so, how do you see yourself now as different from before you started dialysis? How would you say you have changed?

11. What about compared to before you had kidney disease?

12. What about the way other people see you?

    Prompt: members of your family, friends? changed?

C. Coping

13. What does the term 'illness' mean to you? How do you define it?

14. How much do you think about your own physical health?

15. Do you see yourself as being ill?

    Prompt: always, sometimes? Would you say you were an ill person?

16. On a day-to-day basis, how do you deal with having kidney disease (the illness)?

    Prompt: Do you have particular strategies for helping you? Ways of coping: practical, mental.

17. Do you think about the future much?

what we think/hope the interview might cover. More specifically, it enables us to think of difficulties that might be encountered, for example, in terms of question wording or sensitive areas, and to give some thought to how these difficulties might be handled. Thinking in advance about the different ways the interview may proceed allows us, when it comes to the interview itself, to concentrate more thoroughly and more confidently on what the respondent is actually saying. For example, Box 3.2 presents a schedule from a project one of us conducted on kidney disease patients' responses to their illness. The participants are undergoing dialysis treatment for their kidney disease – an extremely demanding treatment regimen which involves going to hospital three or four times a week and being attached to a dialysis machine for about three hours.

The following list suggests a sequence for producing an interview schedule. This is intended to be only suggestive, not prescriptive. Note also that doing this sort of work is often iterative rather than linear, and you may find your ideas of what the interview should cover changing or developing as you work on the schedule.

1. Having determined the overall area to be tackled in the interview, think about the broad range of issues you want your interview to cover. The three issues in the kidney dialysis project are description of dialysis, effect on the self and coping strategies.

2. Put the topics in the most appropriate sequence. Two questions may help here: What is the most logical order in which to address these areas? Which is the most sensitive area? In general, it is a good idea to leave sensitive topics until later in the interview to allow the respondent to become relaxed and comfortable speaking to you. Thus, an interview on political affiliations might begin with questions on what the different political parties represent, and then move on to the question of societal attitudes to politics, before, in the final section, asking about the person's own voting behaviour – thus leaving the most personal and potentially most sensitive area until last. In the dialysis project, one could say that all the material is sensitive – but then the respondents know the project is about their health condition and have agreed to talk about it. It was decided that talking about the illness itself was the best way into the interview, and to allow discussion of the effect on the respondent's sense of self to come later.

3. Think of appropriate questions related to each area in order to address the issue you are interested in.

4. Think about possible probes and prompts which could follow from answers that might be given to some of your questions.

A strategy often employed in this type of interviewing is to encourage the person to speak about the topic with as little prompting from the interviewer as possible. One might say that you are attempting to get as close as possible to what your respondent thinks about the topic, without them being led too much by your questions. Good interview technique therefore often involves a gentle nudge from the interviewer rather than being too explicit. This aspect of the methodology runs counter to most of the training received for more orthodox psychology methodologies. Thus, you may well find that, in the course of constructing your schedule, some of your first draft questions are too explicit. With redrafting, these become gentler and less loaded but sufficient to let the respondents know what the area of interest is and recognize that they have something to say about it. It may be useful to try out possible questions with a colleague and get some feedback on the level of difficulty and tone.

Sometimes this initial question will be insufficient to elicit a satisfactory response. This may be for various reasons – the issue is a complex one or the question is too general or vague for this particular participant. To prepare for this, you can construct *prompts* that are framed more explicitly. Indeed, some of your first draft questions may serve as these prompts. You do not have to prepare prompts for every question, only those where you think there may be some difficulty. So, for example, after question 4 in the dialysis schedule (Box 3.2), there is a prompt to remind the interviewer to ask about each of these domains. After question 8, a prompt is provided in case the respondent has difficulty with the main question itself.

Thus, the interviewer starts with the most general possible question and hopes that this will be sufficient to enable the respondent to talk about the subject. If respondents have difficulty, say they do not understand, or give a short or tangential reply, the interviewer can move to the prompt, which is more specific. Hopefully, this will be enough to get the participant talking. The more specific-level questions are there to deal with more difficult cases where the respondent is more hesitant. It is likely that a successful interview will include questions and answers at both general and more specific levels and will move between the two fairly seamlessly. If an interview is taken up with material entirely derived from very specific follow-up questions, you may need to ask yourself how engaged the respondent is. Are you really entering the personal/social lifeworld of the participant, or are you forcing them, perhaps reluctantly and unsuccessfully, to enter yours?

Funnelling is a related technique. For certain issues, it may well be that you are interested in eliciting both the respondents' general views and their response to more specific concerns. Constructing this part of the schedule as a funnel allows you to do this. Thus, in Box 3.3, the first question attempts to elicit the respondent's general view on government policy. Having established that, the interviewer probes for more specific issues. The general point is that by asking questions in this sequence, you have allowed the respondents to give

BOX 3.3   FUNNELLING

1. What do you think of current government policies?

2. What do you think of current government policies towards health and welfare issues?

3. Do you think the government record in this area is okay, or should it be doing anything different?

4. If so, what?

5. It has been suggested that government policy is moving towards one of self-reliance, the welfare system being there only as a safety net for people unable to finance their own provision. What do you think of this as a policy?

their own views before funnelling them into more specific questions of particular concern to you. Conducted in the reverse sequence, the interview is more likely to produce data biased in the direction of the investigator's prior and specific concerns. Of course, it is possible that when answering the first question the respondent may also address the targeted issue and so make it redundant for you to ask the more specific questions.

Below we provide some more tips on good practice for constructing the interview schedule:

- *Questions should be neutral rather than value-laden or leading.*

    Bad: Do you think that the prime minister is doing a good job?

    Better: What do you think of the prime minister's record in office so far?

- *Avoid jargon or assumptions of technical proficiency.* Try to think of the perspective and language of the participants in your study and frame your questions in a way with which they will feel familiar and comfortable.

    Bad: What do you think of the human genome project?

    Better: What do you know about recent developments in genetics?

    Obviously, the first question would be fine if one were talking to biologists!

- *Use open, not closed, questions.* Closed questions encourage Yes/No answers rather than getting the respondent to open up about their thoughts and feelings.

    Bad: Should the manager resign?

    Better: What do you think the manager should do now?

    It all depends on intent and context, however. It is possible to ask what seems like a closed question in such a way and at such a point in the interview that it is actually unlikely to close down the response.

Having constructed your schedule, you should try to learn it by heart before beginning to interview so that, when it comes to the interview, the schedule can act merely as a mental prompt, if you need it, rather than you having constantly to refer to it.

Interviewing

Semi-structured interviews generally last for a considerable amount of time (usually an hour or more) and can become intense and involved, depending on the particular topic. It is therefore sensible to try to make sure that the interview can proceed without interruption as far as possible, and usually it is better to conduct the interview with the respondent alone. At the same time, one can think of exceptions where this would be neither practical nor sensible. For example, it may not be advisable with young children. The location of the interview can also make a difference. People usually feel most comfortable in a setting they are familiar with, as in their own home, but there may be times when this is not practicable and a different venue will need to be chosen.

It is sensible to concentrate at the beginning of the interview on putting respondents at ease, to enable them to feel comfortable talking to you before any of the substantive areas of the schedule are introduced. Hopefully, then, this positive and responsive 'set' will continue through the interview.

The interviewer's role in a semi-structured interview is to facilitate and guide, rather than dictate exactly what will happen during the encounter. If the interviewer has learnt the schedule in advance, he or she can concentrate during the interview on what the respondent is saying, and occasionally monitor the coverage of the scheduled topics. Thus, the interviewer uses the schedule to indicate the general area of interest and to provide cues when the participant has difficulties, but the respondent should be allowed a strong role in determining how the interview proceeds.

The interview does not have to follow the sequence on the schedule, nor does every question have to be asked, or asked in exactly the same way, of each respondent. Thus, the interviewer may decide that it would be appropriate to ask a question earlier than it appears on the schedule because it follows from what the respondent has just said. Similarly, how a question is phrased, and how explicit it is, will now partly depend on how the interviewer feels the participant is responding.

The interview may well move away from the questions on the schedule, and the interviewer must decide how much movement is acceptable. It is quite possible that the interview may enter an area that had not been predicted by the investigator but which is extremely pertinent to, and enlightening of, the project's overall question. Indeed, these novel avenues are often the most valuable, precisely because they have come unprompted from respondents and, therefore, are likely to be of especial importance for them. Thus quite a lot of latitude should be allowed. On the other hand, of course, the interviewer needs to make sure that the conversation does not move too far away from the agreed domain.

Here are a few tips on interviewing techniques:

- *Try not to rush in too quickly.* Give the respondent time to finish a question before moving on. Often the most interesting questions need some time to respond to, and richer, fuller answers may be missed if the interviewer jumps in too quickly.

- *Use minimal probes.* If respondents are entering an interesting area, minimal probes are often all that is required to help them to continue, for example: 'Can you tell me more about that?' or 'How did you feel about that?'

- *Ask one question at a time.* Multiple questions can be difficult for the respondent to unpick and even more difficult for you subsequently, when you are trying to work out from a transcript which question the respondent is replying to.

- *Monitor the effect of the interview on the respondent.* It may be that respondents feel uncomfortable with a particular line of questioning, and this may be expressed in their non-verbal behaviour or in how they reply. You need to be ready to respond to this, by, for example, backing off and trying again more gently or deciding it would be inappropriate to pursue this area with this respondent. As an interviewer, you have ethical responsibilities towards the respondent.

We provide a sample of an interview transcript in Box 3.4. Watch the unfolding rhythm of the interview and how this facilitates the development of the participant's account of his experience.

Audio recording and transcription

It is necessary to decide whether to audio record the interview or not. Our view is that it is not possible to do the form of interviewing required for IPA without audio recording. If one attempts to write down everything the participant is saying during the interview, one will only capture the gist, missing important nuances. It will also interfere with helping the interview to run smoothly and with establishing rapport.

Of course, the respondent may not like being recorded and may even not agree to the interview if it is recorded, though in our experience this is extremely rare. It is also important not to reify the recording. While the record it produces is fuller, it is not a complete, 'objective' record. Non-verbal behaviour is excluded, and the recording still requires a process of interpretation by the transcriber or any other listener.

If you do decide to record and transcribe the interview, the normal convention is to transcribe the whole interview, including the interviewer's questions (see Box 3.4 again for a sample of how this is done). Leave a margin wide enough on both sides of the page to make your analytic comments. For IPA, the level of transcription is generally at the semantic level: one needs to see all the words spoken, including false starts; and significant pauses,

---

BOX 3.4   SAMPLE OF TRANSCRIPTION FROM DIALYSIS PROJECT

Q   I would like to start with some questions about dialysis, okay? And a very basic one just to start with, can you tell me what you do, physically do, when you're dialysing?

R   What I actually do with myself while I'm sat there?

Q   Yeah.

R   Well, what I tend to do is, I always have a paper, or I watch TV, you mean actually just sat there?

Q   Yeah.

R   I read the papers, I always take two papers from work or a magazine and read those.

Q   Do you mean work papers or?

R   No, just normal everyday papers cos the problem I've got is because I'm right-handed and the fistula (?) is on the right-hand side, which is the one annoyance but I can't write.

Q   Because you can't write, yeah.

R   Or else I would be able to, so I read the papers or take as many magazines as I can and I always keep myself busy or watch TV. If I'm getting a good enough sound from the television point

(Continued)

(Continued)

I watch the news, I always do it the same way, get in, get on, read the news daily papers, any magazines I've got, then if I've got a good enough sound on the TV I watch the news from half-six to half-seven, that's during the week when I'm in there, on the Sunday now I do it on a morning, I just buy a Sunday paper and I always read the paper or read a magazine. Always the same, just so I can keep my mind occupied. I always need to do that.

Q   So you are able to concentrate enough to be able to do?

R   Yeah. And sometimes if I'm tired I can go to sleep for an hour.

Q   Right.

R   Or if I've run out of papers and sometimes I just shut me eyes for an hour, and I can fall asleep but normally if I can I always make sure I get a magazine or a paper and read that and do something.

Q   And that sounds as though you're, that's quite a determined routine.

R   Yeah.

Q   Do you, what's behind that, what what why do you feel the necessity to be so methodical?

R   I think what I try and do is, yeah, so that I treat it as part of normal routine, I think that's what I do it for, I'm sometimes, I always get a paper from work, the same papers, always try and borrow a magazine and read and keep myself, a way not thinking about it while I'm on, that is why I do it and watch TV, so I don't think about the machine or I get bored if I'm just sat there doing nothing, but mainly not so I don't think about it.

laughs and other features are also worth recording. However, for IPA, one does not need the more detailed transcription of prosodic features of the talk which are required in conversation analysis (see Chapter 6). Transcription of interviews takes a long time, depending on the clarity of the recording and one's typing proficiency. As a rough guide, one needs to allow between five and eight hours of transcription time per hour of interview.

ANALYSIS

In IPA the researcher wants to learn something about the participant's lived experience. It is the meaning of experience that is important and the aim is to try to understand the content and complexity of those meanings rather than measure their frequency. This involves the investigator engaging in an interpretative relationship with the transcript. While one is attempting to capture and do justice to the meanings of the respondents, to learn about their mental and social world, those meanings are not transparently available – they must be obtained through a sustained engagement with the text and a process of interpretation.

The following section describes a step-by-step approach to the analysis in IPA, illustrated with a worked example from a study on the impact of chronic benign pain on the participant's self-concept. Chronic benign low back pain is a useful subject for IPA, as the context and personal meanings of the pain to the sufferers are critical to their experience. Participants were interviewed in the style outlined above and the transcripts subjected to IPA. The full study is reported in Smith and Osborn (2007).

This is not a prescriptive methodology. It is a way of doing IPA that has worked for us and our students, but it is there to be adapted by researchers, who will have their own personal way of working. It is also important to remember that qualitative analysis is inevitably a personal process, and the analysis itself is the interpretative work which the investigator does at each of the stages.

A project may take the form of a single case design or involve a number of participants. In IPA, however, one always begins by looking in detail at the transcript of one inter-view before moving on to examine the others, case by case. This follows the idiographic approach to analysis, beginning with particular examples and only slowly working up to more general claims.

A powerful way of thinking of what is going on in IPA is in terms of the hermeneutic circle. The hermeneutic circle refers to the way in which interpretation involves a dynamic move between looking at the part and looking at the whole. Part of the dynamism comes from the fact that what counts as a part and what as a whole are in flux during the analysis. Thus when reading a sentence, one interprets each word in relation to the whole sentence in which it is embedded but that word in turn illuminates the interpretation of the whole sentence. Then, as one moves on, the sentence becomes a part within the bigger whole of the paragraph. So each sentence contributes to the understanding of the paragraph as a whole but the unfolding paragraph in turn helps the interpretation of each sentence. And then this paragraph becomes a part within the whole of the interview, this interview a part within the whole of the corpus of interviews and so on.

Actually there are various hermeneutic circles at work when one is conducting this type of experiential research. Let's think of another one. The early part of the research process when doing IPA is primarily one of zooming in/focusing down. One concentrates on this particular person in this particular context as they unfold this particular account. Then dur-ing analysis one begins to look in detail at the microscopic details which go to make up the whole case, and this can be seen as involving considerable fragmentation. Importantly, how-ever, this is a circular process, so in the second part of the endeavour the individual pieces of analysis slowly come together in clusters and patterns and one ends up with another whole – a complete analysis of this person's or this group's experience. And this new whole is both different from and intimately connected to the whole that one started with – the individual person being talked to in the interview.

Analysing the first case

The transcript is read a number of times, one margin being used to annotate what is interesting or significant about what the respondent said. It is important in the first stage of the analysis to read and reread the transcript closely in order to become as familiar as possible with the account. Each reading has the potential to throw up new insights. This is close to being a free textual analysis. There are no rules about what is commented upon, and there is no requirement, for example, to divide the text into meaning units and assign a comment for each unit. Some parts of the interview will be richer than others and so warrant more commentary. Some of the comments are attempts at summarizing or paraphrasing, some will be associations or connections that come to mind, and others may be preliminary interpretations. It is crucial to keep in mind here what the purpose is. You are trying to make sense of what is important in the participant's experience, and your initial notes are attempts to document this sense-making. You may also find yourself commenting on the use of language by the participants and/or the sense of the persons themselves which are coming across. As you move through the transcript, you are likely to comment on similarities and differences, echoes, amplifications and contradictions in what a person is saying.

The extract which follows shows this first stage of analysis for a small section of the interview with Helen, who was the first participant in our study:

Int. How long has it been like that?

Aggression
Not who I am – identity

H. Since it started getting bad, I was always snappy with it but not like this, it's not who I am it's just who I am if you know what I mean, it's not really me, I get like that and I know like, you're being mean now but I can't help it. It's the pain, it's me, but it is me, me doing it but not me do you understand what I'm saying, if I was to describe myself like you said, I'm a nice person, but then I'm not am I, and there's other stuff, stuff I haven't told you, if you knew you'd be disgusted I just get so hateful.

Being mean
Can't help it – no control

Me doing it but not me
Conflict, tension
Me vs nice
Shame, if you knew – disgust
Fear of being known

Int. When you talk about you and then sometimes not you, what do you mean?

H. I'm not me these days, I am sometimes, I am all right, but then I get this mean bit, the hateful bit, that's not me.

Not always me, part of herself that is rejected – hateful, the 'not me'

Int. What's that bit?

H. I dunno, that's the pain bit, I know you're gonna say it's all me, but I can't help it even though I don't like it. It's the mean me, my mean head all sour and horrible, I can't cope with that bit, I cope with the pain better.

Not me = pain; defending against implications that it is 'me'

Helpless
Mean/sour – worse than the pain

Int. How do you cope with it?

Tearful/distressed, avoidant/resistant

Unbearable, shocked at self

H. Get out the way, [tearful] sit in my room, just get away, look do you mind if we stop now, I didn't think it would be like this, I don't want to talk any more.

This process is continued for the whole of the first transcript. Then one returns to the beginning of the transcript, and the other margin is used to document emerging themes. Here the initial notes are transformed into concise phrases which aim to capture the essential quality of what was found in the text. The themes move the response to a slightly higher level of abstraction and may invoke more psychological terminology. At the same time, the thread back to what the participant actually said and one's initial response should be apparent. So the skill at this stage is finding expressions which are high-level enough to allow theoretical connections within and across cases but which are still grounded in the particularity of the specific thing said. From our analysis of Helen's account, related above, the following themes emerged:

Int. How long has it been like that?

H. Since it started getting bad, I was always snappy with it but not like this, it's not who I am it's just who I am if you know what I mean, it's not really me, I get like that and I know like, you're being mean now but I can't help it. It's the pain, it's me, but it is me, me doing it but not me do you understand what I'm saying, if I was to describe myself like you said, I'm a nice person, but then I'm not am I, and there's other stuff, stuff I haven't told you, if you knew you'd be disgusted I just get so hateful.

Anger and pain
Struggle to accept self and identity – unwanted self

Lack of control over self

Responsibility, self vs pain
Shameful self – struggle with unwanted self
Fear of judgement

Int. When you talk about you and then sometimes not you, what do you mean?

H. I'm not me these days, I am sometimes, I am all right, but then I get this mean bit, the hateful bit, that's not me.

Unwanted self rejected as true self

Int. What's that bit?

H. I dunno, that's the pain bit, I know you're gonna say it's all me, but I can't help it even though I don't like it. It's the mean me, my mean head all sour and horrible, I can't cope with that bit, I cope with the pain better.

Attribution of unwanted self to the pain
Defence of original self

Ranking duress, self vs pain

Int. How do you cope with it?

H. Get out the way, [tearful] sit in my room, just get away, look do you mind if we stop now, I didn't think it would be like this, I don't want to talk any more.

Shame of disclosure

This transformation of initial notes into themes is continued through the whole transcript. It may well be that similar themes emerge as you go through the transcript and where that happens the same theme title is therefore repeated. During this stage, the entire transcript is treated as data, and no attempt is made to omit or select particular passages for special attention. At the same time, there is no requirement for every turn to generate themes. The number of emerging themes reflects the richness of the particular passage.

The emergent themes are listed on a sheet of paper in the order they appear in the transcript (Box 3.5).

BOX 3.5   INITIAL LIST OF THEMES

Anger and pain

Struggle to accept self and identity – unwanted self

Lack of control over self

Responsibility, self vs pain

Shameful self – struggle with unwanted self

Fear of judgement

Unwanted self rejected as true self

Attribution of unwanted self to the pain

Defence of original self

Ranking duress, self vs pain

Shame of disclosure

Rejection of change

Avoidance of implications

Struggle to accept new self

Undesirable, destructive self

Shame

Undesirable behaviour ascribed to pain

Lack of compassion

Conflict of selves, me vs not me

Living with a new 'me'

So, in the initial list, the order provided is chronological – it is based on the sequence which they came up with in the transcript. The next stage involves a more analytical or theoretical ordering, as the researcher tries to make sense of the connections between themes which are emerging.

Some of the themes will cluster together, and some may emerge as superordinate concepts. Imagine a magnet with some of the themes pulling others in and helping to make sense of them.

The traditional way of doing this part of the analysis is by cutting up the individual themes and placing them on a large surface and then physically moving them around as one begins to look for patterns. We would still recommend this method to the novice. Of course there are different ways of looking for patterns and some more experienced researchers will, for example, choose to do this part of the work on the computer.

BOX 3.6   CLUSTERING OF THEMES

Undesirable behaviour ascribed to pain

Struggle to accept self and identity – unwanted self

Shameful self – struggle with unwanted self, fear of judgement

Shame of disclosure

Struggle to accept new self

Undesirable, destructive self

Conflict of selves, me vs not me

Living with a new 'me'

Unwanted self rejected as true self

Attribution of unwanted self to the pain

Defence of original self

Lack of control over self

Rejection of change

Avoidance of implications

Responsibility, self vs pain

Shame

Lack of compassion

Anger and pain

Ranking duress, self vs pain

Shame of disclosure

BOX 3.7   TABLE OF THEMES FROM FIRST PARTICIPANT

1. *Living with an unwanted self*

    –   Undesirable behaviour ascribed to pain   1.16   'it's the pain'
    –   Struggle to accept self and identity –
        unwanted self   24.11   'who I am'
    –   Unwanted self rejected as true self   24.24   'hateful bit'
    –   Struggle to accept new self   1.8   'hard to believe'
    –   Undesirable, destructive self   5.14   'mean'
    –   Conflict of selves, me vs not me   7.11   'me, not me'
    –   Living with a new self   9.6   'new me'

2. *A self that cannot be understood or controlled*

    –   Lack of control over self   24.13   'can't help'
    –   Rejection of change   1.7   'still same'
    –   Avoidance of implications   10.3   'no different'
    –   Responsibility, self vs pain   25.25   'understand'

3. *Undesirable feelings*

    –   Shame   5.15   'disgusting'
    –   Anger and pain   24.09   'snappy'
    –   Lack of compassion   6.29   'don't care'
    –   Confusion, lack of control   2.17   'no idea'
    –   Ranking duress, self vs pain   25.01   'cope'
    –   Shame of disclosure   25.06   'talk'

    (1.16 = page 1, line 16)

In our sample study, the themes were clustered as shown in Box 3.6. In this particular case, it will be seen that many of the themes recorded for the whole interview occurred in the passage we have looked at. This is quite unusual but it happened in this case that this individual extract was dense with meaning and encapsulated most of the important themes of the whole interview.

As the clustering of themes emerges, it is checked against the transcript to make sure the connections work for the primary source material – the actual words of the participant. This form of analysis is iterative and involves a close interaction between reader and text. As a researcher, one is drawing on one's interpretative resources to make sense of what the person is saying, but at the same time one is constantly checking one's own sense-making against what the person actually said. As an adjunct to the process of clustering, it may help to compile directories of the participant's phrases that support related themes. This can easily be done with the cut and paste functions on a standard word-processing package. The material can be printed to help with the clustering, and as the clustering develops so the extract material can be moved, condensed and edited.

The next stage is to turn the clustering into a table of themes (Box 3.7). Thus, the above process will have identified some clusters of themes which capture most strongly the respondent's concerns on this particular topic. The clusters are themselves given a name and at this stage these higher-level units can be called superordinate themes. The table lists the themes which go with each superordinate theme, and an identifier is added to each instance to aid the organization of the analysis and facilitate finding the original source subsequently. The identifier indicates where in the transcript instances of each theme can be found by giving key words from the particular extract alongside the page number of the transcript. During this process, certain themes may be dropped: those which neither fit well in the emerging structure nor are very rich in evidence within the transcript. Box 3.7 presents the final table of themes for Helen.

Continuing the analysis with other cases

A single participant's transcript can be written up as a case study in its own right or, more often, the analysis can move on to incorporate interviews with a number of different individuals. If one is analysing more than one interview, then from an IPA perspective it is important to begin each transcript afresh, allowing the material to speak in its own terms rather than being overly influenced by what other participants have said. Below we see the first stage of the analysis process with Tony's transcript:

	T. Yeah, you know that *Desert Island Discs*?
	Int. The radio show?
Withdrawal, relief	*T.* I'd love that, don't get me wrong I'd miss my kids and I don't mean it, but to be away from people
Change in role, putting on an act	and not have to be something else you're not, that
No people = bliss	would be bliss.
	Int. You'd be happier that way?
Miserable but no cost	*T.* Yeah, no, well, no I'd still be a miserable old git
People = duress	but it wouldn't matter, it's only when other people come around that it matters, if you can just be yourself it doesn't matter what you

People = cannot be yourself
Front, façade, demands of social role and convention

do, I'd probably shout and swear all day but it wouldn't matter I wouldn't have to put on that front so it'd be easier.

Int. So a lot of how you feel depends on who's around?

T. I suppose it does, but not the pain, that just happens. Dealing with the pain, I suppose, is different. You could say if I didn't have kids I wouldn't be like this.

Pain and relationships, kids affected experience

These initial comments were transformed into the following themes.

T. Yeah, you know that *Desert Island Discs*?

Int. The radio show?

T. I'd love that, don't get me wrong I'd miss my kids and I don't mean it, but to be away from people and not have to be something else you're not, that would be bliss.

Pain and social context
Conflict in identity
Conforming to role despite pain

Int. You'd be happier that way?

T. Yeah, no, well, no I'd still be a miserable old git but it wouldn't matter, it's only when other people come around that it matters, if you can just be yourself it doesn't what you do, I'd probably shout and swear all day but it wouldn't matter I wouldn't have to put on that front so it'd be easier.

Self in public domain

Managing the self in public

Destructive social consequences of pain

Int. So a lot of how you feel depends on who's around?

T. I suppose it does, but not the pain, that just happens. Dealing with the pain, I suppose, is different. You could say if I didn't have kids I wouldn't be like this.

Self independent of pain
Self/identity and relationships define pain experience

One continues in the same way as for the first case, documenting connections between themes and producing a separate table of themes for each case. Once each transcript has been analysed by the interpretative process, a final master table of group themes is constructed. Deciding which themes to focus upon requires the analyst to prioritize the data and begin to reduce them, which is challenging. The final themes are not selected purely on the basis of their prevalence within the data. Other factors, including the richness of the particular passages that highlight the themes and how the theme helps illuminate other aspects of the account, are also taken into account. From the analysis of the cases in this study, four main group themes were articulated (Box 3.8).

BOX 3.8   MASTER TABLE OF THEMES FOR THE GROUP

	Helen	Tony
1. *Living with an unwanted self in private*		
Undesirable behaviour ascribed to pain	1.16	3.27
Struggle to accept self and identity – unwanted self	24.11	2.13
Rejected as true self	6.3	7.15
Undesirable, destructive self	5.14	2.17
Conflict of selves	7.11	12.13
Living with a new self	9.6	2.14
2. *Living with an unwanted self, in public*		
Shame	5.15	10.3
Lack of compassion	6.29	3.7
Destructive social consequences of pain	8.16	10.9
3. *A self that cannot be understood*		
Lack of control over self	24.13	11.8
Rejection of change	1.7	4.16
Responsibility, self vs pain	25.15	13.22
4. *A body separate from the self*		
Taken for granted	21.15	15.14
Body excluded from the self	23.5	16.23
Body presence vs absence	18.12	19.1

One can see here how the analysis of pain and identity has evolved and, as the analytic process in this example continued, the theme of 'living with an unwanted self' and 'undesirable feelings' transmuted to become 'living with an unwanted self in private' and 'living with an unwanted self in public'. The fourth theme, 'a body separate from the self', emerged late in the analysis. Consonant with the iterative process of IPA, as the analysis continued, earlier transcripts were reviewed in the light of this new superordinate theme, and instances from those earlier transcripts were included in the ongoing analysis. Box 3.8 shows identifiers for the themes for the two participants looked at in the chapter. In practice, each of the seven participants in the study was represented for each superordinate theme.

Sometimes students worry they won't be able to find convergences between their individual case tables of themes. In our experience, this is an intellectual opportunity rather than a difficulty. It is often possible to see higher-level convergences across seemingly disparate cases so this process pushes the analysis to an even higher level. The resulting analysis respects both theoretical convergence and, within that, individual idiosyncrasy in how that convergence is manifest.

It is worth thinking about terminology for a moment. We are using the theme as a primary unit of analysis and this clearly has some overlap with thematic analysis (Chapter 10). In qualitative psychology, one often finds these sorts of conceptual overlaps. So what makes an IPA theme distinctive? First, thematic analysis can be used to address a huge array of research questions and with a wide range of theoretical perspectives and therefore it has very wide parameters for the content area of themes. For IPA, a theme is always experiential – it is a way of marking or capturing an element of the participant's lived experience and sense-making in regard to that experience.

Second, because of IPA's microscopic, idiographic analysis, it is initially concerned with what one might think of as micro themes – little pieces of experiential material. Thus a single interview is making manifest a large number of experiential themes for that participant. In the next phase of analysis, the patterning of themes is captured within what we describe as superordinate themes within the case. Only in a third phase does one begin to look for relationships between themes and superordinate themes across cases. Because thematic analysis has a less microscopic lens in play and is more concerned with features apparent at the group level, themes are usually invoked at something akin to this third phase in IPA. Of course this is not a hard-and-fast rule and in practice one does find considerable commonalities in the working practices of different qualitative approaches. Indeed, when using a particular qualitative approach, one can sometimes usefully draw on technical suggestions offered by other methodologies. What is important to keep in mind is what theoretical position one is working from and what research question one is attempting to answer.

WRITING UP

The final section is concerned with moving from the final themes to a write-up and final statement outlining the meanings inherent in the participants' experience. This stage is concerned with translating the themes into a narrative account. Here the analysis becomes expansive again, as the themes are explained, illustrated and nuanced. The table of themes is the basis for the account of the participants' responses, which takes the form of the narrative argument interspersed with verbatim extracts from the transcripts to support the case. Care is taken to distinguish clearly between what the respondent said and the analyst's interpretation or account of it.

The division between analysis and writing up is, to a certain extent, a false one, in that the analysis will be expanded during the writing phase. When one sees the extracts again within the unfolding narrative, often one is prompted to extend the analytic commentary on them. This is consonant with the processual, creative feature of qualitative psychology. The dynamic circular process of writing and thinking means that the structure of the analysis itself may undergo considerable changes during writing. This happened in the back pain study. As we were writing, we became aware of a developmental process in the debilitating impact of chronic pain on sense of self being articulated in the accounts, and we modified our write-up to reflect this process. A brief extract from the final version is shown in Box 3.9. The full analysis can be found in Smith and Osborn (2007).

BOX 3.9   EXTRACT FROM FINAL WRITE-UP OF THE BACK PAIN STUDY

The negative impact of pain on the self

We will start with the detailed examination of one passage from one participant – Helen. We are placing this here as it illustrates all the main features which also crop up in the other accounts though of course each instance also has its own idiosyncratic flavour. The effect of the passage is cumulatively therefore to vividly demonstrate the central thesis of this paper – that pain can have dramatic effect on the patient's sense of self and identity:

> It's not who I am it's just who I am if you know what I mean, it's not really me, I get like that and I know like, you're being mean now but I can't help it. It's the pain, it's me, but it is me, me doing it but not me do you understand what I'm saying? If I was to describe myself like you said, I'm a nice person, but then I'm not, am I? And there's other stuff, stuff I haven't told you, if you knew you'd be disgusted I just get so hateful. [...] I know your gonna say it's all me, but I can't help it even though I don't like it. It's the mean me, my mean head all sour and horrible, I can't cope with that bit, I cope with the pain better. [...] [Tearful] Look do you mind if we stop now, I didn't think it would be like this, I don't want to talk any more.

(Continued)

(Continued)

There is a great deal going on in this extract. Helen introduces two selves, 'a nice person' and the 'mean me, my mean head all sour and horrible,' and seems to be engaged in a wrestle over the degree to which each applies to her. At this point the status of the different selves seems somewhat equivocal. It may be that Helen is convinced that she is still a nice person but is worried that publicly other people perceive her to be something else – and that negative image can therefore be attributed to something outside the self – the pain itself. Alternatively and more distressing, she may see herself as engaged in a battle for her identity itself, an attempt to retain the old 'nice' self against the onslaught of the new 'mean' self. What is striking in the extract is just how far the self-denigration goes. She is already describing herself in considerably pejorative terms and yet insists it is in fact even worse but that shame prevents her revealing the full extent of the depravity.

The way the passage unfolds strongly suggests that this is not a cool detached account of herself Helen has come to live with, but rather is something that she is still wrestling with in the present. This is reflected in how she works through the contradictions in real time at the beginning of the extract and then in the way in which she draws the interviewer into the debate: 'Stuff I haven't told you … I know you're gonna say' and then most dramatically at the end where she asks for the interview to be stopped. Helen's battle comes alive in the contemporaneous interview with the researcher.

Helen neatly encapsulates the essence of her distress when she says: 'I can't cope with that bit, I cope with the pain better.' Remember this is a person who has a high level of disability from her pain. Yet she argues that the pain itself is not the main problem. Rather, what is worse is the impact it is having on her sense of self and the struggle she is having to retain a good self.

As suggested earlier, this passage in some way speaks for all the participants – each of whom echoes Helen's struggle. See this passage from Kevin:

> The bits that aren't me, I can't be me. The hardest part is the pain obviously, but the fact that I'm like this monster, I get mean, I do things and I think things which are mean, things which I'd never tell anyone and I'll not tell you so don't ask, […] that's the hardest part now you ask.

We see a similar mental struggle in relation to identity. There is the same unspeakable shame and loathing; the same invocation of the interviewer. And finally a similar plea that the effect on self is more distressing than the pain itself.

(From Smith and Osborn, 2007: 522–3)

This passage illustrates the detailed interpretative commentary that one finds in good IPA. It also shows how particular extracts from participants' accounts come to play a central and integral role in the unfolding analysis. This can be seen to be related to the concept of *the gem* which Jonathan has been articulating. Even more starkly than in this illustration, short pieces of text from participants can become key components in the analysis of the corpus as a whole. (See Smith, 2011, where the idea of the gem is presented and illustrated in full.)

A final note on organization: Usually in IPA, the results section presents one's unfolding interpretative analysis supported with extracts from participants. Then in the discussion section, one makes links between this analysis and the extant literature, thus helping to place the work in a context and point to the mutual illumination process which can occur as the new work helps cast light on what went before and that previous work helps make sense of the new findings. An alternative strategy is to discuss the links to the literature as one presents each superordinate theme in a single 'results and discussion' section.

CONCLUSION

This chapter has aimed to present the reader with an accessible introduction to IPA. We have outlined a series of steps for conducting a research study using the approach. Doing qualitative research may seem daunting at first, but, ultimately, it is extremely rewarding. We hope you may be encouraged by what we have written to attempt a project using IPA yourself. Box 3.10 presents three good examples of IPA in action.

BOX 3.10   THREE GOOD EXAMPLES OF IPA

Migration and threat to identity

This paper by Timotijevic and Breakwell (2000) explores the impact of migration on identity. Immigrants to the UK from the Former Yugoslavia were interviewed about their perceptions of the countries they had left, the one they had joined, and the decision to move. Their accounts point to a rich patterning of identifications. Different people used different category membership strategies in relation to their former home. Some stressed their own ethnic identity at the expense of the greater national Yugoslavian, while others identified as Yugoslavian and emphasized their own ethnic group as being an important element in that Yugoslavian identity. Thus the category Yugoslavian was not fixed and could therefore be invoked in different ways as part of the process of asserting one's identity. Their relationship to the UK was similarly complex. The paper neatly captures this multifaceted and dynamic process of identification and relates it to various theories of identity, including identity process theory and social identity theory.

Anger and aggression in women

Eatough and Smith (2006) present a detailed case study of one woman's account of anger and aggression. It is therefore a useful illustration of IPA's commitment to the idiographic. The paper aims to show

(Continued)

(Continued)

how the individual attempts to find meaning for events and experiences within the context of her life and how this meaning-making can be hard and conflictual. The analysis begins by demonstrating how dominant cultural discourses are used to explain anger and aggression. These include hormones, alcohol, and the influence of past relationships on present action. It then goes on to examine how the participant's meaning-making is often ambiguous and confused, and how she variously accepts and challenges meanings available to her. Finally, the analysis shows how meaning-making can break down and the consequences of this for the individual's sense of self.

The psychological impact of chronic fatigue syndrome

Dickson, Knussen and Flowers (2008) offer a moving analysis of the lived experience of chronic fatigue syndrome based on interviews with 14 participants. The methodology is clearly presented and the results are very well written. The paper is able to deftly manage a balance between speaking to the general patterns for the group of participants while retaining a concern with individual nuance. The three main themes in the paper are 'Identity crisis: agency and embodiment', 'Scepticism and the self' and 'Acceptance, adjustment and coping'. The first is particularly strong. For example, one participant says: 'It was like a death-trap – there was no life going on anymore' (2008: 464). A number of powerful quotes like this provide vivid evidence for the researcher's account.

FURTHER READING

Moran, D. (2000) *Introduction to Phenomenology*. London: Routledge.
This is a very accessible introduction to the philosophical phenomenology literature.

Smith, J.A. (1996) 'Beyond the divide between cognition and discourse: using interpretative phenomenological analysis in health psychology', *Psychology and Health*, 11: 261–71.
This paper is the original position piece for IPA, outlining its theoretical basis and pointing to what it can offer psychology.

Smith, J.A., Flowers, P. and Larkin, M. (2009) *Interpretative Phenomenological Analysis: Theory, Method and Research*. London: Sage.
This is the definitive text on IPA, offering a guide to its theoretical position and giving detailed guidance to conducting a study.

Eatough, V. and Smith, J.A. (2008) 'Interpretative phenomenological analysis', in C. Willig and W. Stainton-Rogers (eds), *Handbook of Qualitative Psychology*. London: Sage.
This chapter discusses the theoretical foundations of IPA and considers a range of pertinent issues.

4 Grounded Theory

Kathy Charmaz

Consider the following statement from a lengthy interview about experiencing chronic illness.[1] Susan Nelson, a 47-year-old woman, has multiple chronic medical problems, including diabetes, depression, vision loss, and congenital myopathy (a disease affecting her muscles). Her declining health affects her everyday life and how she views herself. When responding to the interviewer's first question about her health, Susan explained what congenital myopathy meant:

> Mine was adult onset, so it's milder – it's most common in children. But they don't live to adulthood because it eventually affects the muscles of the respiratory system and – and so then they die because they can't keep breathing. Mine just affects basically my extremities. Extreme muscle pain, extreme fatigue. Any repetitive use of any set of muscles just causes almost instant pain and fatiguing. Now I have managed to work around it – working and resting and working and resting and working and resting – um, but I couldn't get on an exercise bike and pedal it for 30 seconds. Just, it's – I never understood why when I would go on walks with my friends, you know, you're supposed to increase your endurance, you know, and I never got to feeling better. I always hurt so hard after I got home, I'd have to lie down and the next day I was, you know, just real, you know I wasn't able to do a whole lot of anything, and I thought this is really weird, you know. I don't understand this, and I complained about a lot of symptoms for a lot of years and it took me a long time for the doctors to take me seriously. Because I'm a Lab Tech, all my conditions, I've discovered on my own by running my own blood tests.

Susan's statement contains detailed medical information, but also reveals feelings, implies a perspective on self and situation, and offers insights about her illness history. Note her clarity when she first explains her health status and her bewilderment as she later describes experiencing symptoms. Susan's words foretell an interview filled with detailed information and intriguing views.

As a novice researcher, how can you analyse research participants' views and experiences such as Susan describes? How can you give all your data a fair reading? Which methodological guidelines can assist you throughout the research process?

This chapter answers these questions by showing you how to use the grounded theory method to collect and analyse qualitative data. Grounded theory is a comparative, iterative, and interactive method that provides a way to study empirical processes. It consists of flexible methodological strategies for building theories from inductive data. As a comparative method, grounded theory keeps you interacting with the data and your emerging ideas about them. You could compare Susan's statements about experiencing pain and fatigue with similar statements from other people who also had no medical validation, as well as with those who received a quick diagnosis. While you examine Susan's statements, you label them with codes, such as 'experiencing increasing pain', 'feeling mystified', 'working around it', and 'lacking validation'. Subsequently you can compare these codes with codes from other research participants' interviews. As the research proceeds, you can compare these data and codes with the tentative categories you develop from your codes.

Grounded theory demystifies the conduct of qualitative inquiry. Rather than applying a preconceived theoretical framework, your ideas about the data guide how you construct the theoretical analysis. The distinguishing characteristics of grounded theory (see Glaser, 1992; Glaser and Strauss, 1967) include:

- collecting and analysing data simultaneously
- developing analytic codes and categories from the data, not from preconceived hypotheses
- constructing middle-range theories to understand and explain behaviour and processes
- memo-writing – that is, analytic notes to explicate and fill out categories
- making comparisons between data and data, data and concept, and concept and concept
- theoretical sampling – that is, sampling for theory construction to check and refine conceptual categories, not for representativeness of a given population
- delaying the literature review until after forming the analysis.

The logic of grounded theory influences all phases of the research process although the method focuses on analysis, which I emphasize here. Before outlining the analytic strategies of grounded theory, I provide a brief history of the method and an introduction to the theoretical perspective with which grounded theory is most closely aligned. Qualitative methods foster making unanticipated discoveries that shift earlier research questions and designs, so I describe how grounded theorists form research questions and construct research designs. I next discuss how grounded theory shapes data collection in pivotal ways that advance theoretical analyses. Subsequently, I detail specific grounded theory strategies and show how they foster theory construction. A brief discussion of criteria for evaluating grounded theory studies ends the chapter along with several examples of how researchers have used the method.

HISTORY AND THEORETICAL BACKGROUND

The emergence and development of grounded theory

Grounded theory methods emerged from the collaboration of sociologists Barney G. Glaser and Anselm L. Strauss (1965, 1967) during the 1960s and took form in their pioneering book *The Discovery of Grounded Theory* (1967). Sociology has had a long tradition of ethnographic fieldwork, interview, and case studies from its beginnings to the present (see, for example, Adler and Adler, 2011; Allahyari, 2000; Dunn, 2002, 2010; Fine, 2010; Glaser and Strauss, 1965; Goffman, 1959; Lois, 2010; Thomas and Znaniecki, 1918; Whyte, 1943/1955). However, this tradition had eroded by the 1960s, as sophisticated quantitative methods gained dominance.

Quantitative methods were rooted in positivism, or the assumption of a unitary scientific method of observation, experimentation, logic and evidence. Positivist methods assumed an unbiased and passive observer, the separation of fact from value, the existence of an external world separate from scientific observers and their methods, and the accumulation of knowledge about the studied topic. Hence, positivism led to a quest for valid instruments, replicable research designs, and reliable findings.

The division between constructing theory and conducting research grew in 1950s and 1960s sociology. At that time, theory informed quantitative research through the logico-deductive model of inquiry, which relied on deducing testable hypotheses from an existing theory. Yet this research seldom led to new theory construction.

Grounded theory holds a special place in the history of qualitative inquiry. In their cutting-edge book, Glaser and Strauss (1967) opposed conventional notions about research, methods, and theory and offered new justifications for qualitative inquiry. They challenged:

- the arbitrary division between theory and research
- prevailing views of qualitative research as a precursor to more 'rigorous' quantitative methods
- beliefs that qualitative methods were impressionistic and unsystematic
- the separation of data collection and analysis phases of research
- assumptions that qualitative research could not generate theory
- views that limited theorizing to an intellectual elite.

Glaser and Strauss built on their qualitative predecessors' implicit analytic strategies and made them explicit. As Paul Rock (1979) points out, early qualitative researchers had taught students through mentoring and immersion in field experience. Glaser and Strauss's written guidelines for conducting qualitative research changed that oral tradition. And, moreover, Glaser and Strauss justified and legitimized conducting qualitative research on its own canons instead of on the criteria for quantitative research.

Glaser's rigorous quantitative training at Columbia University imbued grounded theory with its original positivistic epistemological assumptions, logic and systematic approach. Strauss's training at the University of Chicago linked grounded theory with ethnographic research and symbolic interactionism, the sociological descendant of pragmatist philosophy. This perspective stresses human reflection, choice and action and is part of the interpretive tradition in sociology.

Grounded theory contains both positivistic and interpretive elements. Its emphasis on using systematic techniques to study an external world remains consistent with positivism. Its stress on how people construct actions, meanings and intentions is in keeping with interpretative traditions. Increasingly, grounded theorists join me (see, for example, Bryant, 2003; Clarke, 1998, 2003, 2005; Keane, 2011, 2012; Thornberg, 2007, 2009, 2010, 2012; Thornberg and Charmaz, 2014) in assuming that a researcher's disciplinary and theoretical proclivities, relationships and interactions with respondents all shape the collection, content and analysis of data. Grounded theory can bridge traditional positivistic and interpretative methods in disciplines such as psychology that have embraced quantification. Grounded theory allows psychologists to study aspects of human experience that remain inaccessible with traditional verification methods. Because grounded theory facilitates studying processes, psychologists can use it to study how individual and interpersonal processes develop, are maintained, or change.

Despite its usefulness, grounded theory is a contested method. Glaser's self-published book, *Theoretical Sensitivity* (1978), contained the most definitive early statement of how to use the method and established it as a type of variable analysis. His book, however, lacked the enormous appeal of Strauss's co-authored books with Juliet Corbin, *Basics of Qualitative Research* (1990, 1998). Strauss and Corbin's books significantly revised grounded theory. Ironically, few readers discerned the disjuncture between their books and the original statements of the method (Bryant and Charmaz, 2007). Unlike Glaser, who emphasized emergent concepts and theory construction, Strauss and Corbin moved grounded theory towards verification and added preconceived technical procedures to be applied *to* the data rather than emerging *from* analysing them. In his scathing response, Glaser (1992) argues that Strauss and Corbin's procedures force data and analysis into preconceived categories, ignore comparative analysis, usurp the method, and impose unnecessary complexity on the analytic process.

Perhaps the major challenge to the early grounded theory works is the constructivist revision (Bryant, 2002, 2003; Charmaz, 2000, 2006, 2014; Clarke, 2005; Mills, Bonner and Francis, 2006) that I first explicitly articulated in 2000 (Charmaz, 2000). Constructivist grounded theory continues the iterative, comparative, emergent and open-ended approach of Glaser and Strauss's (1967) original statement; adopts the pragmatist emphasis on language, meaning and action; counters mechanical applications of the method; and answers criticisms about positivistic leanings in earlier versions of grounded theory.

Constructivist grounded theory preserves the useful methodological strategies of grounded theory but places them on a relativist epistemological foundation (see Charmaz, 2000, 2009, 2014). It also takes into account methodological developments of the past five decades that focus on:

- attending to data collection
- examining researchers' representation of research participants
- acknowledging our co-construction of data with participants
- recognizing the researcher's subjectivity, preconceptions and social locations
- scrutinizing the research situation and process
- engaging in reflexivity.

The constructivist approach illuminates what researchers bring to their studies and do while engaged in them. Constructivists scrutinize the researcher's actions, examine the research situation, and locate the research process in the social, historical and situational conditions of its production.

Several major grounded theorists have aimed to use the method to study processes at the organizational and societal levels. Strauss (1987, 1993) initiated this direction, independently as well as with co-author Juliet Corbin (Strauss and Corbin, 1990, 1998). Adele Clarke (2003, 2005, 2007) has extended their efforts in her 2005 book *Situational Analysis*, which builds a new method from earlier grounded theory precepts.

Two current trends promise to influence future grounded theory studies: the growing interest in mixed methods and the turn towards social justice inquiry (Charmaz, 2005, 2011b, 2012). Grounded theory methods fit mixed methods research well (Johnson, McGowan and Turner, 2010). The flexibility of grounded theory makes it amenable to shaping quantitative instruments, to following up on quantitative findings, and to offering an in-depth view of the studied experience. The turn towards social justice has spawned diverse grounded theory studies that either begin from a value stance or arise through involvement in the research process (see, for example, Furlong and McGilloway, 2012; Karabanow, 2008; Keane, 2011; Mcintyre, 2002; Mitchell and McCusker, 2008; Thornberg, 2007; Thornberg and Jungert, 2014; Veale and Stavrou, 2007; Wasserman and Clair, 2010).

Symbolic interactionism as a guiding theoretical perspective

Researchers with varied theoretical perspectives adopt the grounded theory method. Thus grounded theorists have built on such diverse foundations as critical realism, feminist theory, hermeneutics, and transpersonal psychology – however, the method is most closely intertwined with symbolic interactionism.

As a theoretical perspective, symbolic interactionism rests on several major assumptions and offers general concepts to look at the empirical world rather than providing an explanatory theory. Symbolic interactionists subscribe to this fundamental assumption: people construct selves, social worlds and societies through interaction (Charmaz, 1980). Because the perspective emphasizes understanding why individuals think, feel and act as they do from *their* standpoints, symbolic interactionists focus on how people construct meanings and actions in everyday life.

Symbolic interactionism views shared symbols, cultural meanings and shared language as part of collective life. Our interactions depend on these shared meanings, and our identities and selves arise from them but may change as experience changes. Symbolic interactionists share the following views:

- human life is fluid – in process – and consists of constant action
- meaning and action each influence the other
- meaning-construction, process and action constitute the foci of symbolic interactionist study, not social structure and stability
- individuals can choose their actions and exert some control over their lives
- human beings interpret what happens to and around them and thus can alter their actions
- social structures and constraints exist but people construct and reproduce these structures and constraints through their routine actions.

Symbolic interactionists hold a positive concept of human nature that views people as social, active, reflective and creative. In this view, we human beings are not mere reproductions of our cultures, affiliations and situations. Rather, our ability to reflect and interpret makes us creative and allows personal change. From a symbolic interactionist perspective, possibilities arise for creating novel interpretations and actions. Through articulating three basic premises of symbolic interactionism, Herbert Blumer (1969: 3) clarifies how individuals construct these novel interpretations and actions but do so within a social context.

1. Human beings act towards things on the basis of the meanings that things have for them.
2. The meaning of such things is derived from, or arises out of, the social interaction that one has with one's fellows.
3. These meanings are handled in, and modified through, an interpretative process used by the person in dealing with the things he encounters.

Blumer's first premise turns conventional understandings of meaning inside out. People *confer* meanings on things – whether these things are objects, events or people. Meanings do not inhere in things as individuals ordinarily assume. Nor are meanings singular and shared by all. Instead, meanings are multiple and situated in specific contexts. What you do with something arises from what it means to you – and these meanings have consequences. For example, as long as a young woman could define her fatigue and shortness of breath as a mild condition rather than chronic heart disease, she declined to take heart medications. The meaning she attributed to her symptoms shaped her action and inaction towards them.

The second premise reveals Blumer's view that meanings are social rather than individualistic. Yet this premise also suggests that action and meaning shape each other, and thus supports the pragmatist assumption that meanings arise from what people *do* with things – their actions. Blumer's third premise speaks directly to this point. We *interpret* what things mean when we are involved in dealing with them. This premise reflects Blumer's major interest in the interpretive process and its implications for human life. We are not social robots; we can think, feel and act. People have the ability to assess and reassess things they encounter through thinking about them.

Blumer's depiction of symbolic interactionism may give readers the impression that individuals are constantly indicating what things mean to themselves. Are they? No, much of life is routine and we act accordingly – until our ordinary meanings and actions are called into question or new situations or opportunities arise. In either case, our taken-for-granted meanings and actions no longer fit our current situation, and then we reinterpret what is happening. The logical conclusion of the symbolic interactionist perspective fits Blumer's claim that social interaction *forms* conduct rather than merely expresses it.

Symbolic interactionism has been most closely associated with social psychology although researchers have also used it to study social movements, organizational life and subcultures, such as gangs. But psychologists may resonate most with symbolic interactionist studies of the construction of self, identity, meaning, sexualities and emotions (see, for example, Charmaz, 2011a; Eastman, 2012; Garrett-Peters, 2009; Haworth-Hoeppner and Maines, 2005; Lois, 2010).

FORMULATING A RESEARCH QUESTION AND DESIGNING A STUDY

Grounded theory is an emergent method (Charmaz, 2008). An emergent method begins with the empirical world and builds an inductive understanding of it as events unfold and knowledge accrues. Beyond a few flexible guidelines, grounded theory is indeterminate and open-ended. You draw upon and develop specific methodological tools to answer emerging theoretical and empirical questions during the research process. Your research questions and study design evolve as you proceed, rather than emanating from deducing a hypothesis from an extant theory or following a tightly preconceived plan.

Grounded theorists must keep their research questions and research designs open-ended. We aim to study significant issues that we find in our field settings. Dissertation committees, institutional review boards and granting agencies, however, often require grounded theorists to produce research proposals using a conventional research question and design. Hence, grounded theorists must balance constructing general initial research questions that satisfy external audiences with building possibilities for refining their research design. In one study (Charmaz, 1991a), I started with general questions about how serious chronic illness affected people's lives and how they experienced time. I moved on to develop more refined ideas about self, identity, time and suffering. This approach led to using intensive interviews as the main method of collecting data.

What kinds of research questions can grounded theory methods address? Glaser and Strauss (1967) might answer, 'every kind'. They contend that researchers can adopt grounded theory to study diverse processes. Psychologists can use grounded theory methods to study individual processes, interpersonal relations and the reciprocal effects between individuals and larger social processes. For example, you can study typical psychological topics such as motivation, personal experience, emotions, identity, attraction, prejudice, and interpersonal cooperation and conflict.

With grounded theory, you begin by exploring general questions about a research topic of interest. You collect data about what relevant people for this topic say and do about it. How might you devise your initial research questions? Grounded theorists' background assumptions and disciplinary interests alert them to certain issues and processes in their data from which they can develop research questions. Consistent with Herbert Blumer's (1969) depiction of 'sensitizing concepts', grounded theorists often begin their studies with general concepts that offer open-ended ideas to pursue and questions to ask about the topic. My guiding interests about living with chronic illness and experiencing time brought concepts such as self-concept, identity and duration into the study. I used those concepts as *points of departure* to form interview questions, to look at data, to listen to interviewees and to think analytically about the data. Guiding interests should provide ways of developing, rather than limiting, your ideas. Then you develop specific concepts through studying your data and emergent ideas during successive stages of analysis. Recently, I participated in a demonstration project in qualitative psychology in which five different researchers analysed the same data (Wertz et al., 2011). Our lead author, Fred Wertz, asked us to use the concept of resilience to guide our analyses. Although resilience is a useful concept, I saw it as too definitive – and therefore too restrictive – to begin a grounded theory analysis and could not adopt it.

Sensitizing concepts provide a place to start, not end. Disciplinary perspectives provide such concepts, but grounded theorists must use them with a critical eye. Professional researchers already hold epistemological assumptions about the world, disciplinary perspectives, and often an intimate familiarity with the research topic and the pertinent literature. Yet grounded theorists should remain as open as possible to new views during the research, and critically examine how their own views may enter the research. The open-ended approach of grounded theory gives you an opportunity to learn things you never expected and to gain in-depth understanding of the empirical world. Take this opportunity but scrutinize your views and actions each step along the way.

COLLECTING DATA

The logic of collecting data in grounded theory

Grounded theory methods rely on simultaneous data collection and analysis. Your early analytic work leads you to collect more data around emerging themes and questions. For example, we sense Susan Nelson's efforts to account for her pain and fatigue in the interview excerpt above. Her remarks alert the interviewer to ask about discovering her other conditions and to explore how other people responded to both her search and her conclusions. Following up on an interview participant's comments allows for building further questions into subsequent interviews with other participants.

Simultaneous involvement in data collection and analysis helps you manage your study without being overwhelmed by volumes of unfocused data that do not lead to anything new. If you have already collected a substantial amount of data, begin with it, but subsequently collect additional data about your emerging analytic interests and categories. That way, you can follow up on topics that are explicit in one interview or observation but remain implicit or absent in others. For example, a woman with multiple sclerosis mentioned having 'bad days'.

She said, 'I deal with time differently [during a bad day when she felt sick] and time has a different meaning to me' (Charmaz, 1991a: 52). When we discussed meanings of time, I saw how she connected experiencing time with images of self. On a bad day, her day shortened because all her daily routines – such as bathing, dressing, exercising and resting – lengthened substantially. As her daily routines stretched, her preferred self shrank. After I saw how she defined herself in relation to mundane daily routines, I asked interview questions that addressed this relationship.

The core components of grounded theory studies are analytic categories the researcher develops while studying the data rather than preconceived concepts or hypotheses. These categories move the study towards abstract analyses yet simultaneously elucidate what happens in the empirical world.

From the beginning, researchers actively construct their data with study participants. The first question to ask is, 'What is happening here?' (Glaser, 1978, 1992; Glaser and Strauss, 1967). Then you have to think of ways to find out. Perhaps their enthusiasm for developing a method of theory construction led Glaser and Strauss (1967; Glaser, 1978) to imply that categories inhere in the data and may even leap out. I disagree. Rather, categories reflect interactions between the observer and the observed. Certainly, social researchers' world-views, disciplinary assumptions, theoretical proclivities and research interests influence their observations and emerging categories (see also Charmaz, 2006, 2014; Clarke, 2005; Dey, 1999; Thornberg, 2010; Thornberg and Charmaz, 2014).

Constructing interview guides with open-ended questions is particularly helpful for novices. A well-constructed guide fosters asking open-ended questions, provides a logical pacing of topics and questions, avoids loaded and leading questions, and gives you direction as well as your interview participants (see Charmaz, 2014; Josselson, 2013; Olson, 2011). Constructing interview questions also helps you to become aware of your preconceptions.

Grounded theorists follow leads that we define in the data but may not have foreseen. Thus, I also pursued other topics that my respondents defined as crucial. As I listened to their stories, I felt compelled to explore their concerns about disclosing illness, although I had not anticipated moving in this direction. I studied how, when and why ill people talk about their conditions. My interest in time, however, alerted me to see whether people's accounts of disclosing their conditions changed over time.

What kind of data should you gather for grounded theory studies? To the extent possible, I advocate going inside the studied phenomenon and gathering extensive, rich data about it, while simultaneously using grounded theory strategies to direct data collection. Rich data reveal participants' thoughts, feelings, intentions and actions as well as context and structure. My call for rich, detailed data means seeking full or 'thick' description (Geertz, 1973), such as writing extensive field notes of observations, collecting respondents' written personal accounts, and compiling detailed narratives of experience (such as transcribed tapes of interviews). Seidman (2006) advocates sequential intensive interviewing to build trust and to elicit detailed data. Transcribed tape recordings of interviews provide nuanced details. I find that studying the transcriptions gives me new insights and more codes with which to work. In contrast, Glaser (1998) argues that transcribing wastes time and fosters becoming lost in data.

Grounded theorists take different, sometimes contradictory approaches to data collection, although all assume that the strength of grounded theory lies in its empirical foundation. Glaser (1992, 1998, 2013) consistently stresses discovering what is happening in the setting without forcing the data into preconceived categories. For him, forcing data includes: applying extant theories to the data; assuming the significance of demographic variables (such as age, sex, race, marital status and occupation; also called face-sheet variables) *before* beginning the study; and imposing evidentiary rules (*a priori* prescriptions about what stands as sufficient evidence) on the data. He also advocates short-cuts, such as moving quickly from one empirical world to another to develop a category, and, until recently, urged accepting a group's overt statements about itself. The latter practice can obfuscate members' fundamental concerns or justify their desired public image. Such short-cuts can cause problems. Researchers may obtain only a surface view of a group when they move quickly from one research site to another, and institutional review procedures typically preclude doing so. In addition, people may only state a public relations viewpoint unless they trust the researcher. Furthermore, members may reveal their values and priorities through actions and assumptions, not careful statements. In effect, short-cuts may curtail discoveries, miss basic social processes, overlook subtle meanings and force data into categories prematurely.

Rich data afford views of human experience that etiquette, social conventions and inaccessibility hide or minimize in ordinary discourse. To obtain rich data:

- describe participants' views and actions in detail
- record observations that reveal participants' unstated intentions
- construct interview questions that allow participants to reflect anew on the research topic
- look for and explore taken-for-granted meanings and actions.

'Tell me about', 'how', 'what' and 'when' questions yield rich data, particularly when you buttress them with queries to elaborate on or specify, such as 'Could you describe … further?' (for a sample interview guide, see Charmaz, 2014). Look for the 'ums' and 'you knows'; explore what they indicate. How might they reflect a struggle to find words? When might a 'you know' signal taken-for-granted meanings? What do long pauses indicate? When might 'you know' seek the interviewer's concurrence or suggest that the respondent is struggling to articulate an experience? In my research, however, respondents' stories about illness often spilled out non-stop. For example, Christine Danforth, one of my research participants, stated:

> If you have lupus, I mean one day it's my liver; one day it's my joints; one day it's my head, and it's like people really think you're a hypochondriac if you keep complaining about different ailments. … It's like you don't want to say anything because people are going to start thinking, you know, 'God, don't go near her, all she is – is complaining about this.' And I think that's why I never say anything because I feel like everything I have is related one way or another to the lupus but most of the people don't know I have lupus, and even those that do are not going to believe that ten different ailments

are the same thing. And I don't want anybody saying, you know, they don't want to come around me because I complain. (Quoted in Charmaz, 1991a: 114–15)

Obtaining rich data gives researchers the material for developing a thorough knowledge of their studied empirical worlds or research problems. A thorough empirical grounding in data helps you discern your research participants' meanings of their experiences, and how to interpret these data starting from their situations. You may also see other things in the data, because you bring different perspectives and concerns to them than your participants. (Here I assume that to the best of their ability researchers should find out what is 'happening', and that we can find out because we share language and meanings with those we study, or we can learn them. Ultimately, however, our interpretations shape whatever we find and record and we must be cognizant of our interpretive processes as well as those of the people we study.)

Throughout a grounded theory research project, you increasingly focus your data collection because your analytic work guides which further data you need. *The grounded theorist's simultaneous involvement in data gathering and analysis is explicitly aimed towards developing theory.* Grounded theory ethnographers, for example, move from attempting to capture the whole round of life to focused areas to explore, observe and analyse. Grounded theory interviewers adapt their initial interview guides; they add areas to explore and delete extraneous questions.

Grounded theorists follow leads to develop their emerging theoretical categories (Glaser, 1978). Other qualitative researchers may produce thick description of concrete behaviour without filling out, extending or refining theoretical concepts or making theoretical connections. In contrast, grounded theorists use thick description to ask theoretical questions. For example, young adults agonized over telling room-mates, acquaintances and dates about their conditions. Their stories sparked my interest in dilemmas of disclosing illness. Rather than obtaining thick description only about their difficulties in disclosing, I began to ask analytic questions about disclosing as a process and then gathered data that illuminated that process. These analytic questions included:

- What are the properties of disclosing?
- Which social psychological conditions foster disclosing? Which inhibit it?
- How does disclosing compare with other forms of telling?
- How, if at all, does disclosing change after the person becomes accustomed to his or her diagnosis?
- What strategies, if any, do people use to disclose? When do they use them?

Researchers may adopt several grounded theory strategies to gather descriptive accounts without following the analytic steps that make their work theoretical. Listen closely to your respondents, attempt to learn unstated and assumed meanings of their statements, and shape your emerging research questions to obtain data that illuminate your theoretical categories. Then you will be doing grounded theory.

Data Collection and Studying Meanings and Processes

The grounded theory emphasis on studying processes moves research away from static analyses. We emphasize what people are doing, an emphasis which also leads to understanding multiple layers of meanings of their actions. These layers could include a person's (1) stated explanation of his or her action, (2) unstated assumptions about it, (3) intentions for engaging in it, (4) effects on others, and (5) consequences for further individual action and interpersonal relations. Throughout the research process, look at action in relation to meaning to help you obtain thick description and develop your categories.

How do you study meaning? Some grounded theorists believe they can readily discover what is significant in the research setting simply by looking or asking. However, the most important issues to study may be hidden, tacit or elusive. We probably struggle to grasp them. The data we 'find' and the meanings we attribute to them reflect this struggle. Neither data nor meaningful interpretations of them simply await the researcher. We are part of the meanings that we observe and define. In short, our understanding of respondents' meanings emerges from a particular viewpoint and the vocabulary that we invoke to make sense of them.

A researcher has topics to pursue; research participants have goals, thoughts, feelings and actions. Your research questions and mode of inquiry shape your subsequent data and analysis. Thus, you must become self-aware about why and how you gather data. You learn to sense when you are gathering rich, useful data that do not undermine or demean your respondent(s). Not surprisingly, then, I believe the grounded theory method works best when the grounded theorist engages in data collection as well as data analysis phases of research. This way, you can explore nuances of meaning and process that hired hands might easily miss.

Respondents' stories may tumble out or the major process in which people are engaged may jump out at you. Sometimes, however, respondents may not be so forthcoming and major processes may not be so obvious. Even if they are, it may take more work to discover the subtlety and complexity of respondents' intentions and actions. The researcher may have entered the implicit world of meaning, in which participants' spoken words can only allude to significance, but not articulate it.

Many of my participants spoke of incidents in which their sense of social and personal worth was undermined. They complained, recounted hurtful conversations, and expressed incredulity about how other people treated them. I began to see their accounts as stories of suffering (Charmaz, 1999). These stories reflected more than a stigmatized identity – but what? I pieced together meanings behind their stories in a hierarchy of moral status that catapults downwards as health fails, resources wane and difference increases. Sufferers talked about loss, not moral status. Yet everything they said assumed a diminishing moral status.

The further we go into implicit meanings, the more we may conceptualize them with abstract ideas that crystallize the experiences eliciting these meanings. For example, I defined implicit meanings of 'bad days' according to my participants' evaluations of intensified intrusiveness of illness; reduced control over mind, body and actions; and curtailed choices and actions. I synthesized, condensed and conceptualized participants' statements to make their tacit understandings explicit.

At this point, we grounded theorists speak in our analytic categories rather than reproduce participants' words. Some meanings are so well understood that they remain assumed and unstated. Other meanings are felt, but participants have no words to voice them. For certain topics, close study and direct questioning may suffice. For other topics, you may need to redirect inquiry. Because our language contains few words with which to talk about time, many of my research participants' attitudes towards and actions concerning time remained unspoken and taken for granted. Yet their stories about illness often depended on conceptions of time and referred to implicit qualities of experienced time. Christine Danforth's statement above referred to the quality and unevenness of her days. If researchers plan to explore such areas, then they need to devise ways to make relevant observations or to construct questions that foster pertinent responses. To illustrate, I asked my research participants questions such as, 'As you look back on your illness, which events stand out in your mind?' and 'Could you tell me what a typical weekday is like for you?' At whatever level you attend to your participants' meanings, intentions and actions, you can create a coherent analysis by using grounded theory methods. Hence, the method is useful for fact-finding, descriptive studies as well as conceptually developed theoretical statements.

Perhaps the most important basic rule for a grounded theorist is: *Study your emerging data* (Glaser, 1978, 1992). Studying the data sparks your awareness of respondents' implicit meanings and taken-for-granted concerns. How do you study data? From the very start, transcribe your audiotapes yourself or write your own field notes rather than, say, dictating them to someone else. Studying your data prompts you to learn nuances of your research participants' language and meanings. Subsequently, you learn to define the directions where your data can take you. Through studying interview audiotapes, for example, you attend closely to your respondents' feelings and views. They will live in your mind as you listen carefully over and over to what they were saying. For example, one student in my class remarked:

> What an impact the words had on me when I sat home alone transcribing the tapes. I was more able to hear and feel what these women were saying to me. I realized how, at times, I was preoccupied with thoughts of what my next question was, how my eye contact was, or hoping we were speaking loud enough for the tape-recorder. (Charmaz, 1991b: 393)

If you attend to respondents' language, you can adapt your questions to fit their experiences. Then you can learn about their meanings rather than make assumptions about what they mean. For example, when my respondents with chronic illnesses often talked about having 'good days' and 'bad days', I probed further and asked more questions around my respondents' taken-for-granted meanings of good and bad days. I asked questions such as: 'What does a good day mean to you?', 'Could you describe what a bad day is?', 'What kinds of things do you do on a good day?', and 'How do these activities compare with those on a bad day?' By comparing interview accounts, I discovered that good days meant that participants' temporal and spatial horizons expanded and that possibilities increased for realizing the selves they wished to be. But had I not followed up and asked respondents about the meanings of these terms, their specific properties would have remained implicit.

Certainly, it helps to have strong data-gathering skills. A skilled researcher knows when and how to ask more questions or to make more focused observations. Nevertheless, novices can make remarkable gains in skill during a brief time by attending closely to their methods and by studying their data. By gathering rich data and by making meanings explicit, you will have solid material with which to create your analysis.

ANALYSIS

The grounded theory method consists of several major strategies outlined below. Many grounded theorists now use computer-assisted qualitative data analysis software to help them. Several of these programs have been designed for grounded theory projects. The software can help you organize materials for ready retrieval and synthesis but they cannot do the analysis for you.

Coding the data

Coding is the process of defining what the data are about. Unlike quantitative data, in which *preconceived* categories or codes are applied to the data, grounded theorists *create* their codes by defining what they see in the data. Codes emerge as you scrutinize your data and define meanings within them. This active coding forces you to interact with your data again and ask questions of them. (Thus, the interactive nature of grounded theory research is not limited to data collection, but also proceeds throughout the analytic work.) As a result, coding may take you into unforeseen areas and new research questions.

Coding is the pivotal link between collecting data and developing an emergent theory to explain these data. It consists of at least two phases: an initial phase involving the naming of each line of data, followed by a focused, selective phase that uses the most significant or frequent initial codes to sort, synthesize and organize large amounts of data.

While coding, you use 'constant comparative methods' (Glaser and Strauss, 1967) to establish analytic distinctions – and thus make comparisons at each level of analytic work. At first, you compare data with data to find similarities and differences. For example, compare interview statements within the same interview and with comments in different interviews. When conducting observations of an activity, compare what happens on one day with the same activity on subsequent days. Next, you can ask Glaser's two important analytic questions that separate grounded theory coding from other types of qualitative coding:

- What category or property of a category does this incident indicate? (Glaser, 1992: 39)
- What is this data a study of? (Glaser, 1978: 57; Glaser and Strauss, 1967)

These questions prompt you to think analytically about the fragments of data or incidents that you are coding. You begin to link the concrete data to more abstract ideas and general processes from the beginning, rather than remaining at a topical or descriptive level. Even taking mundane statements apart and looking at their implicit meanings will deepen your understanding and raise the abstract level of your emerging analysis.

Initial coding entails examining each line of data and defining the actions or events that you see as occurring in it or as represented by it – line-by-line coding (see Box 4.1). Compare incident with incident; then, as your ideas take hold, compare incidents to your conceptualization of incidents coded earlier. The code gives you a tool with which to compare other pieces of data. That way you can identify properties of your emerging concept.

BOX 4.1   INITIAL CODING: LINE-BY-LINE CODING

Excerpt 1, *Christine Danforth, age 37, lupus erythematosus, Sjögren's syndrome, back injuries*. Lupus erythematosus is a systemic, inflammatory auto-immune disease of the connective tissue that affects vital organs as ell as joints, muscles and nerves. Sjögren's syndrome is a related auto-immune inflammatory disease characterized by dry mucous membranes of the eyes and mouth.

Shifting symptoms, having inconsistent days Interpreting images of self given by others	If you have lupus, I mean one day it's my liver; one day it's my joints; one day it's my head, and it's like people really think you're a hypochondriac if you keep complaining about different ailments ...
Avoiding disclosure	It's like you don't want to say anything because people are going to start thinking, you know, 'God, don't go near her, all she is – is complaining about this.'
Predicting rejection	
Keeping others unaware Seeing symptoms as connected Having others unaware Anticipating disbelief Controlling others' views Avoiding stigma Assessing potential losses and risks of disclosing	And I think that's why I never say anything because I feel like everything I have is related one way or another to the lupus but most of the people don't know I have lupus, and even those that do are not going to believe that ten different ailments are the same thing. And I don't want anybody saying, you know, [that] they don't want to come around me because I complain.

(Continued)

(Continued)

	Excerpt 2, *Joyce Marshall, age 60, minor heart condition, recent small cerebral vascular accident (CVA) (stroke).* In her case, the stroke left her with weakness, fatigue and slowed responses when tired.
Meaning of the CVA	I have to see it [her CVA] as a warning.
Feeling forced to live one day at a time	I can't let myself get so anxious. I have to live one day at a time. I've been so worried about John [her husband, who had had life-threatening heart attacks and lost his job three years before retirement] and preparing to get a job [her first in 38 years] ... It's just so hard with all this stress ... to concentrate on what I can do today. I always used to look to the future.
Having a worried past	
Earlier losses	
Difficult living one day at a time; concentrate on today	
Giving up future orientation	
Managing emotions through living one day at a time	I can't now; it upsets me too much. I have to live one day at a time now or else there may not be any me.
Reducing life-threatening risk	

Line-by-line coding means naming each line on each page of your written data (Glaser, 1978) – although this data may not always appear in complete sentences. Through line-by-line coding, you take an analytic stance towards your work and, simultaneously, keep close to your data. Coding leads directly to developing theoretical categories, some of which you may define in your initial codes. You build your analysis from the ground up without taking off on theoretical flights of fancy.

In addition, line-by-line coding reduces the likelihood of imputing your motives, fears or unresolved personal issues to your respondents and to your collected data. Some years ago, a young man in my undergraduate seminar conducted research on adaptation to disability. He had become paraplegic himself when he was hit by a car while bicycling. His ten in-depth interviews were filled with stories of courage, hope and innovation. His analysis of them was a narrative of grief, anger and loss. When I noted that his analysis did not reflect his collected material, he realized how his feelings coloured his perceptions of other people's disabilities. His was an important realization. However, had he assiduously done line-by-line coding, he might have arrived at it before he handed in his paper.

From the standpoint of grounded theory, each idea that you adopt from earlier theory or research should earn its way into your analysis (Glaser, 1978). If you apply theoretical concepts from your discipline, you must ensure that these concepts work. Do they help you understand what the data indicate? (If they do not, use other terms that do) Can you explicate what is happening in this line of data?

Line-by-line coding forces you to think about the material in new ways that may differ from your research participants' interpretations. For Thomas (1993), a researcher must take the familiar, routine and mundane and make it unfamiliar and new. Line-by-line coding helps you to see the familiar anew. You also gain distance from both your own and your participants' taken-for-granted assumptions about the material, so that you can see it from new vantage points.

If your codes define another view of a process, action or belief from that held by your respondents, note this. Your task is to make analytic sense of the material. How do you make analytic sense of the rich stories and descriptions you are compiling? First, look for and identify what you see happening in the data. Some basic questions may help:

- What is going on?
- What are people doing?
- What is the person saying?
- What do these actions and statements take for granted?
- How do structure and context serve to support, maintain, impede or change these actions and statements?

Try to frame your codes in as specific terms as possible – and keep them short. Make them active. Gerunds give us linguistic tools to preserve actions because a gerund is the noun form of the verb. Short, specific, active codes help you define processes in the data that otherwise may remain implicit. What you see in these data derives from your prior perspectives and the new knowledge you gain during your research. Rather than seeing your perspectives as truth, try to see them as representing one view among many. That way, you may gain more awareness of the concepts that you employ. For example, try not to assume that respondents repress or deny significant 'facts' about their lives. Instead, look for how they understand their situations before you judge their attitudes and actions through your own assumptions. Seeing the world through their eyes and understanding the logic of their experience brings you fresh insights. Afterwards, if you still invoke previously held perspectives as codes, you will use them more consciously rather than automatically.

In the example of line-by-line coding in Box 4.1, my interest in time and self-concept comes through in the first two codes. Note how I kept the codes active and close to the data.

Initial codes often range widely across a variety of topics. Because even a short statement or excerpt may address several points, it could illustrate several different categories. I could use the excerpt in Box 4.1 to show how avoiding disclosure serves to control identity. I could also use it to show either how a research participant learns that other people see his or her illness as inexplicable or how each day is unpredictable. Having multiple interviews allows me to see how social and emotional isolation begins and progresses.

Initial codes help you to separate data into categories and to see processes. Line-by-line coding frees you from becoming so immersed in your respondents' world-view that you accept it without question. Then you fail to look at your data critically and analytically. Being critical about your data does not necessarily mean being critical of your research participants.

Instead, being critical forces you to ask *yourself* questions about your data. These questions help you to see actions and to identify the significant processes. Such questions include:

- What process is at issue here? How can I define it?
- Under which conditions does this process develop?
- How do the research participant(s) think, feel and act while involved in this process?
- When, why and how does the process change?
- What are the consequences of the process?

Through coding each line of data, you gain insights about what kinds of data to collect next. Thus, you distil data and direct further inquiry early in the data collection. Line-by-line coding gives you leads to pursue. If, for example, you identify an important process while coding your fifteenth interview, you can return to earlier respondents and see whether that process explains events and experiences in their lives. If you cannot return to them, you can seek new respondents who can illuminate this process. Hence, your data collection becomes more focused, as does your coding.

After you have established some strong analytic directions through your initial line-by-line coding, you can begin focused coding to synthesize and explain larger segments of data. Focused coding means using the most significant and/or frequent earlier codes to sift through large amounts of data. Thus, focused coding is more directed, selective and conceptual than line-by-line coding (Glaser, 1978). Focused coding requires decisions about both which initial codes make the most analytic sense and categorize your data most accurately and completely. Yet, moving to focused coding is not entirely a linear process. Some respondents or events make explicit what was implicit in earlier respondents' statements or prior events. An 'Aha! Now I understand' experience prompts you to study your earlier data afresh. Then you may return to earlier respondents and explore topics that had been glossed over, or that may have been too implicit or unstated to discern.

The strength of grounded theory coding derives from this concentrated, active involvement in the process. You *act* upon the data rather than passively read your material. Through your actions, new threads for analysis become apparent. Events, interactions and perspectives that you had not thought of before come into analytic purview. Focused coding checks your preconceptions about the topic.

In the first excerpt in Box 4.2, I selected the codes 'avoiding disclosure' and 'assessing potential losses and risks of disclosing' to capture, synthesize and understand the main themes in the statement. In the second, the following codes were most useful: 'feeling forced to live one day at a time', 'concentrating on today', 'giving up future orientation', 'managing emotions', and 'reducing life-threatening risk'. Again, I tried to keep the codes active and close to the data. Through focused coding, you can move across interviews and observations and compare people's experiences, actions and interpretations. Note how the codes condense data and provide a handle to them.

BOX 4.2   FOCUSED CODING

Excerpt 1, *Christine Danforth, age 37, lupus erythematosus, Sjögren's syndrome, back injuries*

Avoiding disclosure

Assessing potential losses and risks of disclosing

If you have lupus, I mean one day it's my liver; one day it's my joints; one day it's my head, and it's like people really think you're a hypochondriac if you keep complaining about different ailments ... It's like you don't want to say anything because people are going to start thinking, you know, 'God, don't go near her, all she is – is complaining about this.' And I think that's why I never say anything because I feel like everything I have is related one way or another to the lupus but most of the people don't know I have lupus, and even those that do are not going to believe that ten different ailments are the same thing. And I don't want anybody saying, you know, [that] they don't want to come around me because I complain.

Excerpt 2, *Joyce Marshall, age 60, minor heart condition, recent small CVA (stroke)*

Feeling forced to live one day at a time

Concentrating on today
Giving up future orientation
Managing emotions
Reducing life-threatening risk

I have to see it [her CVA] as a warning. I can't let myself get so anxious. I have to live one day at a time. I've been so worried about John [her husband, who had had life-threatening heart attacks and lost his job three years before retirement] and preparing to get a job [her first in 38 years] ... It's just so hard with all this stress ... to concentrate on what I can do today. I always used to look to the future. I can't now; it upsets me too much. I have to live one day at a time now or else there may not be any me.

Strauss and Corbin (1990, 1998) also introduce a third type of coding, axial coding, to specify the dimensions of a category. The purpose is to sort, synthesize and organize large amounts of data and reassemble them in new ways after open coding (Cresswell, 1998). When engaged in axial coding, the researcher also links categories with sub-categories, and asks how they are related. Whether axial coding helps or hinders remains a question. Whether it differs from careful comparisons also is questionable. At best, it helps to clarify; at worst, it casts a technological overlay on the data. Although intended to obtain a more complete grasp of the studied phenomena, axial coding may make grounded theory cumbersome (Robrecht, 1995).

Axial coding is an *a priori* procedure to apply to the data. In contrast, you may find that emergent methodological directions and decisions arise when you study your data. While studying disclosure of illness, I re-examined the data I had coded during open coding. Then I coded for the range between spontaneous statements and staged pronouncements. I linked forms of telling explicitly to the relative absence or presence of strategizing. After discovering that people invoked different forms of telling, I looked more closely at the context of their telling and the conditions affecting how and whom they told, as well as their stated intentions for telling. I coded for how, when and why they changed their earlier forms of telling. These strategies may lead to charting causes and conditions of the observed phenomenon.

Raising focused codes to conceptual categories

Focused coding moves your analysis forward in two crucial steps: (1) it establishes the content and form of your nascent analysis; and (2) it prompts you to evaluate and clarify your categories and the relationships between them. First, assess which codes best capture what you see happening in your data. Raise them to conceptual categories for your developing analytic framework – give them conceptual definition and analytic treatment in narrative form. Thus, you go beyond using a code as a descriptive tool to view and synthesize data.

Categories explicate ideas, events or processes in your data – and do so in telling words. A category may subsume common themes and patterns in several codes. For example, my category of 'keeping illness contained' included 'packaging illness' (that is, treating it 'as if it were controlled, delimited, and confined to specific realms, such as private life') and 'passing' (which means 'concealing illness, maintaining a conventional self-presentation, and performing like unimpaired peers') (Charmaz, 1991a: 66–8). Again, make your categories as conceptual as possible – with abstract power, general reach, analytic direction and precise wording. Simultaneously, remain consistent with your data. By making focused codes brief and active (to reflect what is happening or what people are doing), you can view them as potential categories. Processes gain visibility when you keep codes active. Succinct, focused codes lead to sharp, clear categories. That way, you can establish criteria for your categories to make further comparisons.

Grounded theorists look for substantive processes that they develop from their codes. 'Keeping illness contained', 'packaging illness', and 'living one day at a time' above are three such processes. As grounded theorists create conceptual handles to explain what is happening in the setting, they may move towards defining generic processes (Prus, 1987). A generic process cuts across different empirical settings and problems; it can be applied to varied, substantive areas. The two codes above, 'avoiding disclosure' and 'assessing potential losses and risks of disclosing', reflect fundamental, generic processes of personal information control. Although these processes describe choices people with illness make in disclosing information, people with other problems may treat information control similarly. Thus, a grounded theorist can elaborate and refine the generic process by gathering more data from diverse arenas where this process is evident. In the case of disclosing, homosexuals, sexual abuse survivors, drug users and ex-convicts often face problematic issues in personal information control and difficult disclosure decisions, as well as people with chronic conditions and invisible disabilities.

Concentrate on analysing a generic process that you define in your codes; then you can raise codes relevant to theoretical categories that lead to explanations of the process and predictions concerning it. These categories reflect what you think about the data as well as what you find in them. As Dey (1999) observes, categorization in grounded theory is more complex and problematic than its originators suggest and involves making inferences as well as classifications.

As you raise a code to a category, you begin to write narrative statements in memos that:

- explicate the properties of the category
- specify the conditions under which the category arises, is maintained and changes
- describe its consequences
- show how this category relates to other categories.

Categories may consist of *in vivo* codes that you take directly from your respondents' discourse, or they may represent your theoretical or substantive definition of what is happening in the data. For example, my terms 'good days and bad days' and 'living one day at a time' came directly from my respondents' voices. In contrast, my categories 'recapturing the past' and 'time in immersion and immersion in time' reflect theoretical definitions of actions and events. Furthermore, categories such as 'pulling in', 'facing dependency', and 'making trade-offs' address my respondents' substantive realities of grappling with a serious illness. I created these codes and used them as categories, but they reflect my respondents' concerns and actions. Novice researchers may find that they rely most on *in vivo* and substantive codes. What results is often a grounded description more than a theory. Nonetheless, studying how these codes fit together in categories can help you treat them more theoretically.

Through focused coding, you build and clarify your category by examining all the data it covers and by identifying variations within it and between other categories. You also will become aware of gaps in your analysis. For example, I developed my category of 'existing from day to day' when I realized that 'living one day at a time' did not fully cover impoverished people's level of desperation. In short, I had data about a daily struggle to survive that were not subsumed by my first category of living one day at a time. The finished narrative can be seen in Box 4.3.

BOX 4.3   THE CATEGORY OF 'EXISTING FROM DAY TO DAY'

Existing from day to day occurs when a person plummets into continued crises that rip life apart. It reflects a loss of control of health and the wherewithal to keep life together.

Existing from day to day means a constant struggle for daily survival. Poverty and lack of support contribute to and complicate that struggle. Hence, poor and isolated people usually plummet further and faster than affluent individuals with concerned families. Loss of control extends to being unable to obtain necessities – food, shelter, heat, and medical care.

The struggle to exist keeps people in the present, especially if they have continued problems in getting the basic necessities that middle-class adults take for granted. Yet other problems can assume much greater significance for these people than their illness – a violent husband, a runaway child, an alcoholic spouse, or the overdue rent.

Living one day at a time differs from existing from day to day. Living one day at a time provides a strategy for controlling emotions, managing life, dimming the future, and getting through a troublesome period. It involves managing stress, illness, or regimen, and dealing with these things each day to control them as best one can. It means concentrating on the here and now and relinquishing other goals, pursuits, and obligations (Charmaz, 1991a: 185).

Note the comparisons between the two categories above. To generate categories through focused coding, you need to compare data, incidents, contexts and concepts. Making the following comparisons helps:

- comparing different people (in terms of their beliefs, situations, actions, accounts or experiences)
- comparing data from the same individuals at different points in time
- comparing specific data with the criteria for the category
- comparing categories in the analysis with other categories.

As I compared different people's experiences, I realized that some people's situations forced them into the present. I then looked at how my rendering of living one day at a time did not apply to them. I reviewed earlier interviews and began to seek published accounts that might clarify the comparison. As is evident in the distinctions between these two categories above, focused coding prompts you to begin to see the relationships and patterns between categories.

Memo-writing

In grounded theory, memo-writing consists of taking categories apart by breaking them into their components. Grounded theorists write memos throughout the research process to examine, compare and analyse data, codes and emergent categories. Memo-writing becomes the pivotal intermediate step between defining categories and writing the first draft of your completed analysis. This step spurs you to develop your ideas in narrative fullness and form early in the analytic process. Memo-writing is the logical next step after you define categories; however, it is also useful for clarification and direction throughout your coding. Writing memos prompts you to elaborate processes, assumptions and actions covered by your codes or categories. Memos help you to identify which codes to treat as analytic categories, if you have not already defined them. (Then you further develop your category through more memo-writing.)

Think about including the following points in your memos:

- defining each code or category by its analytic properties
- spelling out and detailing processes subsumed by the codes or categories
- making comparisons between data and between codes and categories
- bringing raw data into the memo
- providing sufficient empirical evidence to support your definitions of the category and analytic claims about it
- offering conjectures to check through further empirical research
- identifying gaps in your emerging analysis.

Grounded theorists look for patterns, even when focusing on a single case (Strauss and Glaser, 1970). Because they stress identifying patterns, grounded theorists typically invoke respondents' stories to illustrate points – rather than provide complete portrayals of their lives. By bringing raw data right into your memo, you preserve telling evidence for your ideas from the start of your analytic narratives. Through providing ample verbatim material, you not only ground the abstract analysis, but also lay the foundation for making claims about it. Including verbatim material from different sources permits you to make precise comparisons. Thus, memo-writing moves your work beyond individual cases through defining patterns.

Begin your memo with careful definitions of each category. This means you identify its properties or characteristics, look for its underlying assumptions, and show how and when the category develops and changes. To illustrate, I found that people frequently referred to living one day at a time when they suffered a medical crisis or faced continued uncertainty. So I began to ask questions about what living one day at a time was like for them. From their responses as well as from published autobiographical accounts, I began to define the category and its characteristics. The term 'living one day at a time' condenses a whole series of implicit meanings and assumptions. It becomes a strategy for handling unruly feelings, for exerting some control over a now-uncontrollable life, for facing uncertainty, and for handling a conceivably foreshortened future. Memo-writing spurs you to dig into implicit, unstated and condensed meanings.

Start writing memos as soon as you have some interesting ideas and categories to pursue. If at a loss about what to write, elaborate on codes that you adopted repeatedly. Keep collecting data, keep coding and keep refining your ideas through writing more and further-developed memos. Some researchers who use grounded theory methods discover a few interesting findings early in their data collection and then truncate their research. Their work lacks the 'intimate familiarity' with the setting or experience that Lofland and Lofland (1995) avow meets the standards for good qualitative research. Cover your topic in depth by exploring sufficient cases and by elaborating your categories fully.

Memo-writing frees you to explore your ideas about your categories. Treat memos as partial, preliminary and eminently correctable. Just note where you are on firm ground and where you are making conjectures. Then go back to the field to check your conjectures. Memo-writing resembles free-writing or prewriting (Elbow, 1981) because memos are for your eyes only; they provide a means of getting ideas down quickly and clearly; and they preserve your natural voice. When writing memos, incorrect verb tense, overuse of prepositional phrases and lengthy sentences do not matter. You are writing to render the data, not to communicate it to an audience.

Use memos to help you think about the data and to discover your ideas about them. Later, after you turn a memo into a section of a paper, revise it for your prospective readers. You can write memos at different levels of abstraction – from the concrete to the highly theoretical. Some of your memos will find their way directly into the first draft of your analysis. Set aside others with a different focus and develop them later.

Direct much of your memo-writing to making comparisons, what Glaser and Strauss (1967: 105) call 'constant comparative methods'. This approach emphasizes comparing incidents indicated by each category, integrating categories by delineating their relationships, delimiting the scope and range of the emerging theory, and writing the theory. As I suggested with Susan Nelson's interview excerpt, you compare one respondent's beliefs, stance, actions or situations with another respondent's, or one experience with another. If you have longitudinal data, compare a participant's response, experience or situation at one point in time with that at another time. Then, as you become more analytic, start to make detailed comparisons between categories and then frame them into a theoretical statement. Through memo-writing, you distinguish between major and minor categories. Thus, you direct the shape and form of your emergent analysis.

At each more analytic and abstract level of memo-writing, bring your data right into your analysis. Show how you build your analysis on your data in each memo. Bringing your data into successive levels of memo-writing ultimately saves time: you do not have to dig through stacks of material to illustrate your points. A section of a memo is provided in Box 4.4. Note that I first defined the category, 'living one day at a time', and pointed out its main properties. Then I developed aspects of living one day at a time, such as its relationship to time perspective, which is mentioned here, and to managing emotions. The memo also covered how people lived one day at a time, the problems it posed (as well as those it solved) and the consequences of doing so.

BOX 4.4   EXAMPLE OF MEMO-WRITING

Living one day at a time

Living one day at a time means dealing with illness on a day-to-day basis, holding future plans and even ordinary activities in abeyance while the person and, often, others deal with illness. When living one day at a time, the person feels that his or her future remains unsettled, that he or she cannot foresee the future or whether there will be a future. Living one day at a time allows the person to focus on illness, treatment and regimen without becoming entirely immobilized by fear or future implications. By concentrating on the present, the person can avoid or minimize thinking about death and the possibility of dying.

Relation to time perspective

The felt need to live one day at a time often drastically alters a person's time perspective. Living one day at a time pulls the person into the present and pushes back past futures (the futures the person projected before illness or before this round of illness) so that they recede without mourning [their loss]. These past futures can slip away, perhaps almost unnoticed. [I then compare three respondents' situations, statements and time perspectives.]

Theoretical Sampling

Memo-making leads directly to *theoretical sampling* – that is, collecting more data to fill out the properties of your theoretical categories. Here, you sample for the purpose of *developing* your emerging theory, not for representation of a population or increasing the generalizability of your results. Conducting theoretical sampling requires already having tentative categories to develop – and test – through rigorous scrutiny of new data. Thus, you seek more cases or ask earlier participants about experiences that you may not have covered before. You need more data to be sure that your category accurately describes the underlying quality of your respondents' experiences. In contrast, quantitative researchers need to have random samples whose characteristics are representative of the population under study. Whereas survey researchers want to use sample data to make statistical inferences about the target population, grounded theorists are interested primarily in the fit between their data and the emerging theory.

When I was trying to figure out how people with chronic illnesses defined the passage of time, I went back to several participants whom I had interviewed before and asked them more focused questions about how they perceived times of earlier crisis and when time seemed to slow, quicken, drift or drag. Because such topics resonated with their experiences, they even responded to esoteric questions. For example, when I studied their stories, I realized that chronically ill adults implicitly located their self-concepts in the past, present or future. These time-frames reflected the form and content of self and mirrored hopes and dreams for self, as well as beliefs and understandings about self. Hence, I made 'the self in time' a major category. Thereafter, I explicitly asked more people whether they saw themselves in the past, present or future. An elderly working-class woman said without hesitation:

> I see myself in the future now. If you'd asked where I saw myself eight months ago, I would have said, 'the past'. I was so angry then because I had been so active. And to go downhill as fast as I did – I felt life had been awfully cruel to me. Now I see myself in the future because there's something the Lord wants me to do. Here I sit all crumpled in this chair not being able to do anything for myself and still there's a purpose for me to be here. [Laughs.] I wonder what it could be. (Charmaz, 1991a: 256)

Through theoretical sampling you can elaborate the meaning of your categories, discover variation within them and define gaps between categories. Theoretical sampling relies on comparative methods for discovering these gaps and finding ways to fill them. I advise conducting theoretical sampling after you have allowed significant data to emerge. Otherwise, early theoretical sampling may bring premature closure to your analysis.

Engaging in theoretical sampling will likely make variation visible within the studied process or phenomenon. One of my main categories was 'immersion in illness' (Charmaz, 1991a). Major properties of immersion include recasting life around illness, slipping into illness routines, pulling into one's inner circle, facing dependency, and experiencing an altered (slowed) time perspective. However, not everyone's time perspective changed. How could I account for that? By going back through my data, I gained some leads. Then I talked with more people about specific experiences and events that influenced their time perspective. Theoretical sampling helped me to refine the analysis and make it more complex. I then added a category, 'variations in immersion', to highlight and account for different experiences of immersion in illness. I filled out this category through theoretical sampling because I sensed variation earlier when comparing the experiences of people with different illnesses, different life situations and different ages, but had not made clear how immersion in illness varied and affected how these people experienced time. Subsequently, for example, I sampled to learn how illness and time differed for people who spent months in darkened rooms and how both varied when people anticipated later improvement or faced continued uncertainty. Thus, initial demographic variations in immersion led to useful theoretical understandings of variations in immersion itself. Making comparisons explicit through successive memos enabled me to draw connections that I did not initially discern. The memo became a short section of a chapter that begins as in Box 4.5 and then goes on to detail each remaining point.

BOX 4.5   VARIATIONS IN IMMERSION

A lengthy immersion in illness shapes daily life and affects how one experiences time. Conversely, ways of experiencing time dialectically affect the qualities of immersion in illness. The picture above of immersion and time has sharp outlines. What sources of variation soften or alter the picture of immersion and time? The picture may vary according to the person's (1) type of illness, (2) kind of medication, (3) earlier time perspective, (4) life situation, and (5) goals.

   The type of illness shapes the experience and way of relating to time. Clearly, trying to manage diabetes necessitates gaining a heightened awareness of timing the daily routines. But the effects of the illness may remain much more subtle. People with Sjögren's syndrome, for example, may have periods of confusion when they feel wholly out of synchrony with the world around them. For them, things happen too quickly, precisely when their bodies and minds function too slowly. Subsequently, they may retreat into routines to protect themselves. Lupus patients usually must retreat because they cannot tolerate the sun. Sara Shaw covered her windows with black blankets when she was extremely ill. Thus, her sense of chronological time became further distorted as day and night merged together into an endless flow of illness (Charmaz, 1991a: 93).

Theoretical sampling helps you to construct more precise, analytic and incisive memos. Because theoretical sampling forces you to check ideas against direct empirical realities, you have solid materials and sound ideas with which to work. You gain confidence in your perceptions of your data and in your developing ideas about them.

   When do you stop gathering data? The standard answer is that you stop when the properties of your categories are 'saturated' and new data no longer spark fresh insights about your emerging grounded theory. But researchers disagree about the meaning of saturation. As Janice Morse (1995) suggests, researchers proclaim saturation rather than prove that they have achieved it. Thus, like other qualitative researchers, grounded theorists may assume their categories are saturated when they may not be. The kinds of analytic questions and the conceptual level of the subsequent categories matter. Mundane questions may rapidly produce saturated but common categories, whereas novel questions may demand more complex categories and more sustained inquiry (Charmaz, 2014; Lois, 2010).

WRITING UP

After you fully define your theoretical categories, support them with evidence, and order your memos about these categories, start writing the first draft of your paper. Writing is more than mere reporting. Instead, the analytic process proceeds while writing the report. Use your now-developed categories to form sections of the paper. Show the relationships between these categories. When you have studied a process, your categories will reflect its phases. Yet you still need to make an argument for your reader as to why this process is significant. That means making *your* logic and purpose explicit. This may take a draft or two. Then outline your draft to identify your main points and to refine how you organize them. (But do not start your draft from an outline – use your memos.) As your argument becomes clearer, keep tightening it by reorganizing the sections of your paper around it.

What place do raw data such as interview excerpts or field notes have in the body of your paper? Grounded theorists generally provide enough verbatim material to demonstrate the connection between the data and the analysis, but emphasize the concepts they have constructed from the data. To date, qualitative researchers do not agree on how much verbatim material is necessary. Compared to those qualitative studies that primarily synthesize description, grounded theory studies are substantially more analytic and conceptual. Unlike some grounded theorists, I prefer to present detailed interview quotations and examples in the body of my work. This approach keeps the human story in the forefront of the reader's mind and makes the theoretical analysis more accessible to a wider audience.

After you have developed your analysis of the data, go to the literature in your field and compare how and where your work fits in with it – be specific. At this point, you must cover the literature thoroughly and weave it into your work explicitly. Then revise and rework your draft to make it a solid finished paper. Use the writing process to sharpen, clarify and integrate your developing analysis. Through writing and rewriting, you can simultaneously make your analysis more abstract and your rendering of it more concrete and precise. In short, you hone your abstract analysis to define essential properties, assumptions, relationships and processes while providing sufficient actual data to demonstrate how your analysis is grounded in people's experience.

CONCLUSION

The inductive nature of grounded theory methods assumes an open, flexible approach that moves you back and forth between data collection and analysis. Your methodological strategies take shape during the research process rather than before you began collecting data. Similarly, you shape and alter the data collection to pursue the most interesting and relevant material without slighting research participants' views and actions. By developing and checking your ideas as you proceed, you not only stay close to the empirical world, but also learn whether and to what extent your analytic ideas fit the people you study.

Grounded theorists aim to develop a useful theoretical analysis that fits their data. The systematic strategies of grounded theory enable qualitative researchers to generate ideas. In turn, these ideas may later be verified through traditional quantitative methods. Nonetheless, as Glaser and Strauss (1967) originally claimed, grounded-theory qualitative studies stand on their own because these works: (1) explicate basic (generic) processes in the data; (2) analyse a substantive field or problem; (3) make sense of human behaviour;

(4) provide flexible, yet durable, analyses that other researchers can refine or update; and (5) hold potential for greater generalizability (for example, when conducted at multiple sites) than other qualitative works.

But do most researchers who claim to do grounded theory research actually construct theory? No, not at this time. At present, most construct conceptual analyses of a particular experience instead of creating substantive or formal theory. These researchers pursue basic questions within the empirical world and try to understand the puzzles it presents. They emphasize analytic categories that synthesize and explicate processes in the worlds they study, rather than tightly framed theories that generate hypotheses and make explicit predictions. Many researchers engage in grounded theory coding and memo-making but, as Hood (2007) points out, do not conduct theoretical sampling or pursue extensive analysis of their categories. However, grounded theory methods provide powerful tools for taking conceptual analyses into theory development. For this reason, grounded theory methods offer psychologists exciting possibilities for re-visioning psychological theory, as well as useful strategies for rethinking psychological research methods. Box 4.6 shows three good examples of grounded theory studies.

BOX 4.6   THREE EXAMPLES OF GROUNDED THEORY STUDIES

Regions of the mind: brain research and the quest for scientific certainty

Susan Leigh Star (1989) analyses how localization theory gained acceptance as the dominant explanation of how the brain functions. By studying the routine work of early brain researchers, Star questions the foundational assumptions of science. Localizationists faced opposition but Star shows that their theoretical take-over did not rest on unassailable scientific proof. Gaps in their research and reasoning can be discerned. The localizationist take-over occurred because of their claims and sustained strategic actions during a particular historical context in which scientists faced and tried to resolve several types of uncertainty, such as the pressure to standardize criteria for disease categories and diagnoses. Star explains how localizationists' routine actions and strategies created definitions of certainty. They controlled the terms of the debate, shifted uncertainties from one realm to another, combined dissimilar data, generalized case results, focused on select problems, and ignored ambiguous findings. Through their routine efforts, localizationists established boundaries that prevented other theories of brain function from gaining credibility. By explicating the interactive and developmental processes that advanced localizational theory, Star constructs a new theoretical explanation for change and stability in scientific theorizing. Her study concludes that scientific theorizing does not result from

(Continued)

(Continued)

unassailable evidence but instead arises from scientists' ideological proclivities and the exigencies of their routine work.

The body, identity and self: adapting to impairment

Kathy Charmaz (1995) outlines the process of altering life and self to accommodate to physical losses and to reunify body and self. This process begins with how chronically ill people experience notice-able physical changes and diminished bodily functions, define them as real, and cope with changes in bodily appearance. Bodily changes and their meanings affect the identity goals of people with chronic illnesses and foster making identity trade-offs. The views and actions of other people figure prom-inently here. When chronically ill people feel devalued, they weigh interactional costs and balance necessary activities against possible identity trade-offs. During illness crises, however, the struggle to realize identity goals may cease and people may surrender to their sick bodies. At this point, the quest for control over illness ceases and the ill person flows with his or her body. Perhaps paradoxically, people who described this kind of surrender felt at one with themselves and able to face uncertainty and the possibility of death. This study shows how relationships between embodiment and identity goals shift as illness progresses, and also questions common beliefs in struggling against illness during crises.

Maintaining integrity in the face of death: a grounded theory to explain the perspectives of people affected by lung cancer about the expression of wishes for end-of-life care

Gillian Horne, Jane Seymour and Sheila Payne (2012) construct a grounded theory, 'maintaining integrity in the face of death', in which patients with advanced lung cancer and their families try to balance the contradictory demands of simultaneously living in the present and facing death. The authors argue that achieving this balance demands that patients and their families act and talk with integrity. Thus these research participants aimed to act and talk in ways that allowed dying individuals to remain 'real' or 'normal' and forestall discussions of death while they still felt relatively well and could work and carry out their usual responsibilities. The authors constructed the following major categories from their data: (1) 'face death when it comes', (2) 'planning for death, not dying', (3) 'only months to live', and (4) 'clinical discussions about the future'. By 'carrying on as normal' and focusing on the present, people can maintain a sense of purpose and hope for themselves and close family members. Horne, Seymour and Payne found that their research participants' concerns about family permeated their responses and fostered living in the present. As dying patients' conditions worsened, their concern for family often spurred practical plans for handling death. In some cases, patients avoided talking about dying with their families to protect them from worry and sorrow.

NOTE

1   The interview was conducted by a trained student assistant for a mini-grant entitled 'Identity
    Hierarchies and Identity Goals: Adaptation to Loss among the Chronically Ill', awarded by Sonoma
    State University. All names of interview participants have been changed.

ACKNOWLEDGEMENTS

This chapter has undergone several iterations. It became part of the foundation for writing
my book *Constructing Grounded Theory* (Charmaz, 2006), which might not have materi-
alized without Jonathan Smith's early interest in my work. I have appreciated receiving his
support for over two decades and thank him and anonymous reviewers for helpful critiques
on versions of this chapter. Thanks are also due to the following students and members
of the Sonoma State University Faculty Writing Program for comments on various drafts:
Judith Abbott, Emiliano Ayala, Tina Balderrama, Jennifer Bethke, Lynn Cominsky, Jennifer
Dunn, Carole Heathe, Jane Hood, Sheila Katz, Sachiko Kuwaura, Erich Lehmann, Catherine
Nelson, Jim Robison, Rocky Rohwedder, and Tom Rosin.

FURTHER READING

Charmaz, K. (2009) 'Shifting the grounds: constructivist grounded theory methods for the twenty-first
century', in J. Morse, P. Stern, J. Corbin, B. Bowers, K. Charmaz and A. Clarke, *Developing Grounded
Theory: The Second Generation*. Walnut Creek, CA: Left Coast Press, pp. 127–54.
This chapter argues for shifting the epistemological foundations of grounded theory from its
objectivist origins to constructivist assumptions that take into account the historical, social,
situational, and subjective conditions of inquiry.

Charmaz, K. (2014) *Constructing Grounded Theory* (2nd edn). London: Sage.
The second edition considerably expands earlier explanations of the grounded theory method,
provides detailed discussions of intensive interviewing, offers clear guidelines and varied examples,
and includes a chapter on symbolic interactionism as a theoretical perspective.

Clarke, A.E. (2005) *Situational Analysis: Grounded Theory after the Postmodern Turn*. Thousand Oaks, CA:
Sage.
This book takes the implications of postmodernism and presents a revised version of grounded
theory that builds on the pragmatist legacy of Anselm Strauss, locating research in the conditions
and situations of its production.

Corbin, J. and Strauss, A. (2008) *Basics of Qualitative Research* (3rd edn). Los Angeles, CA: Sage.
Corbin's updated version of grounded theory reflects her changed epistemological and ontological
perspectives and the integration of recent developments in qualitative inquiry.

Glaser, B.G. (1978) *Theoretical Sensitivity*. Mill Valley, CA: Sociology Press.
This book contains Glaser's definitive statement of how to use the original grounded theory method.

Glaser, B.G. and Strauss, A.L. (1967) *The Discovery of Grounded Theory*. Chicago, IL: Aldine.
Glaser and Strauss provide the original statement of the grounded theory method and present the rationale for it and for qualitative research, more generally.

Strauss, A.L. (1987) *Qualitative Analysis for Social Scientists*. New York: Cambridge University Press.
This book provides a 'hands-on' description of how Anselm Strauss taught grounded theory to graduate students through group participation.

5 Narrative Psychology

Michael Murray

Narrative pervades our everyday life. We are born into a narrative world, live our lives through narrative, and afterwards are described in terms of narrative. Until relatively recently, the study of narrative was considered as being of interest only to literary or folklore researchers, but it increasingly has assumed greater importance in the social sciences. Narrative is concerned with the human means of making sense of an ever-changing world. It is through narrative that we can bring a sense of order to the seeming disorder in our world, and it is through narrative that we can begin to define ourselves as having some sense of temporal continuity and as being distinct from others. The aim of this chapter is to consider some of the theoretical issues around narrative psychology and some methodological issues around forms of narrative research.

HISTORY AND THEORETICAL BACKGROUND

Interest in the study of narrative arose as part of the general turn to language that occurred in the social sciences in the 1980s. Within psychology, four classic texts marked the specific narrative turn. The first was *Narrative Psychology: The Storied Nature of Human Conduct*, edited by Theodore Sarbin (1986). This collection amounted to a manifesto for the transformation of psychology. Sarbin contrasted the machine metaphor that, he argued, underlay much of mainstream psychology with that of the narrative metaphor. He summarized the implications of this alternative model:

> In giving accounts of ourselves or of others, we are guided by narrative plots. Whether for formal biographies or autobiographies, for psychotherapy, for self-disclosure, or for entertainment, we do much more than catalog a series of events. Rather, we render the events into a story. (Sarbin, 1986: 23)

In a later interview with Heaven (1999), Sarbin described how this idea arose in his discussion with theorists in the humanities. At first, he recalled, he did not distinguish between narrative as a mode of representation and narrative as an ontological form. However, over time, he became convinced that the latter, stronger form of narrative was more appropriate. As he emphasized in his interview with Heaven (1999), 'stories have ontological status. We are always enveloped in stories. The narrative for human beings is analogous to the ocean for fishes' (1999: 301). According to this argument, narratives are not just ways of seeing the world; we actively construct the world through narratives and we also live through the stories told by others and by ourselves – they have ontological status.

The book edited by Sarbin (1986) also contains a chapter by Ken and Mary Gergen (1986) on the structure of narratives, in which they argued that narratives are social constructions that are developed in everyday social interaction. They are a shared means of making sense of the world. They also have a certain structure. Gergen and Gergen identified three primary structures: the progressive, in which there is movement towards a goal; the regressive, in which the reverse occurs; and the stable, in which there is little change. This analysis is similar to the classic division of narrative into comedy, romance, tragedy and satire (Frye, 1957). Comedy is a story of progress towards a happy ending; romance is also a progressive tale in which the protagonist overcomes adversity and regains what has been lost; tragedy is more a regressive tale in which the protagonist suffers adversity despite the best of intentions; while satire adopts a more stable stance and considers the absurdity of life.

The second important book was *Acts of Meaning*, by Jerome Bruner (1990), which followed his earlier *Actual Minds, Possible Worlds* (Bruner, 1986). In these books, Bruner argued that there are two forms of thinking: the paradigmatic and the narrative. The former is the method of science and is based upon classification and categorization. The alternative narrative approach organizes everyday interpretations of the world in storied form. The challenge of contemporary psychology is to understand this everyday form of thinking. Bruner identified a number of defining properties of narrative, including the following:

1. It is composed of a unique sequence of events, mental states and happenings involving human beings as characters or actors.
2. It can be 'real' or 'imaginary'.
3. It specializes in the forging of links between the exceptional and the ordinary.

These properties help us understand narrative as ways of constructing reality, of bringing sense to something that is obscure or unusual.

The third influential book was *Narrative Knowing and the Human Sciences*, by Donald Polkinghorne (1988). While this book is wide-ranging in its scope, perhaps one of its most important features was the opening up of hermeneutic philosophy, in particular the work of the French phenomenologist Paul Ricoeur, to more widespread discussion within psychology. Ricoeur has developed an immense body of work on the centrality of narrative for meaning-making. In his classic work *Time and Narrative*, Ricoeur (1984) has argued that, since we live in a temporal world, we need to create narratives to bring order and meaning to the constantly changing flux. Further, not only do we create narratives about the world, but also narrative is central to how we conceive ourselves, to our identity. It is through narrative that we not only construct a particular connectedness in our actions, but also distinguish ourselves from others. This work has been taken up and extended by Freeman (1993, 2010) in a series of books.

Finally, the book entitled *Research Interviewing: Context and Narrative*, by Elliot Mishler (1986), was a deliberate intervention into the growing debate about qualitative research. Mishler argued that many qualitative researchers in their enthusiasm to identify themes in their interviews often disrupted the storytelling nature of interviews or ignored the narrative quality of transcribed interviews.

During the 1980s and 1990s, the study of narrative became much more extensive within various fields of psychology. Within personality and human development studies, Dan McAdams (1985: 11) argued that narrative is central to our self-definition: 'We are all tellers of tales. We each seek to provide our scattered and often confusing experiences with a sense of coherence by arranging the episodes of our lives into stories.' McAdams also developed an approach to the study of narrative based upon a developmental model. The earliest form is the *narrative tone*, which can be either optimistic or pessimistic. The former is characteristic of comic and romantic narratives whereas the latter is character-istic of tragedy and satire. This is followed by *imagery*, which he described as a 'treasure trove of personalized symbols and fantasized objects' (McAdams, 1995: 55) that devel-ops as we mature. At a more advanced level are the story *theme*, which is the 'recurrent pattern of human intention' (1985: 67), and the *ideology*, which is revealed in the values and beliefs underlying the story. Each of these characteristics needs to be considered in investigating narrative.

Within clinical and counselling psychology, there has been a movement towards the development of a form of narrative therapy (e.g., Denborough, 2014; White and Epston, 1990) that is based upon exploring alternative stories. Within health psychology, several researchers (e.g., Crossley, 1999; Murray, 1997a; Murray and Sools, 2014; Squire, 2013) have argued that narrative is an everyday means of making sense of the disruption of illness. Narrative has also been used as an analytic framework within political psychology (Andrews, 2008; Hammack, 2008), sport and exercise psychology (e.g., B. Smith, 2010) and within organizational psychology (e.g., Garcia-Lorenzo, 2010). Of particular note, the study of narrative within psychology encouraged the growth of greater contact with the humanities (e.g., Fulford, 1999; Joy, 1997) and with the other social sciences (e.g., Maines, 1993).

Definition of narrative

According to narrative theory (e.g., Freeman, 1993; Murray, 1999; Sarbin, 1986), we are born into a storied world, and we live our lives through the creation and exchange of narratives. A narrative can be defined as an organized interpretation of a sequence of events. This involves attributing agency to the characters in the narrative and inferring causal links between the events. In the classic formulation, a narrative is an account with three components: a beginning, a middle and an end. Indeed, Bettina Becker (1999) has argued that in our world the number *three* has a special quality. For example, unlike the open-ended nature of a straight line, a triangle is enclosed, finished. In the same way, a narrative offers an integrated account of an event. Unlike an open-ended piece of discourse, a narrative has a finished structure. The full dimensions of this structure may not be detailed in everyday conversation. Rather, depending upon the context, certain endings may be left unfinished, and it is the job of the audience/reader to complete the narrative. Since we live in a storied world, we can draw upon more established social narratives to explain an event or to complete a particular story. This is not a process of which we are always conscious.

Function of narrative

The primary function of narrative is that it brings order to disorder. In telling a story, the narrator is trying to organize the disorganized and give it meaning. This is not a straightforward task. As Ricoeur (1987: 436) says:

> The narrative … is a synthesis of the heterogeneous. But concord cannot be without discord. Tragedy is paradigmatic for this: no tragedy is without complications, without fickle fate, without terrible and sad events, without irreparable error committed in ignorance or by mistake rather than through evil-mindedness. If then concord wins out over discord, surely it is the battle between them that makes the story.

The ongoing tension continues as we try to give meaning to the various challenges to the order of our everyday life. Indeed, the tension intrinsic to narrative continues into the analysis of narrative accounts. This is often tentative and open to further challenge.

The use of narrative is particularly pronounced in everyday understandings of disruption (e.g., Becker, 1997). We all encounter disruptions to our everyday routines. Such disruptions include personal problems, family problems, financial problems and health problems. These challenges to our daily routines encourage attempts by us to restore some sense of order. Narrative is a primary means of restoring this sense of order.

The classic experiment by Heider and Simmel (1944) is an illustration of what can be described as this human urge to narrative. In that experiment, participants were shown a sequence of pictograms of abstract shapes in different positions. When asked to describe the pictograms, the participants replied with short stories. Since Heider and Simmel were interested in how the participants attributed causal connections, they did not consider the structure of the stories they developed. Fortunately, some of these stories were included in their report of the experiment, and it is apparent that, although they were brief, the stories contained the basic elements of the classic narrative with a beginning, a middle and an end.

Although we can use narratives to describe the movements of inanimate objects, such as in Heider and Simmel's experiment, it requires that we give those objects agency. Humans are action centres that strive within bounds to create their own worlds. They provide narrative accounts of their experiences that imply their role or lack of role in shaping these events. The converse of agency is suffering (Ricoeur, 1984). When we are denied the opportunity to express our agency, we experience suffering. Accounts of suffering reveal this restraint on our free agency. Suffering can be due to some personal misfortune, but it can also be due to social oppression that denies the opportunity for true agency.

The need to restore a sense of order following disruption is especially pronounced in Western society, which is bounded by order and rationality. Gaylene Becker (1997) has argued that Western ideas about the life course emphasize linearity. Living in such a world, we try to make sense of inconsistencies. Further, when we try to explain our disruptions to another, we are particularly keen to emphasize our reasonableness.

The central process of bringing order has been termed 'emplotment' by Ricoeur (1984), to denote the organizing of a sequence of events into a plot. This sequence of events can be brief or limitless. We can tell the story of going shopping or the story of the creation of the universe (cf. Polkinghorne, 1996). The common theme is the attempt to give these events a narrative shape. Events do not just happen. In the narrative, there is an interconnected sequence that leads from start to finish. However, the event has ended before the narrator has started to construct a narrative. Freeman (1993: 40) has alerted us to this process: 'Consider again the word "recollection" itself: while the "re" makes reference to the past, "collection" makes reference to a present act, an act … of gathering together what might have been dispersed or lost.' In telling the story, the narrator is aware of the ending and constructs the account from there. In life, all narratives are provisional; they are subject to change as new information becomes available. It is not that the narrator is trying to mislead the listener but rather, from a more extended perspective, different pieces of information become available for the story.

Narrative identity

Narrative not only brings order and meaning to our everyday life but also, reflexively, provides structure to our very sense of selfhood. We tell stories about our lives to ourselves and to others. As such, we create a narrative identity. 'Subjects recognize themselves in the stories they tell about themselves' (Ricoeur, 1988: 247). We can hold a variety of narrative identities, each of which is connected to different social relationships. Each narrative identity not only connects us to a set of social relationships but also provides us with a sense of localized coherence and stability. At times of instability, we can make connections to other aspects of our narrative identities.

It is through narrative that we begin to define ourselves, to clarify the continuity in our lives and to convey this to others. We are active agents who recall the actions we have achieved and also those that have been suppressed by others. Narrative enables us to describe these experiences and to define ourselves. In constructing a personal narrative, we are selecting certain aspects of our lives and connecting them with others. This process enables us to assert that our lives are not a disconnected sequence of events but have a certain order.

This process of narrative identity formation is dynamic and occurs in a changing social and personal context. The values attached to different experiences in that context influence the character of events recalled and thus the shape of the story told. As Ricoeur (1987: 437) emphasized, this indicates that 'we learn to become the *narrator of our own story* without completely becoming the author of our life.' While we can tell our life story, the actual pattern our life takes and indeed the very structure of the story we tell are shaped by a multiplicity of social and psychological forces both conscious and unconscious (Hollway and Jefferson, 2000).

Social dimensions of narratives

Narrative accounts are not emitted in a vacuum; rather, they are encouraged and shaped by a certain social context. Although the narrator tells the story, the character of the story told will depend upon to whom the story is being told, the relationship between the narrator and the audience, and the broader social and cultural context (Murray, 1997a). Thus, the study of narrative breaks down the traditional psychological/social distinction and develops a more complex psychosocial subject. The narrator is an active agent who is part of a social world. Through narrative, the agent engages with that world. Through narrative analysis, we can begin to understand both the narrators and their worlds.

Although narrative is often considered in individual or personal terms, we can also consider group, community or societal narratives. These are the narratives that particular collectives tell about themselves, their histories and their aspirations. In the same way as personal narratives are involved in the creation and re-creation of personal identities, these social narratives define the history of a collective and distinguish it from other collectives. Further, these collective narratives overlap with personal narratives such that individuals can define themselves as part of the group. In discussing narrative analysis, we should think about the level of analysis we are considering (Murray, 2000). Moreover, in analysing the personal narrative, we should attempt to consider the character of the broader social narrative within which it is being created.

In sum, we are enmeshed in a world of narrative; we understand our world and ourselves through narrative. As such, the study of narrative provides the researcher with a means to understand how we make sense of the world and of ourselves. The meaning of different narratives is not always apparent and can be approached in different ways by different researchers.

FORMULATING A RESEARCH QUESTION AND DESIGNING A STUDY

Since narratives are all around us and pervade our very sense of being and our understanding of our world, there are many different research questions that attract narrative research. In particular, much of the research has focused on narrative identity and also how we use narrative as a means of managing traumatic events. Let's consider a few examples. The first is a study of the experience of living in the Alaskan wilderness. This study by Judith Kleinfeld (2012) was concerned with the interpenetration of broader societal narratives with the personal narrative identities of a sample of Alaskan frontiers people. On the one hand, she considered the broader societal frontier narrative of the value of rejecting modern society and adopting a simpler lifestyle. This narrative is pervasive in American literature. The personal narratives she describes are concerned with the processes of rebellion, redemption and rebirth. The methods she adopted were life-story or biographical interviews which she carefully interpreted with reference to the broader societal narrative.

A similar study was conducted by Hammack (2008) on the narrative identity of Israeli and Palestinian youth. In this case, he was concerned with how the young people engaged with the broader national narratives of Israel and Palestine in their own personal narratives. Once again the primary source of data was detailed biographical interviews. He argues that through the process of engagement with what he described as these societal 'master narratives' the youth develop their own personal narratives. Further, these master narratives provide the ideological context and the discursive resources with which the youth construct meaning and identity.

In both studies the aim was to connect the personal narrative with the societal narrative. In both cases the researchers set the scene in describing the broader socio-cultural narrative (frontier narrative and national narrative) and then considered in the life stories how the study participants are defining themselves and their everyday life experiences with reference to this broader social narrative.

Both of these examples are concerned with exploring identity, which is a common theme in narrative research. It is not something which is fixed, but rather develops out of the process of active engagement. This is an ongoing process such that narrative researchers are also not interested in a singular identity but this sense of agency – how do people engage with and manage the myriad challenges in their lives?

COLLECTING DATA

The primary source of material for the narrative researcher is the interview. Unlike the traditional structured interview that has a detailed series of questions to be answered, the narrative interview is designed to provide an opportunity for the participant to give a detailed narrative account of a particular experience. The life-story interview is the most extended version of the personal narrative interview. Gerontologists have particularly favoured this life-story approach as a means of exploring the experience of ageing (e.g., Birren et al., 1996).

As its name implies, the aim of the life-story interview is to encourage the participants to provide an extended account of their lives. The researcher will explain at the outset of the interview that the aim of the study is to learn about the person's life. While this may seem a simple invitation, the participant may, in practice, often be wary and uncommunicative at the outset. It is for this reason that the interviewer may need to meet with some participants on a number of occasions to win their confidence and to encourage them to reflect on their life experiences.

However, narratives are not just life stories in the most general sense, but also stories about everyday experiences, especially disruptions of daily life. We can in the interview setting encourage participants to tell stories about particular experiences of change or disruptive episodes in their lives. Flick (2002) has termed this approach the *episodic* interview. Given the time and the opportunity, participants are often very willing to provide extended narrative accounts of different experiences. See Box 5.1 for examples of interview guides. It is obvious from these that the researcher has a particular focus for the interview but provides lots of latitude for the participant to develop the narrative account.

BOX 5.1   SAMPLE INTERVIEW GUIDES

1. I would like you to tell me about yourself – where you were born, where you grew up, that sort of thing. You should not be in any way inhibited about what to say, but just tell me as much as possible about yourself.

2. I am interested in finding out what happened during the selection interview. You can begin at the time you left home for the meeting and just tell me as much as you can remember.

A challenge for researchers is to convince the participants that they are interested in their narrative accounts but at the same time present a neutral stance so as not to encourage a particular narrative. Thus, the researcher can give encouraging nods and remarks but refrain from overt commentary since this may disturb the narrative. At the close of the interview the researcher may review the participant's narrative and introduce supplementary questions designed to obtain clarification, such as 'Why do you think that is the case?' or 'Could you give an example of that?' It is preferable to keep comment to the end of the interview when the participant's narrative account is reviewed (see Jovchelovitch and Bauer, 2000).

However, some people may be very hesitant about participation in extended interviews and this requires considerable dedication on the part of the researcher. The growth of life-story work in therapeutic settings illustrates how storytelling can be beneficial for the storyteller. This opens up the value of more participatory forms of narrative research.

Sometimes it may be useful to invite participants to a group meeting where they can share in the telling of stories about an event. This focus-group approach provides some participants with a greater sense of control and confidence (see Chapter 9 of this volume; also Wilkinson, 1998a, 1998b). These group interviews can be followed or supplemented with individual interviews. Another approach is for the researcher to provide the participant with details of the issue to be discussed. This helps to alleviate any suspicions the participant might have that there are some trick questions to come.

The interviewer can also use other methods, such as encouraging the participants to keep a personal journal or to collect photographs or even to make a video. The aim is always to find a technique with which the participants are comfortable and which will allow them to develop their narrative account. Further, the researcher can analyse narrative material that is already available. For example, you can analyse published memoirs or films.

Since stories develop out of a particular social context and are told to a certain audience, it is important that such details are recorded when collecting narrative accounts. As Mishler (1986: 82) noted, with reference to the importance of considering the interview setting:

The interviewer's presence and form of involvement – how she or he listens, attends, encourages, interrupts, digresses, initiates topics, and terminates responses – is integral to a respondent's account. It is in this specific sense that a 'story' is a joint production.

The researcher should collect background material about the central participants as well as details about the interviewee. Such information is important when we begin to analyse the narrative accounts.

A useful strategy is for the researcher to keep a detailed log of each interview. This could include some basic demographic details of the participant and when and where the interview occurred. Sometimes after the interview has ended and the tape recorder has been switched off, the participant will make some additional comments that can substantially influence the interpretation of the whole narrative. It is important that the researcher pays careful attention. After the interview has ended, the researchers should record in their logs as much detail and commentary as they can recall about the interview. Even at this early stage the researcher should be considering what the key issues arising are and how the narrative is structured.

There is also the caution about the constraining power of the interview, whereby it encourages a certain shaping of the account into a narrative form. It is for this reason that some researchers prefer a less structured approach whereby the researcher engages with the participant in a more open-ended conversation which may take place over a period of time.

Some logistical issues

It is important that care be taken in setting up the more standard interview. The researcher should make some initial contact with the participants, explain the purpose of the study and obtain their consent. At this stage, they can discuss when it would be most convenient to return for a more extended interview and clarify where would be the most comfortable setting. Sometimes the participants are happy to be interviewed at home; other times they prefer to attend the researcher's office or another setting. It is important to remember that it is the participants' choice and to accommodate their preferences as much as possible.

The researcher should practise with the recording device and test the quality of the recording. Sometimes the quality can be poor because of noise outside the interview room or because the participants are speaking quietly. For these reasons, it is sometimes advisable to use an external microphone. Most recording devices allow the collection of lengthy interviews but make sure the battery is fully charged at the outset. It is a sign of respect to the participant for the researcher to ensure that their account is carefully recorded. Finding that the batteries fail halfway through the interview or discovering afterwards that the microphone did not pick up the participant's voice can be very frustrating.

Often the novice interviewer will be apprehensive about using a recorder and think that this will inhibit the participant. Fortunately, the reverse is often the case. After the researcher has carefully explained the study and assured the participant of confidentiality, the participant is often very enthusiastic. Sometimes, after an initial hesitation, the participants will proceed to talk at length about their various experiences. The very fact that they have an audience for the story can act as a spur to more sustained reflection. It is surprising that even when the interview is being videotaped, many people, once they have agreed to participate, will be only too generous with their time and will be surprisingly detailed in their account. It is for this reason that the researcher should treat the participant with the utmost respect and courtesy. In addition, if the participant becomes distressed, the researcher should be prepared to stop the interview and, if necessary, ensure the participant is aware of appropriate support services.

Afterwards, it is important that the interview be transcribed carefully. It is a great advantage to have a professional transcriber, but this does not mean that the researcher does not have a role to play in the transcription process. Rather, the researcher should carefully review the transcript with the tape recording, correcting any errors in the transcription. This should be done as soon as possible after the interview, since it is easy to forget what the person had to say, especially when interviewing a number of people.

There are different ways of preparing interview transcripts for analysis. This depends upon the analytic frame preferred by the researcher. In narrative analysis, the focus is on getting the main narrative account. The narrative transcription should include, where possible, exclamations, pauses and emphases. You can underline certain parts of the text that the participants have stressed in their speech or add notes to mark paralinguistics such as sighs. The aim is to convey the detail and tenor of the story or stories. The transcription should also include the words of the researcher such that the character of the conversational exchange is apparent. We will see this more clearly in the example given below.

ANALYSIS

There are various ways of analysing narrative accounts and this can be a source of anxiety for the novice researcher. Here I describe an approach which divides the analysis into two broad phases – the first descriptive and the second interpretative. A thorough reading of the transcribed narrative precedes both phases. In reading the narrative accounts, the aim is to familiarize oneself with both their structure and their content. A useful strategy is to prepare a short summary of the narratives that will identify the key features, such as the beginning, the middle and the end. The analysts can highlight key issues in the text and identify narrative linkages that connect different parts. They can also discern sub-plots within the broader narrative and consider connections between these. The summary will highlight the particular features in which the researcher is interested. In reading across the summaries, it is then possible to begin to get an idea of what the main issues being raised are (Mishler, 1986). It is through this process of close reading that a coding frame can be developed that can be applied to the various narratives. This coding frame is designed to capture the overall meaning of the narratives and the various particular issues raised within each.

The second step is to connect the narrative with the broader theoretical literature that is being used to interpret the story. Thus, the researcher goes beyond the descriptive phase to develop the interpretation. This requires a simultaneous familiarity with the narrative accounts and with the relevant literature such that the one can begin to connect with the other. This phase of the analysis can lead to labelling certain accounts as being of a certain type that illustrates their theoretical content. For example, we might be interested in how certain people handle particular crises in their lives. In the reading of the narratives, the central concern is how the narrators describe the various crises in their lives, how they draw on particular sources of support, and how they orient the story to the listener. Each story is examined for particular narrative elements – how the elements in the narrative are linked together (the structure and tone), what issues are the main themes, what images and metaphors are used, and what the underlying beliefs and values are.

Role of the reader

The process of narrative analysis is not a passive process. Rather, the researchers bring to the text certain assumptions and beliefs that they use to analyse the narrative. In discussing the process of reading a text, Ricoeur (1987: 430) makes the same point: 'The meaning or the significance of a story wells up from the intersection of the world of the text and the world of the reader.' Ricoeur (1972) used the term 'appropriation' to describe the process of narrative interpretation. He defined this process as making one's own what has been alien. This is not a one-way process. Not only does the researcher bring to the narrative certain ideas, but also, simultaneously, the narrator is trying to convince the audience of the character of his or her story. As Ricoeur (1972: 90) stresses:

> We play with a project, with an idea, we can equally be played. What is essential is the 'to and fro' (*Hin und Her*) of play. Play is thereby close to dance, which is a movement that carries away the dancer.

Thus, rather than imposing a framework and rather than simply describing the narrative account, narrative analysis requires that the analyst play with the account. In conducting the narrative analysis, it is important to be aware of what theoretical assumptions are guiding the analysis while at the same time being open to new ideas and challenges. This is similar to the concept of abduction whereby the researcher brings to the text certain ideas but does not impose them on it.

Narrative structure and content

A particular concern in narrative analysis is how the narrative is structured or organized. Various schemes have been developed to convey the temporal quality of narratives. The threefold classification scheme developed by Gergen and Gergen (1984) is a useful analytic tool, but it is important to apply it not in a schematic way but rather in a flexible manner so as to encapsulate the various shifts in any narrative account. For example, the tragic narrative begins with a progressive structure, but then, despite struggle, the central character is overcome and the narrative becomes regressive. This regression can be overcome by changing the broad interpretative dimensions that are being used to frame the event. For example, people who are upwardly mobile in their career will probably present a progressive career narrative. However, if they are dismissed from their jobs they may develop a more regressive narrative unless they can redefine their goals and so continue to present a progressive narrative. This redefinition of goals, this turning-point in a narrative, is similar to an epiphany. This is the moment in the account when the narrator sees the world in a different way. Conversely, a comedy is when a regressive narrative is transformed into a progressive narrative, as narrators redefine their values and realize the positive features of the changed life.

In his analysis of the personal narratives of people with multiple sclerosis (MS), Robinson (1990) used this temporal scheme. He found that the MS narratives could be organized into three broad categories. There were those who thought that their lives were ended due to the onset of MS (regressive narrative), those who thought that life had changed but was ongoing (stable narrative) and those who thought that the disease provided new opportunities (progressive narrative).

As mentioned earlier, this concern with narrative structure is similar to the concept of narrative tone that McAdams (1993) and Crossley (2000) place at the centre of narrative analysis. Whereas the structure is concerned with the major components of the narrative and how they are connected, the tone is concerned with the overall emotional flavour of the narrative. Thus a regressive narrative would have an overall pessimistic tone whereas a progressive narrative would have an optimistic tone, while a stable narrative would have a more objective tone and would be more like a chronicle or a listing of events.

Gee (1991) described the value of exploring the poetic structure of popular narrative accounts. He argued that verses are an intrinsic part of everyday narrative accounting and that poetry is merely a more developed form of that accounting. In particular, he was concerned about the use of rhythm and metaphor in popular narratives. The study by Becker (1999) is an example of the successful use of this strategy to explore personal narratives. In reading through the pain narrative of an elderly person, she noted that it had a certain poetic quality. She was then able to recast the narrative account as a series of poetic stanzas that each had a similar structure. In recasting the narrative, the interviewer's questions are omitted and the text is organized into verses by the researcher. This form of analysis requires attention to the overall rhythm that underlies the narrative and the metaphors used to describe particular experiences. For example, the narrator may repeat certain phrases within her account (such as 'and then I') which provide a certain rhythm.

Besides the structure of the narrative there is also the imagery used, the major themes and the values underlying the account. McAdams (1993) argues that the two central themes in life histories centre on power and love, which emphasize the importance of agency and having relationships. The importance of these themes varies across individuals and situations. These themes also underlie the major beliefs and values in a person's narrative account. Thus a focus on agency and power places an emphasis on individual rights and autonomy, while a focus on relationships values the group and interpersonal relationships.

The researcher can also move beyond the personal narrative to consider the interpersonal and societal contexts and how they are connected (Murray, 2000). The personal context is concerned with how narrative draws on the experience of the individual. According to McAdams, the early experiences of attachment and loss colour how we react to situations in our later life. The interpersonal context takes into consideration the audience and the co-construction of narrative; and the societal context considers the broader social narratives which structure our everyday accounts. While it is difficult to integrate all these contextual levels into a single analysis, attention to one or the other may be particularly important in understanding the structure of certain narrative accounts (Stephens, 2010; Stephens and Breheny, 2013).

In this chapter, we will consider the structure of a personal narrative account and the value of different analytic strategies. We will begin by summarizing the case, proceed to how the narrative is structured, and then consider how the narrative is located within a particular social context. Although we will consider in detail only one case, it is useful in developing an argument to explore contrary cases. We will consider briefly a contrary case. This process enables the researcher to clarify particular strategies used by the participants in constructing their narratives.

An example: a breast cancer story

The example is taken from a study of how women handle the disruption of their lives as a consequence of having had breast cancer (Murray, 2002). We were interested in how the women integrated the disease into their everyday lives – how they gave it meaning. We were also interested in how these stories were constructed in a particular social and interpersonal context. In this sense, we were interested in how the broader social context intersects with the personal narratives.

All the women interviewed had had surgery for breast cancer. At their last check-up, there was no sign of recurrence and they had agreed to be interviewed about the experience. The interviews took place in the women's homes or in the researcher's office. A young female research assistant who had no personal experience of breast cancer conducted them. For many of the women, the interview was an emotional experience. Several of them mentioned that they had had limited opportunity to discuss the operation with others. They felt that they had to present a strong face to their husbands and family members. The opportunity to talk freely about the event was largely welcomed. It is important that inexperienced researchers are briefed on the emotional intensity of some narrative interviews and that they have the opportunity to discuss the experience afterwards with their supervisor.

We can begin by preparing a summary of each of the narrative accounts. There were certain commonalties in all of the stories that gave them the standard narrative structure:

1. *Beginning*: this was life before cancer. Different women emphasized particular aspects of their lives – family life, marriage, work, children, etc. The main thing was that cancer did not play a part in their lives. Some of the women tried to identify early experiences that might have contributed to the later development of the disease.
2. *Middle*: the major part of the story centred on the diagnosis of cancer, the surgery (radical or otherwise) and the reaction of the patient and that of their family, friends or colleagues.
3. *End*: this involved looking back on the disruption in their lives; how they began to redefine themselves as a survivor of the disease, and how their life expectations and experiences changed.

For some researchers, summarizing all the interviews can be a tedious task. However, it is an important one, as it makes the researcher familiar with the different narratives. It is also important in developing an analytic frame that can encapsulate all the narrative accounts. Thus, we develop an initial analytic frame and then engage with the other narrative accounts, all the time considering its adequacy and how it can be modified.

Having developed the analysis of the narratives, we can then proceed to writing a report or paper that is grounded in the interviews. It is important to have in mind what the key argument is, or the message that you want to convey from your reading of the narratives. It is then possible to select paradigmatic cases that best illustrate the central argument being developed by the researcher (Becker, 1997; Gray et al., 2002). In this chapter, I have chosen two cases that illustrate how people make sense of illness through connecting their current experiences with earlier life experiences. The selection of the narratives was guided by our understanding of Gergen and Gergen's (1984) temporal model and by McAdam's approach to the study of narrative, which has been further developed by Crossley (1999). An initial reading of the narratives suggested that these models were a useful means of organizing much of the material.

The stable/regressive narratives were those with a pessimistic tone which portrayed life as being a litany of woes. In these narratives, childhood was described as being difficult, with few improvements since becoming an adult. Despite many attempts to overcome various challenges, they seemed to be endless. Not only did these challenges recur, but they also seemed to have little redeeming value. Cancer was another of these bleak challenges. The case of Mrs Brown, which is described in Box 5.2, illustrates this stable/regressive and pessimistic narrative. The dominant theme was that of attachment and loss. In her earlier life Mrs Brown had experienced separation and was now very anxious about the consequences of the cancer on the relationships enjoyed by her children. As a single parent she had had a very close relationship with her children. The thought of them having similar childhood experiences as she had filled her with dread. She emphasized the lack of support she had received from others. A recurrent image was that of being alone: she had been alone as a child; she had not been able to establish a stable relationship with the father of her children or another partner; and she felt very alone when she was initially diagnosed with cancer.

BOX 5.2   STABLE/REGRESSIVE/PESSIMISTIC NARRATIVE

Summary: Mrs Brown was a 50-year-old single mother. She described her upbringing as difficult. Her mother died when she was two, and she and her siblings were sent to different orphanages. There they were very badly treated by the guardians. On leaving the orphanage, she trained to be a nurse. She found it difficult to establish a secure relationship but wanted to have children. She had three children by different partners but never married. Two of the children had grown up and left home. The third was aged 12 years. She had not held a full-time job for about ten years. About ten years ago, she had been diagnosed with breast cancer and had undergone a lumpectomy. Mrs Brown's life was difficult and the diagnosis of cancer was devastating. This summary can be extended into a three-part narrative to help clarify particular features.

Beginning: Throughout her account Mrs Brown emphasized her problems. She described her childhood in the orphanage as a very painful experience. Not only was she separated from her siblings, but she also felt that the teachers were very harsh towards her. After she left the orphanage, she found it difficult to establish relationships. In general, her life was difficult.

Middle: The diagnosis of cancer was yet another ordeal. At the time, she was not working, she had three children and she was finding it difficult to make ends meet. When the surgeon told her she had cancer she was very upset:

Mrs B: It really flipped me right out.

Int.:   Yeah.

Mrs B: It really flipped me out, but it was so quick.

Int.:   Hmm, hmm.

Mrs B: Like, I never had time to stop and think.

Int.:   Right.

Mrs B: Like, they told me, and then I cried for three weeks, and then next week I was in hospital and had it all done.

(Continued)

(Continued)

She had a lumpectomy, and on discharge from hospital she found it very difficult to cope:

Int.:   Was it a mastectomy or a lumpectomy?

Mrs B: No, it was just a lumpectomy.

Int.:   OK.

Mrs B: Right, and so I went through all that, and then I went through a year of chemo and radiation and went through hell, but like by myself.

Int.:   Hmm, hmm.

Mrs B: You know, no husband and three little kids. They were young then, right.

Int.:   Oh, it must have been hard.

Mrs B: And it was terrible, it was absolutely terrible. I had no moral support. I had no one here to help.

Mrs Brown emphasized that, without any social support from family or friends and the fact that she had lost any religious belief because of her difficult childhood experiences, the experience of cancer was frightening.

   End: Looking back, although she had survived, the whole experience was difficult. Sometimes she would blame God for her misfortune.

Int.:   Did you ever think 'why me?'

Mrs B: Oh many times.

Int.:   Yeah?

Mrs B: Many times, like holy, never stops, never stops. I be scrubbing the floor, I be scrubbing out a tub, I be bathing one of the kids, I be like 'why, why?' you know. There's no one here to take these kids.

Int.:   Hmm, hmm.

Mrs B: Why are You taking me? I thought I was going to die.

Int.:   Yeah.

Mrs B: Naturally.

Int.:   Hmm, hmm.

Mrs B: You know, somebody tells you 'you got cancer'. First thing, I'm dead.

The ongoing fear of death pervaded her everyday life: 'You have it, it never leaves you. I don't care what I'm doing. I could be baking bread and I'm always thinking. It was always there with me, maybe it's because I'm alone.' She was very anxious about the implications for her children if there was a recurrence of cancer:

Mrs B: If it happens tomorrow, and he's only 12, I will flip. I will go really, really crazy.

Int.:   Hmm, hmm.

Mrs B: Yeah, because what's going to happen to him?

Int.:   Yeah.

Mrs B: Welfare would come and take him. [I] always worry about that kind of stuff. I worry about all that kind of stuff.

Then, looking forward, she felt despondent about her future life:

Mrs B: Just give me more life and just keep it going and don't take it on me – that's the main thing.

Int.:   Yeah.

Mrs B: You know and like I don't aspire to any greatness or anything.

Int.:   Hmm, hmm.

Mrs B: I really don't. I don't aspire to going back to work and to make another life and to go travelling again. I never think of it. It seems like a dream.

A contrary narrative is one in which life is portrayed as a series of challenges that provide an opportunity for advancement. Even life-threatening events such as the diagnosis of cancer could be characterized as such an opportunity. The case of Mrs Jones, which is summarized in Box 5.3, illustrates this more progressive and optimistic narrative. She had given her 'heart to the Lord' at an early stage, and ever since she had felt her life to be a series of life-enhancing opportunities. Cancer was one of these opportunities. In Mrs Jones's case, attachment was secure, in particular through her attachment to religion. In view of the intensity of this attachment, the threat of cancer was minimized. She adopted a rather fatalistic stance and in some ways her story had tragic features. However, the crises she encountered were perceived as God's will and He would take care of things. Her recovery from cancer was evidence of His power. A recurrent image was that of security and comfort. The crises she experienced seem to strengthen rather than weaken her attachment to religion.

BOX 5.3   PROGRESSIVE/OPTIMISTIC NARRATIVE

Summary: Mrs Jones was a 45-year-old married woman. She had six children. Although she had previously worked as a teacher, since the surgery for breast cancer she had devoted herself full-time to religious work. When she was young, she had not been particularly religious, although she had attended a Catholic church and school. When she was 16 years old, she met her future husband, who was a very devout evangelical Christian. Mrs Jones converted to his religion, and since then her devout religious belief had pervaded her whole life, including her experience of cancer. For her, having breast cancer was an opportunity to strengthen her faith and as such could be welcomed.

Beginning: Early in the interview, Mrs Jones provided a detailed account of her religious conversion: 'I started going to the Salvation Army church first and then started going to the Pentecostal church. So after we got married I kept going to the Pentecostal church and I gave my heart to the Lord and I have been going there since.'

Middle: She was diagnosed with breast cancer and underwent a lumpectomy. Initially, the signs were good, but at follow-up there were signs of recurrence. Mrs Jones described the importance of her faith. The surgery was successful and at the time of the interview there were no signs of recurrence. Mrs Jones felt very optimistic: 'I feel that I'm healed. I feel that the Lord healed me.'

End: Looking back, Mrs Jones emphasized the positive experience of having cancer: 'I think that everything in life has been an experience to make me grow and I think it has brought me closer to the Lord.'

This narrative account was progressive. Although cancer was a major challenge, Mrs Jones had transformed this into an opportunity for heightened religious experience. Her narrative account became almost a testimony in itself. Throughout she gave praise to the Lord and all his glory. Her narrative was one of liberation. The disease strengthened her faith. Her recovery was confirmation of the power of religion.

In terms of narrative structure, Mrs Brown's story is both stable and regressive. Her whole life had been difficult and the diagnosis of cancer only served to highlight these problems. The lack of social support and the lack of religious faith left her feeling isolated. She felt she had substantial family responsibilities, and cancer threatened her ability to live up to these responsibilities. Although she had managed so far, the potential recurrence of cancer remained a threat.

It is important to be flexible and innovative in your analysis such that you are not simply imposing a framework. Although you may be aware of general narrative structures, you want to convey the particular features of the narrative accounts you have collected. For example, Frank (2013) presented three structures which he felt characterized the narrative accounts of people with cancer. These were *quest*, *chaos* and *restitution*. Although these are similar to the narrative accounts presented above, they also have their particularity, which conveys the unique experience of having cancer. A fascinating personal reflection on these different approaches is provided by Weingarten (2001).

Connecting the stories with the context

This example of narrative accounts of the experience of cancer illustrates the way people can use narratives to forge 'links between the exceptional and the ordinary' (Bruner, 1990: 47). When given the opportunity in the interview, the women were eager to provide detailed narrative accounts. Indeed, once she had introduced the topic, the interviewer's role was minimal. Often the women were enthused at the opportunity of providing a detailed narrative account of their experience. Sometimes they mentioned that they felt that the giving of the account was therapeutic.

This eagerness to talk after surviving a personal threat is an established phenomenon. In religious terms, the phenomenon is known as 'giving witness', a term that in Greek is cognate with such terms as 'martyr' and 'testimony' (Scott, 1997). The public display of giving witness has spread from its original religious form to a more secular form in the modern world through the phenomenon of 'coming out', which has extensive currency not only in terms of sexual identity but also in terms of survivors of abuse and torture. This form of public narration is a means of developing a community of support and also of challenging certain repressive societal narratives.

In terms of structure, the women's stories had the classic beginning, middle and end. The beginning set the scene, the middle detailed the experience of breast cancer, and the end concerned the impact of the disease on their lives. In the example, the stable/regressive and pessimistic narrative connected the woman's account of cancer with her previous experiences, the interpersonal context and her broader social beliefs in creating a particular narrative identity. For Mrs Brown, life had been difficult. At a time when she felt she had little support, she was diagnosed as having cancer. This was just not fair. She felt that she did not ask for much out of life. Her narrative ended with almost an appeal to let her be healthy at least until her youngest child had grown.

At the personal level of analysis, the narrative reflects the different experiences of the women. Mrs Brown came from a broken family and felt very insecure in her relationships. The main concern for Mrs Brown was her responsibilities to her children. The onset of cancer was a major threat to this and thus was a threat to her life chances. In developing her narrative account, Mrs Brown works backwards from the present, describing earlier experiences of difficulties and lack of support. There is a coherence in the narrative identity that she presents.

At the interpersonal level, the narrative analyst is interested in how the participant conveys her story to the interviewer. In her story, what issues does she emphasize? Her whole life has been one of trials and she does not expect much in the future. 'I don't aspire to greatness', she says. In comparison to her, the young interviewer was fortunate. She seemed to be healthy and in good employment. The diagnosis of breast cancer was yet another tribulation for Mrs Brown. During the interview, she spent considerable time detailing her childhood experiences of abuse and connecting this to her current circumstances. Her narrative account was developed in opposition to what was perceived as a less painful life history.

At the societal level, these narrative accounts reveal the underlying values of the women (McAdams, 1993). The dominant theme in the lives of the women described earlier was that of relationships, emphasizing the importance of communal values. This finding accords with Gilligan's (1993) idea that women centre their discussions of moral issues on communal care and responsibilities. Thus, in the case of Mrs Brown, it was not right that her children's relationships could be jeopardized as hers had been. In the case of Mrs Jones, her relationship with God was secure and thus she was able to transform her illness into an opportunity for growth. Underlying this transformation was a belief in the agency provided by religious faith.

Further analyses

The examples provide an illustration of the process of narrative analysis. It is not the only way of conducting such an analysis. Unlike other forms of qualitative analysis that break the interviews down into themes, the aim of the narrative analysis is to take the full narrative account, to examine how it is structured and to connect it to the broader context. Murray and Sools (2014) emphasize the importance of not only the central agent in the narrative, but also the other players both immediate and distant, the setting (social, physical and psychological) of the narrative, and the disjunction between elements of the narrative, which can provide dynamism or stasis to the account. The important challenge is that the researcher is explicit in the initial theoretical formulation and then engages with the narrative account.

The narrative researcher can bring different theoretical frameworks to help make sense of the story told. Hollway and Jefferson (2000) compare the process of theoretical engagement with tossing a stone into a pond. An appropriate theory will spread its ripples out through the narrative account, revealing particular features that had been neglected by another theory. They used a psychodynamic framework that considers hidden anxieties as providing an underlying structure in narratives. Applying this framework to the breast cancer narrative previously discussed, we can begin to connect Mrs Brown's anxiety about her early experience of abandonment to her fear about the impact of the cancer on her children. Other researchers were interested in the discursive properties of narrative accounts (DeFina and Georgakopoulou, 2012) which focus on the use of particular features of the language used.

In narrative accounts developed in focus groups, it is important to note how collective stories are developed. The identification of collective terms such as 'we' and 'us' can assist in identifying these more social narratives. They can also be seen in the way some narratives are developed in contrast to the stories of the collective 'other' that are described using terms such as 'they' and 'them'. These terms are also apparent in individual narratives and illustrate to what extent the individual identifies with certain social stories or attempts to develop more oppositional narratives.

The researcher can also involve the participants in the process of narrative analysis. For example, one could ask them to review the narrative transcripts or their personal journals and to highlight certain features of interest, in a way for them to begin to develop a coding scheme. From this review, they, either as individuals or as part of a group, can begin the process of analysis. The researcher could also use the study of the narrative accounts as the beginning of a process of reflection for the participants. An extension to the cancer study described would be to invite the women to participate in a group setting to reflect upon their common experiences. Such a process could be emotionally charged for both the researcher and participants, but it also holds the possibility of converting the narrative research into a form of action research (see Chapter 8 of this volume; Kearney, 2006; Lykes, 1997). In this form of research, the participants can begin to reflect upon the power of dominant societal narratives in shaping their experiences and, as a group, to consider alternative, more enhancing narratives.

WRITING UP

The structure of the research report can vary depending upon the analytic focus. However, the concern must be on conveying the narrative nature of the accounts collected. This can be in terms of its immediate structure and content, how it is shaped in the interpersonal context, and how it connects with the broader societal narratives. One way of doing this is to present one or a small number of case studies which provide an opportunity to detail the nature of particular narrative accounts. You can also consider the use of metaphors and other linguistic devices in conveying ideas. Another interesting extension is to consider the interpenetration of fictional and personal narratives whereby narrative details presented in the media or through novels are taken up and integrated or challenged in personal narratives. Sarbin (1997) takes up how stories heard or read can connect with our own narrative selves and everyday practices.

CONCLUSION

In conclusion, the opportunities provided by narrative research are extensive and are still being developed. In conducting a study, researchers should ask what they are trying to understand, what the participants are trying to say, and why they are trying to say it. The aim is to reveal the underlying structure of narrative accounts that shape not only the way we account for our actions and those of others, but also our very identity.

Box 5.4 presents three examples of narrative analysis in action.

BOX 5.4   THREE GOOD EXAMPLES OF NARRATIVE ANALYSIS

Two Black men with prostate cancer: a narrative approach

Gray, Fergus and Fitch (2005) report details of a study which explored in detail the experiences of two Black men with prostate cancer. The two men participated in extensive interviews at four periods of time. The men were asked to provide details of their changing experience of cancer. The authors of the paper read and discussed the interview transcripts, and agreed on the narrative structure and core aspects of the narrative accounts of the two men. They were concerned to connect the men's accounts with their social experiences. They also considered the linear character of the narrative accounts, in particular, how time is framing the narratives. The authors also consider too the issues of race and gender in interpreting the men's narratives. This paper is recommended because it illustrates in detail the process of conducting narrative analysis, the connection with theory, and the challenge of trying to consider the relevance of just two detailed case studies.

Cancer narratives and the cancer support group

This study by Yaskowich and Stam (2003) develops the idea of illness as biographical disruption. Interviews were conducted with 23 cancer patients who participated in peer support groups. A biographical approach to the interview was adopted. The participants were encouraged to provide details of their experience of being diagnosed and living with cancer. It also considered the unique role of the peer support group. The analysis followed the guidelines of grounded theory, an approach to qualitative analysis that is considered in Chapter 4 of this volume. This analysis produced five preliminary categories and two transformed categories: 'biographical work' and 'a unique and separate culture'. The support group was considered a safe situation within which the participants could do the necessary biographical work which enabled them to integrate the diagnosis of cancer into their identities. This article is selected because it gives detailed information on all stages of the project – participant recruitment, conduct of interviews and analysis of interview transcripts. It is also important because it explicitly links grounded theory with narrative theory and clearly considers the use of grounded theory to explore narrative accounts.

Empowering social action through narratives of identity and culture

Williams, Labonte and O'Brien (2003) consider the use of narrative as a strategy for promoting social action in a community setting. Rather than accepting that narratives are a reflection of reality, the researchers begin to explore their transformative potential. A sample of Pacific Islander women resident in a disadvantaged community in New Zealand agreed to participate in the project. This involved them sharing their stories of exclusion and oppression. Through dialogue and debate the members of the group began to see the commonalities in their stories. They identified a series of benefits of shared storytelling. These included confidence building, reconnection and pride in Tongan and Samoan identities, and group building. They also identified two common narratives: struggles of immigrant women and shared experiences as women. From this process of shared narrative analysis the women began to explore strategies of resistance that brought some of them into conflict with family members. Discussion then moved to how to collectively resist such conflict. The reason why this paper was selected is because it shows the connection between narrative and participatory action research.

FURTHER READING

Andrews, M., Squire, C. and Tamboukou, M. (eds) (2008) *Doing Narrative Research*. Los Angeles, CA: Sage.
An excellent collection illustrating different approaches to narrative analysis.

DeFina, A. and Georgakopoulou, A. (2012) *Analyzing Narrative: Discourse and Sociolinguistic Perspectives*. Cambridge: Cambridge University Press.
A guide to a more discursive approach to the analysis of narratives.

Haaken, J. (2010) *Hard Knocks: Domestic Violence and the Psychology of Storytelling*. London: Routledge.
An exciting example of the role of stories in sustaining and challenging violent relationships.

Riessman, C.K. (2008) *Narrative Methods for the Human Sciences*. Los Angeles, CA: Sage.
A detailed description of different aspects of narrative analysis.

Squire, C. (2013) *Living with HIV and ARVs: Three-Letter Lives*. London: Palgrave Macmillan.
An excellent example of the power of narrative to explore particular issues in everyday lives.

6 Conversation Analysis

Paul Drew

Researchers across a range of disciplines – anthropology, sociology, communication, linguistics, sociolinguistics and pragmatics, as well as psychology – are turning increasingly to the perspective and methods of conversation analysis (CA). They have done so in order to investigate a wide variety of topics, some of which intersect with, or lie within, various fields of psychology. The sheer breadth and richness of these topics begin to give some idea of the adaptability of CA to a great variety of research sites. These topics include: talking about personal troubles and anxieties (Jefferson, 2015); medical interaction, especially interactions between patients and doctors and other healthcare professionals (Drew et al., 2001; Heritage and Maynard, 2006; Heritage et al., 2007; Heritage et al. 2010; Stivers 2007); neurology and the differential diagnosis of seizure (Reuber et al., 2009; Robson, Drew and Reuber, 2012); communicative challenges of interacting with people with Alzheimer's disease (Jones, 2013); emotion in interaction (Hepburn and Potter, 2013); child–adult interaction and the development of mind (Wootton, 1997); news media, such as news interviews, political speaking and debate (Atkinson, 1984; Clayman and Heritage, 2002); speech disorders relating to aphasia, autism and cerebral palsy (Goodwin, 1995); family interactions (Hepburn and Potter, 2011; Mandelbaum, 2014); sexual identity (Kitzinger, 2005a and b); psychiatric consultations in gender identity clinics (Speer and McPhillips, 2013); helplines, such as cancer care and NSPCC child crisis helplines (Hepburn and Wiggins, 2005; Leydon et al., 2013); counselling of various kinds, including family systems therapy applied to HIV/AIDS counselling (Peräkylä, 1995; Silverman, 1997); and mediation (Stokoe, 2014).

Underpinning the diversity of research in 'applied' areas such as these, however, is the programme of CA research into the basic processes of ordinary social interaction, with which this chapter is principally concerned. CA is a largely qualitative methodology (indeed paradigm) for investigating how we interact with one another, and in doing so, how we maintain the intersubjective coherence of our interactions, how we negotiate and sustain mutual understandings about reality, how we conduct social action through talk, and how we fix communicative and interactional problems as they arise, through systems of repair. The materials that we work with – our data – are for the most part ordinary conversational interactions of the kind that most of us are able and have the opportunity to engage in every day. We are therefore exploring the interactional and linguistic/communicative competences that enable us to engage with and understand one another (but see Drew, 2005a, especially the *Prologue: Toma's Paradox*, for what may happen if we don't have the opportunity to interact normally with others). More will be said about this theoretical background and methodology in the next section. For the present:

- CA is applied to a wide range of topics and areas of direct relevance to psychologists, including applied research.
- Underpinning applied topics of research is CA's inquiry into ordinary conversational interaction.
- Our analytic aim is to uncover what makes coherent interaction possible – what are the practices and patterns that enable us to interact meaningfully?

HISTORY AND THEORETICAL BACKGROUND

The origins of CA intersect more closely with psychology – at least with topics which have seemed intrinsically psychological in character – than is perhaps generally appreciated. Having first trained in the law, and then undertaken graduate study at the University of Berkeley, Harvey Sacks (1935–1975) began to develop CA in the course of his investigations at the Center for the Scientific Study of Suicide, in Los Angeles, 1963–1964. Here he was interested initially in psychiatric and psychodynamic theorizing. But staff at the Center were recording suicide counselling telephone calls in an attempt to better understand the problems that callers were facing and thereby to figure out how to counsel callers more effectively. It was Sacks' inquiries into these recordings that provided the stimulus for what was to become CA. Drawn by his interests both in the ethnomethodological concern with members' methods of practical reasoning (arising from his association with Harold Garfinkel), and in the study of interaction (he was taught at Berkeley by Erving Goffman), Sacks began to investigate how callers' accounts of their troubles were produced in the course of their conversations with Suicide Prevention Center (SPC) counsellors. This led him, without any diminished sensitivity to the plight of persons calling the SPC, to explore the more generic 'machineries' or practices of conversational interaction, and of the sequential patterns and structures associated with the management of activities in conversation. (For a definitive account of the origins of Sacks' work in CA, its subsequent development and the range of issues it spawned, see Schegloff (1992a). Edwards (1995) provides a clear and important review not only of Sacks' work, but also of the differences between his interactional approach and psychological perspectives, especially in cognitive psychology. See also Drew and Couper-Kuhlen (2014b); and for an account of these origins, and how CA 'arrived' in Europe see the introduction to Jefferson (2015).

Through the collection of a broader corpus of interactions, including group therapy sessions and mundane telephone conversations, and in collaboration with Gail Jefferson (1938–2008) and Emanuel Schegloff (1937–), Sacks began to show that:

talk can be examined as an object in its own right, and not merely as a screen on which are projected other processes, whether Balesian system problems or Schutzian interpretative strategies, or Garfinkelian commonsense methods. The talk itself was the action, and previously unsuspected details were critical resources in what was getting done in and by the talk; and all this in naturally occurring events, in no way manipulated to allow the study of them. (Schegloff, 1992a: xviii)

At the heart of this is the recognition that 'talk is *action, not communication*' (Edwards, 1995: 579). Talk is not merely a medium, for instance, to communicate thoughts, information or knowledge: in conversation as in all forms of interaction, people are doing things in talk (Austin, 1962; Drew and Couper-Kuhlen, 2014b). We are engaged in social activities with one another – and what is beginning to emerge is a quite comprehensive picture of *how* people engage in social actions in talk-in-interaction. Sacks focused on such matters as the organization of turn-taking; overlapping talk; repair; topic initiation and closing; greetings, questions, invitations, requests, etc. and their associated sequences (adjacency pairs); agreement and disagreement; storytelling; and the integration of speech with non-vocal activities. Subsequent research in CA over the past 50 years has shown how these and other technical aspects of talk-in-interaction are the structured, socially organized resources – or methods – whereby participants perform and coordinate activities through talking together. Thus, they are the technical bedrock on which people build their social lives, or, in other words, construct their sense of sociality with one another.

Essentially, CA is a naturalistic, observation-based science of actual (verbal and non-verbal) behaviour, which uses audio and video recordings of naturally occurring interactions as the basic form of data (Heritage, 1984). CA is distinctive in its approach in the following kinds of ways.

- In its focus on how participants understand and respond to one another in their turns at talk, thereby exploring the social and interactional underpinnings of intersubjectivity – common, shared and even 'collective' understandings between social actors.

- CA empirically develops Goffman's insight that social interaction embodies a distinct moral and institutional order that can be treated like other social institutions (Goffman, 1983). CA explores the practices that make up this institution, as a topic in its own right.

- Conversational organizations underlie social action (Atkinson and Heritage, 1984); CA offers a methodology for investigating how we accomplish social actions.

- It is evident that the performance by one participant of certain kinds of actions, for instance, a greeting, question, invitation, complaint, accusation, etc., sets up certain expectations concerning what the other, the recipient, might or should do in response – particularly whether they respond *affiliatively*.

- The normative character of action and the associated accountability of acting in accordance with normative expectations are vitally germane to the moral order of social life, including ascriptions of deviance.

- CA relates talk to social context. CA's approach to context is distinctive, partly because the most proximate context for any turn at talk is regarded as being the (action) sequence of which it is a part – in particular, the immediately prior turn.

- CA also takes the position that the 'context' of an interaction cannot be exhaustively defined by the analyst *a priori*; rather, participants display in the 'design' of their turns at talk (this will be explained later) their sense of relevant context – including mutual knowledge, what each knows about the other, the setting, relevant biographical information, their relevant identities or relationships, and so on.

- CA (along with other perspectives in sociology, pragmatics and linguistics) recognizes that interaction is fundamentally organized with respect to cooperation; indeed, the origins of language almost certainly lie in the cooperative undertakings of our ancestors. At any rate, there is clear evidence that interaction is managed in such a way as to enhance cohesion and social solidarity and to minimize conflict – or at least to reduce as far as possible the disintegrative effects of conflict and disharmony. (For a review of this and all these themes in CA's work, see Heritage, 1984.)

- Underlying the methodology of CA is the attempt to capture and document the back-and-forth, contingent and *processual* character of interaction. The analytic aim is to show how conversational and other interactions are managed and constructed in real time, through the processes of production and comprehension employed by participants in coordinating their activities when talking with one another. This involves focusing on the turn-by-turn *contingent* evolution of conversations from one speaker's turn, to the next speaker's, and so on.

Each participant in a dyadic (two-person) conversation (to take the simplest model) constructs or designs a turn to be understood by the other in a particular way – for instance, as performing some particular action (Drew, 2012). The other constructs an appropriate response, the other's understanding of the prior turn being manifest in that response. Hence, the first speaker may review the recipient's response to check whether the other has 'correctly' understood his or her first turn; and if the first speaker finds from that response that the other appears not to have understood his or her utterance/action correctly, that speaker may initiate repair to remedy the other's understanding (Schegloff, 1992b). The first speaker then produces a response, or a relevant next action, to the other's prior turn – and so the conversation proceeds, each turn being sequentially connected to its prior turn, but simultaneously moving the conversation forward by forming the immediate context for the other speaker's next action in the sequence (this is the 'context-shaped and context-renewing' character of conversational turns/actions described by Heritage, 1984: 242).

CA's methodology is naturalistic and largely qualitative, and is characterized by four key features:

1. Research is based on the study of naturally occurring data (audio or video recordings). These recordings are usually transcribed in considerable detail, though the precise level and type of detail (such as whether certain phonetic and prosodic features of production are included) will depend on the researcher's particular focus.

2. Phenomena in the data are generally not coded. The reason for this is that tokens which have the appearance of being 'the same' or equivalent phenomena may turn out, on closer inspection, to have a different interactional salience, and hence not to be equivalent. For example, repetitions might be coded in the same category, and hence regarded as undifferentiated phenomena. But different prosodic realizations of

repeats (Couper-Kuhlen, 1996) or the sequential circumstances in which something is being repeated, and specifically what object is being repeated (Schegloff, 1996), can all crucially influence the activity being conducted through a repeat. Coding tokens on the basis of certain manifest similarities runs the risk of collecting, in the same category, objects which in reality have a quite different interactional significance.

3. CA's methodology is generally not quantitative. This is not a rigid precept, but rather a corollary of the risks attendant on coding – following from which, it is clear that quantifying the occurrence of a certain object is likely to result in the truly interactional properties of that object being overlooked. Those interactional properties can be uncovered only by thorough qualitative analysis, particularly of the sequential properties of that object, and how variations in speech production are related to their different sequential implicature (on reasons for being cautious about, or avoiding, quantification, see Schegloff, 1993).

4. CA's methods attempt to document and explicate how participants arrived at understandings of one another's actions during the back-and-forth interaction between them, and how in turn they constructed their turns so as to be suitably responsive to prior turns. Therefore, CA focuses especially on those features of talk that are salient to participants' analyses of one another's turns at talk, in the progressive unfolding of interactions.

But all this is pretty abstract. It is time to give a more concrete, practical guide to CA's methodology.

FORMULATING A RESEARCH QUESTION AND DESIGNING A STUDY

CA research tends not to formulate or address research questions in the way that is conventional for most other methods. We generate research topics in one of four principal ways:

- by identifying a phenomenon emerging from data
- by focusing on a particular kind of action (e.g., requesting) or aspect of interaction (e.g., emotion)
- by designing a study to investigate a particular kind of interaction, or interactions, in a particular kind of setting (e.g., the dynamics of family mealtimes)
- by conducting research in a practical or applied topic area, often addressing issues that practitioners want to explore.

I have mentioned that Sacks developed CA out of his study of telephone calls made to a suicide prevention agency. In that respect he adopted the fourth of these strategies, by conducting research into interactions in a highly practical setting; it is unclear, however, whether his investigations and findings were subsequently 'applied' to altering or improving the ways in which calls were handled (though his findings did tally with, and provided another perspective on, some of what was known about the demographics associated with suicide and attempted suicide). In the early stages, CA research generally took the first route above, by identifying something that began to be apparent and recurrent in the data on which one happened to be working. For instance, some years ago I began to notice how frequently speakers would make a claim, but then back down from the strength of that claim. Their initial claims seem to be exaggerated, when compared with the version that emerged. I'll consider some examples later when discussing how we approach data analysis; so for the present I'll note only that this pattern, and the practices associated with it, emerged through 'unmotivated inquiry' – it just kept showing up in a range of conversational data.

By contrast, other projects evolved from a decision to focus on requesting, for example (Curl and Drew, 2008). We noticed early in the project that speakers use different forms or constructions with which to make a request. It appeared that in our ordinary social conversation data, between family and friends, speakers generally used modal forms (*Could you bring up a letter when you come up*), while in out-of-hours calls to the doctor, callers asked *I wonder whether you could come and give me something for it*, using a conditional form that indicated their understanding that they were not as entitled to ask (as a son might be to ask his mother to bring up a letter for him), and that greater contingency might be involved in granting the request. Then again, other research directions have emerged from the needs and interests of practitioners who may have sponsored the research; so the topics and issues on which we focused in research into how unemployed benefits claimants are interviewed in Job Centres in the UK arose from the aim of the government department which commissioned this research to improve the effectiveness of these interviews (Drew et al., 2014).

The research design or strategy one adopts will follow from which of these four routes the research focus has emerged. But broadly speaking, it is best to focus on what participants are doing, what actions or activities they are engaged in; then investigate how they construct and manage those actions. So, for example, in the research on Jobcentre Plus interviews between advisers and claimants, we focused on the core activities conducted during what are called 'work focused interviews', such as establishing a claimant's three job goals, doing a 'better off calculation', establishing barriers to work, and so on. In research into primary care medical interactions, real progress has been made by focusing on the key activities of the consultation, such as eliciting the patient's account of the problem, the medical examination, making the diagnosis and considering treatment (Heritage and Maynard, 2006). Identifying and exploring the key activities in an interaction or a given setting then provides a framework within which one can develop more specific research strategies and aims.

COLLECTING DATA

I mentioned that the data which researchers in CA use are always recordings of naturally occurring interactions: data are not gathered through simulations, through experimental or quasi-experimental tasks, and are not fabricated. Nor, generally, are interviews treated as data, although, for certain analytic purposes or enterprises, some interviews may be considered as naturally occurring interactions (as, for instance, the interviews I mentioned between advisers and claimants in Jobcentre Plus offices). There is no easy guide to making recordings in the field, the difficulties of which include access (and the ethical standards of obtaining consent), technical aspects and attendant frustrations. (I once videotaped an open-plan architects' office in the north of England over one week; when we checked the recording of one day, of possibly the best 'action' we'd seen all week, there was no audio – loose connections can drive you crazy! But see Goodwin (1993) on technical aspects of recording.) And one can learn only from experience how to handle the personal relationships and expectations that can develop from extended involvement with those whom one is recording.

Once recordings have been obtained, the next step is to transcribe (all or some portions of) the data collected. Later, in the next section, I will introduce CA's approach to analysing data by focusing on a brief extract from a telephone call between Emma (all names are pseudonyms) and a friend, Nancy, whom she has called. This extract begins about eleven minutes into the call when, after they have talked for some time about a class which Nancy is taking at a local university (as a mature student, in middle age), Emma abruptly changes the topic. To give you some idea of what we try to put into and convey through our transcripts, here first is a simple standard orthographic transcription of what the participants say to one another (Box 6.1).

BOX 6.1   SIMPLE TRANSCRIPTION

(1)	[NB:II:2:9]
Emma:	... some of that stuff hits you pretty hard
Nancy:	Yes
Emma:	And then you think well do you want to be part of it What are you doing?
Nancy:	What am I doing?
Emma:	Cleaning?
Nancy:	I'm ironing would you believe that
Emma:	Oh bless its heart.
Nancy:	In fact I I started ironing and I I somehow or another ironing just kind of leaves me cold
Emma:	Yes
Nancy:	You know
Emma:	Want to come down have a bite of lunch with me?
Nancy:	It's just
Emma:	I've got some beer and stuff
Nancy:	Well you're real sweet hon
Emma:	Or do you have something else
Nancy:	Let I No I have to call Roul's mother ....

BOX 6.2   TRANSCRIPTION SYMBOLS

The relative timing of utterances

Intervals either within or between turns are shown thus (0.7).

A discernible pause which is too short to be timed mechanically is shown as a micro-pause (.).

Overlaps between utterances are indicated by square brackets, the point of overlap onset being marked with a single left-hand bracket.

Contiguous utterances, where there is no discernible interval between turns, are linked by an equals sign. This is also used to indicate a very rapid move from one unit in a turn to the next.

Characteristics of speech delivery

Various aspects of speech delivery are captured in these transcripts by punctuation symbols (which, therefore, are not used to mark conventional grammatical units) and other forms of notation, as follows:

A period (full stop) indicates a falling intonation.

A comma indicates a continuing intonation.

A question mark indicates a rising inflection (not necessarily a question).

The stretching of a sound is indicated by colons, the number of which correspond to the length of the stretching.

.h indicates inhalation, the length of which is indicated by the number of h's.

h. indicates outbreath, the length of which is indicated by the number of h's.

(hh) indicate audible aspirations in the speech in which they occur (including in laughter).

°° (degree signs) indicate word(s) spoken very softly or quietly.

Sound stress is shown by underlining, with those words or parts of a word which are emphasized being underlined.

Particularly emphatic speech, usually with raised pitch, is shown by capital letters.

Marked changes in pitch are shown by ↑ for changes to a higher pitch, and ↓ for a fall in pitch.

If what is said is unclear or uncertain, this is placed in parentheses.

Box 6.1 is the kind of transcript that might be produced by *Hansard*, as a record of Parliamentary debate, or by court stenographers as they write down what's said during a trial. It records, in standard orthography, the words that were spoken – or, rather, as they should have been spoken. But it does not record what was actually said. It does not, for instance, record the difference between words that were fully articulated and those that were abbreviated or run together (for instance, we'll see that Emma does not say *bite of* in the eleventh line: she runs them together, as *bahta*). Nor does it record the way in which things were said, the pacing, intonation and emphasis in their talk. Finally, it does not capture anything about the relationship between one person's turn at talk and the next – such as overlapping speech or pauses/silences. In order to represent these and other aspects of talk, CA has developed a transcription system which aims to capture faithfully features of speech which are salient to the interaction between participants, including – as well as characteristics of speech delivery (such as emphasis, loudness/softness, pitch changes, sound stretching and curtailment, etc.) – aspects of the relationship between turns at talk. This relationship includes whether, and when, one speaker talks in overlap with another, and whether there is a pause between one speaker's turn and the next (see Atkinson and Heritage, 1984: ix–xvi; Jefferson, 1985; ten Have, 1999: Chapter 5). To capture these features, we use the symbols shown in Box 6.2.

Using these symbols to transcribe the same extract results in something that, although formidably difficult to comprehend at first sight, captures a considerable amount of detail that may be relevant to our analysis of the interaction between them. It is important to note in this respect that our transcriptions are 'pre-analytic', in the sense that they are made before the researcher has any particular idea about what phenomena, patterns or features in the data might be investigated. Indeed, the purpose of the transcript, used in conjunction with the recording, is that it should be a resource in developing observations and hypotheses about phenomena. The following shows the same extract from the conversation between Emma and Nancy as was shown in Box 6.1, transcribed using the conventions that were just outlined (this has been extended to include a little more of their conversation than was shown in Box 6.1). Try not to be put off by the detail, which, to begin with, will look like Ancient Egyptian: if you read it through a couple of times, you'll quickly begin to follow it.

---

(2)   [NB:II:2:9]

1   Emm:........ so[me a'° s]ome a'that stuff <u>hits</u> yuh pretty <u>ha:</u>rd=

2   Nan: [°<u>Ye:</u>ah°]

3   Emm: = 'n then: °yuh thin:k <u>we:</u>ll d'y<u>ou</u> wanna be°

4   (0.7)

```
 5    Nan: hhhhhh[hh

 6    Emm:        [↑PA:R:T of ut.w;Wuddiyuh ↑DOin.

 7         (0.9)

 8    Nan: What'm I do[in?

 9    Emm:               [Cleani:ng?=

10    Nan: =hh.hh I'm ironing wouldju belie:ve ↑tha:t.

11    Emm: Oh: bless it[s ↓hea:rt.]

12    Nan:            [In f a :c]t I: ire I start'd ironing en I: d-

13         I: (.) Somehow er another ahrning js kind of lea:ve me:

14         co:[ld]

15    Emm:    [Ye]ah,

16               (.)

17    Nan: [Yihknow, ]

18    Emm: [Wanna c'm] do:wn 'av [a bah:ta] lu:nch w]ith me?=

19    Nan:                      [° It' s j s ] (       )°]

20    Emm: =Ah gut s'm beer'n stu:ff,

21         (0.3)

22    Nan: ↑ Wul yer ril sweet hon: uh:m

23        (.)

24    Emm: [Or d'y] ou'av] sup'n [else °(    )°

25    Nan: [L e t-] I : ] hu.   [n:No: i haf to: uh call Roul's mother,h

26         I told'er I:'d call'er this morning I [ gotta letter ] from'er en
```

27   Emm: [°(Uh huh.)°]

28   Nan: .hhhhh<u>h</u> <u>A</u>:nd uhm

29   (1.0)

30   Nan: .tch u.-So: she in the <u>le</u>tter she said if you c<u>a</u>:n why (.)

31   y<u>i</u>hknow c<u>a</u>ll me Saturday <u>mor</u>ning en I jst h<u>a</u>ven't. h

32   [.hhhh]

33   Emm: [°Mm <u>h</u>]m:°=

34   Nan: ='T's like t<u>a</u>kin a b<u>eat</u>ing.

35   (0.2)

36   Nan: kh[hh ↑<u>h</u>nhh hnh]-hnh- [hnh

37   Emm: [°M <u>m</u> :   : :, °]   [No one heard a <u>wo</u>:rd hah,

38   Nan: ><u>Not</u> a word,<

39   (0.2)

40   Nan: H<u>a</u>h ah,

41   (0.2)

42   Nan: n:N<u>o</u>t (.) n<u>o</u>t a word,h

43   (.)

44   Nan: N<u>o</u>t et all, ex<u>cep</u>t Roul's m<u>o</u>ther gotta call.hhhhhh (0.3)

45   °I think it wuss:: (0.3) th'Mond<u>ee</u> er the <u>Tue</u>:sday

46   after <u>Mo</u>ther's Da<u>:y</u>,

This telephone conversation is, of course, like any other, quite unique – in terms of time and place, and its having been held by these two participants, with whatever relationship and history they have with each other, and in whatever circumstances the call happened to be made. Notice that we can begin to see something of their relationship in Nancy's referring to 'Roul's mother', thereby assuming that Emma will recognize to whom she is referring when she names her ex-husband. Furthermore, it is evident that Emma already knows something about the circumstances associated with the difficulties Nancy is having with her ex-husband, when in response to Nancy's reference in line 34 to 'takin a beating', she (Emma) asks in line 37, 'No one heard a wo:rd hah,'. And finally, in lines 18–20, Emma invites Nancy over for lunch ('Wanna c'm *do:wn*' av a bah:ta lu:nch with me?=Ah gut s'm *beer'n* stu:ff,'); presumably, there are not many people Emma could or would call mid-morning to invite over for an informal lunch that same day (that Roul is Nancy's ex-husband and that it is 11.15 am emerge later in the call). Thus, details in their conversation reveal something of their relationship and the uniqueness of what they know about each other.

ANALYSIS

Despite the uniqueness of this conversation, we can make out some familiar things in extract (2), things that we recognize to be happening in other conversations. Foremost among these is perhaps what seems central to this extract: Emma's invitation. There are various ways to begin to approach analysing data (see Pomerantz and Fehr, 1996, for a useful and more extended outline than can be provided here). But an initial – and quite essential – starting point is to consider the ways in which participants are not 'just talking', but engaged in social activities. Whenever we are examining talk in conversation, we look to see what activity or activities the participants are engaged in – what are they doing? Here the activity being managed or conducted in this sequence is Emma's invitation. The *social character* of such an action or activity cannot be too strongly emphasized. People's engagement in the social world consists, in large part, of performing and responding to such activities. So again, when we study conversation, we are studying not language idling, but language employed in the service of doing things in the social world. And we are focusing on the social organization of these activities being conducted in conversation.

In referring to the *management* of Emma's invitation, I mean to suggest that we can see how Emma manages the interaction in such a way as to give herself the opportunity to make the invitation. Looking at what occurs immediately before, it is clear that Emma's invitation in lines 18–20 follows her having inquired about what Nancy was doing (line 6). It appears that Nancy's response – indicating that she *started* doing something (line 12) but might rather not continue it (*ironing just kind of leaves me cold*, lines 13–14) – encourages Emma to make her invitation. Now, we cannot be sure whether Emma asked what Nancy was doing with the intention of finding out whether she was free, and, if so, to invite her; or whether, having asked an innocent question, perhaps about their daily chores, and finding that Nancy was at a loose end, Emma decided at that point (that is, after Nancy's response) to invite her. This illustrates the difficulty in trying to interpret participants' cognitive or other psychological states on the basis of verbal conduct. In short, we cannot know whether her inquiry in line 6 was 'innocent', and therefore that the invitation was interactionally gener-ated by Nancy's response, or whether she made the inquiry specifically in order to set up the invitation she had already planned (and that, indeed, she might have made the call with the purpose of inviting Nancy over for lunch). All that we can say at this stage is that invitations, and similar actions such as requests, are regularly preceded by just such inquiries. Here are two quite clear cases, in which an initial inquiry receives an 'encouraging' response, after which the first speaker makes the invitation which the recipient might well have been able to anticipate.

---

(3)   [:CN:1]

    1   A: Watha doin'

    2   B: Nothin'

    3   A: Wanna drink?

(4)   [JGII(b):8:14]

    1   John: So who'r the boyfriends for the week.

    2   (0.2)

    3   Mary:.k.hhhhh- Oh: go::d e-yih this one'n that one yihknow,jist,

    4   yihknow keep busy en go out when I wanna go out John

    5   it's nothing .hhh I don' have anybody serious on the string,

    6   John: So in other words you'd go out if I:: askedche out one a'

    7   these times.

    8   Mary: Yeah! Why not.

Such inquiries as are made in extracts (3) and (4) are termed *pre-invitations*: they may be designed to set up the invitation which they presage, or may happen to provide an opportunity to make an invitation – by finding out whether, if the invitation were made, it is likely to be accepted.

Whether or not Emma had in mind, when making her inquiry, to invite Nancy (and hence whether her inquiry in line 6 was designed as a pre-invitation), we can see that the invitation did not come out of the blue. It was preceded by, and arose out of, an interactional sequence (lines 6–17) from which Emma could discern that Nancy might be free to come for lunch. Another aspect of the management of her invitation is the way in which it is constructed or designed as a casual, spontaneous idea. This is conveyed, not only in the timing of the invitation (only an hour or so beforehand), but also in using phrases like 'come down' and 'bite of lunch'. The sociability being proposed is not portrayed as a luncheon party, an occasion to which others have been invited, or for which one should dress up, or an RSVP event; rather, it is an impromptu affair, on finding that Nancy might welcome some diversion from her chores. So the kind of invitation it is, and the concomitant expectations and obligations that might attach to the recipient of such an invitation, are manifest in the specific design of the turn in which the invitation is made.

Therefore, having outlined a first step in analysing data:

1. Look to see what activity or activities the participants are engaged in. We can add the second and third steps.
2. Consider the sequence leading up to the initiation of an action, to see how the activity in question may have arisen out of that sequence (and even whether a speaker appears to have laid the ground for the upcoming action).
3. Examine in detail the design (the specific words and phrases used, including prosodic and intonational features) of the turn in which the action is initiated.

This latter point concerning turn design can be developed in the context of a fourth step:

4. Consider how the recipient responds to the 'first' speaker's turn/action.

In this respect, we can notice a number of features of Nancy's response. First, she does not answer immediately: there is a 0.3-second delay (line 21) before she begins to speak.

---

(5) [From (2)]

18 Emm: [Wanna c'm] <u>do:wn</u> 'av [a bah:ta] <u>lu:</u>nch w]ith me?=

19 Nan: [°It's js] (   )°]

20 Emm: =Ah gut s'm <u>beer</u>'n stu:ff,

```
21          (0.3)

22  Nan:    ↑Wulyer ril sweet hon: uh:m

23          (.)

24  Emm:    [Or d'y] ou'av] sup'n else °(   )°

25  Nan:    [L e t-]I  :  ] hu.
```

Bearing in mind the first analytic step, to consider what action a speaker is doing in a turn (or sequence), we can notice here that, when she does respond, Nancy does an *appreciation* of the invitation (line 22, 'Wul yer ril sweet hon: uh:m'). She could, of course, simply have accepted Emma's invitation, with something like 'Oh, that'd be lovely', which would have simultaneously both *appreciated* and *accepted* the invitation. Here, though, Nancy appreciates the invitation without (at least yet) accepting. Two further observations about Nancy's turn/appreciation in line 22: it is prefaced with 'Wul' (that is, *Well*); and then she hesitates before continuing, as indicated by 'uh:m' and the slight (micro) pause (line 23) before she begins with 'Let-' (line 25).

Of course, having invited Nancy over for lunch, Emma is listening for whether Nancy will accept. It is quite plain from her turn in line 24, 'Or d'y ou'av sup'n else', that already Emma anticipates that Nancy might have some difficulty in accepting: having *something else to do* is a standard reason to decline an invitation.

A way to think about Emma's anticipating Nancy's difficulty/possible declining is that Emma *analyses* what Nancy has said. This again is fundamental to our investigations of conversation: we are focusing on *the analyses which participants make of each other's talk and conduct* – on how they understand what the other means or is doing. Looking at what it is that has led Emma to anticipate that Nancy might be going to decline, we can see that the only basis Emma has so far for making this analysis is the delay before Nancy speaks (in line 21), her appreciating the invitation without yet accepting it, and Nancy beginning her turn with 'Well'. Taken together, these three features indicate to Emma that Nancy might, after all, not be free to come over for lunch.

I mentioned before that, although this is a unique conversation, many features of their talk are quite familiar. Nancy's *appreciation* is one of the familiar features, and appreciations are familiar, particularly when one speaker is declining another's invitation (or offer). Here is another example.

```
(6)  [SBL:1:1:10:14]

1  Ros:    And uh the: if you'd care tuh come ovuh, en visit u
```

2		little while this morning I'll give you[cup a'c<u>o</u>ffee.
3	Bea:	[khhh
4	Bea:	<u>Uhhh</u>-huh hh W'l that's <u>awf</u>'lly <u>sweet</u> of yuh I don't
5		think I c'n <u>ma</u>ke it this m<u>o</u>rning, hheeuhh uh:m (0.3)
6		'tch I'm <u>ru</u>nning en <u>a</u>:d in the p<u>a</u>per 'nd an:d uh hh I
7		haftih stay near the ph<u>o</u>::ne,

Bea's declination of Rose's invitation to come over for coffee that morning consists of three components:

[appreciation] + [declines] + [account]

Her [appreciation] is 'W'l that's awf'lly *sweet* of yuh' (line 4): she explicitly [declines] the invitation when she says 'I don't think I c'n *make* it this morning' (lines 4–5). (Note that Bea's declination is softened, or mitigated, by her saying 'I don't think', rather than just 'I can't make it'), after which she offers an [account] for being unable to make it, which is that 'I'm *running* en a:d in the paper 'nd an:d uh hh I haftih stay near the pho::ne' (lines 6–7). This illustrates the way in which an [appreciation] can be done to preface or lead into declining an invitation. One thing which the [appreciation] does is to delay the declination; and this is consistent with the 0.3-second pause (line 21) before Nancy's response to Emma's invitation. So this is another feature of Nancy's response which may give Emma the clue that Nancy is about to decline: her 'decision' is delayed, both by the pause and by the prefatory [appreciation]. But it is important that the [appreciation] is itself prefaced by *Well*: it is possible to use an [appreciation] as a way to accept an invitation (as in *That's very good of you*), but in such cases the [appreciation] is not prefaced by the disjunctive *Well*.

Just parenthetically, before taking stock of where we are, it is worth noticing something about Emma's turn in line 24. Up to now, we have been considering what basis she had for anticipating that Nancy might be going to decline her invitation – focusing on details of what Nancy said in line 22, and the delays in her responding which are evident in lines 21 and 23. But when she anticipates Nancy's possible declination, Emma achieves something else: she also *pre-empts* that declination. If we compare the sequence in lines 24–37 of extract (2) with Bea's declination in lines 4–7 of (5), it is apparent that there is *no explicit declination of Emma's invitation*.

(7)   [From (2)]

22   Nan: ↑Wul yer ril sweet hon: uh:m

23   (.)

24   Emm: [Or d'y] ou'av] sup'n [else °( )°

25   Nan: [L e t-] I :] h u.   [n:No: i haf to: uh call Roul's mother,h

26   I told'er I:'d call'er this morning I [gotta letter] from'er en

27   Emm: [°(Uh huh.)°]

28   Nan: .hhhhhh A:nd uhm

29   (1.0)

30   Nan: .tch u.-So: she in the letter she said if you ca:n why (.)

31   yihknow call me Saturday morning en I jst haven't. h

32   [.hhhh]

33   Emm: [°Mm h]m:°=

34   Nan: ='T's like takin a beating.

35   (0.2)

36   Nan: kh[hh ↑hnhh hnh]-hnh- [hnh

37   Emm: [°M m : : :,   °]   [No one heard a wo:rd hah,

The square brackets at the beginning of lines 24 and 25 indicate that Emma and Nancy start to speak simultaneously. It appears that Nancy was going to continue with her response to Emma's invitation, but Emma manages to come in with her inquiry, anticipating that she might have *something else* to do before Nancy does any more explicit rejection, of the kind which Bea does when she says 'I don't think I c'n *make* it this morning'. And the way in which the sequence develops finds them moving on to the topic of Nancy's difficulties with her ex-husband (line 37), without having resolved the matter of whether Nancy is coming over for lunch. The point to notice here is not only that Emma's turn in line 24 displays her analysis or understanding of Nancy's response thus far, but also that she manages to forestall the declination that she anticipates. And if a declination has not been explicitly or officially made, then perhaps a decision about the invitation is still open (and, indeed, later in the call they do return to the possibility of Nancy's coming over for lunch).

Analytic reprise

In beginning to analyse this brief extract from a telephone call, I have suggested four initial steps. Focusing initially on a turn at talk, here on Emma's turn in lines 18–20 of extract (2), a way to begin to see *what* is going on in the talk, and *how* that is being done, is to:

1. Identify what activity or actions the participants are engaged in.

Here Emma has invited Nancy for lunch, so that we have an invitation sequence, in which Nancy's response should be to accept or decline the invitation.

2. Consider the sequence leading up to the initiation of an action, to see how the activity in question may have arisen out of that sequence (and even whether a speaker appears to have laid the ground for the upcoming action).

We saw that Emma's inquiry *may* have been a pre-invitation inquiry, designed to determine whether Nancy might be free to come for lunch. But we cannot be sure: her inquiry may have been 'innocent'. Nevertheless, she does make the invitation in an environment – after Nancy's less-than-enthusiastic report about a chore she would rather not be doing – which encourages her to believe that Nancy might be free/willing to take a break and come for lunch.

3. Examine in detail the design (the specific words and phrases used) of each of the participants' turns.

For instance, Emma designs her invitation so as to indicate that it is an impromptu, casual affair – which is a way of formulating the kind of occasion being proposed (which may have further implications as regards the recipient's 'commitment' or obligations).

4. Consider how the recipient responds to the 'first' speaker's turn/action.

This involves a combination of the first and third steps, applied to the next turn. Emma's invitation has set up an expectation concerning what Nancy will do next (that is, what action her next turn will constitute): she can be expected either to accept the invitation (preferably) or to decline it. Instead, what she does is to *appreciate* the invitation. That, coupled with two other aspects of the design of Nancy's turn – her delay before starting to speak and prefacing her appreciation with the disjunctive *Well* – are all indications of her trouble in accepting, and are the basis on which Emma anticipates that Nancy might be going to decline.

In summary, we are looking at the data for the ways in which, through their turns at talk, participants manage activities. Our focus is on social conduct, and how conduct is constructed through precisely what participants say – through the *design* of their turns. Turn design involves speakers selecting from alternative possible ways of saying something. For instance, selecting the prefatory *Well* in line 22 gives Nancy's appreciation its declination-implicative character: without *Well*, and without the delay which precedes her response, the 'same' appreciation would presage acceptance. Finally, it is fundamental to CA's approach that we are investigating the ways in which speakers themselves, during the conversation, understand and analyse what the other is doing/meaning: so we focus on participants' analyses of one another's conduct.

In addition to these four analytic steps, another has been taken in what until now has been rather an implicit manner. The observations about the construction of turns at talk, and understandings of/responses to them, have supposed that what we are observing in this conversation are not features that are idiosyncratic to these speakers. I suggested that while this conversation was unique in terms of its occurrence (time, place, participants and circumstances), nevertheless, what goes on in the talk, the activities the speakers are engaged in and how they manage those activities are familiar – by which I was implying that these features of the data are *common* to a speech community and are *systematic* properties of talk-in-interaction. The intelligibility of social action in conversation arises from participants employing intersubjective, common or shared forms and patterns of language. Recall that, at two points during these preliminary observations, I have introduced extracts from other conversations in which the same feature or pattern is evident. Extracts (3) and (4) are examples of inquiries which were plainly *pre-invitations*. Though the specific words and content of each are different, and the nature of the invitation is different in each case, the inquiries themselves serve the same function in terms of the sequence: the questions are asked in the service of an upcoming invitation, to see whether, if the invitation were made, it is likely to be accepted. And subsequently another extract (5) was shown to illustrate that a *Well*-prefaced [appreciation] was used in cases where the speaker is declining an invitation. It is evident that these observations draw on our knowledge about what occurs in other similar sequences of actions (here, invitation sequences) in other conversations between other participants. Hence, we are beginning to build a case for there being *patterns* in talk, and that these patterns are systematic in so far as they arise from certain general contingencies which people face when interacting with one another. But, in order to explore and demonstrate this, we need to build *collections* of instances. This is the final and quite essential stage in the development of an analysis of a conversational phenomenon – so let us see what a collection can look like.

Collections and systematic patterns in interaction

The aim of CA research is to investigate and uncover the *socially organized practices* through which people make themselves understood, and through which they manage social activities in talk. We can begin to see in the preliminary account of extract (2) that participants design their talk in ways that are organized (for instance, the combination of a delay in answering, together with prefacing an appreciation with *Well*) and shared (Emma anticipates from this that Nancy may be going to decline her invitation). These are not idiosyncrasies belonging to individuals, nor are these practices associated with the particular personalities of speakers. CA research aims to identify the shared organizations that are manifest in *patterns* of talk. Patterns only become apparent when one collects instances – as many instances as can be found – of a phenomenon, and examine these for the properties that cases have in common. Therefore, CA's methodology connects together

- identifying a possible phenomenon
- making a collection
- discerning the sequential pattern associated with the phenomenon.

In order to illustrate how these are interconnected, and what a central role *collections* play in CA's methodology, I will take up something that occurs in the extract we have been considering in which Emma invites Nancy over for lunch. This is not directly related to the invitation itself, but arises from Nancy's account of having to call her mother-in-law. That is, the phenomenon I will examine is quite incidental to the invitation response which we have been looking at so far: it is something which initially caught my eye as curious, as in some respect puzzling.

Recall that Emma takes up the topic of the difficulties Nancy has been having with her ex-husband (parenthetically, managing thereby to consolidate the move away from an explicit or formal rejection of her offer).

I mentioned that clearly Emma knows something of the situation involving Nancy's ex-husband, when she asks 'No one heard a wo:rd hah,' (line 37). Nancy confirms this, in a fairly

(8)   [From (2)]

25   Nan: n:No: I haf to: uh call Roul's mother,h I told'er I:'d call'er

26   this morning I [gotta letter] from'er en

27   Emm: [° (<u>U</u>h huh.) °]

28   Nan: .hhhhh<u>h</u> <u>A</u>:nd uhm

29   (1.0)

30   Nan: .tch u.-So: she in the l<u>e</u>tter she said if you c<u>a</u>:n why (.)

31   y<u>i</u>hknow c<u>a</u>ll me Saturday <u>mor</u>ning en I jst h<u>a</u>ven't. h

32   [.hhhh]

33   Emm: [°Mm h]m:°=

34   Nan: ='T's like <u>ta</u>kin a b<u>ea</u>ting.

35   (0.2)

36   Nan: kh[hh ↑ <u>h</u>nhh hnh]-hnh- [hnh

37   Emm: [°M m : : :, °   ]   [No one heard a <u>wo</u>:rd hah,

38   Nan: >N<u>o</u>t a word,<

39   (0.2)

40   Nan: H<u>a</u>h ah,

41   (0.2)

42   Nan: n:N<u>o</u>t (.) n<u>o</u>t a word,h

43   (.)

44   Nan: N<u>o</u>t et all, ex<u>ce</u>pt R<u>ou</u>l's m<u>o</u>ther gotta call.hhhhhh (0.3) °I

45   think it wuss:: (0.3) th'M<u>o</u>nd<u>ee</u> er the <u>Tu</u>e:sday after

46   M<u>o</u>ther's Da:<u>y</u>,

strong fashion. Nancy adds three further confirmations (lines 40, 42 and at the start of 44). Notice that what Nancy repeats and confirms is a quite categorical version, 'no one' and 'not a word', both indicating the completeness of her ex-husband's lack of communication. However, in line 44, she proceeds to qualify that, when she says '*except* Roul's mother gotta call' (she then proceeds to tell what happened during this telephone call). Having initially claimed that no one had heard from him, Nancy changes her story! This, then, is what I found puzzling – how is it that Nancy comes up with what are apparently inconsistent or contradictory versions?

Now, one might attribute the change in her account, and the inconsistency which results, to some kind of personal or psychological factor, such as a disposition to hyperbole, or that she forgot for the moment, or that her initial version sprang from her being bitter about her ex-husband. Such attributions would treat her 'inconsistency' as generated by factors associated with the individual and her psychology, in the circumstances she finds herself in. But once I had noticed Nancy's shift from *not a word* to *except Roul's mother got a call* in this extract, I began to find many similar instances in which a speaker initially claims a strong, categorical or dramatic version, but then qualifies this in some way that backs down from the strength or literalness of the initial version. And, of course, once one begins to find a number of cases, the phenomenon – the production of 'inconsistency' – begins to look less like a psychological attribute, and more like something which, for some reason (or, to deal with some contingency), is being systematically generated in interaction. Here are some of the other instances that I collected.

---

(9)   [Holt 289:1–2]

```
1   Sar:    1-> O:h yes (.) well we've done all the peaks.

2               (0.4)

3   Les:    Oh ye:s

4               (0.5)

5   Sar:    A::h

6               (0.5)

7   Sar:    2-> We couldn't do two because you need ropes and that
```

(10)   [Holt:2:15:4–5]

1 Les: Only: one is outst↓andingly clever wuh- an:' the other-.hh

2   1->   an:'°Rebecca didn't get t'college,°

3   (0.4)

4 Joy: Didn't ↓she:,

5 Les: 2->   Well she got in the end she scraped into a buh-

6   business management,

(11)   [Drew:St:98:1] (Sandra's friends are going out that evening to a disco/night club; she
       has said she isn't going)

1 San: I don't know hhh hu hu.hhh I dunno it's not really me

2 Bec: Mw:rh

3 San: 1->(   ) like it.hh I've never been to one yet,

4 Bec: You ↑HAven't.

5 San: No

6 Bec: Not even t'Ziggy:s

7 San: 2->Nope (.) I've bin twi- no ( ) a bin twi:ce at home to:: a place

8   called Tu:bes which is really rubbi:sh and then I've been

9   once to a place in ( ) Stamford called erm: (.) Crystals (.)

10   which i:s o::kay: <b- n- Olivers> sorry Olivers (.) which is

11   okay: ( ) but nothi:ng special,

> (12)   [NB:IV:13:18]
>
> 1   Emm: 1->I <u>ha</u>ven't h<u>a</u>d a p<u>ie</u>ce a'<u>mea</u>:t.
>
> 2   (1.0)
>
> 3   Emm: 2->Over et <u>Bill</u>'s I had <u>ta</u>:cos M<u>o</u>ndee ni::ght little bitta
>
> 4   m<u>ea</u>:t th<u>e</u>*:re. B't n<u>o</u>t m<u>u</u>ch.

In example (6), Sarah initially claims to have 'done' *all the peaks*, and then reveals that they did not do them all. In (7), Lesley first says that one of their friend's daughters did not get into college, but subsequently concedes that she did. Sandra first claims in (8) that she has *never been to one* (a disco/nightclub), but then mentions some to which she has been. And, in (9), Emma first reports that she has not had a piece of meat recently, but then 'admits' to having eaten tacos a few nights before.

In each instance, there appears to be a discrepancy or inconsistency between the speaker's initial and subsequent versions – just as there was between Nancy's initially claiming that no one had heard from Roul, and her later statement that his mother heard from him a day or two after Mother's Day. In their subsequent versions, speakers seem to back down from their initial claims, revealing those to have been in some fashion incorrect, overstated, too strong and the like.

Here then is a phenomenon – a sequential pattern in which a speaker first claims something, and then retracts or qualifies that claim. We can collect cases of this phenomenon in whatever data we happen to be working with: you can listen for this, and find instances in data that you may collect – the phenomenon is not restricted to telephone calls, or conversations between friends, or even to 'ordinary conversation'. When we put together a collection of cases, we can begin to look for features they may have in common. This is the next analytic step.

Identifying common features in a collection

We have now a collection of five instances in which a speaker claims something and subsequently retracts that claim – our original case in (2), together with extracts (6)–(9) (though these are just a few of the many cases I have collected of this phenomenon). The next step is to examine the collection in order to determine whether instances have any features in common. In effect, this involves two of the analytic steps outlined earlier – namely, looking closely at how turns are designed, and considering how each participant responds to the other. Pulling these together, we can discern a number of features that these fragments have in common.

First, the initial versions are very strongly stated, categorical or dramatic – generally through descriptors that are extreme versions (Edwards, 2000; Pomerantz, 1986). Thus, in (6), Sarah claims to have done *all the peaks*; in (8), Sandra claims that she's *never been to one yet*; and, in (9), Emma claims that she *hasn't had a piece of meat* – each of which is an extreme version. In (7) Lesley does something similar, in claiming categorically that Rebecca *didn't get to college*.

Second, the recipients avoid endorsing these initial versions. Indeed, in various ways, they display some (incipient) scepticism – either through initially not responding (silence), as in examples (6), (7) and (9); through only minimal acknowledgements, in (6); or through interrogative elliptical repeats, such as Joyce's *Didn't she* in (7) or Becky's *You haven't* in (8).

Third, the subsequent versions, in which the speakers appear to back down from the original claims, are characterized by explicitly contrasting elements when compared with the original versions. The sense of retraction is manifest, in part, through a direct contrast between the two versions – a contrast that is achieved through some lexical repetition. So *we've done all* in (6) becomes *we couldn't do two*: note the repetition of both the pronoun and the verb; in (7), (*Rebecca*) *didn't get* becomes *she* got; having claimed that *I've never been*, Sandra concedes *I've been*, in (8); and, in (9), *I haven't had* is changed to *I had*. The contrast exhibited through such repetition, and in extracts (9)–(12) through the simple switch between positive and negative forms (for example, *I've never been* becomes *I've been*) highlights the speakers' *retraction* of their initial claims. They begin by claiming something to be the case, and then retract their original claim.

---

(13)   [Expanded form of (9)] [Holt 289:1–2]

    1 Les: .hhh but there's some beautiful walks aren't the::[re

    2 Sar: [O:h

    3   ye̲s (.)well we've do̲ne all the <u>peaks</u>.

    4   (0.4)

    5 Les: Oh ye:s

    6   (0.5)

    7 Sar: A::h

    8   (0.5)

```
 9 Sar: —>   We couldn't do two because you need ropes and that

10 Les:       Ye[:s.

11 Sar: —>   [It's a climbers spot
```

Nevertheless, fourth, the retractions are constructed so as to preserve some consistency with the initial versions, and hence the essential correctness of those first versions. They seem to back down from its strength, though not from the core truth of what is claimed or reported. I will outline this in just two cases.

Sarah and her family are just back from a holiday on a Scottish island, which Lesley has said is her daughter's favourite stamping ground. They are talking about walking (see line 1), in the context of which Sarah claims to have *done* all the peaks. In her subsequent version (lines 9 and 11), Sarah retracts that: they did not do two. However, she constructs this as their being *unable* to do two, explaining that they could not do two peaks because climbing gear is needed to get up them; they are not for walkers. She thereby constructs as *exceptions* the two peaks (note the specific enumeration of how many peaks, that being a small number – rather than that there were *some* they could not do) which they *could* not (rather than did not) do, thereby retaining her original claim as essentially true – they did all the peaks *which could have been walked*.

In example (7), there are more elaborate components through which the subsequent version is constructed so as to be consistent with the claim Lesley originally makes that *Rebecca didn't get to college*.

```
(13a)

 1   Les:   NO::↑: no they're not. Only: one is outst↓andingly clever

 2           wuh- an:' the other-.hh an: '°Rebecca didn't get t'college,°

 3           (0.4)

 4   Joy:   Didn't ↓she:,

 5   Les: —>Well she got in the end she scraped into a buh- business

 6           —>management,
```

There are three components especially which 'reduce the distance' between this and her original claim. First, *she got in the end* portrays her as having had to search for a college to take her, and/or as having been accepted only at the last minute. This is consistent with, indeed merges into, the second component – *she scraped into* – depicting her as only just being sufficiently qualified to gain entry, and therefore as being in that sense among the last to be accepted. These components together portray her as having considerable difficulty in getting a place in college. The final component, *into business management*, depicts her, moreover, as only having been able to get a place to study that discipline: only having scraped into *business management* portrays this discipline as being in the academic bargain basement. The ways in which subsequent versions are designed to be exceptions to, and thereby essentially consistent with, the initial versions are, of course, quite explicit in the case with which we began, Nancy's claim 'Not et all, *except* Roul's mother gotta call'.

So far, we have identified a pattern in which speakers make a strong claim about something, but subsequently – in the face of the other's implicit scepticism (even if that is expressed only through failure to respond) – back down from that claim; however, their retractions are designed so as to preserve the essential correctness of their original versions (through constructing the subsequent versions as exceptions of one kind or another). Then, the question is, what are we to make of this pattern? Do speakers just routinely lie, and retract when they are 'caught out' by their recipients' disbelief? This is the final stage in analysing a conversational phenomenon or pattern – providing an account for the pattern. It is not easy to be prescriptive about how or where one seeks such an account, but, broadly, it involves trying to identify the contingency that the pattern systematically handles, or to which it offers a solution. Very often, this will involve another of the analytic steps outlined earlier, which is to consider where and how the object or pattern in question arose.

If we look at the sequence immediately prior to the over-strong 'incorrect' versions, it is plain that the initial versions are being 'exaggerated' in order to fit with both the sequential environments in which they are produced, and the actions being done in those environments. For example, in (7), Lesley is disagreeing with Joyce's assessment that their friend is clever *mentally*: this is shown here in (11), line 1 – they have been talking previously about how clever she is with her hands, making her family's clothes and so on.

(14)   [Expansion of (7)] [Holt:2:15:4–5]

1   Joy: =eh Well surely she's clever ↓mentally isn't s[he

2   Les: [Oh I don't

3   know'bout ↑that, I mean uh I don't think it's all that

```
  4            difficult really

  5            (0.4)

  6  Joy:      What.

  7            (0.5)

  8  Les:      If you've got- if you got the schooling an' the

  9            back↑grou:nd ih-uh (.) (          )-

 10            (0.4)

 11  Joy:      Oh[no(h)o perhaps that's what it is I don't know

 12  Les:        [(                              )

 13  Les:      ↓No[: : : ,

 14  Joy:           [(   ) Oh well I don't ↓know though I d- I should

 15            imagine she is clever her children'r clever aren't they,

 16            .hhhh yih know I[mean]

 17  Les:                      [NO::]↑: no they're not. Only: one is

 18            outst↓andingly clever wuh- an:' the other-.hh an:'°Rebecca

 19            didn't get t'college,°
```

After Lesley's initial disagreement in lines 2–3, and subsequent elaboration (lines 8–9), Joyce pursues her assessment of their friend's likely cleverness, stating as supporting evidence that *her children are clever* (line 15). Without tracing this in detail, it is reasonably clear that neither is entirely letting go of her position regarding their friend's cleverness, and that they have, in effect, 'upped the ante'. At this point, in line 17, Lesley further pursues and escalates the disagreement by very strongly contesting Joyce's claim that the children are smart: the extent to which she has escalated the strength of her disagreement is evident in its being strongly marked – lexically, through the outright negative tokens and direct rejection of Joyce's statement; prosodically, through raised pitch and amplitude. So it is in this environment, in pursuing her disagreement, and doing so in a strongly marked form, that Lesley produces her rebuttal of Joyce's claim that *her children are clever*. Her rebuttal is designed to equal the strength of her (escalated) disagreement. Thus, the completeness and strength of her rejection ('*NO::↑: no they're not.*') is matched by her claim that one of the children did not even get into college – while the fact that both children are at college (that is, university) would hardly be commensurate with or support her claim, against Joyce, that they are not clever.

What emerges, then, is that these strong, dramatic or perhaps exaggerated claims arise from, or are fitted to, the contingencies of the particular action sequence in which they are produced. They are constructed to 'work' in terms of the 'requirements' of the slots in which they are done. The 'weaker' versions to which they subsequently retreat would not have done the job *in the slot in which they are produced*. That is, the subsequent weaker versions would not have accomplished, in a coherent fashion, the work of reporting, disagreeing, confirming/agreeing, complaining, giving an account, etc. in the particular positions in which speakers construct those actions. Therefore, these initial (over-)strong versions are fitted to the slot in which speakers are announcing, disagreeing, declining, etc.; here, we can see that the speakers are dealing, through these claims, with the exigencies which have arisen in the immediate (prior) sequential environments. Speakers produce versions that are fitted to those sequential moments. When the moment is past, so too is the 'requirement' for that strong version: the speaker can put the record straight and retreat to a 'weaker' version (albeit in a manner which maintains an essential consistency with the initial 'false' claims).

WRITING UP

You will find published accounts of the pattern of exaggerated versions I've been exploring in Drew (2003, 2005b). Which brings us to how we write up CA studies. The best guidance is, I think, to keep it simple – to set out a clear structure based on the 'stages' or themes of the analysis, to select examples which illustrate clearly each of the themes, and to restrict the accounts given of each data example to just what is necessary in order to illustrate and support the analytic point being made.

Therefore, in approaching writing up this analysis of exaggerated versions that were subsequently reduced or retracted, I first identified the principal themes in analysing this phenomenon or pattern (I'm referring here to the 2005b publication). These were:

- First to outline the phenomenon of initial versions that were subsequently 'corrected' and reduced.
- An analysis of the strength or 'intensity' of these initial versions – how they are constructed to be 'strong' versions.
- Evidence of the recipient's scepticism with the speaker's claim or version of events.

- Analysis of the turn(s) in which speakers retract or reduce the initial claim.
- Analysis of how speakers manage, while retracting the initial claim, retract only its strength and not its essential correctness, the construction of a 'lesser' version that is nonetheless consistent with the initial version.
- Accounting for how these initial versions came to be made in the first place – how they were generated out of the prior interaction.

This broadly established the overall structure of the published report. It is worth emphasizing that a research report should always begin by describing and outlining the phenomenon which is the focus of the report. Beginning with a theoretical account only tends to lose focus, and loses your readers – they need to know what it is that you've found. Then you can set out the steps you'll take in accounting for the phenomenon, those steps being the principal themes in your analysis.

Of course some literature will be relevant and should be discussed. Where this is done, and how extensive your literature review will be, will depend on the nature of the phenomenon. A literature review need not always be done in the conventional position, after the introduction. And of course a research report needs to include some account of the data and methods employed; this should be kept to a minimum. Space is at a premium, so you'll want to give most of the available space to the task of analysing the data: the data examples we need to show for CA research take up a lot of words!

So having identified and set out the analytic themes, the next stage is to decide which data examples are to be shown in each section. It is important to consider carefully showing only as many examples as it takes to (1) establish your analytic points clearly (so aim for *transparency*) and (2) enough examples to demonstrate that the aspect you are focusing on in a given section is *recurrent and systematic*. I will generally discuss one or two examples only in any detail, then show perhaps three or four further examples, which in a sense should speak for themselves, so that the reader can see the recurrent and almost mechanical nature of the practice or pattern you are showing.

When discussing and analysing a particular example, don't simply describe what each speaker says, or describe the data line by line. It's a common mistake to find that authors believe that describing the data is analysing the data – it is not. Focus your account of the data specifically and only on features that will play a part in your analysis of how the speakers are doing what they are doing. Avoid mere description and show how things (in the talk or interaction) work in the way they do.

The nature of the conclusion or discussion is very much dependent on the publication context, the specific pattern that's been discovered and shown, and an author's judgement about what should be highlighted and what the implications and significance are of the research findings. One rule to follow, though, is never to introduce 'new' data (i.e., examples that have not been shown in the main body of the report); the conclusion is not the place to introduce new examples or further analysis.

Finally, I might mention that the criteria – which I advise undergraduate students will be used in assessing their work – are relevant to writing up CA research, whether for finals assessment or for publication. They are:

- clarity of the outline of the phenomenon or pattern
- precision and accuracy of observations
- clear and cogent thematic structure
- insight about interaction
- economy of expression
- inclusion of relevant data (and no more than is relevant).

I advise against being too theoretical, being too general and speculating about an individual's psychology. We don't ever know for sure (scientifically) what's in someone's head.

CONCLUSION

I have outlined some of the principal stages of analysis in CA research – the stages involved when developing research findings about the ways in which interaction, and particularly verbal interaction, are organized. Space has not allowed me to say much about the significance of what we are looking for, or about the theoretical standpoint which this perspective adopts towards people's activities in talk: for instance, the reasons for considering talk as action rather than communication; and our identifying patterns associated with manifest behaviour, and *not* inner cognitive states and other states such as intentions, motives, personality, etc. However, I hope that showing how Nancy's apparent inconsistency in extract (8) is simply one in a recurrent pattern in which speakers initially produce over-strong versions in order to fit the contingencies of the particular interactional sequences in which they are engaged, helps to illustrate that CA resists psychological accounts of behaviour which turn out to be general (rather than individual), systematic (and not particularistic) and interactional (rather than arising from the psyche of one of the participants, as though she were acting independently of the other and the interaction between them). What Nancy does here is what people – of whatever psychological dispositions or types – do generally, given these interactional circumstances.

I have tried to convey something of how we cut in to looking at data, and start to make analytic observations about (verbal) conduct. Starting with a transcript of a recording of natural conversation, we begin by looking at the activities which participants may be managing through their talk; then, we examine in as much detail as possible how their talk is designed or constructed, in an effort to map the organized properties through which participants conduct their affairs in talk-in-interaction. And I have illustrated how we develop an analysis of such organized properties (patterns, devices and practices) by focusing on what at first sight appears to be an incidental curiosity in the extract with which I began – that is, Nancy's initially confirming that *no one heard a word* (from her ex-husband), but subsequently reporting that his mother had heard from him. This was to give you some feeling for how we can move from making observations about the details of talk, to developing an analysis of a conversational phenomenon or practice – in other words, arriving at findings about stable and systematic patterns in talk. If only it were as easy as this! I have to admit that the process or steps from beginning to notice things about the detail to be found in talk, to the end product of a publishable research finding, are not nearly as smooth as this account might suggest. For one thing, there is the difficulty of knowing what kinds of details one might begin noticing, and what to say about them. The next hurdle is to decide whether what one is focusing on is actually a phenomenon (that is, a systematically organized pattern or practice). Afterwards, building a collection of the phenomenon can involve comparative questions, including what kinds of cases the phenomenon encompasses and what cases might be used for comparison and contrast – all of which are not dissimilar from the decisions which need to be made in experimental design. This is too brief an account of CA's methodological approach to do any justice to these complexities: the only way to find out more is to read some of the published research (see below), collect some naturally occurring interactional data relating to some topic in which you are interested, and have a go at doing it yourself. See Box 6.3 for three good examples of CA.

BOX 6.3   THREE GOOD EXAMPLES OF CA

Here are three studies illustrating clearly the application of CA's approach to moments in interaction that have a real (social) psychological significance: interacting with someone with Alzheimer's, laughter in the midst of talking about one's troubles, and crying. The common thread in these studies is that they demonstrate that what are generally taken to be purely psychological phenomena – communicative difficulties, laughter and crying – are instead generated through interaction, and are associated with what participants *do* in interactions with one another.

Interacting with someone with Alzheimer's

In a study of the telephone interactions between someone with Alzheimer's and her family, Jones (2013) highlights how Alzheimer's disease irrevocably challenges a person's capacity to communicate with others. Instead of focusing on the language disorders that are said to be associated with

(Continued)

(Continued)

Alzheimer's, Jones adopts a fresh perspective – revealing how the difficulties experienced by a person with Alzheimer's arises from the contingencies of her interactions with her family. These contingencies are generated by the others' (family members') contributions in the interaction, particularly the questions they ask their relative. Their questions (such as 'What did you do today?') presume memory, of course, and the epistemic authority of the one being asked. Jones's analysis reveals the ways in which questions can (quite inadvertently) compromise the epistemic authority of the person being questioned (i.e., the person with Alzheimer's). Jones also shows that someone with Alzheimer's develops strategies for handling these challenging interactional contingencies. So the picture emerges of communication difficulties that are generated interactionally, rather than some putative language deficits.

Laughter in talk about troubles

Jefferson (1984) shows that when someone is telling about their troubles, they may laugh, sometimes after the completion of their turn – but the recipient does *not* laugh. Instead, a recipient 'produces a recognizably serious response', so that the one telling about their trouble and the recipient do not laugh together. In this pattern, recipients do not 'decline to laugh', as would be the case in other topical/sequential positions; rather, they align themselves as recipients of the other's troubles, in response to matters that are not to be laughed about. On the other hand, through their laughter the troubles-teller exhibits that they are being stoical, resisting the trouble, even make light of it. This is set in a penetrating and beautifully observed account of the nuanced patterns of laughter to be found in troubles-tellings, including variations in which the recipient may laugh with the teller (thereby herself resisting the trouble); and including also the other kinds of responses that recipients may make to the teller's trouble, such as reassuring them that all will be well. Emerging from this analysis is a strong sense of laughter as social action, and not simply as the expression of emotion or the response to an emotional stimulus.

Crying

Like laughter, crying is generally considered to spring from an internal psychological (emotional) state, to be a spontaneous expression of the inner state on an individual. However, Hepburn and Potter (2013) approach crying from a perspective that parallels Jefferson's on laughter (above), in exploring the social patterns associated with crying, including how we recognize and respond to another's crying in interaction. Based largely on research they are conducting into the UK National Society for the Prevention of Cruelty to Children's (NSPCC) child-protection helpline, they show that through careful and detailed transcription, they are able to discern patterns in the way crying emerges, the kinds of conduct through which people 'do' crying (which is not to detract at all from the genuineness of their crying), and how recipients respond to and manage the other's crying. They make an important and useful distinction between responding sympathetically and with empathy, showing how each of these is characteristically managed with callers to the helpline. This study exemplifies the message of each of these studies – that what might be taken to be a product of an individual's inner cognitive or psychological and emotional state is best understood as both a product or emergent property of social interaction, and a form of social conduct in that interaction.

FURTHER READING

These offer concise overviews of CA:

Drew, P. (2005a) 'Conversation analysis', in K.L. Fitch and R.E. Sanders (eds), *Handbook of Language and Social Interaction*. Mawah, NJ: Lawrence Erlbaum, pp. 71–102.
Heritage, J. (1984) *Garfinkel and Ethnomethodology*. Cambridge: Polity Press, Chapter 8.
Atkinson, J.M. and Heritage, J. (eds) (1984) *Structures of Social Action: Studies in Conversation Analysis*. Cambridge: Cambridge University Press.
The editors' introduction gives an invaluable, brief guide, and many of the studies (e.g., by Pomerantz, on agreeing/disagreeing) are key works in CA's programme.

Sacks, H. (1992) *Lectures on Conversation* (Vols I and II). Ed. G. Jefferson. Oxford: Blackwell.
Sack's lectures are an essential resource for anyone interested in CA's analytic approach; these are where CA began – highly original, rigorous, humane and unsurpassed. Schegloff's introduction to the first volume is an authoritative account of Sacks' work and the development of the field, and the distinctiveness of CA's approach.

Textbooks that have much to offer include:

Sidnell, J. (2010) *Conversation Analysis*. Chichester: Wiley-Blackwell.
This is the best introductory textbook on the market – clear and mostly accurate, with useful methodological guidance.

Sidnell, J. and Stivers, T. (2013) *The Handbook of Conversation Analysis*. Chichester: Wiley-Blackwell.
This is an outstanding resource: each chapter is written by a real expert in the field and is authoritative. The scope and coverage is comprehensive. It is completely reliable, and many chapters are leading statements in their field.

ten Have, P. (1999) *Doing Conversation Analysis: A Practical Guide.* London: Sage.

As I mentioned in the opening paragraph of this chapter, CA is widely applied to forms of talk-in-interaction other than 'ordinary conversation' – for instance, to interactions in courts, classrooms, medical consultations, news media, counselling and therapy.
    Much of this research is now applied and used by practitioners. These are useful introductions:

Drew, P. and Heritage, J. (eds) (1992) *Talk at Work.* Cambridge: Cambridge University Press.

Heritage, J. and Clayman, S. (2010) *Talk in Action: Interactions, Identities, and Institutions.* Chichester: Wiley-Blackwell.

Heritage, J. and Maynard, D. (eds) (2006) *Communication in Medical Care: Interaction between Primary Care Physicians and their Patients.* Cambridge: Cambridge University Press.

7 Discourse Analysis

Carla Willig

Since its emergence in the 1980s discourse analysis has become a widely used qualitative research method in psychology. As an increasing number of researchers, particularly in the applied psychology domains, turn to the analysis of discourse, it is worth exploring what a discursive analysis can actually deliver and what kinds of research questions it can, and cannot, address.

Psychologists' turn to language was inspired by theories and research which had emerged within other disciplines over a period of time. From the 1950s onwards, philosophers, communication theorists, historians and sociologists became increasingly interested in language as a social performance. The assumption that language provides a set of unambiguous signs with which to label internal states and with which to describe external reality began to be challenged. Instead, language was reconceptualized as productive; that is to say, language was seen to construct versions of social reality, and it was seen to achieve social objectives. The focus of inquiry shifted from individuals and their intentions to language and its productive potential. Wittgenstein's philosophy, Austin's speech-act theory and Foucault's historical studies of discursive practices are important examples of this shift. However, psychology remained relatively untouched by these intellectual developments throughout the 1950s and 1960s. Instead, it was concerned with the study of mental representations and the rules which control cognitive mediation of various types of input from the environment. In the 1970s, social psychologists began to challenge psychology's cognitivism (e.g., Gergen, 1973, 1989), and in the 1980s the 'turn to language' gained a serious foothold in psychology.

In this chapter, I introduce two versions of the discourse analytic method: *discursive psychology* and *Foucauldian discourse analysis*. Even though these two approaches share a concern with the role of language in the construction of social reality, the two versions address different sorts of research questions. They also identify with different theoretical traditions. Burr (1995, 2003) and Parker (1997) provide detailed discussions of the distinction between the two versions of discourse analysis. However, some discourse analysts do not welcome such a strong conceptual separation. For example, Potter and Wetherell (1995: 81) argue that the distinction between the two versions 'should not be painted too sharply', while Wetherell (1998, 2001) also advocates a synthesis of the two versions. This chapter introduces and describes the two approaches to discourse analysis and illustrates each with a worked example. The two versions of discourse analysis are applied to the same interview extract in order to highlight similarities and differences between them. The chapter concludes with a comparison between the two discursive methods (see also Langdridge, 2004: Chapter 18, for more on the relationship between the two approaches).

DISCURSIVE PSYCHOLOGY

HISTORY AND THEORETICAL BACKGROUND

This version of discourse analysis was introduced into social psychology with the publication of Potter and Wetherell's *Discourse and Social Psychology: Beyond Attitudes and Behaviour* in 1987. The label 'discursive psychology' was provided later by Edwards and Potter (1992). As the method evolved, changes in emphasis also emerged. These are largely to do with an increasing emphasis on the flexibility of discursive resources and a preference for the use of naturalistic materials. Recent developments in discursive psychology continue to be strongly influenced by conversation analytic principles (see Wooffitt, 2005; Wiggins and Potter, 2008). Potter and Wetherell's book presented a wide-ranging critique of cognitivism, followed by a detailed analysis of interview transcripts using a discourse analytic approach. Later publications developed the critique of psychology's preoccupation with cognition and its use as an all-purpose explanatory strategy which involved 'claiming for the cognitive processes of individuals the central role in shaping perception and action' (Edwards and Potter, 1992: 13). The critique of cognitivism argues that the cognitive approach is based upon a number of unfounded assumptions about the relationship between language and representation. These include: (1) that talk is a route to cognition; (2) that cognitions are based on perception; (3) that an objective perception of reality is theoretically possible; (4) that there are consensual objects of thought; and (5) that there are cognitive structures which are relatively enduring. Each of these assumptions can be challenged from a discursive psychology perspective.

From a cognitive point of view, people's verbal expression of their beliefs and attitudes provides information about the cognitions which reside in their minds. In other words, *talk is a route to cognition*. As long as the researcher ensures that participants have no reason to lie, their words are taken to constitute true representations of their mental state (such as the beliefs they subscribe to or the attitudes they hold). Discourse analysts do not share this view of language. They argue that when people state a belief or express an opinion, they are taking part in a conversation which has a purpose and in which all participants have a stake. In other words, in order to make sense of what people say, we need to take into account the social context within which they speak. For example, when male participants are interviewed by a female researcher with the aim of identifying men's attitudes towards sharing house-work, their responses may be best understood as a way of disclaiming undesirable social identities (as 'sexist slob', as dependent upon their female partners or as lazy). This is not to say that they are lying to the researcher about the amount of housework they do; rather, it suggests that, in their responses, participants *orient towards* a particular reading of the questions they are being asked (for example, as a challenge, a criticism or an opportunity to complain), and that the accounts they provide need to be understood in relation to such a reading. As a result, we should not be surprised to find that people's expressed attitudes are not necessarily consistent across social contexts.

Ultimately, cognitivism has to assume that *cognitions are based on perceptions*. Cognitions are mental representations of real objects, events and processes which occur in the world. Even though cognitions are abstractions, and therefore often simplifications and distortions of such external events, they do constitute attempts to capture reality. Once established, cognitive schemata and representations facilitate perception and interpretation of novel experiences and observations. By contrast, discourse analysts argue that the world can be 'read' in an unlimited number of ways, and that, far from giving rise to mental representations, objects and events are, in fact, constructed through language itself. As a result, it is discourse and conversation which should be the focus of study, because that is where meanings are created and negotiated.

If cognitions are based on perceptions, as proposed by cognitivism, it follows that *an objective perception of reality is theoretically possible*. Errors and simplifications in representation are the result of the application of time-saving heuristics which introduce bias into cognition. Given the right circumstances, it should be possible to eliminate such biases from cognitive processes. Again, discourse analysts take issue with this assumption. If language constructs (rather than represents) social reality, it follows that there can be no objective perception of this reality. Instead, emphasis is placed upon the ways in which social categories are constructed and with what consequences they are deployed in conversation.

Attitudes describe how people feel about objects and events in the social world, whereas attribution theory is concerned with how people account for actions and events. In both cases, researchers assume that the social object or event towards which participants have different attitudes and which participants attribute to different causes is itself consensual. That is to say, even though people hold different attitudes and attributions in relation to something (for example, European Monetary Union, or same-sex marriages), this 'something' itself is not disputed. In other words, there are *consensual objects of thought*, in relation to which people form opinions. People agree on what it is they are talking about, but they disagree about why it happened (attributions) and whether or not it is a good thing (attitudes). Discourse analysts do not accept that there are such consensual objects of thought. They argue that the social objects themselves are constructed through language and that one person's version of such an object may be quite different from another person's. From this point of view, what have traditionally been referred to as 'attitudes' and 'attributions' are, in fact, aspects of the discursive construction of the object itself.

Finally, cognitivism is based upon the assumption that somewhere inside the human mind there are *cognitive structures which are relatively enduring*. People are said to hold views and have cognitive styles. Cognitive structures can change, but such change needs to be explained in terms of intervening variables such as persuasive messages or novel experiences. The assumption is that – in the normal course of events – beliefs, attitudes, attributions and so forth remain stable and predictable from day to day. Discourse analysts' conceptualization of language as productive and performative is not compatible with such a view. Instead, they argue that people's accounts, the views they express and the explanations they provide depend upon the discursive context within which they are produced. Thus, what people say tells us something about what they are *doing* with their words (disclaiming, excusing, justifying, persuading, pleading, etc.) rather than about the cognitive structures these words represent.

Discourse analysts' challenge to cognitivism shows that discourse analysis is not simply a research method. It is a critique of mainstream psychology; it provides an alternative way of conceptualizing language; and it indicates a method of data analysis which can tell us something about the discursive construction of social reality. Discourse analysis is more than a methodology because 'it involves a theoretical way of understanding the nature of discourse and the nature of psychological phenomena' (Billig, 1997: 43). However, discursive psychology is still a *psychology* because it is concerned with psychological phenomena such as memory, attribution and identity. But, in line with its critique of cognitivism, discursive psychology conceptualizes these phenomena as *discursive actions* rather than as cognitive processes. Psychological activities such as justification, rationalization, categorization, attribution, naming and blaming are understood as ways in which participants manage their interests. They are discursive practices which are used by participants within particular contexts in order to achieve social and interpersonal objectives. As a result, psychological concepts such as prejudice, identity, memory or trust become something people do rather than something people *have*.

The focus of analysis in discursive psychology is on how participants use discursive resources and with what effects. In other words, discursive psychologists pay attention to the *action orientation* of talk. They are concerned with the ways in which speakers manage issues of stake and interest. They identify discursive strategies such as 'disclaiming' or 'footing' and explore their function in a particular discursive context. For example, an interviewee may disclaim a racist social identity by saying 'I am not racist, but I think immigration controls should be strengthened' and then legitimate the statement by referring to a higher authority: 'I agree with the Prime Minister's statement that the situation requires urgent action.' Other discursive devices used to manage interest and accountability include the use of metaphors and analogies, direct quotations, extreme case formulations, graphic descriptions, consensus formulations, stake inoculation and many more (see Edwards and Potter, 1992; Potter, 1996, for a detailed discussion of such devices). Box 7.1 summarizes discursive psychology's major concerns.

BOX 7.1   DISCURSIVE PSYCHOLOGY

Discursive psychology:

- emerged from ethnomethodology and conversation analysis

- is concerned with discourse practices

- emphasizes the performative qualities of discourse

- emphasizes the fluidity and variability of discourse

- prioritizes action orientation and stake

- asks 'What are participants doing with their talk?'

FORMULATING A RESEARCH QUESTION AND DESIGNING A STUDY

Discourse analysis may be described as a way of reading a text. This reading is informed by a conceptualization of language as *performative*. This means that the reader focuses upon the internal organization of the discourse in order to find out what the discourse is doing. It means moving beyond an understanding of its content and to trace its *action orientation*. Discourse analysis requires us to adopt an orientation to talk and text as *social action*, and it is this orientation which directs our analytic work. The research question which underpins any discursive psychology study is 'What are speakers doing with their talk?' Designing a discursive psychology study requires the selection of a discursive phenomenon of interest (e.g., how people conduct mealtime conversations or how symptoms are talked about during a medical consultation). The analysis of the data is then concerned with the ways in which speakers use discursive resources and what is achieved through this within the social interaction. Although there is no universally agreed set of methodological procedures, some guidelines for the analysis of discourse can help the analyst get started (see also Potter and Wetherell, 1987: 160–76; Billig, 1997: 54; Edwards and Potter, 2001, for guidance).

COLLECTING DATA

Ideally, this type of analysis should be used to analyse naturally occurring text and talk (Potter and Hepburn, 2005). This is because the research questions addressed by discursive psychologists are concerned with how people manage accountability and stake in everyday life. For example, tape recordings of naturally occurring conversations in informal (e.g., friends chatting on the telephone, families having meals together) and formal (e.g., medical consultations, radio interviews) 'real-world' settings constitute suitable data for discursive analysis. However, both ethical and practical difficulties in obtaining such naturally occurring data have led many discourse analysts to carry out semi-structured interviews to generate data for analysis. In any case, discourse analysis works with texts, most of which are generated by transcribing tape recordings of some form of conversation (see Potter and Wetherell, 1987; Jefferson, 2004; O'Connell and Kowal, 1995, for guidance on transcription). It is important that the transcript contain at least some information about non-linguistic aspects of the conversation, such as delay, hesitation or emphasis. This is because the way in which something is said can affect its meaning.

ANALYSIS

The extract in Box 7.2 is taken from the transcript of a semi-structured interview with a woman who had recently experienced the break-up of an intimate relationship. The extract represents an exchange between the interviewer (I) and the participant (R) which occurred about halfway through the hour-long interview.

BOX 7.2   EXTRACT FROM BREAK-UP INTERVIEW

```
 1   I:   And when you made the decision um when you were actually working
 2        towards finishing it did you talk to friends about it?
 3   R:   Oh of course
 4   I:   Yeah
 5   R:   All the time yeah it would always be a case of how do I do it
 6   I:   Ah right
 7   R:   How do I say it what do I say I know I've got to do it how do I go about doing
 8        it you know and and just sort of role-playing it through and and you know just
 9        sort of just preparing myself to actually say to him I don't want to go out with
10        you anymore because it's so hard even though you know it's got to be done
11        It is just so hard because there's all these you know ties and emotional
12        baggage which is which you're carrying and you you you're worrying about
13        the other person and you're thinking you invested you know he's invested
14        maybe two years in me
15   I:   Yes
```

16	R:	by going out with me and suddenly I'm dumping him what if he doesn't find
17		anyone else to go out with
18	I:	Oh right yes
19	R:	You you start taking responsibility for them and for how they'll cope
20		afterwards you know maybe to the detriment to your own personal sort of
21		well-being
22	I:	Right
23	R:	And it was a case of how is he going to cope what's going to happen to him
24		what if no one goes out with him what if this and what if that and it's all a
25		case of ifs anyway and you know as far as I was concerned I was I was
26		more concerned about him and how he would be [...] [and a little later in the interview]
27	I:	[...] if you sort of think about it as going on through time um was there
28		anything that changed in the way you behaved towards each other or sex
29		life or anything like that? Could you say you know something changed or
30	R:	No it was the way I saw it was would I want to marry him was the sort of um
31		you know foundation I would use
32	I:	Right
33	R:	because I thought OK we've been going out for two nearly two years if we
34		were going out for another two years would I want to marry him and the
35		answer was no
36	I:	Right
37	R:	And even though [...] I had no intentions of getting married say for another
38		you know four five whatever amount of years it was on that basis I was
39		using the criteria of my wanting to continue going out with him
40	I:	Right
41	R:	because it was a case of where is this relationship going and as far as I was
42		concerned it had hit the the brick wall and it wasn't going any further

Reading

First of all, the researcher needs to take the time to *read* the transcripts carefully. Although the researcher will continue to read and reread the transcripts throughout the process of coding and analysis, it is important that the transcripts are read, at least once, without any attempt at analysis. This is because such a reading allows us to experience *as a reader* some of the discursive effects of the text. For example, a text may come across as an apology even though the words 'I am sorry' are not actually spoken. We may feel that a text 'makes it sound like' there is a war going on even though the topic of the transcribed speech was a forthcoming election. Reading a text before analysing it allows us to become aware of what a text is doing. The purpose of analysis is to identify exactly how the text manages to accomplish this.

An initial reading of the first half of the extract in Box 7.2 (lines 1–26) leaves me feeling weary. The text appears to bear testimony to the speaker's considerable efforts in coming to a decision about how to end her relationship with her partner. It invokes a decision not taken lightly. The speaker comes across as mature and responsible in her way of dealing with the task of breaking up. A first reading of the second half of the extract (lines 27–42) evokes a sense of finality. There appears to be no ambiguity in its message, and its conclusion (the end of the relationship) seems inevitable. The purpose of the analysis is to understand how the text achieves these impressions.

Coding

Reading and rereading of the transcripts is followed by the selection of material for analysis, or *coding*. Coding of the transcripts is done in the light of the research question. All relevant sections of text are highlighted, copied and filed for analysis. At this stage, it is important to make sure that all material which is potentially relevant is included. This means that even instances which are indirectly or only vaguely related to the research question should be identified. Most importantly, use of certain key words is *not* required for selection of textual material. All implicit constructions (MacNaghten, 1993) must be included at this stage.

The need for coding before analysis illustrates that we can never produce a complete discourse analysis of a text. Our research question identifies a particular aspect of the discourse which we decide to explore in detail. Coding helps us to select relevant sections of the texts which constitute our data. There are always many aspects of the discourse which we will not analyse. This means that the same material can be analysed again, generating further insights.

The material for analysis was selected in the light of the research question, which was concerned with the ways in which the participant accounted for the break-up of an intimate relationship. Both parts of the present extract (lines 1–26 and lines 27–42) represent occasions within the conversation which provided the participant with an opportunity to elaborate upon the circumstances surrounding the end of the relationship. This meant that they constituted suitable data for analysis within this context.

ANALYSIS

Discourse analysis proceeds on the basis of the researcher's interaction with the text. Potter and Wetherell (1987: 168) recommend that throughout the process of analysis the researcher asks 'Why am I reading this passage in this way? What features [of the text] produce this reading?' Analysis of textual data is generated by paying close attention to the constructive and functional dimensions of discourse. In order to facilitate a systematic and sustained exploration of these dimensions, *context*, *variability* and *construction* of discursive accounts need to be attended to. The researcher looks at how the text constructs its objects and subjects, how such constructions vary across discursive contexts, and with what consequences they may be deployed. In order to identify diverse constructions of subjects and objects in the text, we need to pay attention to terminology, stylistic and grammatical features, and preferred metaphors and other figures of speech which may be used in their construction. Potter and Wetherell (1987: 149) refer to such systems of terms as 'interpretative repertoires'. Different repertoires are used to construct different versions of events. For example, a newspaper article may refer to young offenders as 'young tearaways', while defending lawyers may describe their clients as 'no-hope kids'. The former construction emphasizes the uncontrollability of young offenders and implies the need for stricter parenting and policing, while the latter both draws attention to the unmet psychological and educational needs of young offenders and highlights the importance of social and economic deprivation. Different repertoires can be used by the same speaker in different discursive contexts in the pursuit of different social objectives. Part of the analysis of discourse is to identify the action orientation of accounts. In order to do this, the researcher needs to pay careful attention to the discursive contexts within which such accounts are produced and to trace their consequences for the participants in a conversation. This can be done satisfactorily only on the basis of an analysis of *both* the interviewer's and the interviewee's contribution to the conversation. It is important to remember that discourse analysis requires us to examine language in *context*.

Interpretative repertoires are used to construct alternative, and often contradictory, versions of events. Discourse analysts have identified conflicting repertoires within participants' talk about the same topic. For example, Potter and Wetherell (1995) found that their participants used two different repertoires in order to talk about Maori culture and its role in the lives of Maoris in New Zealand: 'culture-as-heritage' and 'culture-as-therapy'. Billig (1997) identifies two alternative, and contrasting, accounts of the meaning of history in participants' discussions of the British royal family: 'history as national decline' and 'history as national progress'. The presence of tensions and contradictions among the interpretative repertoires used by speakers demonstrates that the discursive resources which people draw on are inherently dilemmatic (see Billig et al., 1988; Billig, 1991). This is to say, they contain contrary themes which can be pitted against each other within rhetorical contexts. In order to understand why and how speakers are using a particular theme, we need to look to the rhetorical context within which they are deploying it. Again, the analytic focus is upon variability across contexts and the action orientation of talk.

Reflecting the variability of discursive constructions, parts 1 and 2 of our interview extract construct rather different versions of 'breaking-up'.

Part 1 (lines 1–26). In response to the interviewer's question (I: 'did you talk to friends about it?', lines 1–2), the participant uses an extreme case formulation ('all the time'). In this way, her claim (to have discussed the situation with friends) is taken to its extreme in order to provide an effective warrant (Pomerantz, 1986) for her ultimate decision (to end the relationship). It is suggested that this decision is based on careful consideration informed by frequent discussions with friends. In addition, the participant's use of the word 'you' (instead of 'I') in lines 11–21 serves to generalize her experience and to suggest that her actions followed an established procedure for dealing with such matters, a practice which she shares with responsible others and which will be recognized as such by the interviewer. Through the use of list-like sentence constructions and the use of repetition ('How do I do it, how do I say it, what do I say', lines 5–7; and again 'How is he going to cope, what's going to happen to him, what if no one goes out with him, what if this and what if that', lines 23–4), a commitment to thorough and careful consideration of all eventualities is demonstrated. References to 'role-playing' (line 8) and 'preparing myself' (line 9) reinforce this impression by suggesting that such consideration includes the mental anticipation and practical rehearsal of possible scenarios. Use of terminology such as 'ties and emotional baggage ... which you're carrying' (lines 11–12) and repeated references to it being 'so hard' (line 10 and line 11) invoke a sense of sustained effort and serve to counteract any impression of a decision taken lightly. Talk of 'investment' (line 13) and 'responsibility' (line 19) chimes with a construction of breaking up as a serious business. To summarize, part 1 of the extract uses language in such a way as to construct a version of decision-making which involves considerable effort and hard work. It is interesting to note that the interviewer's question ('And when you made the decision, when you were actually working towards finishing it, did you talk to friends about it?', lines 1–2) mobilizes the same discursive construction of relationship endings as 'work'. Such a construction of decision-making constitutes a warrant for the decision actually taken (that is, ending the relationship) because it removes any semblance of lightness or superficiality from the account.

Part 2 (lines 27–42). The text accomplishes its sense of finality through its use of terminology and grammatical and stylistic features such as the use of metaphor. First, the use of the first person in assertions of the speaker's perspective ('the way I saw it', line 30; 'as far as I was concerned', lines 41–2) supports a singular and unambiguous point of view to which the speaker has privileged access. The use of a question ('Would I want to marry him?', line 34) that requires a categorical answer (we cannot get 'a little bit' married or choose to marry 'some of the time') also contributes to the finality of the extract; in the event, the 'answer was no' (lines 34–5), and this leaves no room for doubt or negotiation. References to the 'foundation' (line 31) and the 'basis' (line 38) of her decision to terminate the relationship invoke a bottom line beyond which considerations cannot be made. This serves as a warrant for the finality of the decision. Finally, and most dramatically, the use of the metaphor in the last sentence (line 42) provides a visual image of the inevitability of the end of the relationship: 'it had hit the brick wall and it wasn't going any further'. By invoking the image of an object hitting a physical barrier, the speaker underlines the finality of her decision. There is no room for second thoughts or reappraisals because it is simply too late: the relationship has 'hit the brick wall' and it cannot continue.

Part 2 of the extract uses language in such a way as to construct a version of the participant's decision that is characterized by inevitability and finality. Such a construction of the decision constitutes a warrant for the decision taken (that is, to end the relationship) because it does not allow for the possibility of an alternative outcome.

From a discursive psychology perspective, both parts of the extract serve as a warrant for the participant's decision to terminate her relationship with her partner. However, two different constructions of the decision are produced in the same interview (that is, as involving effort and hard work, and as final and inevitable, respectively), which demonstrates some of the variability that characterizes discourse. A look at preceding sections of text (not reproduced here) can throw further light on the variable deployment of discursive constructions of decision-making within the interview. The portion of text which constructs the decision as the product of considerable effort on the part of the participant is produced in response to a question about the involvement of friends in the decision-making process (lines 20–2, I: 'And when you made the decision um when you were actually working towards finishing it did you talk to friends about it?'). This question, in turn, is preceded by an account of how the participant's friends had 'taken a dislike' to her ex-partner and how they had 'talked about him with disdain'. As a result, the participant pointed out, 'everyone was glad when I'd finished it with him'. The participant's construction of her decision as 'hard work' could be understood, within this context, as a way of disclaiming an undesirable social identity. In order to counteract the impression that she was someone who unthinkingly follows her friends' advice, a construction of the break-up as involving effort and hard work was produced as a way of distancing herself from such negative attributions.

The portion of text which constructs the decision as inevitable and final is produced following the participant's account of how her ex-partner 'didn't think there was a problem that couldn't be worked out'. The construction of her decision to end the relationship as unequivocal and inescapable, therefore, occurs within a particular rhetorical context. It orients to, and at the same time challenges, an alternative view of how relationship difficulties ought to be dealt with (such as working to improve the relationship).

The variability in the participant's account is in line with discursive psychology's view of language as constructive and performative.

FOUCAULDIAN DISCOURSE ANALYSIS

HISTORY AND THEORETICAL BACKGROUND

The Foucauldian version of discourse analysis was introduced into Anglo-American psychology in the late 1970s. A group of psychologists who had been influenced by post-structuralist ideas, most notably the work of Michel Foucault, began to explore the relationship between language and subjectivity and its implications for psychological research. The publication of Henriques et al.'s *Changing the Subject: Psychology, Social Regulation and Subjectivity* in 1984 (re-issued in 1998) provided readers with a clear illustration of how post-structuralist theory could be applied to psychology. In the book, the authors critically and reflexively examine psychological theories (such as those of child development, gender differences, or individual differences) and their role in constructing the objects and subjects which they claim to explain.

Foucauldian discourse analysis is concerned with language and its role in the constitution of social and psychological life. From a Foucauldian point of view, discourses facilitate and limit, and enable and constrain what can be said, by whom, where and when (Parker, 1992). Foucauldian discourse analysts focus upon the availability of discursive resources within a culture – something like a discursive economy – and its implications for those who live within it. Here, discourses may be defined as 'sets of statements that construct objects and an array of subject positions' (Parker, 1994a: 245). These constructions, in turn, make available certain ways of seeing the world and certain ways of being in the world. Discourses offer *subject positions* which, when taken up, have implications for subjectivity and experience. For example, within a biomedical discourse, those who experience ill health occupy the subject position of 'the patient', which locates them as the passive recipient of expert care within a trajectory of cure. The concept of *positioning* has received increasing attention in recent years (Harré and van Langenhove, 1999).

Foucauldian discourse analysis is also concerned with the role of discourse in wider social processes of legitimation and power. Since discourses make available ways of seeing and ways of being, they are strongly implicated in the exercise of power. Dominant discourses privilege those versions of social reality which legitimate existing power relations and social structures. Some discourses are so entrenched that it is very difficult to see how we may challenge them. They have become 'common sense'. At the same time, it is in the nature of language that alternative constructions are always possible and that *counter-discourses* can, and do, emerge. Foucauldian discourse analysts also take a historical perspective and explore the ways in which discourses have changed over time, and how this may have shaped historical subjectivities (see also Rose, 1999). Finally, the Foucauldian version of discourse analysis pays attention to the relationship between discourses and institutions too. Here, discourses are not conceptualized simply as ways of speaking or writing. Rather, discourses are bound up with institutional practices – that is, with ways of organizing, regulating and administering social life. Thus, while discourses legitimate and reinforce existing social and institutional structures, these structures, in turn, also support and validate the discourses. For instance, being positioned as 'the patient' within a biomedical discourse means that one's body becomes an object of legitimate interest to doctors and nurses – that it may be exposed, touched and invaded in the process of treatment which forms part of the practice of medicine and its institutions (see also Parker, 1992: 17).

The Foucauldian version of discourse analysis is concerned with language and language use; however, its interest in language takes it beyond the immediate contexts within which language may be used by speaking subjects. Thus, unlike discursive psychology, which is primarily concerned with interpersonal communication, Foucauldian discourse analysis asks questions about the relationship between discourse and how people think or feel (subjectivity), what they may do (practices) and the material conditions within which such experiences may take place. Box 7.3 provides a summary of the major concerns associated with Foucauldian discourse analysis.

BOX 7.3   FOUCAULDIAN DISCOURSE ANALYSIS

Foucauldian discourse analysis:

- was inspired by Foucault and post-structuralism

- is concerned with discursive resources

- explores the role of discourse in the constitution of subjectivity and selfhood

- explores the relationship between discourse and power

- links discourse with institutions and social practices

- asks 'How does discourse construct subjects and objects?'

FORMULATING A RESEARCH QUESTION AND DESIGNING A STUDY

Foucauldian discourse analysis is concerned with mapping the discursive environment that people inhabit. It seeks to identify the discursive constructions used by research participants and to trace their implications for their experiences of themselves and the world. The general question driving Foucauldian discourse analytic research, therefore, is 'What characterizes the discursive worlds people inhabit and what are their implications for possible ways of being?' In order to identify a suitable discursive focus for a study, the researcher will need to identify a particular discursive object with whose construction they are particularly concerned. For example, a researcher may wish to better understand how people construct meaning around being diagnosed with a health condition. In this case, the research question may be 'What discourses do research participants draw on in their talk about their diagnosis and what are their implications for research participants' experience of their health condition?' A Foucauldian analysis would then be interested in the discursive resources which are available to the research participants and how their availability may shape their experience of living with their health condition.

COLLECTING DATA

Foucauldian discourse analysis can be carried out 'wherever there is meaning' (Parker, 1999: 1). This means that we do not necessarily have to analyse words. While most analysts work with transcripts of speech or written documents, Foucauldian discourse analysis can be carried out on any symbolic system. Parker recommends that we 'consider all tissues of meaning as texts'. This means that 'speech, writing, non-verbal behaviour, Braille, Morse code, semaphore, runes, advertisements, fashion systems, stained glass, architecture, tarot cards and bus tickets' all constitute suitable texts for analysis (1999: 7).

ANALYSIS

In Chapter 1 of *Discourse Dynamics: Critical Analysis for Social and Individual Psychology* (1992), Parker identifies 20 steps in the analysis of discourse dynamics. These 20 steps take the researcher from the selection of a text for analysis (steps 1 and 2) through the systematic identification of the subjects and objects constructed in them (steps 3–12) to an examination of the ways in which the discourse(s) which structure the text reproduces power relations (steps 13–20). Parker provides us with a detailed and wide-ranging guide that helps us to distinguish discourses, their relations with one another, their historical location, and their political and social effects. Other guides to Foucauldian discourse analysis (e.g., Kendall and Wickham, 1999: 42–6) rely on fewer steps but presuppose a more advanced conceptual understanding of Foucault's method. In this section, I set out six stages in the analysis of discourse and apply them to the extract in Box 7.2. These stages allow the researcher to map some of the discursive resources used in a text and the subject positions they contain, and to explore their implications for subjectivity and practice. It is important to bear in mind, however, that they do not constitute a full analysis in the Foucauldian sense. For more guidance on how to address key Foucauldian concerns, such as genealogy, governmentality and subjectification, see Arribas-Ayllon and Walkerdine (2008).

Stage 1: Discursive constructions

The first stage of analysis is concerned with the ways in which discursive objects are constructed. Which discursive object we focus on depends on our research question. For example, if we are interested in how people talk about 'love' and with what consequences, our discursive object would be 'love'. The first stage of analysis involves the identification of the different ways in which the discursive object is constructed in the text. It is important that we do not simply look for key words. Both implicit and explicit references need to be included. Our search for constructions of the discursive object is guided by shared meaning rather than lexical comparability. The fact that a text does not contain a direct reference to the discursive object can tell us a lot about the way in which the object is constructed. For example, someone may talk about a relative's terminal illness without directly naming it. Here, references to 'it', 'this awful thing' or 'the condition' construct the discursive object (that is, terminal illness) as something unspeakable and perhaps also unknowable.

Since the study from which the interview extract is taken was concerned with how people describe and account for the break-up of an intimate relationship (Willig and dew Valour, 1999, 2000), it makes sense to ask questions about the ways in which 'the relationship' is constructed through language. In the extract above, 'the relationship' is constructed as a clearly identifiable social arrangement with a beginning and an end, which offers security in return for investment of time and emotion (lines 2–26). In the second half of the extract, 'the relationship' is also constructed as a step on the way to marriage (lines 30–42). Thus, the relationship is constructed in two different ways. On the one hand, the relationship is constructed as a mutually beneficial social arrangement between two people who agree to invest resources (such as time and emotion) in order to gain mutual support and security. Such an arrangement is hard to extricate oneself from ('It's hard … it's just so hard', lines 10–11) because 'ties and emotional baggage' have grown over time. On the other hand, the relationship is constructed as a testing ground for, and a step on the way to, a superior form of involvement – namely, marriage. Here, the relationship has to be 'going somewhere' for it to be worthwhile ('it had hit the brick wall and it wasn't going any further', line 42), and its quality is judged in the light of its future direction ('And even though … I had no intentions of getting married for another you know four five whatever amount of years it was on that basis I was using the criteria of my wanting to continue going out with him', lines 37–9).

Stage 2: Discourses

Having identified all sections of text which contribute to the construction of the discursive object, we focus on the differences between constructions. What appears to be one and the same discursive object can be constructed in very different ways. The second stage of analysis aims to locate the various discursive constructions of the object within wider discourses. For example, within the context of an interview about her experience of her husband's prostate cancer, a woman may draw on a biomedical discourse when she talks about the process of diagnosis and treatment, a psychological discourse when she explains why she thinks her husband developed the illness in the first place, and a romantic discourse when she describes how she and her husband find the strength to fight the illness together. Thus, the husband's illness is constructed as a biochemical disease process, as the somatic manifestation of psychological traits, and as the enemy in a battle between good (the loving couple) and evil (separation through death) within the same text.

Let us attempt to locate the two constructions of the relationship identified in stage 1 of the analysis (as 'mutually beneficial social arrangement' and as 'a step on the way') within wider discourses surrounding intimate relationship. The construction of interpersonal relationships as mutually beneficial social arrangements resonates with economic discourse. Notions of investment of resources in return for long-term security, and the expectation that social actors exchange goods and services with one another, are prominent in contemporary talk about the economy. For example, the term 'partner', now widely used to refer to one's significant other, also describes those we share business interests with. By contrast, the construction of the relationship as 'a step on the way' to marriage draws on a romantic discourse. Here, the relationship is not conceptualized as a mutually beneficial arrangement but rather as a way of moving towards the ultimate goal: marriage. Marriage itself is not defined or explored within the text. It is interesting that there appears to be no need to account for why the participant uses suitability for marriage as a 'foundation' (line 31), a 'basis' (line 38) and 'the criteria' (line 39) in her account. She even points out that she has no intention of actually getting married in the near future. However, marriage as a goal forms part of a romantic discourse in which 'love', 'marriage' and 'monogamy' are inextricably linked with one another. By invoking one, we invoke them all. As a result, suitability for marriage becomes a legitimate basis for making decisions about intimate relationships even where there is no suggestion that marriage is a realistic option in the near or medium future.

Stage 3: Action orientation

The third stage of analysis involves a closer examination of the discursive contexts within which the different constructions of the object are being deployed. What is gained from constructing the object in this particular way at this particular point within the text? What is its function and how does it relate to other constructions produced in the surrounding text? These questions are concerned with what discursive psychology refers to as the *action orientation* of talk and text. To return to our example of a wife talking about her husband's cancer, it may be that her use of biomedical discourse allows her to attribute responsibility for diagnosis and treatment to medical professionals and to emphasize that her husband is being taken good care of. Her use of romantic discourse may have been produced in response to a question about her own role in her husband's recovery after surgery and may have served to emphasize that she is, in fact, contributing significantly to his recovery. Finally, psychological discourse may have been used to account for her husband's cancer in order to disclaim responsibility for sharing in a carcinogenic lifestyle (for example, 'I told him to slow down and take better care of himself but he wouldn't listen'). A focus on action orientation allows us to gain a clearer understanding of what the various constructions of the discursive object are capable of achieving within the text.

A closer examination of the discursive context within which our two different constructions of the relationship are deployed allows us to find out more about them. When are they used and what might be their function within the account? How do they position the speaker within the moral order invoked by the construction? (See also Stage 4: Positionings.) The portion of text which constructs the relationship as a 'mutually beneficial social arrangement' is produced in response to a question about the involvement of friends in the decision-making process (lines 1–2, I: 'And when you made the decision um when you were actually working towards finishing it did you talk to friends about it?'). This question, in turn, is preceded by an account of how the participant's friends had 'taken a dislike' to her ex-partner and how they had 'talked about him with disdain'. As a result, the participant pointed out, 'everyone was glad when I'd finished it with him'. The participant's use of a discursive construction of the relationship as a 'mutually beneficial social arrangement' could be seen, within this context, as a way of emphasizing her sense of responsibility for her ex-partner's well-being. Talk about her friends' dislike of her ex-partner and their joy at seeing the relationship break up may have created the impression that he, disliked and rejected, was the victim of a callous act of abandonment on the participant's part. In order to counteract such an impression, a construction of the relationship as a 'mutually beneficial social arrangement' draws attention to its mutually supportive nature and to the participant's awareness of the emotional significance of the break-up ('It's hard … it's just so hard', lines 10–11).

The portion of text which constructs the relationship as a 'step on the way' is produced following the participant's account of how her ex-partner 'didn't think there was a problem that couldn't be worked out'. The use of romantic discourse at this point allows the participant to ward off the charge that she did not give her ex-partner a chance to 'work out' the problems and to save the relationship. From within a romantic discourse, no amount of work can transform 'liking' into 'love', or an 'OK-relationship' into 'the real thing'. The acid test of romantic love (line 30, 'would I want to marry him?') renders attempts to work out problems redundant, because, if marriage is not a goal that can be envisaged, the relationship is not worth saving (lines 41–2, 'and as far as I was concerned it had hit the brick wall and it wasn't going any further'). From within a romantic discourse, the participant cannot be blamed for not trying hard enough to make the relationship work.

Stage 4: Positionings

Having identified the various constructions of the discursive object within the text, and having located them within wider discourses, we now take a closer look at the *subject positions* which they offer. A *subject position* within a discourse identifies 'a location for persons within the structure of rights and duties for those who use that repertoire' (Davies and Harré, 1999: 35). In other words, discourses construct *subjects* as well as objects, and as a result make positions within networks of meaning available, which speakers can take up (as well as place others within). Subject positions are different from roles in that they offer discursive locations from which to speak and act rather than prescribing a particular part to be acted out. In addition, roles can be played without subjective identification, whereas taking up a subject position has direct implications for subjectivity (see stage 6 below).

What are the subject positions offered by our two discursive constructions of 'the relationship'? A construction of relationships as 'mutually beneficial social arrangement' positions partners as highly dependent on each other. Involvement in such a relationship undermines the individual's freedom and mobility; partners are tied to each other through investments, history and emotions (line 11, 'there's all these you know ties and emotional baggage which … you're carrying'). As a result, whoever decides to withdraw from the arrangement is going to cause the other person considerable disruption, inconvenience and probably a great deal of distress. The subject positions offered by this construction are, therefore, those of responsible social actors who depend on each other for support and who are faced with the difficult task of realizing their interests within relationships of interdependence.

The romantic construction of intimate relationships as 'a step on the way' offers provisional subject positions to lovers. While involved in unmarried relationships, lovers are not fully committed to the relationship. Their involvement contains an opt-out clause which allows them to withdraw from the relationship without penalty. Everything that occurs between lovers within such an arrangement is permanently 'under review' and there is no guarantee that the relationship has a future. Therefore, the subject positions offered by this construction are those of free agents who reserve the right to withdraw from the relationship at any time and without moral sanction.

Stage 5: Practice

This stage is concerned with the relationship between discourse and practice. It requires a systematic exploration of the ways in which discursive constructions and the subject positions contained within them open up and/or close down opportunities for action. By constructing particular versions of the world, and by positioning subjects within them in particular ways, discourses limit what can be said and done. Furthermore, non-verbal practices can, and do, form part of discourses. For example, the practice of unprotected sex can be bound up with a marital discourse which constructs marriage and its equivalent, the 'long-term relationship', as incompatible with the use of condoms (Willig, 1995). Thus, certain practices become legitimate forms of behaviour from within particular discourses. Such practices, in turn, reproduce the discourses which legitimate them in the first place. In this way, speaking and doing support one another in the construction of subjects and objects. Stage 5 of the analysis of discourse maps the possibilities for action contained within the discursive constructions identified in the text.

What are the possibilities for action mapped by our two discursive constructions of relationships? What can be said and done by the subjects positioned within them? Constructions of relationships as 'mutually beneficial social arrangements' and their subject positions of responsible social actors require those positioned within them to act responsibly and with consideration for the consequences of their actions. Being part of a mutually beneficial social arrangement means that whatever we do affects the other party within the arrangement, and that we need to take responsibility for these effects. The participant's account of how she rehearsed breaking up (lines 5–10) and how hard it was for her to 'actually say to him I don't want to go out with you anymore' (lines 9–10) demonstrates her positioning as a responsible social actor. Taking responsibility for one's partner's well-being (line 19) and breaking up in a way that demonstrates concern for that partner's future are practices which support a construction of relationships as 'mutually beneficial social arrangements'. By contrast, being positioned within a relationship as 'a step on the way' does not require the same preoccupation with the other's well-being. Note that the section of text which constructs the relationship as 'a step on the way' (lines 30–42) does not contain any references to the participant's ex-partner. Instead, it talks about the nature of the relationship and the criteria by which to assess its value. The subject position of a free agent who reserves the right to withdraw from the relationship at any time and without moral sanction involves a focus upon the self and its interests. This is demonstrated in lines 30–42 (note the consistent use of the first-person singular and the references to 'foundation', 'basis' and 'criteria' for decision-making in this section).

Stage 6: Subjectivity

The final stage in the analysis explores the relationship between discourse and subjectivity. Discourses make available certain ways of seeing the world and certain ways of being in the world. They construct social as well as psychological realities. Discursive positioning plays an important role in this process. As Davies and Harré (1999: 35) put it:

Once having taken up a particular position as one's own, a person inevitably sees the world from the vantage point of that position and in terms of the particular images, metaphors, storylines and concepts which are made relevant within the particular discursive practice in which they are positioned.

This stage in the analysis traces the consequences of taking up various subject positions for the participants' subjective experience. Having asked questions about what can be said and done from within different discourses (Stage 5), we are now concerned with what can be felt, thought and experienced from within various subject positions.

This stage in the analysis is, of necessity, the most speculative. This is because here we are attempting to make links between the discursive constructions used by participants and their implications for subjective experience. Since there is no necessary direct relationship between language and various mental states, we can do no more than delineate what can be felt, thought and experienced from within various subject positions; whether or not, or to what extent, individual speakers actually do feel, think or experience in these ways on particular occasions is a different question (and one we probably cannot answer on the basis of a discourse analysis alone). It could be argued that feelings of guilt and regret are available to those positioning themselves within a construction of relationships as 'mutually beneficial social arrangements' (lines 19–21, 'You start taking responsibility for them and for how they'll cope afterwards you know maybe to the detriment to your own personal sort of well-being'), while taking up a position as free agent within a construction of relationships as 'a step on the way' may involve a sense of time urgency in relation to decision-making (lines 33–5, 'because I thought OK we've been going out for two nearly two years if we were going out for another two years would I want to marry him and the answer was no').

WRITING UP

Writing up discourse analytic research is not a process which is separate from the analysis of the texts. Both Potter and Wetherell (1987) and Billig (1997) draw attention to the fact that writing a report is itself a way of clarifying analysis. The attempt to produce a clear and coherent account of one's research in writing allows the researcher to identify inconsistencies and tensions which, in turn, may lead to new insights. Alternatively, the researcher may have to return to the data in order to address difficulties and problems raised in the process of writing.

Much of the analysis presented above emerged from the process of writing about my interaction with the interview transcript. Impressions based upon my initial encounter with the text had to be worked into an account of how the text achieved its discursive objectives. Having picked out metaphors, expressions and terms which fed into particular versions of how the participant's relationship came to an end, I wrote about the ways in which the participant's account produced these versions. As a result, the process of analysis is really a deconstruction (through the identification of interpretative repertoires and discursive constructions that make up the text) followed by a reconstruction of discourse (through writing about and thus re-creating the constructions and functions that characterize the text), and writing itself is an essential part of this process.

CONCLUSION

Both versions of the discourse analytic method share a concern with the role of language in the construction of social reality. However, as I hope has become clear, there are also important differences between the two approaches. To conclude this chapter, I want to make a direct comparison between the two versions of discourse analysis and the analytic insights each one of them can generate. Key differences between the two versions are presented under three headings: 'Research questions', 'Agency' and 'Experience' (see Box 7.4 for a summary).

Research questions

Discursive psychology and Foucauldian discourse analysis are designed to answer different types of research question. Discursive psychology projects typically ask 'How do participants use language in order to manage a stake in social interactions?', while Foucauldian discourse analysis answers the question 'What characterizes the discursive worlds people inhabit and what are their implications for possible ways of being?' Our discursive analysis of the interview extract was designed to answer questions about what the participant was doing with her talk. It allowed us to observe that the extract served as a warrant for the participant's decision to terminate her relationship with her partner. By contrast, our Foucauldian analysis was concerned with the nature of the discursive constructions used by the participant and their implications for her experience of the relationship break-up. We were able to identify both economic and romantic discourses in her account, each of which offered different subject positions and different opportunities for practice and subjectivity.

Agency

Discursive psychology and Foucauldian discourse analysis emphasize different aspects of human agency. Even though discursive psychology is concerned with language and its performative aspects, rather than with speaking subjects and their intentions, its focus on action orientation presupposes a conceptualization of the speaker as an active agent who uses discursive strategies in order to manage a stake in social interactions. In line with this, our discursive analysis focused upon the participant's use of discourse in the pursuit of an interpersonal objective which was to justify her decision to leave her partner within the context of a research interview. By contrast, Foucauldian discourse analysis draws attention

BOX 7.4   KEY DIFFERENCES BETWEEN DISCURSIVE PSYCHOLOGY (DP) AND FOUCAULDIAN DISCOURSE ANALYSIS (FDA)

Research questions

- DP asks 'How do participants use language in order to manage a stake in social interactions?'
- FDA asks 'What characterizes the discursive worlds that participants inhabit and what are their implications for possible ways of being?'

Agency

Discursive psychology:

- The speaker is an active agent
- The speaker uses discourse
- Discourse is a tool.

Foucauldian discourse analysis:

- The speaker is positioned by/in discourse
- Discourse makes available meanings
- Discourse constructs its subjects.

Experience

Discursive psychology:

- DP questions the value of the category 'experience'
- DP conceptualizes invocations of 'experience' as a discursive move.

Foucauldian discourse analysis:

- FDA attempts to theorize experience
- Discourse is implicated in experience
- Discourse makes available ways of being.

to the power of discourse to construct its objects, including the human subject itself. The availability of subject positions constrains what can be said, done and felt by individuals. Reflecting this concern, our Foucauldian analysis was interested in the discursive resources which were available to the participant and how their availability may have shaped her experience of the break-up.

Experience

Discursive psychology questions the value of the category 'experience' itself. Instead, it conceptualizes it (along with others such as 'subjectivity' and 'identity') as a discursive move whereby speakers may refer to their 'experiences' in order to validate their claims (as in 'I know this is hard because I've been there!'). Here, 'experience' is a discursive construction, to be deployed as and when required. Anything more than this is seen to constitute a return to cognitivism and this would, therefore, not be compatible with discursive psychology. By contrast, Foucauldian discourse analysis does attempt to theorize 'experience' (and 'subjectivity'). According to this approach, discursive constructions and practices are implicated in the ways in which we experience ourselves (such as 'sick' or 'healthy', 'normal' or 'abnormal', 'disabled' or 'able-bodied', and so on). As a result, an exploration of the availability of subject positions in discourse has implications for the possibilities of selfhood and subjective experience. This difference was reflected in our worked example. Our discursive analysis was concerned with what the respondent was *doing* with her talk, whereas our Foucauldian analysis was more interested in the implications of her use of discourse for her *experience* of the break-up.

Discourse analysis is a relatively recent arrival in psychology. However, despite its short history, it has already generated a large body of literature. As researchers use discourse analytic approaches within different contexts, they encounter new challenges which lead them to develop new ways of applying a discursive perspective. For example, early work in discourse analysis tended to concern itself with social psychological topics such as prejudice (e.g., Potter and Wetherell, 1987; Wetherell and Potter, 1992). In the 1990s, health psychologists started to use the method, leading to the formulation of a material-discursive approach (e.g., Yardley, 1997a), while others attempted to find ways in which discourse analysis could inform social and psychological interventions (e.g., Willig, 1999). In recent years, attempts have been made to understand what may motivate individuals to invest in particular discursive constructions and to occupy particular habitual subject positions. This has led to the emergence of a psychosocial approach which further develops some discourse analysts' concern with the relationship between discourse and subjectivity (e.g., Frosh and Saville Young, 2008; Frosh, 2010). Another way of linking the study of discourse with an interest in subjectivity and experience is being explored by researchers who attempt to combine Foucauldian discourse analysis with interpretative phenomenological analysis (e.g., Colahan et al., 2012). There have also been developments in relation to the analysis of non-linguistic 'texts' and the use of visual methods in the analysis of discourse (see Reavey, 2011).

Wetherell (2001) identifies as many as six different ways of doing discourse analysis while Glynos et al. (2009) and Wodak (1996) provide overviews of a wide range of perspectives on the study of discourse. This demonstrates that discourse analysis is not a method of data analysis in any simple sense. Rather, it provides us with a way of thinking about the role of discourse in the construction of social and psychological realities, and this, in turn, can help us approach research questions in new and productive ways. The two versions of the discourse analytic method introduced in this chapter are ways of approaching texts rather than recipes for producing 'correct analyses'. The choice of approach should be determined by the research question we wish to address; in some cases, this means that a combination of the two approaches is called for. The most ambitious discourse analytic studies may wish to pay attention to both the situated and shifting deployment of discursive constructions, as well as to the wider social and institutional frameworks within which they are produced and which shape their production (e.g., Edley and Wetherell, 2001). In this case, both discursive resources *and* discourse practices need to be explored in detail so that we can understand how speakers construct and negotiate meaning (discourse practices), as well as why they may draw on certain repertoires rather than others (discursive resources) (Wetherell, 1998). In any event, our choice of analytic method(s) should always emerge from careful consideration of our research question(s).

Box 7.5 presents three examples of discourse analysis in action.

BOX 7.5   THREE GOOD EXAMPLES OF DISCOURSE ANALYSIS

Eating practices

Wiggins, Potter and Wildsmith (2001) examine eating practices through the analysis of tape-recorded conversations from family mealtimes. The analysis demonstrates how evaluations of food, norms around eating practices and even participants' physiological states are negotiable and flexible products of discourse. The paper focuses on three discursive processes: (1) constructions of food; (2) constructions of the individual (i.e., as consumer of food); and (3) constructions of behaviour (i.e., eating/not eating). Using extracts from the transcripts of mealtime conversations, the authors demonstrate how discursive constructions are bound up with discursive practices such as urging, offering, resisting, rejecting, accepting, and so on. They conclude that food is not simply an object to be individually appraised (e.g., in terms of its taste and texture), but rather that it can be negotiated, defined, and constructed jointly, in talk. This paper is recommended because it constitutes a clear and systematic illustration of research informed by discursive psychology principles.

(Continued)

(Continued)

GPs and male patients

Seymour-Smith, Wetherell and Phoenix (2002) are concerned with the interpretative repertoires through which doctors and nurses construct their male patients. The analysis presented in the paper is based on transcripts of interviews with general practitioners and their nursing colleagues. The authors identify three linked interpretative repertoires which offer a range of subject positions. Each of these repertoires constructs a contrast between men and women, representing masculinity and femininity as obviously dichotomous binary categories. Within these repertoires, men were positioned as child-like with women as their carers and health supervisors. Hegemonic masculinity was both criticized (for preventing men from being more health-conscious) and reinforced (by colluding with the idea that to be a man one has to resist health care). The authors conclude that these repertoires constitute powerful cultural resources readily available to healthcare professionals, which inform the ways in which male patients are positioned in relation to healthcare practices. This paper is recommended because it demonstrates how discursive analysis can be grounded in the micro-analysis of data *and* speak to wider socio-cultural patterns and concerns.

Women talking about heavy drinking

Rolfe, Orford and Dalton (2009) explore the use of discursive constructions of drink and drinking in the accounts of women who drink heavily. The accounts were obtained by conducting semi-structured interviews with 24 women who were heavy drinkers, consuming over 35 UK units of alcohol per week. Critical discourse analysis was used to analyse the interview transcripts. The analysis identified two dominant constructions: 'drink as self-medication' and 'drink as pleasure and leisure'. The authors note that the women used discourse in order to justify their drinking, moving between the two dominant constructions in order to protect their moral status as 'good women'. The research describes the various discursive strategies the women used in order to do this. These included negotiating and resisting stigmatizing subject positions, contrasting their own actions with those of other (less 'good') women, and employing discourses of self-control. The authors argue that the women's deployment of discursive constructions reflects a wider cultural ambivalence about women's drinking. The paper concludes with a discussion of the consequences of the discursive dynamics identified in the research and some recommendations for health promotion practice.

The paper is recommended because it constitutes a good example of a critical approach to discourse analysis which starts with the analysis of interview transcripts and then moves on to make links with wider theory and macro-level discourses (in this case, of drinking and gender).

FURTHER READING

Hepburn, A. and Wiggins, S. (eds) (2007) *Discursive Research in Practice: New Approaches to Psychology and Interaction*. Cambridge: Cambridge University Press.
This book contains many good examples of a discursive psychology approach to discourse analysis.

Wetherell, M. (1998) 'Positioning and interpretative repertoires: conversation analysis and post-structuralism in dialogue', *Discourse & Society*, 9: 387–413.
In this paper, Wetherell argues in support of an integration of the two versions of discourse analysis.

Willig, C. (1998) 'Constructions of sexual activity and their implications for sexual practice: lessons for sex education', *Journal of health Psychology*, 3(3): 383–92.
This paper illustrates a systematic Foucauldian approach to discursive analysis and its concern with the relationship between discursive constructions, subjective experience and behavioural practice.

Willig, C. (2013) *Introducing Qualitative Research in Psychology* (3rd edn). Buckingham: Open University Press.
Chapters 10 and 11 of this book provide a more detailed discussion of the two versions of discourse analysis.

8 Cooperative Inquiry: An Action Research Practice

Sarah Riley and Peter Reason

The primary tradition of research in psychology has emphasized the separation of subject and object, observer from what is observed, in a search for objective truth. In this tradition, it is the researcher who makes all the decisions about what to study, how to study it, and what conclusions may be drawn; and the 'subjects' contribute only their responses to the situation in which they are observed, without knowing anything about the ideas that inform the inquiry. However, another inquiry tradition, which we can broadly call action research, has placed a contrasting emphasis on collaboration between 'researcher' and 'subject' to address practical issues of shared concern. In the full flowering of the approach, this distinction between researcher and subject fades away and *all* those involved in the inquiry endeavour act as co-researchers, contributing both to the decisions that inform the research and to the action that is to be studied. Further, the purpose is to reach not for a transcendent or objective truth in the tradition of Cartesian science (Toulmin, 1990), but for what is called 'practical knowing' – being better able to flourish and enable others around you to flourish (Heron, 1996b; Reason and Bradbury, 2001a).

In this chapter we focus on one approach – cooperative inquiry (CI) – which is part of the wider, rich and diverse family of action research approaches. If you are reading this, then you may well be thinking about the possibility of using cooperative inquiry for your dissertation, and during this chapter we will give you examples of how others have done this so that you can develop your own project. But for now, it's useful to get a sense of the breadth of action research. For some, action research is primarily an individual affair through which professionals can address questions of the kind 'How can I improve my practice?' For others, action research is strongly rooted in practices of organization development and improvement of business and public sector organizations. For many in the majority world, action research is primarily a liberationist practice aiming to redress imbalances of power and restore to ordinary people the capacities of self-reliance and ability to manage their own lives – to 'sharpen their minds' as villagers in Bangladesh described it to Peter. For some, the key questions are about how to initiate and develop face-to-face inquiry groups, while for others the primary issues are about using action research to create change on a large scale and influence policy decisions. And for some, action research is primarily a form of practice in the world, while for others it belongs in the scholarly traditions of knowledge generation. According to Reason and Bradbury (2006: xxii), what these approaches all share is a view of research that does the following:

- responds to practical and often pressing issues in the lives of people in organizations and communities
- engages with people in collaborative relationships, opening new 'communicative spaces' in which dialogue and development can flourish
- draws on many ways of knowing, both in the evidence that is generated and in diverse forms of presentation as we speak to wider audiences
- is strongly value-oriented, seeking to address issues of significance concerning the flourishing of human persons, their communities, and the wider ecology in which we participate
- is a living, emergent process which cannot be predetermined but changes and develops as those engaged deepen their understanding of the issues to be addressed and develop their capacity as co-inquirers both individually and collectively.

The many dimensions of action research are explored in the *Handbook of Action Research* (Reason and Bradbury, 2001b, 2006, 2008) and the excellent *Introduction to Action Research* by Davydd Greenwood and Morten Levin (1998, 2006). But for now, what a would-be cooperative inquiry psychology student needs to know is that CI involves learning with a small group of other people who are as committed to exploring an issue as you are – only they won't have to write up a dissertation about it afterwards.

HISTORY AND THEORETICAL BACKGROUND

A science of persons

The fundamental argument behind this action research tradition is that it is not possible to have a true science of persons unless the inquiry engages with humans *as* persons. And since persons are manifestly capable of making sense of their behaviour, the distinction between a 'researcher' who does all the thinking, and 'subjects' who do the behaving, is completely inappropriate. From a participatory perspective, the 'subjects' of the traditional form are really objects – curiously the word 'subject' wraps around itself to mean both the autonomous human person and the one who is 'subject to' God, the monarch, or a scientific researcher. In a science of persons, all those engaged in the inquiry process enter the process as persons, bringing with them their intelligence, their intentionality, their ability to reflect on experience and to enter relations with others – and of course also their capacity for self-deception, for consensus collusion, for rationalization, and for refusal to see the obvious, which also characterizes human persons.

A participative world-view

A science of persons also rests on a participative view of the world:

> [O]ur world does not consist of separate things but of relationships which we co-author. We participate in our world, so that the 'reality' we experience is a co-creation that involves the primal givenness of the cosmos and human feeling and construing. The participative metaphor is particularly apt for action research, because as we participate in creating our world we are already embodied and breathing beings *who are necessarily acting* – and this draws us to consider how to judge the *quality* of our acting.
>
> A participatory worldview places human persons and communities as part of their world – both human and more-than-human – embodied in their world, co-creating their world. A participatory perspective asks us to be both situated and reflexive, to be explicit about the perspective from which knowledge is created, to see inquiry as a process of coming to know, serving the democratic, practical ethos of action research. (Reason and Bradbury, 2001a: 6–7)

A science of persons in this sense is not a science of the Enlightenment. It does not seek a transcendental truth, which Descartes and his fellows would have us pursue. A science of persons embraces a 'postmodern' sentiment in attempting to move us beyond grand narratives towards localized, pragmatic and constructed practical knowings that are based in the experience and action of those engaged in the inquiry project. Toulmin (1990) argues persuasively that this can be seen as a reassertion of Renaissance values of practical philosophy.

An 'extended' epistemology and the primacy of the practical

As researchers, our epistemology frames the way we make sense of the knowledge we produce. An epistemology is the standpoint we take towards the nature of knowledge: for example, whether we think our research is producing facts about the world or understandings about how people interpret the world. The epistemological standpoint of cooperative inquiry, located as it is as a participative form of inquiry, is what is called an 'extended epistemology' – extended beyond the positivist concern for the rational and the empirical to include diverse ways of knowing as persons encounter and act in their world, particularly forms of knowing which are experiential and practical.

As Eikeland (2001) points out, this notion goes right back to Aristotle; and in modern times Polanyi (1962) clearly described his concept of tacit knowledge, a type of embodied know-how that is the foundation of all cognitive action. Writing more recently, Shotter argues that in addition to Gilbert Ryle's distinction between 'knowing that' and 'knowing how', there is a 'kind of knowledge one has *only from within a social situation*, a group, or an institution, and thus takes into account … the *others* in the social situation' (Shotter, 1993: 7, emphasis in original). It is significant that Shotter usually uses the verbal form '*knowing* of the third kind' to describe this, rather than the noun *knowledge*, emphasizing that such knowing is not a thing, to be discovered or created and stored up in journals, but rather arises in the process of living and in the voices of ordinary people in conversation.

Many writers have articulated different ways of framing an extended epistemology from pragmatic, constructionist, critical, feminist and developmental perspectives. While these descriptions differ in detail, they all go beyond orthodox empirical and rational Western views of knowing, and embrace a multiplicity of ways of knowing that start from a relationship between self and other, through participation and intuition. They assert the importance of sensitivity and attunement in the moment of relationship, and of knowing not just as an academic pursuit but as the everyday practices of acting in relationship and creating meaning in our lives (Reason and Bradbury, 2001a).

The methodology of cooperative inquiry draws on a fourfold extended epistemology: *experiential knowing* is through direct face-to-face encounter with a person, place or thing (it is knowing through empathy and resonance, the kind of in-depth knowing which is almost impossible to put into words); *presentational knowing* grows out of experiential knowing, and provides the first form of expression through story, drawing, sculpture, movement, dance, drawing on aesthetic imagery; *propositional knowing* draws on concepts and ideas; and *practical knowing* consummates the other forms of knowing in action in the world (Heron, 1996a; Heron and Reason, 2008). In some ways the practical has primacy since:

> most of our knowledge, and all our primary knowledge, arises as an aspect of activities that have practical, not theoretical objectives; and it is this knowledge, itself an aspect of action, to which all reflective theory must refer. (MacMurray, 1957: 12)

A liberationist spirit

As well as being an expression of an extended epistemology within a participative worldview, a science of persons has a political dimension. The relationship between power and knowledge is well argued by Habermas, Foucault, Lukes and others (Gaventa and Cornwall, 2001). Participative forms of inquiry start with concerns for power and powerlessness, and aim to confront the way in which the established and power-holding elements of societies world-wide are favoured because they hold a monopoly on the definition and employment of knowledge:

> This political form of participation affirms peoples' right and ability to have a say in decisions which affect them and which claim to generate knowledge about them. It asserts the importance of liberating the muted voices of those held down by class structures and neo-colonialism, by poverty, sexism, racism, and homophobia. (Reason and Bradbury, 2001a: 9)

So participatory research has a double objective. One aim is to produce knowledge and action directly useful to a group of people – through research, through adult education, and through socio-political action. The second aim is to empower people at a second and deeper level through the process of constructing and using their own knowledge: they 'see through' the ways in which the establishment monopolizes the production and use of knowledge for the benefit of its members. This is the meaning of consciousness-raising or *conscientização*, a term popularized by Paulo Freire (1970) for a 'process of self-awareness through collective self-inquiry and reflection' (Fals Borda and Rahman, 1991: 16). As Daniel Selener (1997: 12) emphasizes, while a major goal of participatory research is to solve practical problems in a community, '[a]nother goal is the creation of shifts in the balance of power in favour of poor and marginalized groups in society'. Greenwood and Levin (1998: 3) also emphasize how action research contributes actively to processes of democratic social change. Participative research is at its best a process that explicitly aims to educate those involved to develop their capacity for inquiry both individually and collectively.

These dimensions of a science of persons – an orientation to the practical, treating persons as persons, a participative world-view, an extended epistemology and a liberationist spirit – can be seen as the basis of contemporary action research. Action research itself is currently undergoing an exciting resurgence of interest and creativity, and there are many forms of inquiry practice within this tradition. In one attempt to provide some order to this diversity, we have elsewhere described three broad pathways to this practice. First-person action research/practice skills and methods address the ability of the researcher to foster an inquiring approach to his or her own life, to act awarely and choicefully, and to assess effects in the outside world while acting. Second-person action research/practice addresses our ability to inquire face-to-face with others into issues of mutual concern. Third-person research/practice aims to extend these relatively small-scale projects to create a wider community of inquiry involving a whole organization or community (Reason and Bradbury, 2006: xxv).

Cooperative inquiry is one articulation of action research. The original initiatives into experiential inquiry were taken around 1970 by John Heron (Heron, 1971). This developed into a practice of cooperative inquiry as a methodology for a science of persons (Heron, 1996a) which places an emphasis on first-person research/practice in the context of supportive and critical second-person relationships, while having the potential to reach out towards third-person practice.

The understanding of participants as co-researchers and the focus on solving problems, and thus enabling social change, make cooperative inquiry an exciting method for researchers in psychology. There is a range of concerns for researchers who tend to employ qualitative methods in psychology. For some, these issues are about doing radically different psychology that is not co-opted back into the 'mainstream'; for others the project is less political, and concern is on developing the discipline to include a broader, more humanist outlook (Stainton Rogers et al., 1995). Cooperative inquiry offers something to both 'types' of researcher. For those who are less critical of the psychology project, cooperative inquiry offers an additional method that produces new ways of knowing through a systematic yet flexible method. In drawing on multiple levels of knowing and focusing on applying knowledge at a local level, cooperative inquiry can therefore be used to broaden the remit of psychology, without challenging that remit.

Cooperative inquiry also opens up the possibilities for a more radical psychology that celebrates multiple ways of knowing. This multiplicity shifts the understanding that both researchers and participants are people from a 'methodological horror' to a 'methodological virtue' (Parker, 1994b, 1999). A more radical aspect is also incorporated through championing the use of research for political ends. Critical and feminist psychologists, for example, may find cooperative inquiry a useful approach in engendering social change.

Regardless of whether a more humanist or more radical approach is taken, cooperative inquiry has the potential to re-energize research in psychology (Box 8.1 offers an account of the experience of one psychology teacher). Cooperative inquiry has been used in educational, health and organizational psychology, but is also particularly relevant for social psychologists looking for ways to develop their sub-discipline and discursive, critical and feminist psychologists who seek ways of using their work to address oppressive practices and facilitate inquiry into issues of concern (Riley and Scharff, 2013; see also Willig, 1999). And with its emphasis on producing knowledge and action directly useful to a group of people, cooperative inquiry offers a unique approach to engaging with the impact agenda that characterizes contemporary research within the UK and elsewhere.

In the rest of this chapter we first set out the logics of the cooperative inquiry method, and then endeavour to show how this takes place within the learning community that is a cooperative inquiry group.

BOX 8.1   A COMMENT FROM A PSYCHOLOGY TEACHER

One of our colleagues wrote to tell us of her experience of teaching cooperative inquiry to a psychology class (Jennifer Mullett, personal communication):

I just wanted to tell you that I have just finished teaching a fourth year class in Community Psychology and Action Research (based on Nelson and Prilleltensky's, 2005, value-driven *Community Psychology* and your work). Your work not only allows Psychology students to discover a human psychology (after learning the experimental method and statistics for four years) but also that they can make a difference in the world through inspiring and engaging research. The comments made to me at the end of the class indicated that, for some, their thinking had been transformed and they were rethinking their careers in light of the possibilities opened by Action Research. Others found an approach that resonated with their values. I gently moved them from the experimental method using the four ways of knowing as a guide: starting with propositional knowing, introducing them to major theorists in the field of Psychology to situate action research in their own field; then experiential knowing by giving them case studies from my practice to work on, problem solve and critique; next,

(Continued)

(Continued)

presentational knowing by trying out Freire's triggers in the form of 'life statues' or tableaus, in which half the students used their bodies to create a 'still life' example of a situation where there was an unequal balance of power, the other half of the class 'decoded' the example and described what they saw; and finally, practical knowing by presenting community issues and looking at particular methods to investigate them. If I had started with the methods some of them might have thought action research was 'flaky' and not real science (a few did have trouble with the presentational knowledge). I also used the four ways of knowing heuristic to review and reflect on what we were learning as I felt it might appear as chaos to those who are used to following a text chapter by chapter. Their other classes in Psychology had taken this more traditional approach. It was also reassuring to me to hear that they were appreciating the significance of the participatory orientation of this approach. I didn't have to 'sell it' too vigorously.

I anticipated more resistance (e.g., this isn't science) than I experienced. From the first day they embraced the ideas and in fact appeared hungry for a 'human psychology'. I was very careful not to begin with a critique of the experimental paradigm, as I felt I would be telling them that all they had studied and worked hard to master for four years was trivial or irrelevant, but instead to present an alternative approach as just that and to win them over with my enthusiasm and case studies. Also I tried to indicate in what ways the experimental method was useful while at the same time generating excitement for the type of knowledge and change possible with action research. One thing surprised them: they were not aware that the field of action research has a long history going back to Lewin; nor of the extensive use of action research around the world. In their four years of university classes in psychology action research had not been discussed.

Jennifer Mullett is Director at the Centre for Healthy Communities Research, Vancouver Island University.

DESIGNING A STUDY

The logics of cooperative inquiry

Cooperative inquiry can be seen as cycling through four phases of reflection and action. In phase one, a group of co-researchers come together to explore an agreed area of human activity. They may be professionals who wish to develop their understanding and skill in a particular area of practice or members of a minority group who wish to articulate an aspect of their experience which has been muted by the dominant culture; they may wish to explore in depth their experience of certain states of consciousness, to assess the impact on their well-being of particular healing practices, and so on. In this first phase they agree on the focus of their inquiry, and together develop tentative questions or propositions they wish to explore. They agree to undertake some action, some practice, which will contribute to this exploration, and agree to a set of procedures by which they will observe and record their own and each other's experience.

Phase one is primarily in the mode of propositional knowing, although it will also contain important elements of presentational knowing as group members use their imagination in story, fantasy and graphics to help them articulate their interests and to focus on their purpose in the inquiry (see section on examples of cooperative inquiry at the end of this chapter for examples of activities that help participants represent their propositional knowledge). Once they have clarified sufficiently what they want to inquire about, group members conclude phase one with planning a method for exploring this in action, and with devising ways of gathering and recording evidence from this experience.

In phase two, the co-researchers engage in the actions agreed. They observe and record the process and outcomes of their own and each other's experience. In particular, they are careful to hold lightly the propositional frame from which they started, to notice how practice both does and does not conform to their original ideas and also notice the subtleties of experience. This phase involves primarily practical knowledge: knowing how (and how not) to engage in appropriate action, to bracket off the starting idea, and to exercise relevant discrimination.

Phase three is in some ways the touchstone of the inquiry method as the co-researchers become fully immersed in and engaged with their experience. They may develop a degree of openness to what is going on, so relatively free of preconceptions that they see it in a new way. They may go deeper into the experience so that superficial understandings are elaborated and developed. Or they may be led away from the original ideas and proposals into new fields, unpredicted action and creative insights. It is also possible that they may get so involved in what they are doing that they lose the awareness that they are part of an inquiry group: there may be a practical crisis, they may become enthralled, they may simply forget. Phase three involves mainly experiential knowing, although it will be richer if new experience is expressed, when recorded, in creative presentational form through graphics, colour, sound, movement, drama, story or poetry.

In phase four, after an agreed period engaged in phases two and three, the co-researchers reassemble to consider their original propositions and questions in the light of their experience. As a result, they may modify, develop or reframe them, or reject them and pose new questions. They may choose, for the next cycle of action, to focus on the same or on different aspects of the overall inquiry. The group may also choose to amend or develop its inquiry procedures – forms of action, ways of gathering data – in the light of experience. Phase four again emphasizes propositional knowing, although presentational forms of knowing will form an important bridge with the experiential and practical phases.

In a full inquiry the cycle will be repeated several times. Ideas and discoveries tentatively reached in early phases can be checked and developed; investigation of one aspect of the inquiry can be related to exploration of other parts; new skills can be acquired and monitored, experiential competencies realized. The group itself may become more cohesive and self-critical, more skilled in its work and in the practices of inquiry. Ideally, the inquiry is finished when the initial questions are fully answered in practice, when there is a new congruence between the four kinds of knowing. It is, of course, rare for a group to complete an inquiry so fully. It should be noted that actual inquiry practice is not as straightforward as the model suggests: there are usually mini-cycles within major cycles; some cycles will emphasize one phase more than others (some practitioners have advocated a more emergent process of inquiry which is less structured into phases). Nevertheless, the discipline of the research cycle is fundamental.

The cycling can really start at any point. It is usual for groups to get together formally at the propositional stage often as the result of an invitation from an initiating facilitator. However, such a proposal is usually birthed in experiential knowing, at the moment that curiosity is aroused or incongruity in practice noticed. And the proposal to form an inquiry group, if it is to take flight, needs to be presented in such a way as to appeal to the experience of potential co-researchers.

THE HUMAN PROCESS OF COOPERATIVE INQUIRY

In a science of persons, the quality of inquiry practice lies far less in impersonal methodology, and far more in the emergence of a self-aware, critical community of inquiry nested within a community of practice. So, while cooperative inquiry as method is based on cycles of action and reflection engaging four dimensions of an extended epistemology, as described above, cooperative inquiry as human process depends on the development of healthy human interaction in a face-to-face group. Would-be initiators of a cooperative inquiry must be willing to engage with the complexities of these human processes as well as with the logic of inquiry. This requires us to recollect our understanding of group processes.

Many theories of group development trace a series of phases of development in the life of a group. Early concerns are for inclusion and membership. When and if these needs are adequately satisfied, the group focuses on concerns for power and influence. And if these are successfully negotiated, they give way to concerns for intimacy and diversity in which flexible and tolerant relationships enable individuals to realize their own identity and allow the group to be effective in relation to its task (see, for example, Srivastva, Obert and Neilson, 1977). This phase progression model of group behaviour – in which the group's primary concern moves from issues of inclusion to control to intimacy, or from forming to norming to storming to performing (Tuckman, 1965), or from nurturing to energizing to relaxing (Randall and Southgate, 1980) – is a valuable way of understanding group development (although every group manifests these principles in their own unique way, and the complexity of an unfolding group process will always exceed what can be said about it). In what follows we will use Randall and Southgate's (1980) model of creative group process as a vehicle for describing the process of a successful cooperative inquiry group and to indicate the kinds of leadership or facilitation choices that need to be made.

Randall and Southgate differentiated between the creative group in which there is an exciting interaction between task and people – a 'living labour cycle' – and the destructive group in which primitive emotions arise, swallow up and destroy both human needs and task accomplishment – Bion's 'basic assumption group' (Bion, 1959). The life of a creative group follows the creative organismic cycle which can be seen in all life-affirming human processes, such as sexual intercourse, childbirth, preparing food and feasting, and doing good work together. In contrast, the destructive group lumbers between the basic group assumptions identified by Bion – dependency, flight/flight and messianic pairing – in its search for relief of its overwhelming anxiety. In between the creative and destructive group process is the intermediate group which is neither completely satisfying nor completely destructive, but which represents the everyday experience.

The creative group can be described as a cycle of nurturing, energizing, a peak of accomplishment, followed by relaxing (see Figure 8.1).

- The nurturing phase draws people together and helps them feel emotionally safe and bonded. At the same time, early, preparatory aspects of the group task and the organizational issues which allow the group to continue its life and work are attended to. The nurturing phase is about creating a safe and effective container for the work of the group, and leadership is primarily focused on those concerns.

- In the energizing phase, interaction intensifies as the group engages in its primary task. A degree of healthy conflict may arise as different views, experiences and skills are expressed. Leadership concerns are with the requirements of the task at hand – with containing and guiding the increasing levels of emotional, physical and intellectual energy which are being expressed.

- The peak in the creative group occurs at points of accomplishment, those moments when the emotional, task and organizational energy of the group come together and the main purpose to hand is achieved. These are moments of utter mutual spontaneity.

- In the relaxing phase, members attend to those issues which will complete the emotional, task and organizational work of the group. Emotionally, the group needs to wind down, to celebrate achievements, to reflect and learn. The task needs to be completed: there are always final touches that differentiate excellence from the merely adequate. And the organizational issues need completion – putting away tools, paying bills. Leadership makes space for these issues to be properly attended to, and usually those naturally gifted as 'finishers' come forward to lead celebrations and complete the task.

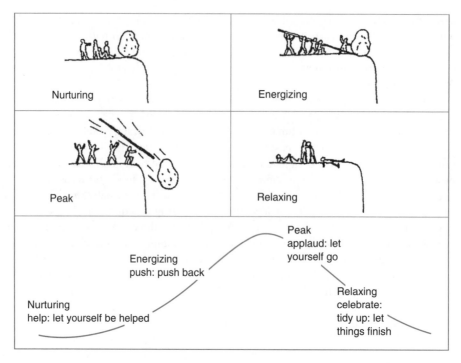

Figure 8.1   The living labour cycle and the creative group cycle (Randall and Southgate, 1980)

A group which lasts over a period of time will experience cycles at different levels: mini-cycles associated with particular tasks and major cycles of action and reflection. These will be set in the context of a long-term developmental cycle of birth, maturation and death. Early concerns focus on issues of inclusion; this is often followed by a struggle for influence, with conflicts and cliques emerging; if issues of influence are successfully negotiated a mature group may emerge characterized by intimacy and mutuality. This creative group nurturing/ energizing/relaxing cycle interacts with inquiry phases of action and reflection to produce a complex rhythm of cooperative inquiry.

A creative group is also characterized by an appropriate balance of the principles of hierarchy, collaboration and autonomy – deciding for others, with others, and for oneself (Heron, 1999). Authentic hierarchy provides appropriate direction by those with greater vision, skill and experience. Collaboration roots the individual within a community of peers, offering basic support and the creative and corrective feedback of other views and possibilities. Autonomy expresses the self-directing and self-creating potential of the person. The shadow face of authority is authoritarianism: that of collaboration, peer pressure and conformity; that of autonomy, narcissism, wilfulness and isolation. The challenge is to design institutions which manifest valid forms of these principles, and to finds ways in which they can be maintained in self-correcting and creative tension.

Establishing cooperative inquiry: focus on nurturing

The key issues in the nurturing phase are:

- identifying potential group members and establishing a group emotional atmosphere in which potential members feel sufficiently at home to begin to contribute their creative energy
- introducing and explaining the process of cooperative inquiry
- agreeing a framework of times and places for meeting which will provide an organized framework for the major cycles of action and reflection.

A key consideration is to provide sufficient time, to create relaxed conversational spaces, and to provide sufficient information for potential group members to make a considered choice about membership. Experience suggests that most inquiry groups are brought together specifically for the inquiry process – they come together around a shared interest or concern, or are members of an occupational group or an organization, so that when they assemble they will recognize their commonality and potential shared purpose. Some inquiry groups are actual work or living groups who choose to devote time to inquiry to address an issue of particular concern. For example, an established team of five hospital-based social workers explored the tension between prescription and discretion in front-line social work practice (Baldwin, 2001). However, it is the initiating energy of one person that brings people together and creates a potential group.

For example, Kate McArdle's doctoral research used cooperative inquiry to work with young women managers in large organizations.

> At the end of October I took part in a day celebrating 'diversity' within XYZ. I was given half of a stand promoting women's interests. I covered it with bright yellow posters asking questions such as: 'What is it like to be a twenty-something woman in XYZ?', 'Does gender matter?' I littered the entire floor with bright orange flyers, which asked the same questions, gave the date of an introductory session and my contact details. I was expected to remain on the stand, but I had little interest in being interrogated or speaking to people who were not in the age bracket of my inquiry. I needed to use my voice in the right kind of conversations. I wandered around talking to people who looked as if they were in my 'target audience'. We sat on couches, drank coffee, shared stories about my research and their work and exchanged contact details. (McArdle, 2002: 180)

Several of Sarah's undergraduate students have set up cooperative inquiry projects for their dissertations. These have involved relatively small numbers of participants, between three and six, where students have used informal and formal methods of advertising their project to potential participants. For example, a project looking at older women's experiences of beauty involved a student asking her mum, who in turn asked her friends, while a project on street harassment recruited participants from a psychology student subject pool.

Whether the inquiry group arises as an independent initiative or from within an established group, the first proposal to initiate inquiry is a delicate matter: it needs to be clear enough to catch the imagination, address a felt need or interest, attract people's curiosity and interest, and at the same time be sufficiently tentative for potential members not to feel invaded or put upon by yet another demand on their busy lives. Many initiating facilitators of inquiry have spent considerable time talking through their ideas with potential members, sowing seeds in informal conversation. Some have established a reputation in their organization or community as initiators of interesting new projects, and are trusted to take a lead; and others are able to attract people to their idea, and then have to work to establish an atmosphere of trust and inquiry.

One approach is to write a letter or an email that attractively summarizes the proposal and the method on one side of a sheet of paper, and invites people to come to a meeting to discuss the idea in greater depth. It can be a substantial, all-day meeting, with some profile within relevant communities, or a more intimate, face-to-face affair. For example, Agnes Bryan and Cathy Aymer, black social work lecturers, were concerned to address issues in the development of professional identity among black social workers in the UK, issues they had identified on the basis of their experience and some prior research. They invited a large group of black social work professionals – practitioners, managers and teachers – to a day-long meeting at their university to discuss the issues and explore the establishment of inquiry groups (see Aymer, 2005; Bryan, 2000).

An introductory discussion meeting, as described above, is often the first occasion at which a potential inquiry group meets, and thus can be seen as the beginning of the creative process, and as needing to address the emotional, task and organizational requirements of the nurturing phase.

The *emotional needs* of group members are, first of all, to feel safe, included and welcomed. The early stages of any group are characterized by free-floating anxiety in which every group member feels more or less isolated and is seeking to know that there are others around sufficiently like them to connect with. They will be asking questions about identity and inclusion ('Who am I to be in this group?' and 'Who is like me?') questions about purpose ('Will this group meet my needs and interests?') and questions about intimacy ('Is this a place where I will be liked and valued?'). If group members are part of an organization, there may be other questions about potential conflict between individual and organizational needs. These questions are rarely fully articulated in consciousness: they are acted out in everyday chitchat and stereotypical interaction. However, they are powerful influences on the group. It follows that careful attention to these questions is essential.

It is usually helpful if the meeting starts with opportunities for people to meet each other. There is nothing more off-putting than the silence that a new group can generate as people come into a room for the first time; and if this is followed by a meeting which launches immediately into a task agenda without hearing why people have come together, the new group can be off to a really bad start. In a small group, it may be sufficient for the facilitator to introduce people as they come in; for a large group, some structure of meeting in pairs and trios can be helpful. This can be followed by a round in which everyone is asked to say their name and what attracted them to the meeting, or some form of 'name game' that gives people an initial sense of knowing who others are. The physical arrangements for a first meeting can be important:

> I arrived to find a beautiful conference room filled with large wooden tables arranged in a square, on top of which at regularly spaced intervals were a mixture of mineral waters, glasses arranged in diamond shapes and small dishes of mints on paper doilies ... I wanted a circle of chairs. I phoned Facilities to remove the tables. Two big men in overalls arrived ... removed the tables and put the chairs back in a square. Then they all left and I was alone again. I wheeled the huge plush chairs into a circle and wondered what the women would think when they arrived. Would they be as bemused by what I had created, as I had been by what I'd seen when I'd arrived? (McArdle, 2002: 181)

The *task needs* of the group in this first meeting are to initiate people into the cooperative inquiry method, and explore together the potential focus of the proposed inquiry. Of course, these are closely related to the emotional needs explored above, because people's sense of insecurity is in part associated with uncertainty as to whether the group will meet their needs and interests. Usually both of these will have been briefly described in the invitation to the meeting, but it is likely that most people's interest will be diffuse and unformed at this stage. In particular, the methodology of cooperative inquiry can be confusing because most people associate 'research' with filling in questionnaires designed by the researcher, not with becoming co-researchers in a relationship of mutual influence.

It is here that the initiators of the inquiry need to exercise authentic authority in setting out as clearly as they can the principles and practices of cooperative inquiry, and in responding to questions and comments from the group. It is important that at this stage potential inquiry group members understand the logic of the inquiry method and also the personal and emotional investment that needs to be made if the inquiry is to be truly transformational. One approach is to talk through different phases of the inquiry cycle, emphasizing the different kinds of knowing that are primary at each stage, and emphasizing that the quality of the inquiry comes from the quality of engagement that group members have with the issues and their willingness to be experimental in their practices. It can be helpful to give a ten-minute talk, and then invite people to chat in pairs for a few minutes to clarify their questions before opening a general discussion. In terms of the extended epistemology we described earlier, this will give people an opportunity to draw on their tacit experiential knowing, and articulate this through a narrative (presentational knowing) which will contribute to the articulation of questions and issues that people want to address (propositional knowing). While clarity at this stage is important, one must also realize that cooperative inquiry, as an experiential process, can only be fully learned through engagement – there are important tacit learnings that take place as people enter the cycles of action and reflection, and as the group develops as a community of inquiry.

This introductory meeting needs also to attend to the inquiry topic proposed in order to generate at least an initial agreement as to the focus. Usually the initiating facilitator has done some preparatory work: they may be fired up themselves with concern for some issues, have had preliminary conversations with potential inquiry participants, and by proposing a set of questions or an arena for inquiry be playing a valuable role in initiating and focusing attention. It is important that the potential inquiry topic is put forward with clarity as an attractive and exciting venture; it is also important that a dialogue is initiated in which the initiator's vision can be explored and amended so that it becomes more generally owned and genuinely adopted by those who will join the inquiry. Geoff Mead was clear that:

> Improving the quality of leadership is a crucial issue for the police service. Learning *about* theories of leadership is not enough. What really matters is for each of us to understand and improve our own unique practice as leaders. (Mead, 2002: 191)

He therefore initiated a series of briefing meetings:

> designed to help people make a positive decision to opt into the action inquiry or to decide, without any stigma, that it was not for them. The underlying principle was that of voluntary, informed self-selection. I spoke a little about the rationale for offering this opportunity to focus on leadership and said something about the participative and democratic ethos of action inquiry. I talked about the possibility of transformative learning and asked people to decide if they wanted to take part using their head (Do you have enough information? Does it make *sense* for you to do it?), heart (Are you intrigued, curious, drawn? Does it *feel* right for you to do it?), and will (Are you able and willing to meet the commitment? Do you really *want* to do it?). (Mead, 2002: 196)

This early process of clarifying the inquiry focus, so that the group in time meets with a clear and agreed sense of its own purpose, is a crucial stage in the establishment of an inquiry group. It is not to be rushed. Experience suggests that at least two pre-meetings, as well as informal conversations, are necessary.

The *organizational needs* of the inquiry group must also be met in these early meetings, and again these overlap with the emotional needs of nurturing the group into being, since people will feel more comfortable if they know they can meet the demands, such as time and money. A first introductory meeting is often so fully engaged with discussions of method and topic that the organizational details can only be touched on, to be revisited at a second meeting. The most significant decision usually concerns how often the group should meet and for what period of time. Ideally, the group will need: enough time in meeting together at the beginning to fully clarify the topic area and details of the inquiry method; enough time during the main body of the inquiry to thoroughly reflect on the information and experiences gathered; and enough time at the end to draw some conclusion and agree about any writing or other reporting that is desired – and in addition enough time to maintain a healthy group process through social activities (eating together and going for walks are common practices) and more formal group review sessions. Similarly, the group needs sufficient time between meetings for members to try out and observe their own and each other's behaviour, to gather experience with a thoroughness that matches the complexity of the inquiry topic.

In practice, these decisions are made pragmatically, not on the basis of what is perfect but on what is good enough under the circumstances and for the task at hand. A substantial amount of work can be accomplished in a series of 6–8 half-day meetings, but more time is desirable. As with all aspects of cooperative inquiry, the issue is not one of getting it right, because every decision has its own consequences; rather, it is a matter of being clear about the choices that are made, and their consequences for the quality of inquiry. So if a relatively small amount of time is available, it is probably better to be modest in the aims of the inquiry group, and to keep the group small, remembering always that the purpose of cooperative inquiry is to generate information and understanding that are capable of transforming action rather than generating valid but impersonal and abstract understanding on a large scale.

In practice, these decisions are usually made on a 'propose and consult' basis: the initiator, with some sense of what is required from the inquiry topic itself, may propose to the group a number of different formats for meeting, and from the group's reaction to these will come to a decision which best approximates a consensus. For further examples of good studies, see Box 8.3 at the end of this chapter.

In summary, in the introductory meetings that launch a cooperative inquiry the emotional, task and organizational needs of the group are closely intertwined. The initiating facilitator must work to establish qualities of interaction that will allow the group to grow towards a full expression of the creative cycle. This includes: helping potential group members feel included in an emerging group which can meet their needs; finding a sense of purpose for the inquiry to which people can subscribe; and making organizational arrangements that enable the inquiry task to fit into people's lives. Thus the introductory meetings are both part of phase one on the inquiry cycle, in which the inquiry questions are clarified, and an essential grounding for the whole inquiry process is provided.

We want to emphasize the value and importance of spending time and giving careful attention to these early contracting arrangements, which is why this section on nurturing the group is substantially longer than those that follow. If you get this right (or at least 'good enough', to borrow from Winnicott), the rest will follow. We believe that more attempts at participative research fail because not enough attention is given to these early stages than for any other reason.

Cycles of action and reflection: moving into energizing

Following these initial meetings, which establish the existence of the inquiry project, the group is ready to move into the inquiry proper. In terms of the major phases of the group endeavour, this means moving from a primary focus on nurturing towards greater energizing. This doesn't mean that the work of nurturing the group has been done: every meeting, almost every interaction, involves a creative cycle; and this always includes bringing the group together with a clear sense of purpose as a foundation for good work together.

Throughout the life of a group the business of nurturing continues – 'Who is feeling left out?', 'Who might be feeling oppressed?', 'Are we clear about our purposes?' In particular, the first full meeting will probably be longer than subsequent ones and it may be the first occasion when the whole group is assembled: it is worth spending a good length of time on deepening the sense of mutual knowing and discussing in more detail the dimensions of the inquiry task.

However, if the group remains in a nurturing mode, the task of inquiry doesn't get done (and the group will be at risk of smothering itself in destructive nurturing mode). The key task need is for the group to establish cycles of action and reflection since this is the major vehicle for moving the inquiry forward. This research cycling carries a fundamental rhythm of learning through which group members deepen their engagement with the inquiry, open themselves to more subtle understandings, engage with previously unsuspected aspects of the inquiry task, and so on. The research cycling, moving through the four ways of knowing described above, complements the creative group cycle.

A significant chunk of time at the first full meeting of the group is usually taken up with discussing in detail the basic ideas on which the inquiry will be founded, converting the sense of joint purpose into a practical task that can be accomplished (phase one of the inquiry cycle). This may involve sharing experiences, concerns, hopes and fears so that group members raise their awareness and establish a sense of solidarity about what questions are important (Douglas, 2002). More formally, the group may establish a model, or a set of questions, to guide the inquiry:

> The holistic medicine group, established to explore the theory and practice of holistic medicine in the NHS, spent much of its first meeting with members in small groups reflecting on their practice as doctors, and drawing from this experience themes which defined the nature of holistic practice. By the end of the weekend a tentative five-part model of holistic practice had been developed which was to guide the rest of the inquiry. (see Reason, 1988)

These ideas then need to be translated into plans for the practical actions (propositional to practical knowing) which will form the basis of members' activities while away from the group. Some groups will simply agree to carefully notice aspects of their experience that fall within the scope of the inquiry:

> We ended with an agreement that the time until the [next] session would be an 'exploratory' cycle, rather than taking one of the themes discussed and working solely with that. We talked about today's session as being an 'awareness-raising' one and the coming six weeks as time to mull over, digest and notice more awarely. I encouraged an already present sense of not wanting to rush the process. I believe in order for our questions to be meaningful, we have to give ourselves time to find them and give them space to grow. (McArdle, 2002: 185)

On the other hand, it may be appropriate to start more systematically:

> The Hospital Group focused on a specific bureaucratic procedure to investigate differences of practice. The document chosen was a form that had to be signed by a potential service user, to give consent for the social worker to contact third parties to seek information about the user. Consent was seen by the authority as good practice in that it reflected partnership. Social workers in the Hospital Group were concerned that requesting a signature was a threatening practice for some people. When they felt that to be the case, they did not ask for a signature, even though they knew they *ought* to …The group devised a technique of investigation and recording. Every time one of the forms *should* have been completed, participants recorded the reason why they did or did not ask service users to sign the form. In effect, they were required to justify their actions, both to themselves and to their peers in the co-operative inquiry group. (Baldwin, 2002: 290)

> The holistic medicine group brainstormed ways in which each dimension of the five-part model could be applied in practice and how records of experience could be kept. Each doctor chose activities that were of greatest relevance to themselves and contracted with the rest of the group to study these. (see Reason, 1988)

It may be appropriate for all members of the group to undertake the same activity, or for each to choose their own idiosyncratic path of inquiry. Whichever way, cycles of action and reflection are established. Group members leave the group with more or less specific plans: they may agree to some very specific activities, as with the social work group, or more generally to observe particular aspects of experience; they may choose to experiment with novel activities, or to deepen their understanding of their everyday practice; they may record their experience through diaries, audio or video recordings, or mutual observation; they may choose to collect quantitative data where relevant. After the agreed period, the group reassembles to reflect on the experiences, to revise and develop their propositional understandings, and to enter a second cycle:

> We found that the simple act of sharing our stories, telling each other how we had been getting on with our inquiries, was enormously powerful – both to deepen the relationships between us and as a way of holding ourselves and each other to account. We quickly got into the habit of tape-recording our sessions and sending copies of relevant sections of the tapes to individuals to aid further reflection. Most sessions began with an extended 'check in' of this sort and then followed whatever themes emerged. On one occasion, following a 'spin-off' meeting arranged by several women members of the group, this lead to a fascinating exploration of gender and leadership. We learned to trust the process of action inquiry and that, in an organisational setting at least, it needs to be sustained by careful cultivation and lots of energy. (Mead, 2002: 200)

Some group members will not find it easy to enter this inquiry cycle. They may enjoy the group interaction and enter fully into the discussions about the inquiry, but be unwilling to commit in practice. Others may rush off into new activity without giving sufficient attention to the reflective side of the inquiry. The inquiry facilitator has a crucial role to play here in initiating people into the iteration of action and reflection and helping people understand the power of the research cycle.

Heron (1996a) suggests that inquiry groups need to draw on both Apollonian and Dionysian qualities in their research cycling. Apollonian inquiry is planned, ordered and rational, seeking quality through systematic search: models are developed and put into practice; experiences are systematically recorded; different forms of presentation are regularly used. Dionysian inquiry is passionate and spontaneous, seeking quality through imagination and synchronicity: the group engages in the activity that emerges in the moment, rather than planning action; space is cleared for the unexpected to emerge; more attention is paid to dreams and imagery than to careful theory building; and so on. Apollonian inquiry carries the benefits of systematic order, while Dionysian inquiry carries the possibility of stretching the limits through play. To the extent that co-inquirers can embrace both Apollo and Dionysus in their inquiry cycling, they are able to develop diverse and rich connections with each other and with their experience.

Research cycling builds the energetic engagement of the group with its inquiry task and with each other, and thus meets the *emotional needs* of the group as it moves into energizing. As the group adventures into deeper exploration of the inquiry topic, to the extent that nurturing has built a safe container, members will become more deeply bonded and more open to conflict and difference. Deep and lasting friendships have started in inquiry groups, and relationships which are already stressed may fracture. When conflict arises between members, the group needs to find a way of working through differences, rather than ignoring or burying them, and different members will be able to offer skills of mediation, bridge-building, confrontation and soothing hurt feelings. The deepening engagement with the inquiry task may itself raise anxieties, for as people start to question their taken-for-granted assumptions and to try out new forms of behaviour, they can disturb old patterns of defence, and unacknowledged distress may seriously distort inquiry. Inquiry groups will need to find some way to draw the anxieties which arise from both these sources into awareness and resolve them; one of the best ways of doing this is to allow group process time in every meeting for such issues to be raised and explored.

The *organizing needs* of the group often revolve around maintaining the schedule of meeting, and within the meetings agreeing together how much time should be devoted to different activities. Typically, the structure for a meeting will be planned collaboratively, with different members taking increasing responsibility for leading different aspects. As the inquiry progresses, questions arise as to how best to complete the inquiry task – questions which often concern the validity and quality of inquiry. John Heron has explored the theoretical and practical aspects of validity in cooperative inquiry in detail (Heron, 1996a) (see Box 8.2). These may helpfully be seen within the wider context of validity in action research (Bradbury and Reason, 2001; Reason, 2006). Often the initiating facilitator will introduce these validity procedures and invite the group to consider the implications for their inquiry.

This may raise questions about the appropriate balance of convergent and divergent cycling, the quality of interaction within the group, the amount of attention paid to anxiety, the degree to which the group may be colluding to avoid problematic aspects of the inquiry, and so on.

BOX 8.2   INQUIRY SKILLS AND VALIDITY PROCEDURES

Cooperative inquiry is based on people examining their own experience and action carefully in collaboration with people who share similar concerns and interests. But, you might say, isn't it true that people can fool themselves about their experience? Isn't this why we have professional research-ers who can be detached and objective? The answer to this is that certainly people can and do fool themselves, but we find that they can also develop their attention so they can look at themselves critically – their way of being, their intuitions and imaginings, their beliefs and actions – and in this way improve the quality of their claims to fourfold knowing. We call this 'critical subjectivity'. It means that we don't have to throw away our personal, living knowledge in the search for objectivity, but are able to build on it and develop it. We can cultivate a high-quality and valid individual perspective on what there is, in collaboration with others who are doing the same.

We have developed a number of inquiry skills and validity procedures that can be part of a cooperative inquiry and which can help improve the quality of knowing. The skills include:

- *Being present and open*. This skill is about empathy, resonance and attunement – being open to the meaning we give to and find in our world.
- *Bracketing and reframing*. The skill here is holding in abeyance the classifications and constructs we impose on our perceiving, and trying out alternative constructs for their creative capacity; we are open to reframing the defining assumptions of any context.
- *Radical practice and congruence*. This skill means being aware, during action, of the relationship between our purposes, the frames, norms and theories we bring, our bodily practice, and the outside world. It also means being aware of any lack of congruence between these different facets of the action and adjusting them accordingly.
- *Non-attachment and meta-intentionality*. This is the knack of not investing one's identity and emotional security in an action, while remaining fully purposive and committed to it.
- *Emotional competence*. This is the ability to identify and manage emotional states in various ways. It includes keeping action free from distortion driven by the unprocessed distress and conditioning of earlier years.

(Continued)

(Continued)

The cooperative inquiry group is itself a container and a discipline within which these skills can be developed. These skills can be honed and refined if the inquiry group adopts a range of validity procedures intended to free the various forms of knowing involved in the inquiry process from the distortion of uncritical subjectivity.

- *Research cycling*. Cooperative inquiry involves going through the four phases of inquiry several times, cycling between action and reflection, looking at experience and practice from different angles, developing different ideas, and trying different ways of behaving.

- *Divergence and convergence*. Research cycling can be convergent, in which case the co-researchers look several times at the same issue, maybe looking each time in more detail; or it can be divergent, as co-researchers decide to look at different issues on successive cycles. Many variations of convergence and divergence are possible in the course of an inquiry. It is up to each group to determine the appropriate balance for their work.

- *Authentic collaboration*. Since intersubjective dialogue is a key component in refining the forms of knowing, it is important that the inquiry group develops an authentic form of collaboration. The inquiry will not be truly cooperative if one or two people dominate the group, or if some voices are left out altogether.

- *Challenging consensus collusion*. This can be done with a simple procedure which authorizes any inquirer at any time to adopt formally the role of devil's advocate in order to question the group as to whether any form of collusion is afoot.

- *Managing distress*. The group adopts some regular method for surfacing and processing repressed distress, which may get unawarely projected out, distorting thought, perception and action within the inquiry.

- *Reflection and action*. Since the inquiry process depends on alternating phases of action and reflection, it is important to find an appropriate balance, so that there is neither too much reflection on too little experience (which is armchair theorizing), nor too little reflection on too much experience (which is mere activism). Each inquiry group needs to find its own balance between action and reflection.

- *Chaos and order*. If a group is open, adventurous and innovative, putting all at risk to reach out for the truth beyond fear and collusion, then, once the inquiry is well under way, divergence of thought and expression may descend into confusion, uncertainty, ambiguity, disorder and tension. A group needs to be prepared for chaos, tolerate it, and wait until there is a real sense of creative resolution.

(Adapted from Heron and Reason, 2001: 184)

Thus, in the major working phase of a creative cooperative inquiry, group members will continue to pay attention to nurturing each other and the group, while more attention is given to developing energetic cycles of inquiry. The task of the inquiry becomes figural, but it is nevertheless important to maintain attention for the continued health and authenticity of group interaction.

The creative peak

Randall and Southgate (1980) suggest that the peak is an important aspect of the creative group process, a moment when the 'living labour cycle' reaches a particular point of task accomplishment. In a cooperative inquiry group, which may be extended over weeks or months, there may be many 'mini-peaks' and if the group is successful there is likely to be an overall sense of accomplishment rather than a sharply defined moment in time. However, such moments do occur, particularly when members bring stories from the lives which show how the group is transforming their experience and practice.

Relaxing, appreciating and completing

Randall and Southgate (1980) call the third phase of the creative group 'relaxing', which in emotional terms means stepping back from the task, celebrating and appreciating achievements; in organizational terms, it means tying up loose ends; and in task terms, adding the final touches to group activities that move it to completion. Relaxing in this sense is an active, energetic engagement, different in quality from the feeling of 'getting out of the room and down to the pub', which so often characterizes our group experience.

We have also found that many groups express the emotional side of relaxing by choosing to give time to social activities – eating together, maybe going for walks – which provide a contrast to the intensity of inquiry and continue to build and deepen relationships:

> After this first [midwives inquiry group] meeting, having tea and coffee with cake or biscuits while we talked seemed such a normal thing to do. After all, people do this ordinarily at any social gathering where conversation is to be the primary activity. Food and fluid as a 'social lubricant' made sense for subsequent meetings as participants were in the middle of working days and their bodies needed nourishment to keep going. (Barrett and Taylor, 2002: 242)

The organizational side of relaxing often involves keeping the group's records in good order, transcribing tapes of meetings, keeping flip-chart records together, providing summary statements of what has happened in meetings, and so on. This may be undertaken by each person looking after their individual records, or by one or more people taking care of this for the group:

> I found that it took a considerable amount of energy and attention to hold the whole process together. Although we shared the tasks of arranging venues and of 'rounding

people up' for meetings, a good deal of the work came my way – from negotiating a budget to cover our costs for the year, to writing innumerable letters keeping members in touch with developments and making sure that those who could not get to particular meetings were kept in the picture. (Mead, 2002: 199–200)

The task requirement of the relaxing phase involves doing whatever is required to complete the inquiry, which often centres on how the learning from the project will be written up or otherwise reported to a wider audience. Sometimes groups attempt to write collaboratively, but more often one person or a small group does the actual writing in consultation with other group members (e.g., Maughan and Reason, 2001). It is important to agree the basis on which group members can use the material generated by the group, attending to issues of both confidentiality and ownership. A good rule of thumb is to agree that anyone may use the experience in any form they wish, so long as they include a clear statement about how the material has arisen (e.g., 'This is my account of the XYZ inquiry group; as far as I know I have represented the group's learning but I have not checked in detail with all members').

If the inquiry project has formed part of a higher degree or other formal publication that the initiator is undertaking, ensuring an authentic representation is particularly important:

Agnes Bryan and Cathy Aymer initiated and facilitated several inquiry groups of black professionals. Agnes subsequently worked with the transcripts of the groups as part of her PhD dissertation, finding immense difficulties in arriving at an authentic representation. She offered her findings to as many group members as she could, received challenging feedback and rewrote much of her text. She recorded and explored these difficulties of sense-making at length in her dissertation. (Bryan, 2000)

The relaxing phase of a creative group also involves winding down emotionally, saying farewells, and dealing with unfinished business. It is always tempting, particularly if the group has been successful, to avoid finishing properly, colluding to pretend that the group will meet again (this hints at a destructive dimension to the group's life, placing hopes in a future ideal state rather than dealing with the messy present reality). So time must be given for group members to have their final say as they separate from the group – it is often helpful to have a final 'round' at which each person can say what they have taken from the group, and leave behind any resentments or unfinished business.

By way of comment

We have offered two ways of seeing the inquiry process: through the logic of the inquiry process, cycling through propositional, practical, experiential and presentation knowing; and through the dynamics of the creative group cycle of nurturing, energizing, peak and relaxing. Please don't try to map these two descriptions onto each other in simple ways, but rather allow the two descriptions to interact and illuminate different aspects of the overall process. In the early life of the group, when the interpersonal emphasis will be on nurturing, the group will most likely engage with the inquiry cycle in mechanical and tentative ways. As the group matures, it will be able to engage in inquiry more energetically and robustly, adapting it to members' own needs and circumstances. There is always a complex interplay between the logic of inquiry and the process of the human group, as is described in many of the accounts of cooperative inquiry (for a collection of these, see Reason, 2002).

OUTCOMES

If, as we argued at the beginning of this chapter, action research places a primacy on practical knowing – on localized, pragmatic, constructed, practical knowings – what is the 'outcome' in terms of a research product? Are 'research reports' (in whatever form) illegitimate, misguided, epistemologically in error? Clearly not, or the accounts of cooperative inquiry processes referred to in this chapter would never have been written. But the outcome of an inquiry is far more than can be written.

The practical knowing which is the outcome of a cooperative inquiry is part of the life experience and practice of those who participated: individual experience will be unique and reflect shared experience. The inquiry will continue to live (if it is successful), and the knowledge will be passed along, in the continuing practice of participants as informed by the inquiry experience: doctors practise differently and it affects their patients, colleagues and students; black women discover more about how to thrive, and it changes how they are as professionals and as mothers; police professionals see how leadership is a practice of continued learning with others; young women are empowered to speak from their experience, and so on.

So the first thing to remember about all forms of representation is not to confuse the map with the territory. The knowing (the territory) is in the experience and in the practice, and what we write or say about it is a *re-presentation*. Sometimes action research is seen – wrongly in our view – as primarily a means to develop rich qualitative data that can be put through the processes of grounded theory or some other form of sense-making; but in action research the sense-making is in the process of the inquiry, in the cycles of action and reflection, in the dialogue of the inquiry group.

Nevertheless, we may want to write. We may want to write for ourselves, for first-person inquiry, to keep records, to help make sense, to review or to deepen experience. Inquiry group members keep journals, dream diaries, write stories, draw pictures, and engage in all kinds of representation as part of their inquiry. We may want to write 'for us', for the inquiry group and for the community that it represents, to pull together ideas, create frameworks of understanding, and communicate what it is we think we have discovered. We may want to write for an outside audience to inform, to influence, to raise questions, to entertain. In these writing projects it is important to be clear about both authorship and audience. Rather than write in the 'voice from nowhere' (Clifford and Marcus, 1986), reports from inquiry groups are clearly authored by members and directed to a particular purpose.

THINKING ABOUT USING COOPERATIVE INQUIRY FOR YOUR DISSERTATION?

Cooperative inquiry is an exciting method that should provide you with a rewarding dissertation experience, in part because both you and 'your' participants are engaged with the process. However, the difference between you and the other members of the group is that their engagement in the inquiry isn't tied into meeting institutional requirements for a dissertation, whereas yours will be. So it's useful to think through how you can both engage in inquiry in a deep way that is informed by the principles of cooperative inquiry (participatory, flexible, process oriented, employing cycles of action and reflection to facilitate flourishing and change) *and* write an excellent dissertation. Here is one way in which you might do this.

Start with a broad issue that you know/think a small group of relatively homogeneous people would be interested in meeting with you and each other on at least three occasions to discuss, reflect and develop ideas about.

Advertise or invite them through personal networks to meet with you and/or each other to learn about the inquiry process and if they want to participate in your study. Discuss what your and their time boundaries are to the inquiry. You will need to discuss with your supervisor what will be considered appropriate 'data collection' time for your institution, but what has worked for Sarah's students is a group size of 3–6 people who meet for an agreed period of time between 3–6 sessions, when a session lasts approximately an hour. Typically, if the participants/co-inquirers are students, this means that they will meet together once a week during term time for the agreed number of sessions. It doesn't sound like much, but some people will find that a lot to commit to and there will be at least one session that some people can't make and will need to be rescheduled, so build extra time into your planning.

Once you have volunteers and an agreed structure for the inquiry in terms of time, then you will need to meet your institutional ethical requirements, including consent forms and participant information sheets. Your challenge will be managing this administration well, while also allowing participants to feel energized and enthusiastic about the project. You may want to consider, for example, doing the paperwork before your first meeting, and then verbally reminding participants of what they have consented to and their rights (for example, to stop participating at any time without giving a reason).

While you are setting up the inquiry, discuss with your participants and your supervisor some potential content for the inquiry sessions. Then plan the first one in detail with the aim of providing a safe container for participants to explore their propositional knowledge about the issue and develop a sense of nurturing and trust in the group. Try to include an energizing activity so that the experience is enjoyable and they want to come back. Conclude with a summary activity that allows the participants to share a sense of where they are and what action they might want to explore over the week. Meet with your supervisor after each session and talk through the issues raised and also the energy in the room (did people seem enthusiastic, anxious, etc.? What do you need to do to help them feel supported enough to explore this issue further?). Consider your own emotional responses in the meeting and how these might either enable or limit you in your facilitation. Cooperative inquiry is an emotional business – as a facilitator you need to provide a safe container from which the group can do good work. This will involve emotional work and it's important to talk through your emotional responses with the group. Often cooperative inquiry facilitators have a mentor with whom they can discuss their experiences and feelings, so use your supervisor as your mentor.

After your first session, plan the subsequent sessions in response to the discussions you have with your supervisor and any other lead from your participants, so that you have something to suggest if they turn to you. But hold this plan lightly – it's there for when your participants look to you for direction. Often inquiry members enjoy someone else making the effort to structure a session, but try to create opportunities for your participants to take the lead so that it is a participatory inquiry, and don't push an activity if people don't seem to want to engage with it.

With a four-week inquiry, week one is focused on setting up and week four on drawing discussions together and finding a way to close the inquiry. Between that you have two sessions to develop reflection on the issue. That's not a lot of time, but it is enough to see some changes. Typically, participants highlight various issues in the earlier sessions which they return to in later ones, perhaps thinking about them differently or more deeply; this allows the inquiry to develop a more focused approach to the issue at hand. Group members may also outline actions for change either during the inquiry or afterwards. For example, a student of Sarah's ran a group with older women about their issues around beauty. One thing that emerged was that the group members, who were already friends, realized that they ignored each other's compliments, but that these compliments were spoken genuinely. The group resolved that after the inquiry they would not dismiss a friend's positive comments, but instead would choose to enjoy them.

There is a potential tension between your role as an inquiry group member facilitating the participants in developing a focused inquiry, and you as a student needing to complete a project that can be written up as a dissertation. Cooperative inquiry in its fullest sense is cooperative: everyone is involved in the sense-making and that includes activities and outputs from the inquiry. Torre et al. (2001), for example, wrote up a participatory project located in a prison that involved training inmates in research methods so that a community of researchers was formed within the inquiry. All were authors of their publication. However, it might be that the outputs from your work move down the participatory continuum, with you applying a form of qualitative analysis on the audio recordings of the meetings in a less collaborative way to meet the requirements of your dissertation.

If you have participants' permission to audiorecord the meetings (always with the possibility of turning the recorder off), then a relatively straightforward approach is to transcribe these recordings, which gives you a data set. You will also need to formulate a research question, which you can answer using this data set and with an appropriate form of analysis. This question may not be the same question that you started with, or expected to end with, or which your participants are inquiring into, and it might be driven by your own methodological and theoretical interests as much as the content of the data set.

For example, if your participants started their inquiry asking 'How do older women make sense of beauty issues in their lives?' and developed this into 'How do older women negotiate pleasure in their appearance?', in the process they will have discussed their meanings of beauty and age at great length. A student interested in taking a social constructionist approach might then consider analysing this data using Foucauldian discourse analysis or social constructionist-informed thematic analysis to explore constructions of age and beauty, whereas a student more interested in experiential understanding might employ a phenomenologically informed thematic analysis with the question 'How do older women experience their feminine identity?', and thematically explore how this experience is tied up within understandings of age and beauty.

This tactic, of applying a qualitative method of analysis to the recordings of your inquiry sessions, has the potential to pull you back into the observer/subject dichotomy of research that participatory approaches resist. In effect, you could take the data and run. To avoid this, work with your participants on the inquiry so that they can be as engaged with the analysis and outputs as they want to be. Bring the transcriptions to the meetings, perhaps leaving longer gaps between meetings so that you have time to transcribe and share the transcriptions. If your inquiry group is interested in exploring their transcriptions with you, look at developing an analysis collaboratively. It can be part of an action–reflection cycle. If your group is less interested in applying qualitative techniques, then a distinction between shared sense-making and applying qualitative techniques to that sense-making may emerge in your study. In effect, following this procedure means that your dissertation becomes one inquiry among many going on in the group and the process is experienced as participatory at the level that people want to engage.

This is not the only way that cooperative inquiry can be produced as a dissertation, but as long as you have permission from the group to explore their talk in the way you envisage, then this approach allows a cooperative inquiry to meet the needs of a dissertation in a relatively straightforward way. There are other ways (see Chowns' example of participatory video research at the end of this chapter), but at this stage most students will find enough challenges in helping to facilitate a dynamic and fully immersed inquiry. The benefits of doing an 'academic inquiry' within the inquiry are also evident when writing up, as students can follow the normative format for the chosen method of analysis (e.g., discourse analysis), although the method might be longer and with named quality criteria specific to cooperative inquiry also included (e.g., on group processes).

To increase your confidence that you are doing a good cooperative inquiry, focus on your process. In particular, consider the following:

- Group processes: take care of the process and the outcome will take care of itself.
- Extended epistemology: try to focus on experiential knowledge. Cycling between experiential and presentational knowledge for as long as possible will prevent shifting too quickly to propositional knowledge and reproducing frameworks with which you are already familiar.

- Cycles of action and reflection: structure your design to include cycles of action and reflection so that your group can experiment with the ideas they are developing, and review and reflect on how valuable they are in changing a system or helping them to understand it differently.
- Build in consultation time: share your analysis ideas with your participants/co-inquirers so that they may contribute, concur or have the fact that they disagree with your analysis recorded in your thesis.

Top tip: given that your dissertation markers may be unfamiliar with cooperative inquiry, make it easier for them to know how to assess your report by stating in your method section the quality criteria by which your cooperative inquiry should be judged.

And note that while many of the examples we offer in this chapter come from a series of projects that Sarah has supervised on women's experience of appearance issues, cooperative inquiry can be used for a range of projects, including those in educational, health, organizational and social psychology. For example, Sarah supervised a cooperative inquiry project on the experiences of mature students at university. A similar inquiry could be done by students in organizations where they have done a work placement or in their own university, if you can identify a group of people who would like to inquire into their work practices. This could include how to be more environmentally sustainable or how to work creatively within organizational constraints.

CONCLUSION

Cooperative inquiry offers a radical, empowering approach to research that can move flexibly in the direction that most suits the participants. It has the potential to contribute to a range of questions in which psychology students may be interested, and offers exciting opportunities for new and established psychology researchers.

Cooperative inquiry provides a different way of thinking about and doing research, focusing on working with people collaboratively to learn and enhance lives – both the lives of those involved in the inquiry and, in some cases, the lives of those affected by the institutions to which the co-inquirers belong (see, for example, the legacy of Piran's (2001) cooperative inquiry with ballet school pupils that changed an institutional culture). As such, cooperative inquiry research is particularly timely, addressing as it does recent drives for research that impacts and benefits individuals or organizations outside academia (for UK examples, see the impact requirements for the Research Excellence Framework or those of the Economic and Social Research Council). Its spirit, though, is less on addressing current concerns of research review bodies and more on imagining into being new ways of engaging in and with the world in ways that allow people to flourish – a rationale that is behind many people's decisions to study psychology, but one that is often lost in the drive for systematic, validated knowledge. Cooperative inquiry offers students and researchers the possibility of doing quality research while not forgetting the values that brought them there in the first place.

BOX 8.3   THREE GOOD EXAMPLES OF COOPERATIVE INQUIRY

Dilemmas of femininity

Riley and Scharff (2013) participated in an inquiry with six other academics to explore their experience of contemporary gendered identities. The participants were all white women working in British universities, able-bodied and feminist-identified, but they differed in terms of sexuality, original nationalities, personal histories, understandings of feminism, levels of participation in beauty practices, and motherhood. The group met for eight all-day meetings over a six-month period. The meetings followed a similar pattern: a checking-in activity to get sense of what was being brought to the group; a review of any actions or reflections since the last meeting; reflection activities to develop experiential or presentational knowing on a topic that had emerged from previous meetings or which had been introduced in the warm-up activities of that day; and closing activities. The paper clearly describes its application of the cooperative inquiry method before applying a form of discourse analysis to the recordings of the meetings. Focusing on one theme that emerged in this talk, the paper explores a dilemma between the participants' feminist-informed critical understanding of beauty practices, such as wearing makeup, and their own participation in such beauty practices. The paper reports how the group explored this dilemma, considering their own pleasures in meeting culturally defined beauty norms while also feeling that somehow their feminist consciousness should mean that they were able to resist these. They also brainstormed strategies to resist or engage differently with this dilemma, providing interesting examples of change possibilities from both the successful and less successful solutions.

Fixed by gaze and space

This was a Master's in Research dissertation project led by Stephanie Stafford Smith and supervised by Sarah Riley (Stafford Smith, 2010). Its focus was on exploring body image development through a cooperative inquiry with 14- and 15-year-old girls, supporting them to ask critical and reflective questions about when and where they felt conscious of their bodies. It highlighted for both the participants and the researchers the social aspects of body image development. It is a good example of how to provide structure and support for critical thinking, while enabling participants to have a sense of being in a nurturing and energizing environment of which they had ownership. Friendship groups were recruited to facilitate a safe space for a three-meeting inquiry. A range of activities aimed at evoking memories of experiences were offered to allow experiential, presentational and propositional knowing, and themes that emerged in one meeting were developed in subsequent meetings. The focus of the meetings was to identify where participants felt self-conscious of their bodies and to develop strategies for dealing with these situations. Techniques included a 'learning pathways grid' (Rudolph et al., 2001) adapted for use with young people, which was further developed in a subsequent project (see Figure 8.2). Using the questions on the grid, participants were encouraged to reflect on and challenge their frameworks for making sense of an experience. In the process, they identified different ways of making sense of the experience and discussed ideas for how they might respond differently should it occur again. The grids were used as a solution-focused strategy to develop practical knowing, thus giving the inquiry sustainability.

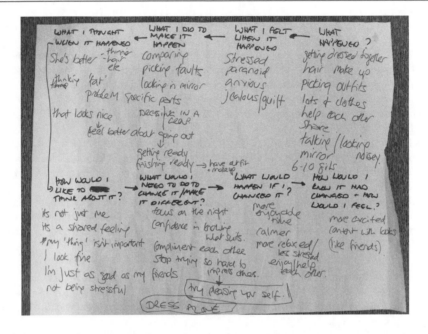

Figure 8.2   Recent example of a learning pathways grid adaptation for working with young people (designed by Stephanie Stafford Smith). The example is taken from a project led by Sarah Riley with young women aged 16–17, who were discussing the stress of getting ready for a night out with friends. Stages of this learning pathways grid include: What happened? What I felt when it happened? What I did to make it happen? What I thought when it happened? How would I like to think about it? What would I need to do to change it and make it different? What would happen if I changed it? How would I know it had changed and how would I feel?

No you don't know how we feel

Cooperative inquiry can also be combined with participatory video so that one output of the project is a video made by the group members that articulates an issue of importance to them. For example, Gillian Chowns, a social worker engaged in palliative care with children and families, convened a group of children, each of whom had a parent dying of cancer, as a cooperative inquiry group to research the experience of these children as they saw it. Chowns chose cooperative inquiry as an approach that offered a more ethical, respectful and democratic way of working with these children, a marginalized group in the world of palliative care. The group worked together to produce a video to help make findings more readily accessible, as well as being a contemporary, attractive medium for the young co-researchers (Chowns, 2006, 2008). For further discussion of participatory video, see: http://betterpvpractice.wordpress.com/the-webinars-2/, and Lunch and Lunch (2006).

FURTHER READING

Piran, N. (2001) 'Re-inhabiting the body from the inside out: girls transform their school environment', in D.L. Tolman and M. Brydon-Miller (eds), *From Subjects to Subjectivities: A Handbook of Interpretive and Participatory Methods*. New York: New York University Press, pp. 218–38.

Riley, S. and Scharff, C. (2013) 'Feminism vs femininity? Exploring feminist dilemmas through cooperative inquiry research', *Feminism & Psychology*, 23(2): 207–23. DOI: 10.1177/0959353512454615.

Torre, M.E., Fine, M., Boudin, K., Bowen, I., Clark, J., Hylton, D., Martinez, M., Roberts, M.R.A., Smart, P. and Upegui, D. (2001) 'A space for co-constructing counter stories under surveillance', *Under the Covers: Theorising the Politics of Counter Stories*. Special issue of *The International Journal of Critical Psychology*, 4: 149–66.

The above three readings represent research produced by psychologists using cooperative inquiry. They discuss aspects of the method and offer examples that show the possibilities of cooperative inquiry in terms of producing new knowledge and actions that change the lives of the participants.

Heron, J. (1996a) *Co-operative Inquiry: Research into the Human Condition*. London: Sage.

Heron, J. and Reason, P. (2001) 'The practice of co-operative inquiry: research "with" rather than "on" people', in P. Reason and H. Bradbury (eds), *Handbook of Action Research: Participative Inquiry and Practice*. London: Sage.

Reason, P. (2002) *The Practice of Co-operative Inquiry*. Special issue of *Systemic Practice and Action Research*, 15(3): 169–270.

The above three readings are work from originators and leading figures of cooperative inquiry, John Heron and Peter Reason. They detail the principles of the method and offer interesting examples of its application. Publications by Peter Reason can be found at: peterreason.eu

9 Focus Groups

Sue Wilkinson

Focus groups are a popular and widely used method in qualitative research across the social sciences. Although the method dates back some 75 years, it was relatively uncommon until a major resurgence of interest in the late 1970s. It has become popular in psychology only within the last 15 years or so, as qualitative research has burgeoned and become more generally accepted within the predominantly quantitative discipline.

Focus group methodology is, at first sight, deceptively simple. It is a way of collecting qualitative data, which – essentially – involves engaging a small number of people in an informal group discussion (or discussions), 'focused' on a particular topic or set of issues. Focus group projects in which I have been involved, for example, include young women exploring how to negotiate sexual refusals; young men talking about body modification practices, such as hair removal, piercing and tattooing; nurses evaluating different types of ward management; lesbian parents discussing their children being bullied at school; women comparing their experiences of vaginal examinations and cervical smears; and partners of women with breast cancer sharing information about 'coping' with life on a day-to-day basis. There is a common misconception that people will be inhibited in revealing intimate details in the context of a group discussion. In fact, focus groups are well suited to exploring 'sensitive' topics, and the group context can sometimes actually facilitate personal disclosures (Farquhar, with Das, 1999; Frith, 2000).

The discussion that takes place in a focus group is usually based around a series of questions (the focus group 'schedule'), and the researcher generally acts as a 'moderator' for the group: posing the questions, keeping the discussion flowing, and encouraging people to participate fully. Although focus groups are sometimes referred to as 'group interviews', the moderator does not ask questions of each focus group participant in turn, but rather facilitates group discussion, actively encouraging group members to interact *with each other*. This interaction between research participants is a key feature of focus group research, and the one which most clearly distinguishes it from one-to-one interviews (Kamberelis and Dimitriadis, 2013; Morgan, 1997). Compared with interviews, focus groups are much more 'naturalistic' (that is, closer to everyday conversation), in that they typically include a range of communicative processes – such as storytelling, joking, arguing, boasting, teasing, persuasion, challenge and disagreement. The dynamic quality of group interaction, as participants discuss, debate and (sometimes) disagree about key issues, is generally a striking feature of focus groups.

Typically, the focus group discussion is audio- or video-recorded (video-recording is far preferable as it allows for a more in-depth analysis of interactions between participants). The recorded data are transcribed and then analysed by conventional techniques for qualitative data – most commonly, content or thematic analysis. Focus groups are distinctive, then, primarily for the method and type of data *collection* (that is, informal group discussion), rather than for any particular method of data *analysis*.

HISTORY AND THEORETICAL BACKGROUND

The early use of focus groups can be traced back to the 1920s, when the psychologists Emory Bogardus and Walter Thurstone used them to develop survey instruments – although their 'invention' is more often credited to sociologist Robert Merton and his colleagues Patricia Kendall and Marjorie Fiske in the 1940s. Merton's research team developed 'focused group interviews' to elicit information from audiences about their responses to radio programmes. Since then they have also been known (variously) as 'group interviews' or 'focus group interviews', but the term 'focus groups' is the most commonly used and serves (if nothing else) to distinguish the approach from more psychodynamically oriented forms of group work.

Prior to the late 1970s, the main use of focus groups was as a market research tool, and most published studies were in the field of business and marketing – this is still an active area of focus group research today (e.g., Greenbaum, 2000). In the 1980s, health research-ers pioneered the use of focus groups in social action research, particularly in the fields of family planning and preventive health education. The method was then widely used to study sexual attitudes and behaviours, particularly in relation to HIV/AIDS, and it continues to be used extensively today in the areas of health education and health promotion as well as in health research more generally (Hennink, 2007; Wilkinson, 1998a). A *Web of Knowledge* search for articles published in 2013 or 2014 using focus group methodology revealed that more than 90 per cent of them were in the field of health.

From the 1990s on, the growing popularity of focus group research created a substantial literature on the method across a much wider range of disciplines, including education, com-munication and media studies, feminist research, sociology and psychology (see Morgan, 1996; Wilkinson, 1998b, for reviews).

Alongside new editions of 'classic' texts on focus group methodology (e.g., Krueger and Casey, 2009; Morgan, 1997; Stewart and Shamdasani, 2014), brand new texts continue to appear (e.g., Barbour, 2007; Hennink, 2014; Kamberelis and Dimitriadis, 2013).

One possible reason for the contemporary popularity of focus group research is the flexibility of the method. Focus groups can be used as a stand-alone qualitative method or combined with quantitative techniques as part of a multi-method project. They can be used within the psychology laboratory or out in the field, and to study the social world or to attempt to change it – that is, in action research projects (see Wilkinson, 1999, for a review; also Chapter 8 of this volume). At almost every stage of a focus group project there are methodological choices to be made. A good way to get a sense of this flexibility and variety is to look through one of the edited collections of focus group research (e.g., Barbour and Kitzinger, 1999; Morgan, 1993).

FORMULATING A RESEARCH QUESTION AND DESIGNING A STUDY

Given their flexibility, focus groups are obviously a multi-purpose method. However, they are not, as is sometimes assumed, 'a method for all seasons'. Like any other method, they have particular advantages and disadvantages, and are demonstrably more suited to some kinds of research questions than others. Focus groups are a good choice of method when the purpose of the research is to elicit people's own understandings, opinions or views; or when it seeks to explore how these are advanced, elaborated and negotiated in a social context. They are less appropriate if the purpose of the research is to categorize or compare types of individual and the views they hold, or to measure attitudes, opinions or beliefs (although they are sometimes used in this way).

Once you have decided that focus groups are an appropriate way to address your research question (more about this below), here are some of the main considerations in designing an effective focus group study.

First, you will need to decide on the broad parameters of your project – that is, the overall timescale; how many focus groups you will run; what kind of focus groups they will be; the number and types of participant you will have (and how you will recruit them); and how you will record, transcribe and analyse your data. These parameters need to be set before you can address the more detailed practical issues in setting up the study itself. In almost all cases, the design of the research is likely to be a compromise between what would be ideal and what is actually feasible, given the practical constraints of time, resources and your own expertise and energy.

A focus group project can involve a single group of participants meeting on a single occasion, or it can involve many groups, with single or repeated meetings. Participants need not even be physically co-present: a recent development is the use of online focus groups (Fox, Morris and Rumsey, 2007; Stewart and Williams, 2005). It can involve as few as two or as many as a dozen or so participants (the norm is between four and eight). These participants may be pre-existing groups of people (such as members of families, clubs or work teams), or they may be brought together specifically for the research, as representative of a particular population, or simply on the basis of shared characteristics or experiences (for example, middle-aged men, sales assistants, and sufferers from premenstrual tension).

In addition to (or instead of) a set of questions, the moderator may present group members with particular stimulus materials (such as video clips and advertisements); and, in addition to (or instead of) discussing particular questions, they may be asked to engage in a specified activity (such as a card-sorting task or a rating exercise). Kitzinger (1990) provides examples of a range of such activities in the context of researching AIDS media messages. The moderator may be relatively directive or relatively non-directive. Proceedings may be audiotaped or videotaped.

Data transcription may be more or less detailed, ranging from simple orthographic transcription, which preserves just the words spoken, to the more complex form of transcription favoured by conversation analysts (see Chapter 6), which also preserves a range of linguistic and paralinguistic features, such as false starts, self-corrections, overlapping speech, pauses, volume and intonation. If you have video-recordings, you can also transcribe gaze, gesture and other body behavioural features of the interaction (if you are interested in these).

Data analysis may be by hand (as in cutting and pasting sections of transcript) or computer assisted (using programs such as NUD*IST or The Ethnograph). A wide variety of different types of data analysis may be undertaken, including content, thematic, phenomenological, narrative, biographical, ethnographic, discursive or conversation analysis (some of which are discussed in more detail in other chapters of this book).

The type of analysis used depends upon the theoretical framework of the researcher rather than upon any particular feature(s) of focus group data. One particular strength of focus group research is that it is not tied to a specific theoretical framework: the method can be used either within an 'essentialist' or within a 'social constructionist' framework.

Focus group research conducted within an essentialist framework, like most psychological research, rests on the assumption that individuals have their own personal ideas, opinions and understandings, and that the task of the researcher is to access or elicit these 'cognitions'. Within this framework, the particular advantage of focus groups is the more comprehensive elicitation of individuals' ideas, opinions and understandings than is possible in one-to-one interviews (that is, more comprehensive in the sense that co-participants are likely to trigger memories, stimulate debate, facilitate disclosure and generally encourage the production of elaborated accounts).

Focus group research conducted within a social constructionist framework does *not* assume pre-existing cognitions located inside people's heads, but rather presupposes that sense-making is produced collaboratively – in the course of social interactions between people. Within this framework, the particular advantage of focus groups is the opportunity they offer for the researcher to observe how people engage in the process of collaborative sense-making: how views are constructed, expressed, defended and (sometimes) modified within the context of discussion and debate with others.

The theoretical framework of the research will influence the kind of data analysis undertaken. Essentialist research is likely to utilize content or thematic analysis, while social constructionist research is more likely to use ethnographic, discursive or conversation analysis.

Focus group data are voluminous, relatively unstructured, and do not readily lend themselves to summary analysis. While such data can be subjected to some limited quantification (as in some forms of content analysis – see below), they are best reported in ways which preserve (at least some of) the participants' own words – for example, by using illustrative quotations. Ideally, too, there should be some analysis of group interactions (although, sadly, this is all too rare in the published literature: see Wilkinson, 2006, for some examples).

Focus groups are unlikely to be the method of choice when statistical data and generalizable findings are required: samples are usually small and unrepresentative, and it is difficult to make a good theoretical case for aggregating data across a number of diverse groups or for making direct comparisons between groups (although, again, this is sometimes done).

There are also practical advantages and disadvantages to the use of focus groups. They have been seen as a way of collecting a large volume of data relatively quickly and cheaply. However, it can be difficult to recruit and bring together appropriate participants; moderating a group effectively is a skilled technique, which (ideally) requires training and practice; and data transcription and analysis (of whatever kind) is an extremely painstaking and time-consuming process, which requires a range of data-handling and interpretative skills.

The focus group literature includes a substantial number of 'handbooks' that offer a wealth of general information and advice about the process of doing focus group research, as well as a consideration of issues specific to particular types of focus group. The most useful of these guides for the psychologist are by Bloor et al. (2001), Fern (2001), Krueger and Casey (2009), Morgan (1997), Stewart and Shamdasani (2014) and Vaughn et al. (1996); the most comprehensive is by Morgan and Krueger (1998). Here, I draw both on the advice offered by these handbooks and on my own experience of focus group research, to review the key stages of a focus group project and to suggest the key practical considerations at each stage.

In particular, I illustrate each stage of a focus group project with examples from my research on women's experiences of breast cancer (Wilkinson, 1998a, 1998b, 2000a, 2000b, 2006, 2007, 2011). In this project, a total of 77 women took part in 13 focus groups, each lasting 1–3 hours. Participants were recruited through a symptomatic breast clinic at a general hospital in the north of England. Most were working-class, middle-aged or older, and within five years of diagnosis. The focus groups were held in a university setting, and each woman attended only one group on a single occasion. Discussion ranged across the women's feelings on diagnosis, their relationships, their experiences of treatment, and the changes that cancer had created in their lives. Data were audiotaped and transcribed orthographically in the first instance, and later re-transcribed in more detail and analysed by a variety of techniques (see Wilkinson, 2000b, for a comparison of three methods of analysis of one of the focus groups).

Ethical issues

Focus group research, like any other psychological research, must be conducted in accordance with the ethical guidelines of the relevant professional body (in the UK, the British Psychological Society). Broadly speaking, you need to obtain the necessary permissions and ethical clearances from the institution where you are based (such as a university research ethics committee), and from the institution where you will collect your data (such as a National Health Service research ethics committee), as well as from any key 'gatekeepers' within it (such as consultant or service manager). You must also obtain your participants' informed consent to take part. You are responsible for protecting their confidentiality, and you should take all reasonable steps to ensure that they will not be subjected to any stress or anxiety beyond and above what they might reasonably experience in their everyday lives.

Part of the informed consent procedure is ensuring that your participants know, and have agreed to, the particular use(s) you intend to make of the data. This may range from simply using short quotes from transcripts in a report or publication, through putting supporting audio or video clips on a website, to placing entire audio- or video-recordings in an open access archive. They should have the opportunity to withhold consent from any or all of such uses, and also to withdraw consent at a later date.

Confidentiality is a particular issue within focus groups because of the number of participants, and 'ground rules' must be set to ensure that personal details and potentially sensitive material are not discussed outside the context of the group (that is, participants should be requested to respect and preserve the confidentiality of others). There are also some ethical issues specific to the interactional nature of focus group research. For example, very occasionally a participant may be visibly worried or distressed by the experiences or opinions being aired; an argument may 'turn nasty'; or several focus group members may collude to silence or intimidate a particular individual. It is important to handle such a situation immediately, within the group (this may include, in the last resort, terminating the session). It may also be necessary to address it further with the individual(s) involved once the group has finished. In practice, though, focus group research is usually an interesting and often enjoyable experience for all concerned, and such 'difficult situations' rarely occur. Finally, as with any research, it is a good idea to have contact details available for relevant counselling services, helplines, self-help groups and other sources of information, in case they are needed or requested following the group.

COLLECTING DATA

For any focus group to provide the best possible data (and to be a rewarding experience for the participants), two things – at least – are necessary: an effective moderator and meticulous preparation. Preparation for data collection includes preparing and piloting the materials you intend to use, recruiting participants, choosing the venue, and preparing for the session itself. After the focus group you will also need to do some data management and transcription before embarking on analysis.

The focus group moderator

Ideally, the moderator should have some basic interviewing skills, some knowledge of group dynamics, and some experience of running group discussions. Although some of the skills involved in moderating a focus group are similar to those involved in one-to-one interviews (for example, establishing rapport, effective use of prompts and probes, and sensitivity to non-verbal cues), the number of research participants involved in a focus group requires more in terms of active 'people management'. The shy participant must be encouraged to speak, the talkative one discouraged at times, and instances of discomfort and/or disagreement must be handled with care. The handbooks provide substantial detail on the principles of 'people management', but they are no substitute for the experience of moderating a focus group in practice. The most common mistakes of novice and/or nervous moderators are a failure to listen (and to follow up appropriately), an inability to tolerate silence, talking too much and sequential questioning.

You should not embark on a focus group project without some kind of practice run or, preferably, a full-scale pilot study. Proper preparation for, and efficient planning of, the focus group session itself is just as essential as moderator skills for obtaining high-quality data. A well-run focus group session might *look* effortless, but it almost certainly is not: a surprising amount of preparatory work is needed before, during and after the session itself.

Preparing and piloting materials

You will need (at least) a focus group schedule, perhaps also written or pictorial materials, or audio or video materials. In devising a schedule, make sure that it is likely to engage the participants, that it uses appropriate vocabulary, that the questions flow logically, that it provides the opportunity for a variety of viewpoints to be expressed, and that it allows participants to raise points which may not have occurred to the researcher. Box 9.1 shows the schedule used in my breast cancer project.

BOX 9.1   SAMPLE FOCUS GROUP SCHEDULE: WOMEN'S EXPERIENCE OF BREAST CANCER

Introduction (recap on purpose of project, procedure, ground rules)

Questions (used in all groups)

1. How did you feel when you first became aware of a breast problem?

2. How did you feel when you were first told it was breast cancer?

3. How did people around you react to knowing you had breast cancer? (Partner/family/friends/others)

4. What kind of support did you need?

   - When you were first aware of a problem?

   - When you knew for sure it was cancer?

(Continued)

(Continued)

5. What kind of support did your partner/family/others close to you need?

   • When you were first aware of a problem?

   • When you knew for sure it was cancer?

6. What do you think caused your breast cancer?

7. What kind of effect has having breast cancer had on your life?

   • Including your general outlook on life?

   • On you personally?

   • On those around you?

Supplementary questions (used in some groups, when time)

8. What is the worst thing about having breast cancer?

9. Has anything good come out of having breast cancer?

   • What?

10. Have you been concerned about your appearance?

    • In what way?

    • Those around you? In what way?

11. Is there anything else you would like to say about your experience of breast cancer?

    • Or about this research project?

Conclusion (summary, thanks and debriefing)

Try out all the materials you intend to use – to ensure they are intelligible, legible, visible and the right length. If you are intending to use audio or video materials, make sure that the appropriate sound systems/projectors are readily available and that you know how to operate them. Have back-ups available in case of equipment failure. Write out your introduction to the session (include a recap on the project, the procedure to be followed and the 'ground rules' for the focus group) and your closing comments (include a summary of the session, any necessary debriefing and a reiteration of thanks). (See also the procedural points covered in 'the session itself' below.)

Recruiting participants

This is much harder than the novice focus group researcher ever imagines. Make sure that potential participants know what is involved in the focus group procedure – this is part of giving informed consent. Consider whether you will pay them (or offer other incentives; for example, simple refreshments are almost always appropriate) and/or reimburse travel expenses. Always over-recruit by about 50 per cent (that is, recruit nine participants for a six-person group). However much enthusiasm/commitment participants express, some of them always fail to turn up on the day for one reason or another. Make sure they have clear directions for finding the venue and (particularly if you recruit some time in advance of the session) issue several reminders, including – most crucially – a telephone call the day before the focus group meets.

Choosing the venue

Sometimes – particularly in action research projects – there is no choice of venue: you have to conduct the focus group on the group's own 'territory' (that is, wherever the participants usually meet, or wherever they are prepared to meet you), which may not be an ideal research environment. Where there is a choice, however, the main consideration is balancing participant comfort and a good recording environment. A few universities now have purpose-built 'focus group suites' (more often in the business school than the psychology department), and most psychology departments have a laboratory with a one-way mirror – this might be worth considering, particularly if observation/video-recording is part of the project. Most important is a relatively comfortable, quiet room where you will not be disturbed or under time pressure to finish. Participants should be seated in a circle, either in easy chairs or around a table (your choice may depend on what participants will be asked to do, but note the different 'feel' of these two options). Easy access to lavatories and to a telephone is essential.

Preparing for the session itself

There are two aspects to this: thinking through the logistics of the day and preparing supplementary materials. It is ideal to have an assistant, especially for larger focus groups. Whether or not this is possible, think through how you will handle arrivals and departures (including late arrivals and early departures), refreshments, dealing with unforeseen queries or problems, and taking notes and/or operating the recording equipment while moderating the group. Remember that Murphy's Law (if anything can go wrong, it will) holds as much for focus groups as other types of research, but it seems to apply particularly to recording equipment! This should be checked and double-checked before every group. Highly specialized recording equipment is unnecessary: a small digital recorder or MP3 player with a recording facility is fine. However, if possible, use an omnidirectional microphone in order to produce a recording clear enough for transcription. To minimize the risk of recording failure, it is also desirable to use *two* sets of recording equipment, if possible – this is much easier to manage if you have an assistant.

In terms of supplementary materials, you will need some or all of the following:

- refreshments: water at least, preferably tea/coffee and biscuits (*not* alcohol); depending on time of day and length of session, possibly simple food (such as sandwiches and pizza), but nothing crunchy (this obscures the recording)
- writing materials (paper and pens) – for yourself and the participants
- informed consent forms; expenses claim forms
- a box of paper tissues
- name badges or cards (and marker pens to complete them)
- recording equipment (including spare batteries and/or memory cards, as appropriate).

Set up the room well in advance, if possible, and check the recording equipment (again) just before using it.

The focus group session itself

You need to allow 1–3 hours (depending on the topics/activities to be included and the availability/commitment of the participants). The beginning and end of the focus group session entail specific practical considerations.

The following activities are needed at the *beginning* of the session (not necessarily in this exact order):

- offering thanks, a welcome and introductions
- attending to participants' comfort (refreshments, toilets, any special needs)
- signing consent forms (if not done at recruitment), including permission to record, and for various uses of the data
- reiterating issues of anonymity/confidentiality
- completing name badges
- recapping purpose of study
- outlining procedure (including confirming finishing time)
- setting ground rules for running the group
- providing an opportunity to ask questions.

You then move into the discussion proper. You should aim to create an atmosphere in which participants can relax, talk freely and enjoy themselves. Although it may take a while to 'warm up', once it gets going, a good focus group discussion will appear almost to run itself. The discussion will 'flow' well – and it will seem to move seamlessly through the schedule – sometimes even without the moderator needing to ask the questions. Such apparent 'effortlessness' rests substantially upon good preparation and effective moderating skills (as well as a measure of good luck). Although your main energies should be directed towards effective moderation of the group discussion, it is also desirable to keep notes of the main discussion points and, if recording audio only, of any events which may not be captured on the recording – for example, the occasion when one of my focus group participants reached inside her bra, pulled out her prosthesis (artificial breast) and passed it around the table. (It's hard to think of a better example of why you really need video!) An assistant will be able to take more comprehensive notes, which could include a systematic list of the sequence of speakers (this helps in transcription, especially with larger groups). It is also worth noting that a good focus group often overruns: always allow participants to leave at the agreed time, even if you have not finished.

The following activities are needed at the *end* of the focus group (again, not necessarily in this exact order):

- reiterating thanks
- reiterating confidentiality
- giving a further opportunity for questions
- providing further information or possible sources of information (as appropriate)
- debriefing (as appropriate), including on an individual basis as necessary
- checking that participants have had a good experience (possibly formal evaluation)
- completing expenses claim forms (and making payment arrangements)
- offering appropriate farewells and/or information about any follow-ups.

Data management and transcription

The next step is to make back-up copies of all notes and data files (which should be clearly labelled with the date, time, length and nature of the session). Keep the copies in a separate place from the originals. If you are transcribing your own data (as is usually the case), try to do this as soon as possible after the session, while it is still fresh in your mind. Specialized transcription/editing software is not necessary, although many such programs are available (Audacity and Amadeus are popular and relatively simple to use).

Transcription is really the first stage of data analysis, and a careful, detailed transcription will facilitate the next steps, although the level of detail preserved in the transcription will depend on your research question and the type of data analysis you plan to use (see earlier discussion). Note that whenever you present extracts from your data, you should append a transcription key listing the precise transcription conventions you have used. Box 9.2 shows a typical (simple) transcription key covering the data extracts presented in this chapter; a more elaborate transcription key, of the type used in conversation analytic studies, can be found in Atkinson and Heritage (1984) (see also Chapter 6).

BOX 9.2   SAMPLE TRANSCRIPTION KEY

Transcription conventions used for data extracts in this chapter:

- underlining – emphasis
- hyphen at end of word – word cut off abruptly
- ellipsis (. . .) – speaker trails off
- round brackets – used when transcriber is uncertain what was said but is able to make a reasonable guess, for example (about)
- square brackets – enclose comments made by transcriber. Such comments include inability to make out what was said [indistinct] and sounds that are difficult to transcribe, such as [tch] and [stutters], as well as interactional features of note, such as [laughs], [pause], [cuts in], [turns to Edith].

Whatever type of transcription you undertake, the transcription process is likely to take much longer than you might expect. A skilled transcriber typically needs 3–4 hours' transcription time per hour of discussion to produce a simple orthographic transcript; a novice transcriber is likely to take two or three times as long. Transcription suitable for conversation analysis typically takes many hours per *minute* of discussion. (For this reason, whole discussions are rarely transcribed in this way. Rather, extracts relevant to the particular phenomenon under study are selected for transcription.) Transcription of gaze, gesture and body behavioural features is still more specialized, and takes still longer.

Focus group data are harder to transcribe than one-to-one interview data because of overlapping talk (although the degree of accuracy with which you need to transcribe this will depend on whether it is a feature of your planned analysis). Make back-up copies of your transcripts, too, and store them separately from the originals, all appropriately labelled.

Transcripts should generally be anonymized to remove all names and other potentially identifying features (unless participants specifically wish to be identified). If you have obtained consent to use audio- or video-recordings, you need to consider whether/how to anonymize these. A simple 'beeping out' of a name may be enough, or you may need to pixellate faces (a variety of pixellating tools can be downloaded for free). More elaborate video anonymization tools, involving techniques such as animation, are also available.

ANALYSIS

You should have decided long before this stage how you will analyse your data in relation to your theoretical framework and your specific research question (see earlier for a range of possibilities). Here, I will give examples of two contrasting ways of analysing focus group data – content analysis and ethnographic[1] analysis – again, drawn from my breast cancer project.

Both of the analyses presented below are concerned with the possible 'causes' of breast cancer. The content analysis (conducted within an essentialist framework – see above) rests on the assumption that people have (relatively stable and enduring) beliefs or opinions about the causes of breast cancer, and that these can reliably be inferred from an analysis of what they say. Its aim, then, is to identify participants' beliefs or opinions about the causes of breast cancer. The ethnographic analysis (conducted within a social constructionist framework – see above) rests on the claim that people's ideas about the causes of breast cancer are produced collaboratively, in social interactions between people, and that these collaborative productions can be observed, as they actually happen, in the course of focus group interaction. Its aim, then, is to identify the ways in which people actively construct and negotiate ideas about the causes of breast cancer.

Content analysis

Content analysis is a commonly used approach to analysing qualitative data, including focus group data. It involves coding participants' open-ended talk into closed categories, which summarize and systematize the data. These categories may be derived either from the data themselves (perhaps using grounded theory – see Chapter 4; this is known as a 'bottom-up' approach) or from the prior theoretical framework of the researcher (this is known as a 'top-down' approach, and requires prior familiarity with the literature on the topic under investigation in order to derive the categories, as in the worked example below). The end point of the analysis may be simply to illustrate each category by means of representative quotations from the data, presented either in a table (see Box 9.3a); or written up as consecutive prose (e.g., Fish and Wilkinson, 2000a, 2000b). Box 9.3a provides an example of a content analysis based on the transcript of a breast cancer focus group with three participants. All talk in this focus group about the 'causes' of breast cancer has been categorized systematically. The categories (and sub-categories) are derived from Mildred Blaxter's (1983) classic study on women talking about the causes of disease, with the addition of an 'Other' category. Box 9.3a illustrates each category used by the participants with representative quotations from their talk.

The procedure for this analysis entailed making a list of the categories used by Blaxter (e.g., 'Infection', 'Heredity or familial tendencies', 'Agents in the environment', and so on) and then working systematically through the transcript looking for instances where the participants referred to a possible cause for breast cancer that fell into one of these categories. So, for example, when one of them said 'I mean there's no family history', this statement was placed in the 'Heredity or familial tendencies' category, and when another said 'I was once told that if you use them aluminium pans that cause cancer', this statement was placed in the 'Agents in the environment' category. (Statements not fitting into one of Blaxter's 11 categories were placed in the 'Other' category.) The results of this analysis are displayed in a table, in which all of the focus group talk relating to causes is arranged under 12 category headings, with the quotations displayed under each heading providing the evidence for the existence of that category in the data.

BOX 9.3A   CONTENT ANALYSIS –
PRESENTED QUALITATIVELY

Women's beliefs about the causes of breast cancer

1. *Infection*

   Not discussed

2. *Heredity or familial tendencies*

   - 'I mean there's no family history'

3. *Agents in the environment:*

   a) *'Poisons', working condition, climate* (see also Box 9.3b)

   - 'I was once told that if you use them aluminium pans that cause cancer'

   - 'Looking years and years ago, I mean, everybody used to [laughs] sit about sunning themselves on the beach and now all of a sudden you get cancer from sunshine'

   - 'I don't know (about) all the chemicals in what you're eating and things these days as well, and how cultivated and everything'

   b) *Drugs or the contraceptive pill*

   - 'I mean I did t-, you know, obviously I took the pill at a younger age'

4. *Secondary to other diseases*

   Not discussed

5. *Stress, strain and worry*

   Not discussed

6. *Caused by childbearing, the menopause*

   - 'Inverted nipples, they say that that is one thing that you could be wary of'

   - 'Until I came to the point of actually trying to breastfeed I didn't realize I had flattened nipples and one of them was nearly inverted or whatever, so I had a lot of trouble breastfeeding, and it, and I was several weeks with a breast pump trying to uhm get it right, so that he could suckle on my nipple, I did have that problem'

- 'Over the years, every, I couldn't say it happened monthly or anything like that, it would just start throbbing this [pause] leakage, nothing to put a dressing on or anything like that, but there it was, it was coming from somewhere and it were just kind of gently crust over'

- 'I mean, I don't know whether the age at which you have children makes a difference as well because I had my [pause] 8-year-old relatively late, I was an old mum'

- 'They say that if you've only had one that you're more likely to get it than if you have a big family'

7. *Secondary to trauma or to surgery*

- 'Sometimes I've heard that knocks can bring one on'

- 'I then remembered that I'd banged my breast with this, uhm [tch] you know these shopping bags with a wooden rod thing, those big trolley bags?'

- 'I always think that people go into hospital, even for an exploratory, it may be all wrong, but I do think, well the air gets to it, it seems to me that it's not long afterwards before they [pause] simply find that there's more to it than they thought, you know, and I often wonder if the air getting to your inside is- [pause] brings, brings on [pause] cancer in any form'

8. *Neglect, the constraints of poverty*

Not discussed

9. *Inherent susceptibility, individual and not hereditary*

Not discussed

10. *Behaviour, own responsibility*

- 'I was also told that if you eat tomatoes and plums at the same meal that-'

11. *Ageing, natural degeneration*

Not discussed

12. *Other*

- 'He told them nurses in his lectures that everybody has a cancer, and [pause] it's a case of whether it lays dormant'

- 'I don't think it could be one cause, can it? It must be multi, multifactorial'

BOX 9.3B   CONTENT ANALYSIS – PRESENTED QUANTITATIVELY

Women's beliefs about the causes of breast cancer

1. *Infection*: 0 instances

2. *Heredity or familial tendencies*: 2 instances

   family history (×2)

3. *Agents in the environment*:

   a) *'Poisons', working condition, climate: 3 instances*

   aluminium pans; exposure to sun; chemicals in food

   b) *Drugs or the contraceptive pill: 1 instance*

   taking the contraceptive pill

4. *Secondary to other diseases*: 0 instances

5. *Stress, strain and worry*: 0 instances

6. *Caused by childbearing, the menopause*: 22 instances

   not breastfeeding; late childbearing (×3); having only one child; being single/not having children; hormonal; trouble with breastfeeding – unspecified (×4); flattened nipples (×2); inverted nipples (×7); nipple discharge (×2)

7. *Secondary to trauma or to surgery*: 9 instances

   knocks (×4); unspecified injury; air getting inside body (×4)

8. *Neglect, the constraints of poverty*: 0 instances

9. *Inherent susceptibility, individual and not hereditary*: 0 instances

10. *Behaviour, own responsibility*: 1 instance

    mixing specific foods

11. *Ageing, natural degeneration*: 0 instances

12. *Other*: 5 instances

    'several things'; 'a lot'; 'multifactorial'; everybody has a 'dormant' cancer; 'anything' could wake a dormant cancer

One particular advantage of content analysis (for some researchers) is that it also allows for the conversion of qualitative data into a quantitative form. This is done by means of counting the number of responses falling within each category (that is, their frequency or 'popularity') and then summarizing the number (or percentage) of responses for each category, usually in tabular form. Box 9.3b illustrates this. It is based on the same data and the same categories as Box 9.3a, but the results of the content analysis are presented quantitatively, rather than qualitatively. Box 9.3b records the frequency with which 'causes' falling into each category is mentioned.

The procedure for this analysis was exactly the same as that described for the qualitative content analysis above, plus the addition of one extra step: that is, counting the number of instances of talk that fall into each category. The results of this analysis are displayed in a table, in which only the *number* of instances in each category – derived from the 'extra step' of counting them – is displayed. This gives the reader a quick way of examining the frequency with which each type of cause is mentioned. (It is easy to see, for example, that responses falling into the category 'Caused by childbearing, the menopause' are the most frequent.)

The main advantages of undertaking a content analysis of these data, then, are that it provides a useful summary of women's beliefs about the causes of breast cancer, and offers an overview of the range and diversity of their ideas. It also offers easy comparison with other studies undertaken within a similar framework. If the potential for quantification is taken up, content analysis also gives a sense of the relative significance women attach to different causes (if, as in Blaxter's (1983) analysis, frequency of mention is equated with perceived importance). The main disadvantages are that a great deal of detail is lost; it can be hard to select quotations which are both representative of the categories and compelling to the reader ('naturalistic' talk doesn't come in sound bites!); and, particularly in the quantified version, one loses a sense of individual participants and – especially – the interaction between participants, which is so distinctive in focus group data. (It may be possible to preserve this by doing a separate 'sweep' of the data for interactional phenomena and attempting to 'map' these onto the content analysis in some way.)

There is also a range of coding problems associated with content analysis. For example the analysis above categorizes, as equivalent, causes which the women say *do* apply to them (for example, 'I took the pill at a younger age') and those which they say *do not* (for example, 'there's no family history'). It also categorizes, as equivalent, statements which the women present as their own beliefs or opinions (for example, 'I always think...', 'It must be...') and those which they attribute to others (for example, 'I was once told...', 'He told them...', 'They say...'). Finally, it is unable to deal with inconsistencies in expressed beliefs or apparent changes of opinion during the course of the focus group because each mention of a cause is treated as an isolated occurrence, taken out of context. These apparent 'coding problems' are actually epistemological issues arising from the framework within which this type of analysis is undertaken. As such, they are key to what can (and cannot) be said about the data (see Wilkinson, 2000b, for a more extended discussion). The point will become clearer as we move to a second example of focus group analysis, again drawing on some of my breast cancer data.

Ethnographic analysis

The data extract on which the second analysis is based is shown in Box 9.4 (note that this is a simple orthographic transcription of a small part of a focus group). There are three participants in this focus group, in addition to myself as researcher/moderator. Doris and Fiona are both pub landladies (although Doris has recently retired). They arrived early for the session, met each other for the first time, and discovered their shared occupation while waiting for the other participants to arrive. During this pre-focus-group conversation, they developed a joint theory about the possible role of their work in causing their breast cancer. Specifically, Doris and Fiona co-constructed the explanation that 'pulling' (drawing beer from a cask by means of a handpump, which is quite a strenuous activity) was to blame. Immediately prior to the extract presented here, I asked the focus group participants if they had any idea about what might have caused their breast cancer.

Doris and Fiona answer my question by presenting their joint theory to the group; note that they simply continue as if everyone had been present at their earlier conversation, making no concession to Edith's later arrival – it is left to me, as group moderator, to 'fill Edith in' on what has gone before. Edith is, however, very quick to catch on (asking a clarificatory question – 'Is it at the side where...?' – which I, as researcher, would certainly not have thought to ask). Doris and Fiona respond to Edith's question by pooling their similar experiences: Fiona even completes Doris's sentence for her, in expounding their joint theory. Fiona then offers additional information: she has two friends who are also pub landladies, and *they too* have breast cancer on the same side as they pull beer. This strengthens their joint theory still further: with the evidence of *four* pub landladies all with breast cancer on the same side as they pull beer, who could doubt that 'pulling' is a contributory factor? However, Doris then offers an alternative or additional contributory factor for breast cancer in pub landladies: 'the atmosphere of the smoke in the pub'.

There are several possibilities open to Fiona at this point: she can *reject* this new information out of hand in favour of the 'pulling' theory (in which case she will need to defend 'pulling' as the stronger contender, perhaps offering more evidence to support 'pulling' or to refute the 'smoky atmosphere' theory); she can elaborate the 'pulling' theory to incorporate 'smoky atmosphere' as an *additional* possible cause; she can engage with the new information as offering a possible *alternative* theory (perhaps exploring the parameters and implications of a 'smoky atmosphere', or challenging Doris to provide examples or additional evidence of its effects); or she can simply accept 'smoky atmosphere' as a better explanation for breast cancer. In the event, her hesitant and qualified response ('Well I, I'm not, I don't know, I'm not so sure about that one') implies disagreement (or, at the very least, uncertainty).

Fiona's apparent disagreement leads Doris to marshal supporting evidence for the 'smoky atmosphere' theory, in the form of a recent television documentary featuring a celebrity with cancer. Fiona has seen the documentary too, and in her response to Doris, we see the possible beginning of a shift in her views (or at least a willingness to engage seriously with the 'smoky atmosphere' theory): she recognizes – and names (as 'passive smoking') – the phenomenon Doris has identified. Doris accepts this label and goes on to relate it to the case of the TV celebrity.

BOX 9.4   DATA EXTRACT FOR ETHNOGRAPHIC ANALYSIS

In the following data extract, two pub landladies (Doris and Fiona) consider the possible role of their profession in 'causing' their breast cancer (another focus group participant [Edith] and the researcher/moderator [SW] also contribute to the discussion).

Doris: Well, I uhm, like you

Edith: [Cuts in] It's not in the family

Doris: [Turns to Fiona] Like you I wondered if it was with <u>pulling</u>, you know

Fiona: Yeah

SW: [Turns to Edith] These two were talking about being pub landladies and whether that contributed

Edith: Well that, oh [indistinct]

Fiona: Yeah, you know, yeah

Edith: Is it at the side where . . .?

Doris: Mine's at the side where [indistinct]

Fiona: where you pulled

Doris: Yes

Fiona: and mine's the same side, and I've got two friends who are both pub landladies down south

Doris: And then

Fiona: and they're sisters and both of them have got breast cancer, both on the same side as they pull beer

Doris: And then there's the atmosphere of the smoke in the [stutters] pub

Fiona: Well I, I'm not, I don't know, I'm not so sure about that one

Doris: Well, I think I lean to that more in, what do they call him? The artist, Roy Castle

Fiona: Oh Roy Castle, yeah, with passive smoking

Doris: Mm hm, he said he got his through being in smoke, smoke-filled rooms

This ethnographic analysis illustrates the collaborative production and negotiation of ideas about the causes of breast cancer. In its focus on the processes of constructing notions of cause through ongoing social interaction, it is epistemologically very different from a content analytic approach that sees ideas about cause as internal 'cognitions'. It is also worth noting that, although ethnographic analysis has an affinity with narrative methods (see Chapter 5), from an ethnographic perspective, a narrated story – or other contribution to a discussion – is never just a stand-alone. Rather, it is a form of social action, produced for a specific purpose (such as to amuse, inform, illustrate or explain) within the particular interactional context of a particular focus group discussion.

The exact procedure for undertaking an ethnographic analysis like the one above is hard to specify. It depends upon the researcher having some familiarity with the approaches of conversation and discourse analysis (see Chapters 6 and 7), so that they can first 'spot' some phenomenon of interest, and then undertake a detailed examination of how this plays out in the interactions between participants as the focus group progresses. So the analysis presented here depends upon noticing that the participants are together exploring and developing a theory about a possible cause of breast cancer (at least in pub landladies). It then involves working through the interactions between participants, turn by turn, considering what occasioned each specific utterance (e.g., was it perhaps a confirmation of what had gone before, or perhaps a challenge to it?) and what each utterance contributes to the evolving discussion (e.g., does it perhaps offer further confirmation of the theory, or perhaps dismiss a challenge to it?). In this way, the researcher builds up a detailed picture of exactly how these particular people, in this particular context, develop their theory about one possible cause of breast cancer. The specific analysis may also enable the researcher to make some more general (and potentially testable) suggestions about the ways in which people develop, challenge or defend these kinds of theories.

The main advantages of undertaking an ethnographic analysis of focus group data such as these, then, are that it takes the fullest possible account of the social context within which statements about cause are made; it does not treat such statements as unitary, static or non-contingent; and it preserves both a sense of individual participants and – particularly – the details of their interaction, which here become a central analytic concern. If video (rather than audio) data are available, a broader analysis of the group dynamics within which particular conversations are located becomes a real possibility. The very different epistemological framework of ethnographic analysis also accounts for many of the 'coding problems' identified in relation to content analysis (for example, the inconsistency and variability of accounts) – see Wilkinson (2000b) for a more extended discussion. The main disadvantages of ethnographic analysis are that it does not easily permit either a summary overview of a large data set or a detailed focus on the lives of individuals outside the focus group context (for this, see Chapters 3 and 5 on phenomenological and narrative research). Only a very small sample of data can be analysed in detail in this way, and traditional concerns about representativeness, generalizability, reliability and validity (often levelled at qualitative research) may be difficult to counter (but see Chapter 12 for ways in which qualitative researchers have reconceptualized these traditional concerns).

WRITING UP

Writing up focus group research is not – in most respects – much different from writing up qualitative research more generally. Following an introduction to the topic area, including a review of key studies, the methods section of a good write-up of a focus group study will cover: design, ethics, participants, data collection materials and procedure, and method of data analysis. It will be followed by a results section reporting the key findings of the research, and then a discussion of these, related to the literature.

The format of the 'results' section will depend on the type of data analysis undertaken. The worked example above shows the kind of tables that may be produced in reporting the results of a content analysis (either qualitatively or quantitatively) and the kind of extract from a focus group transcript that may be used to support an ethnographic analysis. Examples of how to report a thematic analysis (of focus group data or of interview data) can also be seen in Chapter 10.

If you illustrate your findings using quotes from the focus group participants, the key thing to remember is that those quotes must fit the categories you propose (in a content analysis) or illustrate the themes you propose (in a thematic analysis). The quotes constitute the *evidence* to support your findings (your category system or your main themes).

It is also worth remembering that the *interaction* between participants is the hallmark of focus group research, and that, ideally, you should select quotes that reflect this, and – at least if doing an ethnographic project – analyse the interaction itself (as well as the content of individuals' talk).

CONCLUSION

I hope that the practical guide to focus group research presented above does not look too daunting. This kind of research does demand a great deal of planning and organization (and often also considerable development of analytic skills), but in my experience it is also immensely rewarding, both for the researcher and for the participants.

I also hope to have illustrated through the worked example from my breast cancer research that there is no single canonical – or even preferred – way of analysing focus group data. Rather, such data can be analysed in a number of (very different) ways, each of which has specific costs and benefits. The particular method of analysis chosen depends centrally upon your theoretical framework and the type of research question you hope to address.

Box 9.5 presents three further illustrative examples of focus group research in action.

NOTE

1 There are a number of different terms that could be used for this type of analysis, which draws on the approaches of discourse analysis/discursive psychology (see Chapter 7), conversation analysis (see Chapter 6), and the sociological field of ethnomethodology (e.g., Garfinkel, 2002). For clarity and consistency, I have chosen to follow Morgan (1988: 64) in using the term 'ethnographic' here.

BOX 9.5   THREE GOOD EXAMPLES OF FOCUS GROUP RESEARCH

Focusing on sex

These three examples illustrate the value of focus groups in exploring 'sensitive' topics and facilitating self-disclosure.

Sexual refusal

O'Byrne, Rapley and Hansen (2006) is an important contribution to the literature on so-called 'date rape'. It draws on two focus groups with young heterosexual male students to explore their understanding of sexual refusal. The authors demonstrate that these young men perfectly well understand young women's refusals to have sex with them, even when such refusals do not explicitly contain the word 'no', or when they are expressed non-verbally, through 'body language' alone. This is a good illustration of an 'ethnographic' analysis of focus group data, drawing on discursive psychology.

Alcohol and sexuality

Livingston et al. (2013) used 15 focus groups to explore young women's understandings of the relationships between alcohol use and heterosexual sexual behaviour. Participants recognized both advantages and risks of combining alcohol and sex: advantages included facilitating sexual interactions and excusing sexual behaviour; disadvantages included increased likelihood of sexual regret and coercion through impaired judgement. The paper concludes with a discussion of implications for education and prevention.

Harassment

A Canadian study (Welsh et al., 2006) is a good example of the use of focus groups in researching the views of socially excluded and often-hard-to-reach groups: here, among others, Filipina domestic workers and African-Canadian women. The focus groups provided a safe, supportive context for exploring definitions of harassment. The study revealed that, for these women, isolation due to lack of citizenship and racialized harassment are central factors in their harassment experience, which may or may not be experienced as sexual.

FURTHER READING

Wilkinson, S. (1998) 'Focus group methodology: a review', *International Journal of Social Research Methodology*, 1: 181–203.
Good brief introduction to the method and the range of ways in which it has been used in various disciplinary contexts.

Barbour, R. and Kitzinger, J. (eds) (1999) *Developing Focus Group Research: Politics, Theory and Practice*. London: Sage.
A very useful edited collection, with a wider range of examples than most.

Krueger, R.A. and Casey, M.A. (2009) *Focus Groups: A Practical Guide for Applied Research* (4th edn). Newbury Park, CA: Sage.
One of the best introductions to doing focus group research; very practical.

Hennink, M.M. (2014) *Focus Group Discussions.* New York: Oxford University Press.
Another useful, and up-to-date, introduction to doing focus group research.

Wilkinson, S. (2000) 'Women with breast cancer talking causes: comparing content, biographical and discursive analyses', *Feminism & Psychology*, 10: 431–60.
Useful for more examples of different types of data analysis, and discussion of their implications.

Wilkinson, S. (2006) 'Analysing interaction in focus groups', in P. Drew, G. Raymond and D. Weinberg (eds), *Talk and Interaction in Social Research Methods*. London: Sage, pp. 50–62.
Collects together some of the (few) examples of focus group research to analyse interaction, and offers a more sustained example of this.

10 Thematic Analysis

Victoria Clarke, Virginia Braun and Nikki Hayfield

This chapter provides an introduction to thematic analysis (TA). We highlight the unique features of TA, including its flexibility and its status as a technique that can be used within a wide variety of approaches to qualitative research. We then provide a detailed description of doing TA, using Virginia Braun and Victoria Clarke's six-phase approach to coding and theme development (Braun and Clarke, 2006), illustrated with worked examples from Nikki Hayfield's interview research on bisexual women's (visual) identities. This study has been reported in two papers – one focused on bisexual identities and marginalization (Hayfield, Clarke and Halliwell, 2014) and one focused on appearance (Hayfield et al., 2013) – and we use examples from both. We conclude with additional guidance on successfully completing a high-quality TA of qualitative data.

HISTORY AND THEORETICAL BACKGROUND

Since the term appeared about 40 years ago, 'thematic analysis' has had many different meanings. As well as referring to a method for analysing the concepts underpinning the production of scientific knowledge (Holton, 1973), and a quantitative measure of cognitive complexity (Winter and McClelland, 1978), the term has described a wide variety of methods for analysing qualitative data. It has often been used interchangeably with terms like 'content analysis' to name everything from methods that allow for the quantification of qualitative data (Woodrum, 1984), to more interpretative forms of analysis based on the identification of recurrent themes or patterns in data (Baxter, 1991; Dapkus, 1985). In addition, countless qualitative papers make reference to 'organising sections of the data into recurrent themes' (Kitzinger and Wilmott, 2002: 330) or note simply that 'themes *emerged* from the data' – often without any discussion of the precise analytic procedures followed or reference to methodological literature. Given this, there has been confusion about what TA is and whether it *is* a particular approach, and considerable variation in advice around how you go about doing it.

Thankfully, the situation has changed considerably in the last decade, and TA has become a very widely used and recognized method in psychology and the social and health sciences.

The most commonly used approach to TA – that outlined by Virginia and Victoria (Braun and Clarke, 2006, 2012, 2013) – provides an accessible, systematic and rigorous approach to coding and theme development (Howitt, 2010). This is the approach we focus on in this chapter. There are, however, two main approaches to TA that have been developed, and we will briefly outline the differences between these, as they are important.

Our approach can be described as a 'Big Q' approach to TA. Big Q refers to qualitative research conducted within a qualitative *paradigm* (Kidder and Fine, 1987a). Big Q approaches to qualitative research share in common a rejection of the possibility of discovering universal meaning, because meaning is understood as always being tied to the context in which it is produced. Big Q approaches also emphasize the active role of the researcher in the research process, and the importance of embracing researcher subjectivity, rather than viewing it as a 'problem' to be managed (Braun and Clarke, 2013). Our approach to TA is Big Q because we advocate the use of an organic approach to coding and theme development, one that is informed by the unique standpoint of the researcher, and that is fluid, flexible and responsive to the researcher's evolving engagement with their data.

In contrast, 'small q' qualitative research uses qualitative techniques in a (post)positivist paradigm (Kidder and Fine, 1987a). Key motivations in developing small q approaches to TA include making qualitative methods acceptable to quantitative researchers, and seeking to 'bridge the gap' between qualitative and quantitative approaches (Boyatzis, 1998). Small q TA is underpinned by quantitative conceptions of reliability; authors advocate the use of a (predetermined and fixed) 'code book' or coding frame (e.g., Boyatzis, 1998; Guest, MacQueen and Namey, 2012; Joffe, 2011), which is *applied* to the data (the coding frame is typically developed after data familiarization). The use of a coding frame facilitates the use of multiple, independent coders, which allows for the calculation of inter-coder or inter-rater reliability scores. These scores provide a quantitative measure of coding 'accuracy', offering reassurance of the reliability of the analysis (if a kappa of $>.80$ is calculated). From a Big Q perspective, the notion that coding can be more or less 'accurate' is problematic. It appears to be underpinned by the problematic assumptions that the analysis is *in* the data, waiting to be found (see below), and that if two or more researchers agree about coding, it is somehow 'better'. From our Big Q perspective, a 'good' inter-rater reliability score only shows us that the researchers have been trained to apply a coding frame in a similar way, not that the coding is 'reliable' or 'accurate' (Braun and Clarke, 2013). These emphases in small q TA necessarily limit its claimed theoretical flexibility (Boyatzis, 1998; Guest et al., 2012; Joffe, 2011).

Our Big Q approach to TA *is* theoretically flexible, and one of the key elements that distinguishes it from many other qualitative analytic approaches is that it is a method rather than a methodology. What do we mean by this? A *methodology* refers to a theoretically informed framework for research; and qualitative approaches like interpretative phenomenological analysis (IPA), grounded theory, discourse analysis and conversation analysis are methodologies rather than methods. Methodologies are like package holidays – you select the package, not the individual elements of the package. Alongside guidelines for data analysis, methodologies like IPA and discourse analysis come complete with guiding theoretical assumptions and recommendations or prescriptions for particular kinds of research questions

BOX 10.1   DEFINING REALIST, CRITICAL REALIST AND RELATIVIST TA

Type	Definition	Example study
Realist/ essentialist	Reality is 'out there' and discoverable through the research process; people's words provide direct access to reality.	Rance et al.'s (2014) study of women with anorexia assumes that anorexia is a real condition.
Critical realist/ contextualist	Reality is 'out there' but access to it is always mediated by socio-cultural meanings, and, in the case of qualitative analysis, the participant's and the researcher's interpretative resources (so *direct* access to reality is never possible). People's words provide access to their *particular* version of reality; research produces interpretations of this reality.	Hayfield et al.'s (2014) study reports bisexual marginalization from bisexual women's perspectives, but also locates their experiences within a wider interpretative context where sexuality is normatively understood in dichotomous 'either/or' terms.
Relativist/ constructionist	There is no external reality discoverable through the research process. Instead, versions of reality are created in and through research. The researcher cannot look through people's words to find evidence of the psychological or social reality that sits behind it. Rather, people's words become the focus of research, and the researcher interprets how these words produce particular realities.	Braun's (2008) study explored the explanatory frameworks that 'lay' people provide for sexual health statistics in New Zealand. Taking a constructionist approach, it treated these accounts as reflecting and rein-forcing a certain reality that needs to be taken into account if sexual health promotion is to be successful.

and ideal methods of data collection. In contrast, TA provides a *method* – a set of theoretically independent *tools* for analysing qualitative data. This means doing TA is like arranging your own holiday: you choose which flights you take, where you stay and how you get around. When you use TA, you have to decide what theoretical assumptions will guide your research, what your research question will be, what type(s) of data you will collect and how exactly you will implement TA.

Qualitative analytic methodologies often have unique aspects that set them apart from other approaches and make them ideally suited to *particular* kinds of qualitative research. In grounded theory, for example, it is theory development (Birks and Mills, 2011); in IPA, it is idiography (Smith, Flowers and Larkin, 2009). TA's status as method means that its hallmark is flexibility – you can do it in a wide range of ways, guided by different theoretical frameworks. TA can be used to address most types of research questions (see Box 10.2 below) and to analyse most types of qualitative data, everything from interviews (e.g., Hayfield and Clarke, 2012) and focus groups (e.g., Braun, 2008) to qualitative surveys (e.g., Moller, Timms and Alilovic, 2009), diaries (e.g., Malinen, Rönkä and Sevón, 2010), story completion tasks (e.g., Whitty, 2005), and secondary sources such as newspaper articles and official documents (e.g., Ellis and Kitzinger, 2002). TA can be deployed within a wide range of theoretical frameworks. It can be realist/essentialist (e.g., Malik and Coulson, 2008), critical realist/contextualist (e.g., Hayfield et al., 2014) or relativist/constructionist (e.g., Braun, 2008) (see Box 10.1 for more details). So theoretical independence doesn't make TA *non-theoretical* (as is often assumed) or an implicitly realist/essentialist method (another common assumption).

TA can also take a range of different forms:

- *Inductive TA* refers to analysis primarily grounded in the data, rather than existing theories and concepts. Although pure induction is not possible in most forms of qualitative research – analysis is always shaped by a researcher's theoretical assumptions, disciplinary knowledge, research training, prior research experiences, and personal and political standpoints – inductive TA aims to stay as close as possible to the meanings in the data.

- *Deductive TA*, by contrast, views the data through a theoretical lens so that existing theoretical concepts inform coding and theme development, and the analysis moves beyond the obvious meanings in the data. For instance, in our research area – critical sexuality studies – a widely used concept has been the notion of a 'male sex drive discourse'. Introduced by feminist psychologist Wendy Hollway (1984) to capture the ways accounts around male heterosexuality were often underpinned by the assumption that men want sex 'anytime, anyplace, anywhere' (Farvid and Braun, 2006), this concept has provided researchers with an interpretative frame that has guided the analysis and interpretation of their data (e.g., Farvid and Braun, 2006; Gilfoyle, Wilson and Brown, 1992; Hayfield and Clarke, 2012).

- *Semantic TA* focuses on the surface meaning of the data, the things that are *explicitly stated*. One way of thinking about the notion of semantic meanings (in research involving participants) is as the explicit meanings participants communicate to the researcher: the obvious ideas and concepts in the data. In coding and analysing semantically, the researcher seeks to remain close to the participants' meanings, while maintaining an awareness that these are always viewed through *their* particular interpretative lens (Smith et al., 2009).

- *Latent TA* focuses on meanings that lie under the data surface – assumptions, frameworks or world-views that underpin semantic meanings. So latent meanings can be thought of as those that participants are not explicitly aware of, or explicitly communicating; they are meanings that become apparent from the vantage point of the researcher. Analysing latent meaning requires more interpretative work on the part of the researcher, including asking questions like 'What suppositions are required to make sense of things in *this* way?'
- *Descriptive TA* refers to analysis that aims primarily to summarize and describe patterned meaning in the data.
- *Interpretative TA* goes beyond description, to decipher the (deeper) meanings in the data and interpret their importance.

This variability in the application of TA means that it can range from relatively straightforward descriptive overviews of key features in data to more complex, conceptual readings of data that examine the theoretical implications of the analysis. However, it's not the case that latent and interpretative versions of TA are necessarily 'better' TA. TA that is primarily semantic and descriptive can be highly sophisticated, and make important theoretical or practical contributions. For example, Rance, Clarke and Moller's (2014) largely semantic and descriptive TA of the interview accounts of women with a history of restricting their intake of food (see example study at the end of the chapter) has important theoretical implications for understanding anorexia.

It is worth noting that while many combinations of these forms are possible, commonly they cluster together into one of two 'versions' of TA: (1) a realist/essentialist, inductive, semantic and descriptive approach; and (2) a relativist/constructionist, deductive, latent and interpretative approach.

FORMULATING A RESEARCH QUESTION AND DESIGNING A STUDY

Due to the flexibility of TA the researcher plays an obviously *active* role in designing their TA study: selecting theoretical framework(s), research question(s), method(s) of data collection, and sample, and also in determining how exactly TA will be used, creating an overall good 'fit' in design. Fit is an important principle for qualitative research design (Willig, 2001) and provides an anchor in the sea of possibility that is qualitative research. In achieving 'fit', all the different elements of the research design must be conceptually compatible. Nikki's study, which we discuss in depth below, was guided by both a political commitment to 'give voice' to bisexual women and an academic interest in how bisexual women make sense of their visual identities. A broadly experiential approach to TA (see below), underpinned by a critical realist ontology (Ussher, 1999) and contextualist epistemology (Madill, Jordan and Shirley, 2000), was most appropriate, as was the collection of detailed individual narratives through qualitative interviews. A semantic and inductive approach to coding and analysis meant Nikki stayed close to, and could 'give voice' to, the women's meanings.

BOX 10.2   EXAMPLE RESEARCH QUESTIONS SUITABLE FOR TA STUDIES

Broad type of research	Questions about...	Example studies	Broad TA approach in example study
Experiential qualitative research – assumes language is a tool for communicating people's experiences, perspectives and practices; that such things can be 'read off' people's words; language reflects reality.	People's lived experiences of...	Women's lived experiences of body hair growth (Fahs, 2014)	Essentialist
	People's perspectives on...	Young adults' views on pubic hair (Braun, Tricklebank and Clarke, 2013)	Contextualist (critical realist)
	The factors and social processes that underpin particular phenomena	The role of experiential and gendered embodiment in regulating alcohol consumptions (Lyons, Emslie and Hunt, 2014)	Contextualist (focus on embodied experience in a constructionist-lite framework)
	Practices; the things people *do* in the world	Young lesbian, gay and bisexual people's clothing practices (Clarke and Turner, 2007)	Contextualist
Critical qualitative research – rejects the assumption that the reality of people's experiences sits behind language; rather, reality is constructed in and through language.	Representations of particular subjects and objects in particular contexts	The representation of women's bodies in women's magazines, focusing on 'love your body' discourse (Murphy and Jackson, 2011)	Constructionist (post-structuralist)
	The social construction of a particular topic or issue	The construction of men's talk about weight management on weight loss discussion forums (Bennett and Gough, 2013)	Constructionist

TA is suited to a wide range of research questions – from *experiential* questions about people's lived experiences and perspectives to *critical* questions about the social construction of 'reality' (Box 10.2 offers some appearance- and embodiment-focused example research questions). Research questions that don't fit well with TA are those focused on 'language practice' and 'idiography'. Language-practice questions draw on a theoretically informed and technical body of knowledge about the action orientation of language (Schegloff, 2007; Wiggins and Potter, 2010) – suiting discursive approaches (e.g., discursive psychology, conversation analysis). Although TA *can* productively be combined with some discursive approaches (Murphy and Jackson, 2011), and 'thematic discourse analysis' (Clarke and Braun, 2014), which focuses on generating codes, themes and *discourses* (Taylor and Ussher, 2001), is gaining popularity, TA does not provide the tools for a detailed examination of language use. Neither is TA appropriate for the in-depth scrutiny of the narratives of individual participants (Riessman, 2007; Smith et al., 2009). Because of its focus on patterned meaning, and looking *across* data items to identify themes, it is not suitable for use with a single case or a small number of cases.

The organic and flexible nature of TA coding allows for research questions to evolve throughout the course of the research. Nikki's study, for instance, began with a quite focused research question: 'How do bisexual women make sense of their visual identity?' It quickly became apparent that participants wanted to talk more broadly about their bisexual identity and their experiences of marginalization and stigmatization. As the women's experiences of biphobia provided a wider context for their visual identities (and there is limited research on this topic), Nikki broadened her research question to include bisexual women's experiences of bisexual identity and bisexual marginalization. A more common evolution is for a broader question to become more focused. For example, Victoria and Katharine Spence (Clarke and Spence, 2013) began their analysis of lesbian and bisexual women's clothing practices by asking how lesbian and bisexual women make sense of their clothing practices in relation to their sexualities. During coding and theme development, their research question was refined to how lesbian and bisexual women negotiate pressures to look like an authentic individual and an authentic lesbian.

COLLECTING DATA

Ideally, you'll collect 'good' data to analyse thematically. For TA, like most qualitative approaches, whatever types of data are collected, they should provide detailed and complex insights into the topic in question. Although no guarantee of data quality, careful preparation and planning for data collection is important (see Braun and Clarke, 2013). For example, piloting a data collection tool is a useful way to ensure that it generates appropriate and good quality data, especially if you're collecting a small sample.

'What size sample do I need?' is a common – and vexed – question in TA (and much other qualitative research), with no easy answer. Determining the ideal number of data items depends on your research question and your theoretical approach, as well as practical considerations (such as the time-frame for conducting the research, total time involved in collecting data and preparing it for analysis, and the ease of recruiting participants, if used). The richness of individual data items is also relevant. Generally, fewer are required if individual data items (e.g., an interview) provide detailed, rich data (but keep in mind TA's focus on the generation of themes *across* data items); larger sample sizes can to some extent 'compensate' for shallower data items. Box 10.3 provides some suggestions for *minimum* sample sizes for different types of data in relation to projects of different scopes and sizes. Homogeneity or heterogeneity of sample is another useful question to consider in relation to size. With small TA studies, a more homogeneous, focused sample can help in identifying meaningful themes (Braun and Clarke, 2013). More heterogeneous samples are more practicable in larger TA studies.

Certain data items (e.g., audio-recorded interviews) will require transcription before analysis commences. For TA, a thorough orthographic transcript that captures what was said, and possibly also some basic details of *how* things were said (e.g., particularly notable

---

BOX 10.3   RECOMMENDED SAMPLE SIZES FOR TA STUDIES OF VARIOUS SIZES AND SCOPES

Data type	Small project (e.g., u/g project)	Medium project (e.g., Master's, Prof Doc)	Large project (e.g., PhD)
Interviews	5/6–10	6–15	15–20 (one study); 30+ (sole data source)
Focus groups	1–3	3–6	3–6 (one study); 10+ (sole data source)
Qualitative surveys	20–30	30–100	50+ (one study); 200+ (sole data source)
Story completion tasks	20–40	40–100	100+ (one study); 400+ (sole data source)
Secondary sources (e.g., media texts)	1–100	1–200	3/4–400+

(Adapted from Braun and Clarke, 2013)

pauses or emphasis), are required (see Braun and Clarke, 2013, for guidelines). For example, in the transcript extracts in Boxes 10.5, 10.7 and 10.8 below, underlining is used to signal emphasis on a particular word, and inverted commas to signal the reported speech of self and others.

With your data set collected and prepared, you're ready to begin data analysis. For smaller studies, because the data set is small and focused, we recommended waiting until all data are collected before beginning. In larger TA studies, a more organic, exploratory approach is possible (in which new questions are incorporated and new avenues explored during data collection), and data collection and analysis are conducted simultaneously.

BOX 10.4   SIX PHASES OF THEMATIC ANALYSIS

Familiarization: Data analysis is facilitated by an in-depth knowledge of, and engagement with, the data set. Familiarization – reading and rereading transcripts, listening to audio-recordings, making notes of any initial analytic observations – helps the researcher to move the analysis beyond a focus on the most obvious meanings.

Coding: A systematic process of identifying and labelling relevant features of the data (in relation to the research question). Coding is the first step in the process of identifying patterns in the data because it groups together similar data segments.

'Searching' for themes: The 'search' for themes is not simply one of 'discovery'; the themes are not *in* the data waiting to be uncovered by an intrepid researcher. Rather, the researcher clusters together codes to *create* a plausible mapping of key patterns in the data.

Reviewing themes: The researcher pauses the process of theme generation to check whether the candidate themes exhibit a good 'fit' with the coded data and with the entire data set, and each has a clear, distinct 'essence' – or central organizing concept. Reviewing may lead to no or few changes, or to discarding the candidate themes and restarting the previous phase.

Defining and naming themes: Writing theme definitions (effectively a brief summary of each theme) and selecting a theme name ensure the conceptual clarity of each theme and provide a road map for the final write-up.

Writing the report: The researcher weaves together their analytic narrative and vivid, compelling data extracts. Themes provide the organizing framework for the analysis, but analytic conclusions are drawn across themes.

(Braun and Clarke, 2006)

ANALYSIS

We now describe the six – recursive – phases Braun and Clarke (2006) recommend for TA (see Box 10.4). Each phase is illustrated with examples from Nikki's interview study with bisexual women. Following these steps closely will hopefully reduce the anxiety that analysing qualitative data can generate in new researchers! Keep in mind that each phase provides the foundation for the next; the more solid the foundations you lay in each phase, the more confidence you can have in your developing analysis.

As you begin, it's crucial to remember that the analysis is not *in* the data, waiting to be discovered by a researcher with the correct tools and skills to do so. Themes do not simply 'emerge' from data. Rather, analysis is constructed at the intersection of the data and the researcher's theoretical assumptions, disciplinary knowledge, and research skills and experience. To illustrate this, let's consider a short data extract that we often use when teaching TA (see Braun and Clarke, 2012); see Box 10.5. It comes from Virginia and Victoria's research on lesbian, gay, bisexual and transgender (LGBT) students' experiences of university life, and we encourage you to read this data extract now and make a note of any analytic observations you have.

We're always struck by the myriad of different ways people make sense of this short extract. Psychologists, particularly therapists, tend to focus on Andreas' psychological experience: what it must *feel like* to be in the situation he describes. Critical social psychologists tend to focus on the wider social context, and the ways in which Andreas' account is reflective of social *norms* around sexuality. People with no personal or professional experience around non-heterosexualities, and who are embedded in culturally dominant sense-making frameworks around sexuality (neoliberalism and libertarianism; Brickell, 2001), tend to view Andreas as overly fearful and lacking confidence in his sexuality. By contrast, people with personal or professional experience of non-heterosexualities tend to view Andreas as responding rationally to a heteronormative university environment. These interpretations (and others) are neither 'wrong' nor 'right'; they're analytic observations based on researcher experience. What were your observations? What assumptions underpinned your observations?

Phase 1: Familiarization

Familiarization involves spending quality time with your data! You should read through your *entire* data set at least twice. If you have audio data, listen to it (over and above any listening required to transcribe it, although transcription assists familiarization). Try not to just absorb the data as you might absorb information when reading a magazine or listening to the radio. Read in a *curious and questioning* way. You can facilitate this by asking yourself the following types of questions as you read:

- Why are they making sense of things in *this* way (and not *that* way)?
- What assumptions underpin this account?

- What type of world-view does this account imply or rely on?
- How would I feel in this situation?
- What implications does this account have?

BOX 10.5   A GAY MALE STUDENT RESPONDING TO A QUESTION ABOUT WHETHER HE IS 'OUT' AT UNIVERSITY

Andreas: I sometimes try to erm not <u>conceal</u> it that's not the right word but erm let's say I'm in a in a seminar and somebody- a a man says to me 'oh look at <u>her</u>' (Int: mm) I'm not going 'oh actually I'm <u>gay</u>' (Int: mm [laughter]) I'll just go like 'oh yeah' (Int: mhm) you know I won't fall into the other one and say 'oh yeah' (Int: yep) 'she looks really brilliant' (Int: yep) but I sorta then and after then you hate myself for it because I I don't know how this person would react because that person might then either not talk to me anymore or erm might sort of yeah (Int: yep) or next time we met not not sit next to me or that sort of thing (Int: yep) so I think these this back to this question are you <u>out</u> yes but I think wherever you go you always have to start afresh (Int: yep) this sort of li-lifelong process of being courageous in a way or not

(Braun and Clarke, 2012)

Make notes as you go, recording your observations and insights. You'll almost inevitably start by noting fairly obvious meanings, but the more you read in a curious and questioning way, the greater depth of insight you will achieve. End this phase by making notes on your overall observations on the data set. Box 10.6 provides two examples of familiarization notes from the bisexual women's visual identities study – observations first from one interview, then from the entire data set.

BOX 10.6   FAMILIARIZATION NOTES FROM THE BISEXUAL WOMEN'S VISUAL IDENTITIES STUDY

Familiarization notes from Interview 8 (Roxy):

- *There is no way to look bisexual or identify other people as being bisexual.*
- *It does not seem like there are many bisexual people around (bisexual invisibility).*

- *She felt she belonged within some (non-sexuality-related) communities and this was clearly important to her (belonging/multiple identities - bisexuality as not a master identity).*
- *Her experience of lesbian/LGBT groups is that they are not inclusive of bisexuality, which makes her feel that she does not fit in, AND additionally, heterosexual people do not understand bisexuality.*
- *She distanced her own bisexual identity from how she saw bisexuality being portrayed ('bicuriosity', 'threesomes' and 'promiscuity').*

Familiarization notes from entire data set:

- *Most of the women directly state that it is not possible to communicate bisexuality through dress and appearance.*
- *However, it seems more complex than this - the women talked about trying to look bisexual or not heterosexual and not lesbian, thinking people who look like them might be bisexual, some 'looks' (alternative/hippy/goth) might hint at the possibility of bisexuality.*
- *Dress and appearance are important - to convey individuality, identity, embodiment, performativity, practicality/'comfort', construction of femininity/masculinity and androgyny.*
- *Participants (sometimes reluctantly) acknowledge that they do assess other people's appearance in relation to sexuality and can recognize certain lesbian looks (mainly 'butch lesbians').*
- *Communication of bisexuality difficult (through appearance or otherwise) because often others assume sexuality based on partner gender AND overlook the possibility of bisexuality/multiple partners.*
- *The interviews contain lots of different perspectives on lived bisexuality which seems to relate to involvement with LGBT spaces and bisexual communities/cisgender and transgender/monogamy and polyamory.*
- *Lots of talk about bisexual identity - as a third identity position 'in between' heterosexual and lesbian/gay OR as a breaking down of binaries.*

These bisexual women talked about bisexuality as invisible or, if visible, as represented in ways that do not resonate with their experiences ('bicurious', not really existing, temporary phase, 'sat-on-the-fence', diseased, 'promiscuous', non-monogamous).

Phase 2: Coding

A systematic and rigorous coding process builds solid foundations for theme development. As tempting as it is to skip this phase and start theme identification immediately, coding facilitates deep engagement with the data and the production of an analysis that goes beyond the immediate or obvious. A code identifies and labels something of interest in the data in relation to the research question. As noted above, coding can happen at two levels – semantic

---

BOX 10.7   A CODED DATA EXTRACT FROM THE BISEXUAL WOMEN'S VISUAL IDENTITY STUDY

Do you think that there is a bisexual look? (*long pause*) No. (*long pause*) Not really. Although I'm not one hundred percent sure about that but I (*pause*) slightly struggle with the concept of a bisexual look because I don't know whether that means (*pause*) a lesbian look, as in a clichéd 'I don't want to look (*pause*) attractive to men', or what's cultur-ally seen as attractive to men, so I'm going to defeminize myself' (*pause*) and I would say that there's a percentage of lesbians that wish to do that to identify themselves within their cultural group of, y'know, I want to commu-nicate to other women that I'm a lesbian through having a certain look and I want to make it clear to men that I'm completely	*No bisexual look (initial response)* *Uncertainty about (possibility or necessity of) bisexual look* *Bisexual look difficult to grasp* *Bisexual look may be similar to a lesbian look* *Lesbian look could be a cliché/stereotype* *Appearance as a form of communication (of sexuality)* *Lesbian looks function to communicate sexuality to (heterosexual) men* *Particular appearances attractive to men* *Women feminine, lesbians reject femininity* *Some (not all) lesbians adhere to cliché/stereotype* *Lesbian looks function to communicate sexuality to other lesbians / form community*
unattracted to you, which I would kind of say is a clichéd lesbian look, but I think that's, proba-bly lots of lesbians would, dispute that (*pause*) and I suppose the whole lipstick lesbian thing is another part of that. But I think traditionally there's an aspect of defeminization as a lesbian. (Gemma)	*Lesbian 'look' is an active choice* *Appearance is actively constructed* *Hesitant to assert existence of lesbian look* *Resisting clichés/'stereotypes'* *Lipstick lesbian look* *'Traditional' lesbian look unfeminine/masculine – butch lesbians*

(Hayfield et al., 2013)

and latent – and most analyses will contain some mix of both. For instance, in Nikki's study, her experiential approach led to primarily semantic codes that stayed on the surface of the data (Box 10.7 shows a coded extract from her study). Semantic codes in Box 10.7 include *no bisexual look* and *bisexual look difficult to grasp*; Gemma communicated these directly in the words she used to talk about bisexual appearance. The code *women feminine, lesbians reject femininity* is a more latent code, however, because Gemma's statement that lesbians 'defeminize' is underpinned by an assumption that women *are* fundamentally feminine, and that lesbians actively *reject* an inherent femininity in order to establish a (butch) lesbian appearance. This latent code moves beyond what is explicitly stated to consider the frameworks the participant uses to explain her world.

How you practically manage the coding process is up to you, and there are numerous techniques to choose from: scribbles on the (wide) margins of each data item; the use of specialist software (Silver and Fielding, 2008) to code selected text electronically; creating a Microsoft Word document for each code, and collating data relevant for each code; or very low-tech cutting and pasting of hard copies of data items onto file cards or sheets of paper for each code. Collating the coded data is essential for the next phase – most of these techniques have the advantage of collating as part of the process; with scribbling on the data items, you need to collate after coding.

Whichever technique you use, coding begins with a close reading through a data item. (To avoid viewing your data through the lens of the first item you collected, we encourage you to start with a later item.) When you note something of potential relevance to your research question, you code it – that is, you tag the selected data excerpt with a pithy label (the code). A code is typically a short phrase (see Box 10.7) that clearly captures the key aspect you see as important in that bit of data, either in your own words or using a data quotation. One-word codes like 'gender' or 'realism' may make sense when scribbled on data items, but when you're working 'off' your data item, and trying to identify analytically coherent connections between multiple codes, such vague codes are unlikely to successfully evoke the analytic relevance of the data. Good codes are ones that make analytic sense, without needing to see the data; they provide a shorthand analytic 'take'.

After generating your first code, you keep moving through the data; each time you identify something of potential interest, you need to decide if an existing code captures what is of interest or whether a new code is required. As TA coding is flexible and organic, you can tweak existing codes as you work through the data, expanding or contracting them, splitting them into two or more codes or collapsing similar codes together, to better fit your developing analysis. Continue coding throughout the entire data set. Data excerpts can be coded more than once (it's not a case of fitting the data into the 'correct' code) (see Box 10.8 below). Coding should be over- rather than under-inclusive. If in doubt, code it! But use your research question to judge relevance. Given the fluid and flexible nature of TA coding, we recommend at least two rounds of coding the entire data set, to ensure that your coding is thorough. This is especially important if you tweak your coding a lot during your first round of coding. Second coding rounds can also facilitate the development of latent codes.

There's no ideal (or limit on) number of codes for a data set: any recommendations for numbers of codes risks being interpreted as a prescription or target. Moreover, the question 'how many codes?' makes no sense – recall the point we made above: you're not finding *the* analysis already evident in the data; you're constructing *an* analysis that is plausible and robust. You should end this phase with your data thoroughly coded, and all your codes, and the data relevant to each code, collated ready for the next phase. Box 10.8 provides some instances of codes and collated data from the example study.

Phase 3: 'Searching' for themes

You now move up a level of abstraction, from coding to theme development. Although we use 'searching' to describe this phrase, you're not looking for something that already exists; rather, you are aiming to *create* a plausible and coherent thematic mapping of your data. In developing themes, you might 'promote' a particularly dense and complex code to a theme (there is no *absolute* distinction between a code and a theme); more commonly, you would cluster together similar codes. The key criteria for determining whether a potential theme *is* in fact a theme is whether it *both* identifies a coherent aspect of the data *and* tells you something about it, relevant to your research question. A theme needs to be under-pinned by a *central organizing concept* – or, more simply put, a key analytic point. Weaker themes group together similar codes but lack a central idea that unifies the codes. Consider a candidate theme you've called *Social Support*. If this simply collated the main things the participants said about this issue, it would lack a key point and focus. Presenting and sum-marizing diverse views does not constitute a theme (especially if summarizing participants' responses to a question – e.g., about social support – because little analytic work has been undertaken). However, if you developed a candidate theme around a central idea that unified participants' various observations about social support, it could work. For instance, *Effective Social Support Facilitates Coping* tells us that views on social support cohered around a relationship between support and coping – a key point. This also highlights the importance of naming themes appropriately (see Phase 5).

It's important to reflect on the relationships between your candidate themes – do they work together to form a coherent analysis? Themes can exist in hierarchical as well as lateral relationships, but we recommend having no more than three theme levels:

- *Overarching themes* tend to be used to organize and structure an analysis; they capture an idea underpinning a number of themes (see Braun and Clarke, 2013).
- *Themes* report in detail on meaning related to a central organizing concept.
- *Sub-themes* capture and develop an important facet of the central organizing concept of a theme (see Braun, 2008).

A very complex thematic analysis, with many different theme levels, suggests a rather frag-mented, underdeveloped analysis that requires further theme development. Reflecting on relationships between themes also helps determine the boundaries of each theme – what

BOX 10.8 COLLATED CODES AND ASSOCIATED DATA EXTRACTS FROM THE BISEXUAL WOMEN'S VISUAL IDENTITY STUDY

Prioritizing practicality	Scary lesbians with attitude	Body size matters	Lesbian appearance: short hair	Bisexual appearance: goth
Betty: That's one of my favourite jumpers at the moment, just cus it's really thick and warm for winter, it's been so cold recently *Berni*: I don't wear sarongs cus I can't walk in them and they just annoy me and I'm too worried about flashing my bits *Rose*: I did buy a pair of heels when I was about seventeen or eighteen and I wore them for about three weeks. I was in so much pain I just thought 'this is insane'. So I got rid of them	*Elizabeth*: You've gotta have this atmosphere of 'don't come anywhere *near* me or I'm gonna beat you up' *Adele*: One of the big things is the attitude. Really. Just 'don't mess with me' kind of attitude (*laughs*). And that's before I've spotted the short hair *Emily*: Not that I y'know, tried to pretend that I was a lesbian when I went out, I wouldn't, but I wouldn't go round broadcasting 'oh yeah I've got a boyfriend at home by the way' in case they like, run you out of the pub	*Lucy*: I mean the attitude of people about women, and women's image, goes across all sexualities and across all of our culture and is massively judgemental of women *Sandy*: I was bullied quite extensively at high school, and then I dropped all this weight in the summer before college and it was like I was a different person, and I was so much more confident and, just like I made so many friends and it was like the best two years of my life	*Blue*: Your archetypal trendy dyke, y'know, skinny, short hair, vest tops, jeans, tattoos *Berni*: it's easy to spot the lesbian that has short hair because of how she looks but that's what you're spotting, you're stereotyping *Elizabeth*: If I saw someone in the street and I was to go 'oh they're gay' these are the reasons why. So yeah, normally short hair, piercings *Adele*: One of the big things is the attitude. Really. Just 'don't mess with me' kind of attitude (*laughs*). And that's before I've spotted the short hair	*Ruth*: I'd be more likely to assume that people who look like goths, or skaters, or emos, or the kind of ... hippy indie rock end of the young people's cultural spectrum. I'd think it was more likely that they would be bi *Eddy*: There is an enormous slew of very femme-y goths *Adele*: Especially in the evening when people dress up it can get very gothy [...] so there's a lot of corsets and a lot of sort of 'striking' looks

(Hayfield, et al., 2013)

each includes and excludes. Good themes are unlikely to be very narrow and restricted in focus (e.g., based on only one or two analytic observations), nor very broad and sprawling – lacking a clear focus and with lots of sub-themes (see Box 10.10 below).

Drawing thematic maps – figurative representations of the relationships between codes and potential themes – is a useful technique both for developing individual themes and for exploring the relationship between themes. Early thematic maps are often rather complex as they can record many potential patterns identified in the data. Nikki used her early thematic map (Figure 10.1) as a way to document the analytic thoughts and ideas developed during coding, and to get a sense of the overall analysis. However, these ideas were refined considerably as theme development progressed (as Figure 10.2 shows), with some themes discarded, and others retained and refined.

This phase ends when you reach a point in theme development where you're only making minor adjustments to your candidate themes and feel confident that your thematic map captures your data coding and provides a coherent answer to your research question. When first starting out with TA, keeping Phases 3 and 4 sequential helps build a robust analysis. With experience, the process of theme development and review can become more recursive, moving fluidly back and forth between the two.

Phase 4: Reviewing themes

You review your themes in two ways: first, in relation to the collated, coded data for each theme; second, in relation to the entire data set. The first stage of review focuses on the individual themes and checks whether they 'work' in relation to the coded data. It involves rereading all the data associated with the codes for each theme and asking whether the candidate theme is a good (enough) fit with the meanings evident in the coded data. If it is, you proceed to the next stage of review. If not, you need to revise your themes. This can range from some minor tweaking, to discarding all the themes and restarting theme development. In Nikki's study, for example, an early candidate theme related to 'body size and shape', as several of the women talked about their bodies (see Box 10.8 and Figure 10.1). However, in review, it was evident that the theme lacked a central organizing concept, as women's discussions of their bodies were disparate: some took pride in defying the dominant 'thin ideal' (Bordo, 1993) and claiming alternative forms of beauty and femininity; others spoke of being happier when thinner. Some considered body size important in relation to sexuality; others did not. And overall, many said very little about their bodies and body size (despite being asked about it). The combination of lack of coherence and limited data led Nikki to discard this as a candidate theme.

Once your candidate themes have 'passed' review against the coded data, you need to return to your entire data set for a final check for fit. You want an analysis that addresses your research question *and* reflects the content of the data. Each analytic phase takes you further and further away from your data. This review stage provides a check to ensure that both the individual themes and the analysis as a whole capture key meanings and patterns in the data. The outcome of this stage of review can range from few or no changes, to

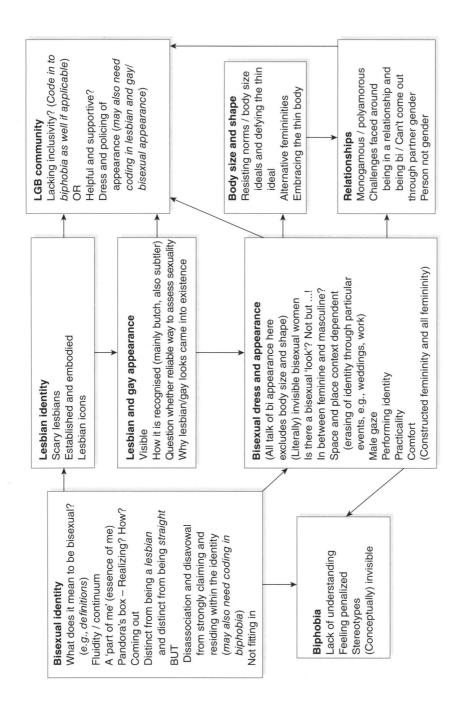

Figure 10.1 First thematic map from the bisexual women's visual identity study (Hayfield et al., 2013)

Bisexual identity
What does it mean to be bisexual? (e.g., definitions)
Fluidity / continuum
A 'part of me' (essence of me)
Pandora's box – Realizing? How?
Coming out
Distinct from being a lesbian and distinct from being straight
BUT
Disassociation and disavowal from strongly claiming and residing within the identity (may also need coding in biphobia)
Not fitting in

Lesbian identity
Scary lesbians
Established and embodied
Lesbian icons

LGB community
Lacking inclusivity? (Code in to biphobia as well if applicable)
OR
Helpful and supportive?
Dress and policing of appearance (may also need coding in lesbian and gay/ bisexual appearance)

Lesbian and gay appearance
Visible
How it is recognised (mainly butch, also subtler)
Question whether reliable way to assess sexuality
Why lesbian/gay looks came into existence

Body size and shape
Resisting norms / body size ideals and defying the thin ideal
Alternative femininities
Embracing the thin body

Bisexual dress and appearance
(All talk of bi appearance here excludes body size and shape)
(Literally) invisible bisexual women
Is there a bisexual 'look'? Not but ...!
In between feminine and masculine?
Space and place context dependent (erasing of identity through particular events, e.g., weddings, work)
Male gaze
Performing identity
Practicality
Comfort
(Constructed femininity and all femininity)

Relationships
Monogamous / polyamorous
Challenges faced around being in a relationship and being bi / Can't come out through partner gender
Person not gender

Biphobia
Lack of understanding
Feeling penalized
Stereotypes
(Conceptually) invisible

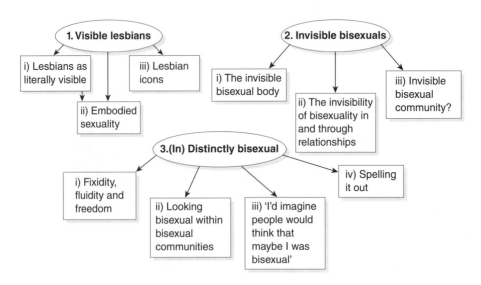

Figure 10.2   Final thematic map from the bisexual women's visual identity study (Hayfield et al., 2013)

discarding candidate themes and returning to theme development. If there is a large mismatch, you may even need to return to coding, to ensure a good match between codes and data content.

Phase 5: Defining and naming themes

Once you are (reasonably) confident that you have generated a robust thematic mapping of your data, understanding both the scope of each theme and how the themes relate together, you begin the process of elaborating each theme and moving towards the write-up of your results. One very useful step is writing *theme definitions*. These are fairly short descriptions (generally a few hundred words in length) explaining the essence (central organizing concept), scope and coverage, and boundaries of each theme (see Box 10.9 for an example). This step helps you to develop and enrich your *analytic narrative* – your (interpretative) commentary on the data. Writing theme definitions also helps you to think about the organization and flow of analysis within each theme, effectively providing a road map for writing up your results.

Finalizing the name of each theme is another part of the theme development process. Good *theme names* capture the essence of each theme – and may use a particularly compelling data quotation to do so (see Hayfield et al., 2014). We enjoy the creative potential of this process, and often develop theme names that are playful or reference popular culture. For example, we have named themes after popular sayings, album and song titles, and even the 'seven deadly sins' (see Braun and Clarke, 2013).

BOX 10.9 *VISIBLE LESBIANS* THEME DEFINITION, FROM THE BISEXUAL WOMEN'S VISUAL IDENTITY STUDY

The theme *visible lesbians* captures participants' observations that lesbian women have a visual identity, if they want it, as well as (some) cultural visibility. Bisexual women identified and described a 'lesbian look', despite being hesitant to do so and trying to 'resist' the notion of appearance stereotypes. The 'butch lesbian', who participants constructed as masculine and highly visible, was the most commonly identified 'lesbian look'. Many participants also named more specific and nuanced lesbian looks (e.g., baby dyke), reflecting a cultural awareness of lesbian communities. The women understood lesbian appearance as both visible on the body and as embodied. It was not only a lesbian's clothes and hair which conveyed her sexuality; it was a combination of this and a lesbian's body, walk and 'attitude'. Participants also noted some cultural visibility and role models for lesbian women, identifying lesbian 'icons' in film and television. However, the women (often) distanced *themselves* from lesbian looks, effectively positioning bisexuality as distinct from lesbian identity.

(Reported in Hayfield et al., 2013)

WRITING UP (TA PHASE 6)

There is no clear separation between analysis and writing in TA. You start writing as soon as you begin your analysis (noting initial observations on the data), so 'writing up' involves compiling and editing existing analytic writing as well as producing new writing. As there are no particular requirements for how you frame and contextualize TA studies, we recommend following general guidance for writing up qualitative research here (e.g., Braun and Clarke, 2013). In the method section of your report, you need to identify how you chose to implement TA, and explain why your choices are appropriate. In the results, how many themes should you cover? There is no precise formula, as it depends on the complexity of your analytic map, the depth of each theme, and the style and focus of your report. That said, we consider six to be the maximum possible, and our analyses often report fewer. A key issue to consider is the order in which you present your themes. If one 'main' theme contextualizes the other themes, present this first (see Braun and Clarke, 2012).

Your theme definitions will help you to identify key points to make in presenting your themes, but writing up will develop the analysis further. The analytic write-up contains two elements: data excerpts and analytic commentary. It's rarely practical (or desirable) to evidence every analytic observation with examples from the data. Instead, provide examples for your key observations (your analytic 'headlines'). It's not unusual to have certain participants who are particularly articulate, but avoid being seduced into just presenting quotations from them. In Nikki's study, she managed this by presenting longer narratives from the more articulate women, balanced with shorter excerpts from others. So although you don't *need* to quote every single data item (and it may not be possible due to sample size), do quote a wide sample of your data items to provide strong evidence of patterning *across* data. There are some other pitfalls to avoid when writing up to produce a good TA. Box 10.10 summarizes these.

BOX 10.10   GOOD AND BAD PRACTICES WHEN REPORTING A TA

Element of the analysis	Bad practices in analysis	Good practices in analysis
Balance between analytic narrative and data extracts	Little in the way of analytic narrative – at the most extreme, we have encountered themes that consisted of one summary sentence followed by a long string of 20 or so data extracts.	A good balance of analytic narrative and data extracts. Main analytic claims appropriately evidenced. The reader has enough information to assess the validity of the author's interpretations.
	Analytic narrative supported by very few data examples – at the most extreme, we have encountered write-ups with no example data extracts *at all*, leaving the reader no basis for 'validation' of the author's analytic observations.	
Selection of data extracts	Most or all of the extracts come from the same (small number of) participants/data items.	The selected extracts powerfully illustrate the analytic claims, and clearly and convincingly demonstrate the patterning of meaning in the data.
	The extracts presented are not particularly vivid or compelling (raising questions about the validity of the analytic claims).	
	Only one data extract provided to evidence patterning in the data.	
Fit between data and analytic claims	There is a poor fit between the data extracts and the analytic claims; the extracts don't clearly demonstrate the author's analytic claims.	There is a good fit between data and analytic claims, and all obvious interpretations of the data are considered.
	Other obvious interpretations of the data are not considered.	

Character of individual themes	Some or all of the themes are thin and sketchy, consisting of one or two analytic observations (closer to a code than a theme).	Each theme is underpinned by a central organizing concept (any sub-themes clearly demonstrate a facet of this central concept), and is of a suitable scope.
	The themes simply identify an area of the data but don't tell the reader something about it; it's not clear if the theme is underpinned by a central organizing concept.	
	The themes are unwieldy and overly complex, and thus lack coherence.	
Relationship between themes	There is lots of overlap between themes and thus the individual themes lack a distinct identity.	Each theme is distinct, and together the themes provide a cogent analysis in relation to the research question.
	There is no clear relationship between the themes presented; the themes do not form a coherent analysis.	

In terms of the balance between analytic narrative and data excerpts, aim for at least a 50:50 ratio (with greater emphasis on the analytic narrative – more like 70:30, or even 80:20 – for more conceptual analyses; for an example, see Nicolson and Burr, 2003). Data extracts can be used either illustratively or analytically (Braun and Clarke, 2013). When used illustratively, extracts provide one possible example of an analytic observation – see Box 10.11. The exact extract could be removed, and substituted with another, without any disruption to the analytic narrative (e.g., Braun, Tricklebank and Clarke, 2013). When used analytically, the specific features of a particular data extract matter, as the analysis develops around them and comments directly on them (e.g., Braun, 2008). Some qualitative approaches (e.g., discursive psychology, conversational analysis) primarily, or exclusively, use data analytically; others use data illustratively (e.g., grounded theory). In TA, both are appropriate, and a single analysis can incorporate both styles (e.g., Braun and Clarke, 2012).

Another major consideration when writing up is whether to weave together your results with the existing literature (a combined results and discussion, followed by a short general discussion/longer conclusion), or to present your results with little or no reference to existing literature, followed by a separate discussion where you contextualize your results in relation to existing scholarships (followed by a short conclusion). Whereas most qualitative approaches encourage the use of one particular format for presenting results,

---

BOX 10.11   EXTRACT FROM BISEXUAL WOMEN'S VISUAL IDENTITY STUDY, SHOWING DATA USED ILLUSTRATIVELY

'The term "bicurious" was often understood to encapsulate the notion of bisexuality as an attention-seeking strategy, which the women also disassociated from their own "genuine" sexuality:

> I think there's a certain type of bisexuality that is visible and I don't think that's real bisexuality [...] There's so much of a focus on, a sort of faux bisexuality as being something to attract men. The actual true sexuality is lost in that [...] I think the media just don't really want to accept it or understand it [...] all the sort of stereotypes, the pornographic stereotypes and the bicurious stereotype is very dismissive, it's like it's not a real sexuality, it's not a real thing [...] because biness is so invisible in society, unless you're bicurious. (Marie)

> There was like about a million people that were bicurious [on the social networking website 'Facebook']. And actually bicurious just means I wanna shag with a woman and a man really, it doesn't mean [laughter] that you're thinking that you might be bisexual and you wish to explore these feelings, because you wouldn't be doing that on a site, wearing nothing but your underwear. (Roxy)

This resonates with quotes from bisexual men and women in various published materials, where the concept of bicuriosity, and those who identify themselves as bicurious, are seen as problematic in shoring up negative media and pornographic portrayals of bisexuality, which are positioned as the underpinnings of negative understandings of bisexuality (Eisner, 2013). Eisner highlights that such logic is problematic, because it represents people who associate with one form of bisexuality marginalizing an alternative form of bisexuality, which in turn creates notions of "good bisexuals" and "bad bisexuals" (Eisner, 2013: 185).'

(From Hayfield et al., 2014)

TA can work with both – the choice depends on the analysis (and, sometimes, external requirements such as the 'house style' of a particular journal). If you have used TA deductively and/or have made greater use of latent coding, it is likely that contextualizing your data in relation to existing theory and concepts is important (e.g., Braun, 2008). If your analysis is more semantic and descriptive, but nonetheless you can spot lots of micro-connections between your analysis and the wider literature, then a combined results and discussion is a good choice (e.g., Huxley, Clarke and Halliwell, 2014). If the connections between your analysis and the literature are more macro and relate primarily to your overall analytic conclusions, then a separate results and discussion is appropriate (see Opperman et al., 2014).

BOX 10.12   15-POINT CHECKLIST FOR A GOOD TA

Process	No.	Criteria
Transcription	1	The data have been transcribed to an appropriate level of detail and the transcripts have been checked against the tapes for 'accuracy'.
Coding	2	Each data item has been given equal attention in the coding process.
	3	Themes have not been generated from a few vivid examples (an anecdotal approach), but instead the coding process has been thorough, inclusive and comprehensive.
	4	All relevant extracts for each theme have been collated.
	5	Themes have been checked against each other and back to the original data set.
	6	Themes are internally coherent, consistent and distinctive.
Analysis	7	Data have been analysed – interpreted, made sense of – rather than just paraphrased or described.
	8	Analysis and data match each other – the extracts illustrate the analytic claims.
	9	Analysis tells a convincing and well-organized story about the data and topic.
	10	A good balance between analytic narrative and illustrative extracts is provided.
Overall	11	Enough time has been allocated to complete all phases of the analysis adequately, without rushing a phase or giving it a once-over-lightly.
Written report	12	The assumptions about, and specific approach to, thematic analysis are clearly explicated.
	13	There is a good fit between what you claim you do and what you show you have done – i.e., described method and reported analysis are consistent.
	14	The language and concepts used in the report are consistent with the epistemological position of the analysis.
	15	The researcher is positioned as *active* in the research process; themes do not just 'emerge'.

(Braun and Clarke, 2006: 96)

CONCLUSION

As noted above, we do not subscribe to the notion that TA can be 'reliable' in the same way that quantitative research aims to be. However, this doesn't mean that 'quality' is not a concern in TA. Throughout this chapter, we have provided guidance on how best to implement TA to produce a 'good quality' analysis. Quality TA is not a question of universal absolutes, but is reliant on the subjectivity of the researcher and their rigour and scholarship. Box 10.12 provides a 15-point checklist for successfully implementing TA.

Although TA is often thought of as a foundational or 'starter' method, we hope we have demonstrated that it's not inherently less sophisticated than approaches that provide fully formed methodologies (e.g., grounded theory, interpretative phenomenological analysis (IPA)). Because of its flexibility, TA does provide a good starting point for your qualitative research journey, and you can apply the skills you learn from TA when using most other qualitative approaches. As TA can run the gamut from fairly basic, descriptive overviews of semantic meaning to highly sophisticated, conceptually informed interpretations of latent meaning, you can both progress from TA to other approaches, and progress from implementing TA in a way that's fairly rudimentary to producing cutting-edge, complex TA. In Box 10.13, we present three good examples of TA studies.

BOX 10.13   THREE EXAMPLES OF GOOD TA STUDIES

To illustrate the range of possibilities with TA, each study offers a different version: experiential/essentialist (Rance et al., 2014), critical realist/contextualist (Hayfield et al., 2014), and critical/constructionist (Braun, 2008).

On eating disorder clients' perceptions of their female therapists' bodies

Women with eating disorders often observe and assess body-related stimuli, but little is known about whether, and if so, how and with what consequences, this occurs in the therapy room. Rance, Clarke and Moller's (2014) inductive/descriptive TA study aimed to explore how women diagnosed with anorexia, or with a history of restricting food, who had been receiving counselling from a female therapist, observed and assessed their female therapist's body. Nicola Rance conducted interviews with 11 women who saw themselves as recovered or 'on the road to recovery'. The interviews included questions about the female therapists' body/weight and shape, and three themes were generated around this topic: (1) *'Wearing eating disorder glasses'* captured the ways women viewed the world through an 'anorexia lens' and had an almost uncontrollable tendency to assess and compare themselves, in a skewed or distorted way, to the bodies of other women; (2) *'You're making all sorts of assumptions as a client'* explored how the women's 'eating disorder glasses' informed their experiences of therapy, including assumptions around their therapist's body and, therefore, professional competence; (3) *'Appearance matters'* explored the impact of the women's assessments on their resistance to, or engagement with, therapy. The results suggest practitioners should reflect on the ways their bodies might be perceived and interpreted by clients.

On bisexual women's experiences of bisexuality and bisexual marginalization

Based on interviews Nikki Hayfield conducted with 20 self-identified bisexual women, Hayfield, Clarke and Halliwell's (2014) inductive and (broadly) semantic, critical realist TA focused on the ways women talked about their experiences of bisexual marginalization or 'biphobia'. Previous research indicates that bisexuality is not well understood by non-bisexual people, is often conceptualized negatively, and the validity of bisexual identity has sometimes been called into question (McLean, 2008; Morrison, Harrington and McDermott, 2010). The three themes identified in women's accounts highlighted and explored: (1) how bisexual women felt excluded from heterosexual society *and* lesbian, gay, bisexual and transgender (LGBT) communities, both of which were portrayed as lacking an understanding of bisexuality and bisexual people; (2) how others dismiss bisexuality as an authentic identity, which the women themselves experienced it as; and (3) how bisexuality is both (hyper)sexualized and also stigmatized through popular cultural representations. The paper recommended that future researchers further explore the impact of bisexual marginalization on bisexual women (and men).

On national identity explanations for sexual health in Aotearoa/New Zealand

New Zealand has very poor sexual health statistics. Virginia Braun ran 15 focus group discussions with younger New Zealanders to identify everyday understandings that might help improve sexual health (Braun, 2008). The latent/deductive and critical/constructionist TA reported in this paper focused on one dominant theme in participants' account: a particular 'New Zealand persona' that was evoked in explaining sexual health statistics. Such explanations, based on a national character/identity, clustered into four distinct, sometimes contradictory, sub-themes: (1) New Zealanders are binge drinkers and are unconcerned about sexual safety when under the influence; (2) New Zealanders are poor communicators, and therefore do not and cannot communicate to ensure sexual safety; (3) New Zealanders are conservative about sex, yet at the same time highly and complacently sexual; and (4) New Zealanders are inherently 'laid back', captured in sayings such as 'she'll be right' and 'no worries', which means they are unconcerned about *personal* sexual health risk. An emphasis on national identity – rather than *personal* – characteristics shifts responsibility for sexual health from the individual, and suggests agency lies beyond the individual. The analysis suggests that if we focus sexual health promotion efforts at the individual level, a mismatch in messages might doom them to failure; promotion based within a national 'identity' framework might offer a fruitful avenue for prevention.

FURTHER READING

Braun, V. and Clarke, V. (2006) 'Using thematic analysis in psychology', *Qualitative Research in Psychology*, 3(2): 77–101.
This is our original TA article.

Braun, V. and Clarke, V. (2012) 'Thematic analysis', in H. Cooper, P.M. Camic, D.L. Long, A.T. Panter, D. Rindskopf and K.J. Sher (eds), *APA Handbook of Research Methods in Psychology, Vol. 2: Research Designs: Quantitative, Qualitative, Neuropsychological, and Biological*. Washington, DC: American Psychological Association, pp. 57–71.
A chapter providing a more detailed worked example of TA.

Braun, V. and Clarke, V. (2013) *Successful Qualitative Research: A Practical Guide for Beginners*. London: Sage.
A book explaining TA (and qualitative research) in much more detail. The companion website for the book, which contains data sets to practise TA with, can be found at: www.sagepub.co.uk/braunandclarke

Our thematic analysis website, which includes FAQs, can be found at: www.psych.auckland.ac.nz/thematicanalysis

11 Choosing your Approach

Michael Larkin

The reader will notice that a thread first established by Peter Ashworth, in Chapter 2, runs throughout the chapters in this book. The thread is concerned with identifying and applying approaches (i.e., epistemologies, methods) which can provide us with a psychologically-focused alternative to the concrete empiricism of cognitive, behavioural and neurological psychologies. In Peter's closing comments, he notes that there is, however, a 'qualitative sensibility', even though, beyond this sensibility, there is a great deal of diversity in the field. So, for example, some of the qualitative approaches outlined in this book provide us with alternatives which are complementary to the mainstream, aiming to address its blindspots; others position themselves in ways which are more concerned with constructing a parallel account, retaining a critical distance from psychology's disciplinary narrative. In this chapter, I'd like to begin by briefly considering the nature of the *shared sensibility* a little further. This will give us a platform for considering what is distinctively psychological about our approaches to qualitative research. From here, we can look at the opportunities provided by the different approaches in this book, and consider a précis of their respective points of focus, before concluding with some final thoughts about the consequences of our choices.

FOCUSING UPON MEANING

When we choose an approach for a qualitative psychological research project, we are choosing a perspective on the world, and on our data. We are choosing to 'slice' it in a particular way. When you slice through an object, such as an orange, you give special privilege to the perspective that you have chosen to take. If you slice the fruit horizontally, for example, you reveal a cross-sectional view through the centre of each segment. If you slice it vertically, you see the segments in a very different form: sliced longways on either side of the central column. Whichever way you choose to slice your orange, you do not entirely rule out the possibility of imagining what the perspective afforded by an alternative slice would look like – but you certainly bring one particular view into the foreground. Choosing a method is like this: different approaches bring different views of the world to our attention.

As we have seen, qualitative research tends to focus on meaning, sense-making and communicative action: it looks at how people *make sense* of what happens, and what the *meaning* of whatever happened might be. It is also concerned with context (Madill, Jordan and Shirley, 2000). Meaning is never context-free, after all, and so all of the approaches outlined in this book would – in different ways – claim to be interested in context. Where they differ from one another is in terms of the way that they bring a particular view of data (and the world from which it originates) into the foreground, for a reader's benefit, through an analyst's efforts.

So, for example, different approaches may conceive the person as the embodied site for experience, or the vector for a set of interpersonal relationships, or the narrator of a suite of interweaving stories, or an agent within a community, or an identity represented within a social structure, or an actor skilled in the management of cultural resources. The research questions that we ask, and the conceptual and epistemological underpinnings of our asking them, will lead us to bring different combinations of these interests to the fore. To choose an appropriate approach, we must first decide what we are interested in. Previous research and theoretical work help us to identify this, by pointing out what is missing and what is assumed, and directing us towards insights which might be useful or helpful.

APPROACHING YOUR CHOICE

Researchers must make informed choices about the approaches which match their interests and questions. As this book shows, a broad range of possibilities are opened up by established approaches, and for the confident and experienced researcher even more options are available.

The routes towards making these choices may depend upon the history of your project, and your relationship to it. Some researchers find a particular way of working to be intrinsically rewarding and interesting, and then go on to immerse themselves in it. Often they find that their chosen approach is consonant with their wider world-view, and so they begin to seek out further opportunities to apply that method, and to learn more about the world through that particular lens. These researchers often relate to their chosen approaches rather as an expert craftsperson might relate to, say, gemcutting skills; they look for projects which will allow them to deepen their knowledge and hone their expertise in their chosen approach.

Some researchers may be a little more eclectic. They may find, for example, that it is qualitative psychology in general, or perhaps a particular epistemological stance, which is attractive to them, and they may go on to explore and apply a range of methodologies from that starting position. These researchers may relate to their research rather as an explorer might relate to planning a new expedition; they look for projects which lend themselves to a general mode and scale of exploration, but may be open-minded about the details beyond this point.

Other researchers will see methods much as one might view the tools in a toolbox: different tasks call for different tools. These researchers develop very eclectic portfolios of work, often because they are very interested in a particular topic. Each project starts with a different research question, and each question leads to an appropriate methodological approach. Many of these researchers also use quantitative methods, too.

Finally, some researchers will find that a given situation simply requires them to use a particular approach. If the constraint is concerned with the training and supervision which is on offer, then it will obviously shape and limit the kinds of research questions which can be asked. But sometimes constraints are linked to the outcome of a particular study. If all of the people with a stake in a particular piece of research agree that its outcomes need to be of a particular type (for example, they might agree that it needs to produce a theoretical model, because the second stage of the study might depend upon being able to test such a model), then inevitably, this will limit the options which the researcher can choose from. In this instance, the researcher's relationship to the project is rather like that of a contractor hired to manufacture a product: in such circumstances we need to understand what our customers want, and we need to know what raw materials are available, and what techniques can be applied to them.

As you might imagine, some qualitative researchers are strong advocates of whichever of these positions they occupy, and may also be critical of the others. From the point of view of this book, and the options which it offers to the reader, I think it is important to be open-minded. What we can say is that each position has consequences and entails certain risks. The risk for the intensely focused gemcutter is that one becomes so familiar with a particular way of seeing the world that one's sense of perspective becomes distorted; the insights offered by other approaches may be overlooked or discounted. The risk for the eclectic explorer is that, while one acquires a very useful broad map of the territory, one does not get so many opportunities to really engage with the world in depth. The risk for the pragmatic toolkit-user is that one is always – to some extent – a novice, and that one may be slow to acquire the confident judgements that come from having used an approach many times before. The risk for the contractor is that one's lack of personal ownership of the project can undermine the sort of reflexive processes which are so important to many forms of qualitative analysis.

CHOOSING YOUR APPROACH

As we have seen already in this book, methodological choices tend to follow from epistemological positions. For the purposes of providing some summary guidance, we can represent the choices as they are characterized in Box 11.1. Here we see a series of questions around the experience of connectedness. Each one provides one example of the way in which a given technique might approach a connectedness-related topic (that is, the list is in no way exhaustive). This hypothetical set of examples allows us to see how formulation of research questions links to choices about the appropriate qualitative approach(es).

BOX 11.1   MATCHING THE QUESTION TO THE APPROACH

Example research question	Key features	Suitable approach
How do people who have chosen to live in a co-housing community make sense of their experience of 'belonging'?	Note the focus on personal meaning and sense-making in a particular context, for people who share a particular experience.	Interpretative phenomenological analysis
What sorts of story structures do romantic partners use to describe the moment when they first met?	Note the focus on how narrative relates to sense-making (e.g., via genre, structure, tone or imagery); this could be related to a general experience or a specific context.	Narrative psychology
Through what process do adoptive families incorporate a new family member?	Note the willingness to develop an explanatory account (factors, impacts, influences, etc.) of a complex social process.	Grounded theory
What communicative patterns characterize the collaborative aspects of the relationship between a psychotherapist and client?	Note the focus on conversation as a form of collaborative social activity which can be used to help us understand how or why a process unfolds in the way that it does.	Conversation analysis
How do people manage their identities when they do 'being in love' in close heterosexual relationships?	Note the focus on enactment and achievement over and above content, the importance of specifying the social context, and the caution about inferring anything about love itself.	Discursive psychology
In legal disputes about parental custody and access to children, how is the relational role of 'parent' constructed?	Note the willingness to use a range of data sources, and the focus on how things 'must be understood' according to the structural conventions of a particular setting.	Foucauldian discourse analysis

Example research question	Key features	Suitable approach
How can we collaborate with young people who have been excluded from school to develop better relationships with education?	Note the importance of a collaborative process which involves people as co-inquirers, and which often aims to feed directly into a local, social change process.	Cooperative inquiry
What are the main themes which can be identified in population X's accounts of being connected to something/someone?	Note the difficulty of specifying a clear epistemological focus: this is not because TA should not have such a focus; it is because the focus is not specified as part of the method (i.e., it is adaptable).	Thematic analysis

Box 11.1 captures a rough spectrum of interest (in terms of the scope of such analyses) from the idiographic (at the top) through the psychosocial (in the middle) to the structural (at the bottom). This isn't precise or definitive (for example, IPA studies using multiple perspective designs expand out from the idiographic to the systemic level), and there are variations within these approaches (for example, there are multiple versions of grounded theory), but as a broadbrush characterization of the field, it captures something useful about the options which are available to us. These options are expanding all the time. For example, due to its flexibility, thematic analysis doesn't quite fit this formulation, but it makes an excellent supplement to it, because it potentially provides a mechanism through which new blends of epistemologies can be developed and applied to qualitative data.

Thus, your strongest reason for choosing one approach over another should be because it is consistent with the epistemological position of your research question:

Implicit in the formulation of any research question is an assumption about what the data can tell us. Thus epistemology is a conceptual issue with a practical impact upon the research that we do. This becomes evident as soon as we have a data transcript in front of us: there are infinite things we could infer, about action, meaning, purpose, etc. How are we to direct our gaze? What are we to code *for*? (Smith, Flowers, Larkin, 2009: 46, original italics)

Alongside this concern, you might take a moment to reflect upon your intended relationship to *theory*. In qualitative psychological research, there is Theory, and there is theory. When people talk about Theory with a capital 'T', they are often invoking the conceptual and epistemological framework which informs the methodological approach itself. A Theory shapes the coding of the analytic work, as we have seen, but it may well offer a wider world-view, with implications for how the results of the analysis process are linked to practice, to recommendations for future work, or to the social and political context.

On the other hand, theory with a small 't' might refer to the more common psychological meaning of the concept; that a theory is an explanation (or proposed explanation) of the relationship between particular observable phenomena. Psychological theories are usually empiricist in their assumptions. As a consequence, most qualitative approaches do not *test* theories, and external theoretical concepts are not typically used in an explanatory capacity within qualitative analysis. They do sometimes have an important role to play in the rationale for a *proposed* study, however, and they are often important for the discussion and wider contextualization of a *completed* study. The outcomes of an analysis might contribute to the development of a new or existing theory; they might offer a critical or deconstructive perspective on some of its assumptions; or they might engage in a dialogue with it. It is worth considering how these issues will be accommodated into your choices.

There are also pragmatic matters to consider. These are secondary to developing a clear and coherent line between question, epistemology and method, but they are important. In the next section, I'll consider some of these issues.

COMPETENCE AND COMPLEXITY

Experienced qualitative researchers will often take these 'off-the-shelf' approaches and then adapt or extend them to meet the needs of their current projects. Researchers who are new to the field will want to work within established structures to begin with. Some methods and approaches (thematic analysis (TA), interpretative phenomenological analysis (IPA), grounded theory (GT), some forms of narrative analysis (NA)) are particularly good at providing this sort of structure, and may thus be especially appealing to new qualitative researchers. However, it is also important to be able to access appropriate supervision and support, and this may be the factor that informs choices when all other things are equal.

Underpinning this is the issue of training. Despite the accepted importance of qualitative methods in applied research (e.g., see Shaw, Larkin and Flowers, 2014) and the large size of the qualitative methods groups which now exist in many psychologists' national and professional organizations, there is still great variation in the coverage given to qualitative research skills in psychology degree courses. Some new researchers will feel that they are well prepared (conceptually and methodologically), while others may feel that they are entering another world! This does mean that we need to have a 'zone of tolerance' around early stage research in qualitative psychology. Partly, this means that examiners need to remember that while dissertations and theses must be 'good enough' (of course), there will also be areas for improvement. Researchers can anticipate this by drawing on the reflective component of qualitative work, as a means of showing what they have learned, and where it is leading. A further consequence of this issue is that, because approaches which offer more structure tend to appeal to newer researchers, they sometimes take the blame for the underdeveloped work which can follow. TA, IPA and GT have all been criticized for this in the past, but I think it misses the point entirely. All of these approaches can support sophisticated and nuanced work. If, sometimes, they also appear to produce less-sophisticated work, this is because methods and approaches in qualitative research are not like experimental protocols (Willig, 2013). That is, no method or approach will *guarantee* a particular outcome; this can only be achieved by the analyst. What methods and approaches do provide is directions and a map. The analogy is thus one of exploration or travel, not testing or production. Qualitative research is hard work. With support and constructive supervision, more-sophisticated work will follow from newer researchers, regardless of which approaches they adopt.

It is also important to consider who your audience is, what you need to do in order to persuade them of your message, and where you need to do it, in order that they receive that message. If you are writing for publication in a peer-reviewed journal, then the focus and the disciplinary identity of the journal will help shape your choices. Some journals encourage sophisticated, reflexive analysis and nuanced recommendations; others (often the 'higher impact' journals) prefer more concrete and direct reporting, with a simpler 'take home' message. In this book, contributors have concentrated for the most part on what Kidder and Fine (1987b) call 'Big Q' approaches. The implicit argument here is that quality in qualitative research is marked by *depth*: that is, insightful attention to detail, thoughtful reflection on process, and open-minded sensitivity to context (e.g., see Lucy Yardley's Chapter 12). However, there is a competing account, prevalent in some areas of medical research, which favours *breadth*: that is, large sample sizes and explanatory-level accounts of relatively 'concrete' features of the data. The split which is emerging between these different kinds of qualitative research may be one reason for the overwhelming number of increasingly detailed 'quality criteria' which have been published, and for the confusing mixed messages which are embedded within some of those which are often held up to 'gold standard' (e.g., see Tong, Sainsbury and Craig, 2007). Whether this schism can be repaired, and whether it will follow the form of disciplinary lines, remains to be seen. In the meantime, qualitative psychologists must engage in these debates, and be explicit about their aims and the criteria against which they should be evaluated.

There are practical and resource implications to your choices too. Different approaches will have different requirements regarding: what to treat as data; how to manage your role 'in the field'; how to access and approach participants; and what constitutes an appropriate sample size and data collection method. The previous chapters in this book will give you an excellent start in thinking through these issues, but do make sure that the different elements of your planned project line up coherently – with each other, and with your aims for the project.

To this end, don't start your project without considering what you would like the outcome of the project to be. A good question to ask yourself is 'What impact will it have?' – on your participants, on the context of your data collection work, on the field to which you will report your analyses, and for future researchers. Think about what you might like to be different. In a cooperative inquiry project, this may be explicit from an early stage, but other approaches may benefit from some prompting here. Looking at some of the examples in Box 11.1, we might notice that the project about understanding the experience of belonging in a community co-housing project is probably less concerned with influencing the community from which data will be collected, than it might be with showing some of the possible benefits of this *kind* of community to a wider audience. It might aim to influence or contribute to debates about housing policy, environmental development or public health.

It is also important to think about how you can involve people who will make that happen, and who will help you to achieve your aims in an acceptable, sensitive and practical manner. There is now a rich literature on user involvement in research which can help you to plan this, and there are many organizations to whom you can turn for help. You may decide that you wish to involve 'service users' or 'research users', or both. For example, in the project example above which is concerned with legal constructions of 'parenthood' in child custody and access cases, the 'research users' might be policy makers and members of the legal profession, and the 'service users' might be families. If there are people, groups or organizations with a stake in your area, and if you are setting out in the hope that your work will be useful to them, then it is often very helpful to get advice and feedback on your ideas at an early stage in the life of the project, and to discuss with them how you might reasonably expect to benefit from their further involvement over the course of the research.

For experienced researchers, as we have seen, a wide range of possibilities are available, not just regarding the approaches but also regarding designs (for example, single cases, theoretical, purposive or multiple perspectival sampling) and data sources (for example, naturally occurring data, face-to-face or email interviews, group discussions, blogs, photographic elicitation, co-production, and so on). The choices are made even more complex by a growing literature on how they can be combined (e.g., see Frost, 2011, on pluralism, or the growing number of interdisciplinary 'hybrids', such as neurophenomenology or conversation analytic roleplay). These are exciting times for qualitative psychology, but they must be balanced against the challenges involved in making more sophisticated work accessible and understandable to 'mainstream' audiences.

Good luck!

12 Demonstrating Validity in Qualitative Psychology

Lucy Yardley

The validity of research corresponds to the degree to which it is accepted as sound, legitimate and authoritative by people with an interest in research findings. This will include other researchers (in particular, those who must judge its worth for the purposes of examination or approval for funding or publication), policy makers and practitioners who use the research, and the lay public. This chapter, first, discusses why there is a need to establish criteria for evaluating the validity of qualitative research, and considers why establishing the validity of research in qualitative psychology can be problematic. A variety of specific methods that can be used to increase and demonstrate the validity of qualitative research are described. Finally, a framework for evaluating the validity of qualitative psychology studies is presented, illustrated by examples of good and bad practice. The framework does not prescribe exactly what you should do in order to show that your study is valid, since each study is different and can be validated in different ways. Nevertheless, if you wish to claim that your research is valid you may find it helpful to show that, in its own way, your study meets each of the key criteria in the framework.

CAN WE JUDGE THE VALIDITY OF QUALITATIVE RESEARCH?

Evaluating the validity of research involves making a judgement about how well the research has been carried out, and whether the findings can be regarded as trustworthy and useful. Such judgements are never easy, but can pose particular problems for qualitative research.

Differing perspectives on validity

Most qualitative researchers believe that different people have different, equally valid perspectives on 'reality', which are shaped by their context, culture and activities (see Chapter 2). But if there is no one 'true' perspective on reality, then which perspective should be used to evaluate the validity of a study? One solution to this problem might be to accept all researchers' perspectives as equally valid and useful. Some years ago I attended a qualitative research conference that appeared to have been based on this principle – it seemed as if the organizers must have accepted all the studies that were submitted for presentation. As a result, they accepted so many papers that they had to be presented in 14 parallel sessions. To fit all these simultaneous talks into one venue, there were talks given in every room and even in the corridors between rooms! No one was happy with this solution, since there were so many talks that only a few people attended each one, and there was no way for people to work out which of the talks would be worth going to. From this experience I concluded that it is necessary to make judgements about the value of qualitative research. Indeed, we all constantly make these judgements individually and informally, for example when we decide whether a talk was 'worth going to' – whether it was convincing, or at least interesting or thought-provoking.

An alternative solution to the problem that we each have different perspectives on whether a study is 'really' valid is to try to agree on common criteria that can be used to judge the validity of qualitative research. However, it is not easy to identify criteria that can be applied to all qualitative studies, since there are numerous different approaches to qualitative research, each based on different assumptions and employing quite different procedures. For example, a valid grounded theory study should theoretically sample a wide enough range of people to be able to develop a detailed description and explanation of the study topic, based on an analysis of all the data obtained (see Chapter 4). In contrast, a valid discourse analysis (see Chapter 7) might be based on an in-depth analysis of just a few illuminating text excerpts. Within each broad approach, such as 'discourse analysis', there are then further differences in the methods thought to be appropriate and valid. For instance, in discursive psychology (as in conversation analysis) it is often considered important to study naturally occurring dialogue and use the way that speakers respond to each 'turn' in the conversation as one way of validating the analysis of the social and linguistic functions of what the previous speaker said. In a valid Foucauldian discourse analysis there is no imperative to use naturally occurring dialogue as data, but it is important to analyse the wider socio-cultural implications of the talk.

Using validity criteria from quantitative research

A further problem in qualitative psychology is that quantitative methods have historically been dominant within the discipline, and so there is a tendency for psychologists to assume that the criteria for validity that are relevant to quantitative studies can also be applied to qualitative studies. There are three criteria, in particular, that are often mistakenly applied to qualitative research: objectivity, reliability and (statistical) generalizability. The reasons why these criteria are relevant to most quantitative studies, but are inappropriate for most qualitative studies, are explained below (for further explanation see Yardley, 1997b).

Most quantitative researchers seek to minimize sources of error in their data, in order to obtain as far as possible an accurate, unbiased observation of reality. Since it is known that the researcher can potentially influence the data and analysis, and this influence is seen as 'bias' or 'error', a variety of methods are used to try to reduce the influence of the researcher. These include impersonal administration of standardized questionnaires so that the researcher cannot influence how questions are asked, and statistical analysis of numerical measures to reduce the extent to which data can be shaped by the researcher's interpretation. However, most qualitative researchers believe that the researcher *inevitably* influences the production of knowledge, by formulating a research question, choosing particular measures and analyses, and interpreting findings. Moreover, attempting to eliminate the influence of the researcher would make it very difficult to retain the benefits of qualitative research, such as disclosure of subjective experiences in an in-depth interview, or insightful analysis of the hidden or oppressed meanings in talk. Consequently, rather than trying to eliminate the influence of the researcher by rigidly controlling the research process, qualitative researchers generally seek to maximize the benefits of engaging actively with the participants in the study. This means allowing the participants to influence the topic and data (for example, by using open-ended questions), while also acknowledging and analysing how the researcher may have influenced the findings of research (see section 'Coherence and transparency' below).

The aim of most quantitative research is to identify predictable causal relationships that can be observed or 'replicated' in different contexts. The reliability of measurements is therefore another important criterion for validity in quantitative research, since it is only possible to replicate a finding if the measurements used give the same results when administered by and to different people at different times. Once again, error is eliminated as far as possible through standardization of the administration and analysis of measures. But whereas quantitative researchers tend to focus on generalizable laws, qualitative researchers are often interested in the effects of context and individual differences. These are the very effects that are excluded as 'error variance' in quantitative research. For example, if you ask someone how bad their pain is, they may give a different answer depending on whether you are their employer, doctor or family member. This will cause problems if you were asking the question in order to test the effect of a treatment (in which case you need a reliable measure), but could provide very interesting insights if you want to understand the meaning and function of talk about pain in different contexts. In practice, when asked to talk about a topic, people very rarely produce 'reliable' responses; instead, they frequently offer a combination of rather different, sometimes contradictory, perspectives. This complexity in people's expressed views is suppressed and ignored when they are obliged to tick just one response to a questionnaire.

Although qualitative researchers are interested in individual differences and contextual variation, both quantitative and qualitative researchers hope that their findings will be generalizable. There would little point in doing research if every situation was totally unique, and the findings in one study had no relevance to any other situation! Quantitative researchers usually try to ensure that their findings can be generalized from a sample to a wider population by carrying out their research in a representative random sample of the target population. However, it is seldom practical to gather and analyse in-depth qualitative data from a large enough sample to be statistically representative of a wider population. In any case, qualitative researchers are typically more interested in examining subtle interactive processes occurring in particular contexts than making generalizations about population trends, and so they tend to intensively study a relatively small number of carefully selected individuals or cases. Qualitative researchers therefore aspire to what can be called 'theoretical', 'vertical' or 'logical' rather than statistical generalization of their findings (Johnson, 1997). This means that they would not expect their findings to be exactly replicated in any other sample or context, but would hope that the insights they derived from studying one context would prove useful in other contexts that had similarities. Since contexts can share some features even if others are quite dissimilar, generalizability in qualitative research is potentially wide-ranging and flexible.

Developing validity criteria for qualitative research

Despite the difficulty of developing criteria for validity that are applicable to all types of qualitative research, there are many reasons why it is necessary to attempt to find some common criteria. Since qualitative methods have not been widely used within psychology in the past, it is essential for qualitative researchers to be able to show that their studies are sound and rigorous, and yield findings that are as valuable as those from quantitative research. Anyone, including lay people and journalists, can interview people and report what they have said, and so if qualitative researchers are to demonstrate the value of their research they need to show that their studies do more than this. The process of agreeing criteria for judging the value of qualitative research is useful in itself, because it involves critically reflecting on how qualitative research should be carried out, and what the essential ingredients of good qualitative research are. Publishing these criteria is an important way of disseminating best practice and improving standards. Published criteria can help novice researchers to carry out their research in a way that avoids the shortcomings and mistakes that more experienced researchers have learned to anticipate. Finally, if studies can demonstrate that they meet criteria that have been agreed and accepted by qualitative experts, this can be used as an assurance of their quality by people who are not qualitative experts. For example, policy makers, research funders and journal editors are often not expert in qualitative methods but need to be able to make important decisions about whether qualitative studies are flawed, acceptable or outstanding.

These motives led in the 1990s and early twenty-first century to the development and publication of a number of guidelines for validity criteria that qualitative studies should meet, both within qualitative psychology (e.g., Elliott, Fischer and Rennie, 1999; Henwood and Pidgeon, 1992; Meyrick, 2006; Stiles, 1993; Yardley, 2000) and in health and social research (e.g., Daly et al., 2007; Malterud, 2001; Spencer, Ritchie, Lewis, and Dillon, 2003; Tong, Sainsbury and Craig, 2007). These guidelines remain extremely useful to this day as a set of suggestions for good practice, but the expert qualitative researchers who have produced these guidelines themselves emphasize that they should not be used as a set of rigid rules for judging qualitative research. Merely following guidelines cannot guarantee good research. Qualitative research is not simply a descriptive science, but also relies on the capacity to evoke imaginative experience and reveal new meanings (Eisner, 2003) – and this core quality is not easily captured by checklist criteria. Moreover, qualitative research is constantly evolving, and it is important for qualitative researchers to be able to be flexible and creative in the way they carry out their research, provided that they can justify their departure from conventions for good practice. The framework for considering the validity of qualitative studies given later in this chapter therefore outlines the quality issues that need to be addressed, but does not restrict the ways in which they can be addressed. However, qualitative researchers have developed a range of procedures that can be used to enhance the validity of their research, and these are described in the next section.

PROCEDURES FOR ENHANCING VALIDITY

The procedures described below will not be suitable for every qualitative study, and specific recommendations for procedures relevant to particular methods are made in many of the chapters in this volume. However, the suggestions below provide a 'toolbox' from which you can select procedures for enhancing validity that are suitable for your study. Many of these procedures are sufficiently flexible that they can be adapted for use with a wide range of methodological approaches. Of course, they will only enhance the validity of your research if you use them thoughtfully to improve the depth, breadth and sensitivity of your analysis (see Barbour, 2001).

Triangulation

Triangulation is a term originally taken from navigation, where it refers to the practice of calculating location from three different reference points. As this metaphor implies, triangulation was initially viewed as a way of trying to corroborate the accounts of one person or group using the accounts of others. For example, to confirm a participant's description of their psychological problems as the consequence of external events, the researcher might interview members of their family. However, this approach to triangulation is inconsistent with the view of most qualitative researchers that people's perspectives may be different, but may each have validity. Triangulation is equally valuable from this point of view, but as a method of enriching understanding of a phenomenon by viewing it from different perspectives rather than converging on a single, consistent account of the phenomenon (Flick, 1992). For example, the participant might give a compelling and phenomenologically revealing account of their experience of external events as a cause of their problems, but family members might contribute useful insights into how the individual's personality and biography may have influenced their experiences of these events.

Enriching understanding through triangulation can be achieved by gathering data from different groups of people, or by gathering data at different times from the same people in a longitudinal study. It is also possible to triangulate different theories or methods (see Box 12.1) in a mixed methods study or 'composite analysis' (Yardley and Bishop, 2007). In addition, triangulating the perspectives of different researchers can enrich the analysis (see next section).

BOX 12.1   TRIANGULATING RESEARCH ON OLDER PEOPLE'S ATTITUDES TO FALLS PREVENTION

Research question: What do older people think of existing advice on falls prevention?

Method: Focus groups and interviews carried out with 66 people aged 61 to 94, purposively sampled to ensure a wide range of physical functioning.

Findings: Most participants (even those over 75 who have fallen) reject falls prevention as only relevant to older, frail people, and believe it means restricting activity to avoid falling (Yardley, Donovan-Hall et al., 2006).

Research question: What motivates older people to take part in falls prevention programmes based on strength and balance training?

Method: Interviewed 69 people aged 68 to 97, purposively sampled from six countries to represent a range of experience of different programmes, including people who had refused or dropped out of programmes.

Findings: Key motivations to take part were improving physical functioning to maintain independence, general health benefits and enjoyment (Yardley, Bishop et al., 2006).

Research question: Is intention to carry out strength and balance training predicted by threat appraisal (fear of falling) or coping appraisal (perceived benefits of programme)?

Method: 558 people completed questionnaires assessing threat and coping appraisal, including beliefs about strength and balance training expressed in interview study.

Findings: Structural equation modelling showed that intention to carry out strength and balance training was much more strongly related to coping appraisal than threat appraisal, including the perceived benefits identified in the interview study (Yardley et al., 2007).

Composite analysis: The first qualitative study revealed the negative meanings that older people associated with 'falls prevention'; the second qualitative study identified positive motivations that could promote uptake of falls prevention programmes; and the quantitative study confirmed that intended uptake was motivated by these perceived benefits. The Prevention of Falls Network Europe (www.ProFaNE.eu.org) and Help the Aged concluded from integrating these findings that to persuade older people to undertake falls prevention we need to emphasize the immediate positive benefits of strength and balance training for functioning, independence, enjoyment and health. Promoting this as 'falls prevention' may be unhelpful since people are reluctant to consider themselves as so old and frail that they need to take precautions to avoid falling.

Comparing researchers' coding

In qualitative research, the purpose of comparing the coding of two or more researchers is usually to triangulate their perspectives. This ensures that the analysis is not confined to one perspective, and makes sense to other people. For example, one researcher might code the data, but discuss the emerging codes in repeated meetings with other members of the research team who had read the transcripts. These discussions could help to identify potential themes in the data that may not yet have been captured by the codes, and highlight clarifications or modifications of codes that might be needed in order to increase the consistency and coherence of the analysis. This kind of inter-rater comparison is suitable for corroboration of complex and subtle coding schemes.

Sometimes a more formal procedure is used, whereby more than one researcher codes the data, and their codes are compared to determine 'inter-rater reliability' (Boyatzis, 1998). The most stringent form of inter-rater reliability requires two researchers to code the data independently. The level of agreement between their codes is then calculated by Cohen's kappa. A kappa of $\geq .80$ indicates a very good level of agreement, indicating that the data coding is reliable. This kind of inter-rater reliability calculation is appropriate if the codes are to be used for a quantitative analysis – for example, to compare the frequency of their occurrence in two groups. In this situation, coding reliability provides an assurance that the occurrence of codes has been recorded in a systematic manner that can be replicated by a second coder. However, this kind of analysis of qualitative data is unusual (except in content analysis); requires samples that are large enough to meet the requirements for statistical analysis; and is only suitable for simple codes that can be strictly defined and easily identified.

Participant feedback

Participant feedback, sometimes known as 'respondent validation', is obtained by asking participants to comment on the analysis (Silverman, 1993). This is a valuable way of engaging participants in the research and ensuring that their views are not misrepresented, but it is not always either feasible or appropriate. Offering participants an opportunity to express their viewpoint is often an important aim of qualitative research, but most analyses go beyond this. Analyses may highlight, for example, differences and contradictions between participants' perspectives, or the suppressed meanings and functions of talk. The theories and methods these analyses draw on may be difficult for lay people to understand. Before seeking participant feedback it is therefore important to consider whether participants will be able to relate to the analysis, and whether feedback from participants can be used constructively.

Disconfirming case analysis

Qualitative analysis typically consists of an inductive process of identifying themes and patterns within the data. This process is inevitably influenced by the assumptions, interests and aims of the researcher. Once a set of themes and patterns have been identified, it can therefore be very useful to engage in the complementary process of seeking 'disconfirming instances', also known as 'deviant cases' or 'negative cases'. This can be considered as the qualitative equivalent of testing your emerging hypothesis, and involves systematically searching for data that does *not* fit the themes or patterns that have been identified (Creswell, 1998; Pope and Mays, 1995).

Disconfirming cases should be paid careful attention and reported whenever possible. Reporting disconfirming cases reassures the reader that you have taken into account and presented all the data, rather than just selecting the parts that fit with your viewpoint. Disconfirming cases can also provide an indication of the limits of the generalizability of the analysis. To illustrate, imagine that you have analysed the data from participants who volunteered to take part in a study of the effects of exercise. The overwhelmingly dominant themes from your interviewees consist of descriptions of how exercise makes them feel happier, healthier and more in control of their lives. However, just two people describe how exercise made them feel ill and inadequate. These two 'disconfirming cases' are an important indication that exercise may not always have positive effects. Indeed, these two cases in your sample might represent a much larger population of people who dislike exercise, and may therefore not have wanted to take part in a study of exercise. These cases could therefore suggest a valuable next step for your research – to explore the circumstances in which people do or do not have positive experiences of exercise.

A paper trail

While researchers are trusted to prepare reports that accurately reflect the data they gathered, it should always be possible to provide evidence linking the raw data to the final report. In qualitative research this can be done by keeping what has been called a 'paper trail' of the analysis (Flick, 1998) – although these days the 'paper trail' can be entirely electronic! If an audit of the analysis was carried out, the paper trail should allow the auditor to retrace all the stages of the analysis, based on a complete set of coded transcripts, together with a description of the development of the codes and interpretations (with records of research questions, memos, notes and diagrams detailing the reasoning behind analytic decisions, together with interim and final definitions of the codes). The paper trail cannot be published, but should be available to other researchers to examine if they want to look closely into your analysis. Availability of a paper trail serves to reassure others that you have completed and documented your study carefully and professionally.

DEMONSTRATING THE VALIDITY OF QUALITATIVE RESEARCH

As the previous sections have explained, it can be useful to be able to refer to published criteria for demonstrating that qualitative research is valid, provided that these criteria are sufficiently flexible to be applied to a wide range of different methods and approaches. The framework outlined below (originally published in Yardley, 2000) sets out a core set of broad principles, summarized in Box 12.2, that are applicable to diverse types of qualitative research – indeed, although they were developed for qualitative research, they can even be applied to quantitative research. Encouragingly, these criteria cover much the same content as emerged from a systematic review of 29 published sets of criteria (Cohen and Crabtree, 2008). Some illustrations of different ways in which each of these principles might be implemented in practice are given below and in Box 12.3. Drawing on many years of experience as a supervisor, reviewer and editor, I also provide some illustrations of common pitfalls in qualitative research to be avoided!

Sensitivity to context

Whereas the value of a quantitative scientific approach lies in hypothesis testing – the isolation and manipulation of pre-defined variables that permit causal inference – a primary motivation for using qualitative methods is to allow patterns and meanings to emerge from the study that have not been strictly specified in advance. The tremendous value of this approach is that it permits the researcher to explore new topics and discover new phenomena; to analyse subtle, interacting effects of context and time; and to engage with participants to create new understandings (Camic, Rhodes and Yardley, 2003). Demonstrating that your study has this vital characteristic is therefore central to demonstrating its validity as an example of high-quality qualitative research.

There are numerous ways in which a qualitative study can be shown to be sensitive to context. An important aspect of the context of any study is the existing relevant theoretical and empirical literature. It may be valuable to draw on basic theory relating to the meanings and concepts that are studied, referring to psychological and philosophical writers who have carried out fundamental analyses of meaning. As noted above (see comments on the generalizability of qualitative research), insights from qualitative research potentially have theoretical relevance to somewhat different contexts. Consequently, there is almost always some previous relevant qualitative research. For example, if you are carrying out research into children's feelings about taking medication for attention deficit hyperactivity disorder, then relevant qualitative research could include studies of children's attitudes to taking other kinds of medication, as well as studies of children and adults' attitudes to being diagnosed and treated for other mental health problems. Note that much good qualitative research is relevant to a range of disciplines, so you might find relevant studies carried out by sociologists, anthropologists and health and social care professionals. Familiarity with the existing literature is necessary in order to formulate a research question that addresses gaps in our current understanding, rather than re-'discovering' what is already known, and can provide comparisons and explanations that may help you interpret your findings.

Good qualitative research must show that it is sensitive to the perspective and socio-cultural context of participants. The way in which researchers engage with participants can have ethical implications as well as potentially influencing the data. At the design stage this often means considering the possible impact on participants of the characteristics of the researcher(s) and the setting in which the research is carried out. For example, if participants are interviewed by someone they see as linked with those in authority (for example, with the school that their child attends), then they may defer to the apparent expertise of the interviewer by expressing only socially acceptable views rather than their personal experiences, and may also be reluctant to disclose information that could lead to negative perceptions of their child. Another crucial way in which the design of qualitative research can demonstrate sensitivity to participants' perspectives is by the construction of open-ended questions that will encourage participants to respond freely and talk about what is important to them, rather than being constrained by the preoccupations of the researcher (Wilkinson, Joffe and Yardley, 2004).

At the analysis stage, sensitivity to the position and socio-cultural context of participants may involve consideration of both the reasons why particular views may or may not be expressed and the ways in which views are expressed. Awareness of insights from discourse analysis can be helpful in this respect, even if no discourse analysis is undertaken in the study. Most importantly, the analysis must show sensitivity to the data. This involves demonstrating that the analysis did not simply impose the researcher's categories or meanings on the data, but was open to alternative interpretations and recognized complexities and inconsistencies in the participants' talk.

Commitment and rigour

As noted in the first section of this chapter, in order to claim that your study has validity as research you cannot simply talk to a few people and present some of what they have said – you need to show that you have carried out an analysis that has sufficient breadth and/or depth to deliver additional insight into the topic researched. The ways in which you do this will be closely linked to the purpose of your study (see next section 'Coherence and transparency'). For example, if your aim is to achieve a thorough description of a phenomenon which will have relevance to many different contexts, then you will need to show that you have recruited a sufficiently broad range of people to have sampled many of the different perspectives that are likely to be encountered. However, if your aim is to study a rare but theoretically important phenomenon, then you need instead to show how and why you have carefully selected one or more individuals that have particular relevance to your research question.

The selection of your sample may be less important than the depth and insight of your analysis – which is often linked to its sensitivity to context. You may achieve unique insights because of the theoretical sophistication of your analysis, or through an empathic understanding of participants' perspectives resulting from extensive in-depth engagement with the topic (for example, based on personal experience or prolonged participant observation). Your analysis may yield insights through the painstaking and skilful application of detailed analytical methods, such as the in-depth micro-analysis of dialogue, or the systematic construction of a grounded theory.

Clearly, it is not necessary or even possible for any single study to exhibit all these qualities, and it may be useful to consider and explain which form(s) of rigour your study aims to excel in. However, a minimum quality threshold will usually be relevant even in areas where your study does not aim to demonstrate excellence. Even if the primary value of your analysis lies in the imaginative depth of your interpretation, you still need to show that you had a reasonable justification for your selection of participants or texts to study. Similarly, however comprehensive your data collection, you still need to demonstrate competence in your analysis of the data. Achieving rigour therefore demands substantial personal commitment, whether to attaining methodological skills or theoretical depth, or to engaging extensively and thoughtfully with participants or data.

Coherence and transparency

The coherence of a study means the extent to which it makes sense as a consistent whole. This is partly determined by the clarity and power of the argument you can make for the study and the way it was carried out. The clarity and power of your argument will in turn depend on the fit between the theoretical approach adopted, the research question, the methods employed, and the interpretation of the data. In order to carry out a coherent piece of qualitative research it is therefore necessary to have a solid grounding in the methods used and their theoretical background, as this will enable you to decide what is or is not compatible with the approach you have chosen. This does not mean that qualitative studies have to follow a rigid formula – it is vital that researchers are able to be flexible and innovative. However, an in-depth understanding of why different approaches employ different procedures is needed in order to coherently select, adapt and justify the methods you employ.

Sometimes using a procedure that could enhance validity in one study may actually reduce the validity of another, if it is inconsistent with the approach adopted. For example, if you have adopted an interpretative approach to your data, it would usually be inconsistent to carry out strict inter-rater reliability checks and report Cohen's kappa for your codes. This is because the purpose of calculating reliability within a realist approach is to demonstrate that the codes are independent of the perspective of the coder. But within an interpretative approach, it is assumed that coding can never be objective, and so even if two people code the data in the same way, this simply shows that the coding manual and training process have enabled them to share one particular perspective on the data.

A common mistake made by novice qualitative researchers is to present their findings in a way that is incompatible with their method. An interpretative qualitative study cannot test hypotheses or correlations. Consequently, while it may be useful to identify differences in the views of participants with different characteristics, or associations between particular sets of views, these should not be reported as if they were firm evidence of group differences or causal relationships. Similarly, since qualitative research typically offers the researchers' interpretation of people's accounts of their experiences, it is generally inappropriate to report analyses as if they are concrete 'findings' corresponding to 'reality'. Often this is simply a question of using language precisely: rather than stating that your study 'found that women were more careful drivers than men', you could report that in your study 'more women than men described themselves as careful drivers and gave examples of cautious driving behaviour'.

Incompatibility between forms of validity relevant to different methodological approaches can pose problems for 'mixed methods' studies that combine qualitative and quantitative research. It may be difficult to find a common language that can coherently integrate quantitative findings and qualitative interpretations. For example, to report the quantitative analyses it may be necessary to treat people's responses to questionnaires as accurate measures of their beliefs, whereas the qualitative analyses may highlight the complex and contradictory meanings and functions of responses to researchers' questions. One solution to this problem is to report studies using different approaches as internally coherent parts of a 'composite analysis' (Yardley and Bishop, 2007), which triangulates the findings from studies which use methods that cannot be coherently 'mixed' (see Box 12.1).

The transparency of a report of a qualitative study refers to how well the reader can see exactly what was done, and why. A clear and coherent argument contributes to transparency, but it is also necessary to provide sufficient details of the methods used, often supported by a paper trail (see section 'Procedures for enhancing validity'). A transparent analysis presents enough data – quotations, text excerpts, and/or tables or figures summarizing themes – to show the reader what the analytic interpretations are based on.

Since qualitative research usually assumes that the researcher will influence the study, 'reflexivity' is often an important part of the transparency of the study. Reflexivity is the term used for explicit consideration of specific ways in which it is likely that the study was influenced by the researcher. This may simply mean openly describing features of the study that may have influenced the data or interpretations (such as the researchers' background and interests). Sometimes it may be appropriate to include a reflexive analysis of how these features could have influenced the conclusions reached.

Impact and importance

There is no point in carrying out research unless the findings have the potential to make a difference – indeed, research funders increasingly demand evidence of impact as a key indicator of worthwhile research. Your study may have direct practical implications, which will be immediately useful for practitioners, policy makers, or the general community. Alternatively, the importance of your research may be entirely theoretical – it may help us to understand something better, which may in turn lead to applications that achieve practical, real-world change. Some qualitative research has had a profound socio-cultural influence, changing the way we think about the position of women in society, or the way we treat people who have psychological problems. Ultimately, the key reason for taking all the steps suggested above to show that your research is valid is so that it can have an impact. Before you embark on any piece of research it may be useful to imagine how you would answer a sceptic who accepted that your findings were based on sound methods but nevertheless asked the question 'So what?'. This question leads back to the issue of being sensitive to the context of your research: your study will have impact and importance if it builds on what we already know, to take us a step further and answer questions that matter to people and to society.

BOX 12.2   CORE PRINCIPLES FOR EVALUATING THE VALIDITY OF QUALITATIVE PSYCHOLOGY

Sensitivity to context

- Relevant theoretical and empirical literature
- Socio-cultural setting
- Participants' perspectives
- Ethical issues
- Empirical data

Commitment and rigour

- Thorough data collection
- Depth/breadth of analysis
- Methodological competence/skill
- In-depth engagement with topic

Coherence and transparency

- Clarity and power of your argument
- Fit between theory and method
- Transparent methods and data presentation
- Reflexivity

Impact and importance

- Practical/applied
- Theoretical
- Socio-cultural

BOX 12.3   SIMILAR HYPOTHETICAL STUDIES THAT DEMONSTRATE OR LACK FEATURES OF VALIDITY

	Study lacks features of validity	Study demonstrates features of validity
Sensitivity to the context of existing theory and research in the development of a research topic	Study sets out to simply 'explore women's experiences of postnatal depression', ignoring relevant theory (e.g., feminist) and previous qualitative studies of experiences of maternity and depression in women.	Study clarifies what is already known from theory and research, formulates a specific research question that has not been addressed: 'How does the family context influence women's experiences following childbirth?'
Sensitivity to how the perspective and position of participants may influence whether they feel able to take part and express themselves freely	Senior male professional carries out interviews with women with postnatal depression in a clinic setting, ignoring the possibility that they may feel less able to express their feelings to a man, and may be intimidated and distressed by a clinical environment.	Participants are given the choice of taking part in focus groups (allowing solidarity with other women with similar experiences) or interviews in their own home (maximizing privacy, security and accessibility), carried out by women of about their own age.
Commitment and rigour in recruitment of participants who will represent an adequate range of views relevant to the research topic	The sample comprises 12 self-selected volunteers. Most of these women are well educated, affluent and married.	Twelve women are purposively sampled to include married, co-habiting and single participants from affluent and socio-economically disadvantaged backgrounds.
Transparency in the analysis of data	Little description is provided of how themes were identified, and no checks on their consistency are reported.	A detailed description is provided of how data were initially coded and how codes were modified through comparison of all instances and discussions between the researchers.

	Study lacks features of validity	Study demonstrates features of validity
Coherence between the qualitative design and the analysis and presentation of data	Based on a frequency count of the occurrence of codes, the researcher highlights the finding that two-thirds of the single women (n = 3) but only one-third of married women complain of lack of social support. Strong quantitative statements of this kind are inappropriate when the sample size is so small and the reliability of the codes is unknown.	Based on a qualitative comparison of all instances of the codes, the researchers note that there was a tendency for single women to report a lack of social support. However, disconfirming instances are discussed as revealing examples of why married and co-habiting women may feel unsupported, and how single mothers may be supported by others.
Impact of the research	The researcher simply notes that the findings are compatible with existing models and research (for example, showing that single mothers feel that they have less social support).	The researchers explain how different family structures and relationships may exert positive or negative influences on the experience of maternity, suggesting questions for further research and ways of identifying and supporting women at risk of depression.

CONCLUSION

It might, at first, seem daunting to contemplate criteria for high-quality research – meeting these standards may appear challenging, especially for novice researchers. It is not always possible for practical reasons to meet some of the criteria. It may be sensible or necessary to take short-cuts, to prioritize some kinds of validity, and acknowledge that it may not be feasible in the circumstances to achieve other kinds. However, the framework outlined above is not meant to intimidate or inhibit researchers, but simply to provide a set of principles that can be referred to when making decisions about how to carry out and justify your research. Published criteria represent the consensus of expert qualitative researchers regarding good practice, and so can be used to support claims that what you have done is valid. These criteria continue to evolve and to provoke debate – as do the criteria for evaluating quantitative research. Nevertheless, the existence of broad principles that we can refer to for showing that our work has integrity and value marks a new confidence that qualitative methods are now sufficiently well developed to take equal place alongside quantitative methods in psychology.

FURTHER READING

Yardley, L. (2000) 'Dilemmas in qualitative health research', *Psychology & Health*, 15: 215–28. This paper originally set out the principles for establishing validity outlined in this chapter, and provides many referenced examples of studies that illustrate a variety of ways in which the criteria might be met.

Elliott, R., Fischer, C.T. and Rennie, D.L. (1999) 'Evolving guidelines for publication of qualitative research studies in psychology and related fields', *British Journal of Clinical Psychology*, 38: 215–29. Another set of guidelines published specifically for qualitative psychologists. This set and mine were developed independently at much the same time, and so it is reassuring to note the close convergence between our recommendations!

Spencer, L., Ritchie, J., Lewis, J. and Dillon, L. (2003) *Quality in Qualitative Evaluation: A Framework for Assessing Research Evidence.* Government Chief Social Researcher's Office. Available at: www.civilservice.gov.uk/wp-content/uploads/2011/09/a_quality_framework_tcm6-38740.pdf (accessed 27/04/2014). This report presents an integrated set of criteria based on a review of published frameworks for validity and wide consultation with qualitative experts.

References

Adler, P. and Adler, P. (2011) *The Tender Cut: Inside the Hidden World of Self-injury*. New York: New York University Press.

Allahyari, R.A. (2000) *Visions of Charity: Volunteer Workers and Moral Community*. Berkeley, CA: University of California Press.

Allport, G.W. (1961) *Pattern and Growth in Personality*. New York: Holt, Rinehart and Winston.

Allport, G.W. (1962) 'The general and the unique in psychological science', *Journal of Personality*, 30: 405–22.

Allport, G.W. (1965) *Letters from Jenny*. New York: Harcourt, Brace and World.

Andrews, M. (2008) *Lifetimes of Commitment: Aging, Politics, Psychology*. Cambridge: Cambridge University Press.

Andrews, M., Squire, C. and Tamboukou, M. (eds) (2008) *Doing Narrative Research*. Los Angeles, CA: Sage.

Arendt, H. (1998) *The Human Condition* (2nd edn). Chicago, IL: Chicago University Press.

Arribas-Ayllon, M. and Walkerdine, V. (2008) 'Foucauldian discourse analysis', in C. Willig and W. Stainton Rogers (eds), *The Handbook of Qualitative Research in Psychology*. London: Sage.

Ashworth, P.D. (1973) 'Aspects of the psychology of professional socialisation', unpublished PhD thesis, University of Lancaster.

Ashworth, P.D. (1979) *Social Interaction and Consciousness*. Chichester: John Wiley and Sons.

Ashworth, P.D. (1985) '*L'enfer, c'est les autres*: Goffman's Sartrism', *Human Studies*, 8: 97–168.

Ashworth, P.D. (1996) 'Presuppose nothing! The suspension of assumptions in phenomenological psychological methodology', *Journal of Phenomenological Psychology*, 27: 1–25.

Ashworth, P.D. (2000) *Psychology and 'Human Nature'*. Hove: Psychology Press.

Ashworth, P.D. (2006) 'Seeing oneself as a carer in the activity of caring: attending to the lifeworld of the person with Alzheimer's disease', *International Journal of Qualitative Studies in Health and Well-being*, 1(4): 212–25.

Ashworth, P.D. (2009) 'William James's "psychologist's fallacy" and contemporary human science research', *International Journal of Qualitative Studies in Health and Well-being*, 4(4): 195–206.

Ashworth, P.D. (2013) 'The gift relationship', *Journal of Phenomenological Psychology*, 44(1): 1–36.

Ashworth, P.D. and Chung, M.C. (eds) (2006) *Phenomenology and Psychological Science: Historical and Philosophical Perspectives*. New York: Springer.

Atkinson, J.M. (1984) *Our Masters' Voices: The Language and Body Language of Politics*. London: Methuen.

Atkinson, J.M. and Heritage, J. (eds) (1984) *Structures of Social Action: Studies in Conversation Analysis*. Cambridge: Cambridge University Press.

Austin, J.L. (1962) *How to Do Things with Words*. Oxford: Clarendon Press.

Aymer, C. (2005) 'Seeking knowledge for Black cultural renewal', unpublished PhD thesis, University of Bath.

Baldwin, M. (2001) 'Working together, learning together: co-operative inquiry in the development of complex practice by teams of social workers', in P. Reason and H. Bradbury (eds), *Handbook of Action Research: Participative Inquiry and Practice*. London: Sage, pp. 287–93.

Baldwin, M. (2002) 'Co-operative Inquiry as a tool for professional development', *Systemic Practice and Action Research*, 14(6).

Bannister, D. and Fransella, F. (1971) *Inquiring Man: The Psychology of Personal Constructs*. Harmondsworth: Penguin.

Barbour, R.S. (2001) 'Checklists for improving rigour in qualitative research: a case of the tail wagging the dog?', *British Medical Journal*, 322: 1115–17.

Barbour, R. (2007) *Doing Focus Groups*. London: Sage.

Barbour, R. and Kitzinger, J. (eds) (1999) *Developing Focus Group Research: Politics, Theory and Practice*. London: Sage.

Barrett, P.A. and Taylor, B.J. (2002) 'Beyond reflection: cake and co-operative inquiry', *Systemic Practice & Action Research*, 14: 237–48.

Bartlett, F.C. (1932) *Remembering: A Study in Experimental and Social Psychology*. Cambridge: Cambridge University Press.

Baxter, L.A. (1991) 'Content analysis', in B.M. Montgomery and S. Duck (eds), *Studying Interpersonal Interaction*. New York: Guilford Press, pp. 239–54.

Becker, B. (1999) 'Narratives of pain in later life and conventions of storytelling', *Journal of Aging Studies*, 13: 73–87.

Becker, G. (1997) *Disrupted Lives: How People Create Meaning in a Chaotic World*. Berkeley, CA: University of California Press.

Benner, P. (ed.) (1994) *Interpretive Phenomenology: Embodiment, Caring and Ethics in Health and Illness*. Thousand Oaks, CA: Sage.

Bennett, E. and Gough, B. (2013) 'In pursuit of leanness: the management of appearance, affect and masculinities within a men's weight loss forum', *Health*, 17(3): 284–99.

Berger, P. and Luckmann, T. (1967) *The Social Construction of Reality*. Harmondsworth: Penguin.

Billig, M. (1991) *Ideology and Opinions: Studies in Rhetorical Psychology*. London: Sage.

Billig, M. (1997) 'Rhetorical and discursive analysis: how families talk about the Royal family', in N. Hayes (ed.), *Doing Qualitative Analysis in Psychology*. Hove: Psychology Press, pp. 39–54.

Billig, M., Condor, S., Edwards, D., Gane, M., Middleton, D. and Radley, A. (1988) *Ideological Dilemmas: A Social Psychology of Everyday Thinking*. London: Sage.

Binswanger, L. (1963) *Being-in-the-World*. New York: Basic Books.

Bion, W.R. (1959) *Experiences in Groups*. London: Tavistock.

Birks, M. and Mills, J. (2011) *Grounded Theory: A Practical Guide*. London: Sage.

Birren, J.E., Kenyon, G.M., Ruth, J.-E., Schroots, J.J.F. and Svensson, T. (eds) (1996) *Aging and Biography: Explorations in Adult Development*. New York: Springer.

Blaxter, M. (1983) 'The causes of disease: women talking', *Social Science and Medicine*, 17: 59–69.

Bloor, M., Frankland, J., Thomas, M. and Robson, K. (2001) *Focus Groups in Social Research*. London: Sage.

Blumer, H. (1969) *Symbolic Interactionism*. Englewood Cliffs, NJ: Prentice-Hall.

Bolton, N. (1977) *Concept Formation*: Oxford: Pergamon.

Bordo, S. (1993) *Unbearable Weight: Feminism, Western Culture, and the Body.* Berkeley, CA: University of California Press.

Boss, M. (1979) *Existential Foundations of Medicine and Psychology.* New York: Jason Aronson.

Boyatzis, R.E. (1998) *Transforming Qualitative Information: Thematic Analysis and Code Development.* London: Sage.

Bradbury, H. and Reason, P. (2001) 'Conclusion: broadening the bandwidth of validity: five issues and seven choice-points for improving the quality of action research', in P. Reason and H. Bradbury (eds), *Handbook of Action Research: Participative Inquiry and Practice.* London: Sage, pp. 447–56.

Braun, V. (2008) '"She'll be right"? National identity explanations for poor sexual health statistics in Aotearoa/New Zealand', *Social Science and Medicine,* 67(11): 1817–25.

Braun, V. and Clarke, V. (2006) 'Using thematic analysis in psychology', *Qualitative Research in Psychology,* 3(2): 77–101.

Braun, V. and Clarke, V. (2012) 'Thematic analysis', in H. Cooper, P.M. Camic, D.L. Long, A.T. Panter, D. Rindskopf and K.J. Sher (eds), *APA Handbook of Research Methods in Psychology, Vol. 2. Research Designs: Quantitative, Qualitative, Neuropsychological, and Biological.* Washington, DC: American Psychological Association, pp. 57–71.

Braun, V. and Clarke, V. (2013) *Successful Qualitative Research: A Practical Guide for Beginners.* London: Sage.

Braun, V., Tricklebank, G. and Clarke, V. (2013) '"It shouldn't stick out from your bikini at the beach": meaning, gender, and the hairy/hairless body', *Psychology of Women Quarterly,* 37(4): 478–93.

Brentano, F. (1874; trans. 1973) *Psychology from an Empirical Standpoint.* London: Routledge.

Brickell, C. (2001) 'Whose "special treatment"? Heterosexism and the problems with liberalism', *Sexualities,* 4(2): 211–36.

Broadbent, D.E. (1958) *Perception and Communication.* London: Pergamon Press.

Bruner, J. (1986) *Actual Minds, Possible Worlds.* Cambridge, MA: Harvard University Press.

Bruner, J. (1990) *Acts of Meaning.* Cambridge, MA: Harvard University Press.

Bryan, A. (2000) 'Exploring the experiences of black professionals in welfare agencies and black students in social work education', unpublished PhD dissertation, University of Bath.

Bryant, A. (2002) 'Re-grounding grounded theory', *Journal of Information Technology Theory and Application,* 4(1): 25–42.

Bryant, A. (2003) 'A constructive/ist response to Glaser', *FQS: Forum for Qualitative Social Research* 4(1): www.qualitative-research.net/fqs/www/qualitative-research.net/fqs/-texte/1–03/1–03bryant-e. htm (accessed 14/03/2003).

Bryant, A. and Charmaz, K. (2007) 'Grounded theory in historical perspective: an epistemological account', in A. Bryant and K. Charmaz (eds), *Handbook of Grounded Theory.* London: Sage, pp. 31–57.

Bugental, J.F.T. (1964) 'The third force in psychology', *Journal of Humanistic Psychology,* 4: 19–25.

Bühler, C. (1971) 'Basic theoretical concepts of humanistic psychology', *American Psychologist,* 26: 378–86.

Burr, V. (1995) *An Introduction to Social Constructionism.* London: Routledge.

Burr, V. (2003) *An Introduction to Social Constructionism* (2nd edn). London: Routledge.

Camic, P., Rhodes, J. and Yardley, L. (2003) 'Naming the stars: integrating qualitative methods into psychological research', in P. Camic, J. Rhodes and L. Yardley (eds), *Qualitative Research in Psychology: Expanding Perspectives in Methodology and Design.* Washington, DC: APA Books, pp. 1–15.

Charmaz, K. (1980) *The Social Reality of Death.* Reading, MA: Addison-Wesley.

Charmaz, K. (1991a) *Good Days, Bad Days: The Self in Chronic Illness and Time.* New Brunswick, NJ: Rutgers University Press.

Charmaz, K. (1991b) 'Translating graduate qualitative methods into undergraduate teaching: intensive interviewing as a case example', *Teaching Sociology*, 19: 384–95.

Charmaz, K. (1995) 'The body, identity and self', *Sociological Quarterly*, 36(4): 657–80.

Charmaz, K. (1999) 'Stories of suffering: subjects' tales and research narratives', *Qualitative Health Research*, 9: 369–82.

Charmaz, K. (2000) 'Grounded theory: objectivist and constructivist methods', in N. Denzin and Y. Lincoln (eds), *Handbook of Qualitative Research* (2nd edn). London: Sage, pp.509–35.

Charmaz, K. (2005) 'Grounded theory in the 21st century: a qualitative method for advancing social justice research', in N. Denzin and Y. Lincoln (eds), *Handbook of Qualitative Research* (3rd edn). Thousand Oaks, CA: Sage, pp. 507–35.

Charmaz, K. (2006) *Constructing Grounded Theory: A Practical Guide through Qualitative Analysis*. London: Sage.

Charmaz, K. (2008) 'Grounded theory as an emergent method', in S.N. Hesse-Biber and P. Leavy (eds), *The Handbook of Emergent Methods*. New York: Guilford Press, pp. 155–70.

Charmaz, K. (2009) 'Shifting the grounds: constructivist grounded theory methods for the twenty-first century', in J. Morse, P. Stern, J. Corbin, B. Bowers, K. Charmaz and A. Clarke, *Developing Grounded Theory: The Second Generation*. Walnut Creek, CA: Left Coast Press, pp. 127–54.

Charmaz, K. (2011a) 'A constructivist grounded theory analysis of losing and regaining a valued self', in F.J. Wertz, K. Charmaz, L.J. McMullen, R. Josselson, R. Anderson and E. McSpadden, *Five Ways of Doing Qualitative Analysis: Phenomenological Psychology, Grounded Theory, Discourse Analysis, Narrative Research, and Intuitive Inquiry*. New York: Guilford Press, pp. 165–204.

Charmaz, K. (2011b) 'Grounded theory methods in social justice research', in N.K. Denzin and Y.E. Lincoln (eds), *Handbook of Qualitative Research* (4th edn). Thousand Oaks, CA: Sage, pp. 359–80.

Charmaz, K. (2012) 'Mixing or adding methods? An exploration and critique', in N.K. Denzin and M. Giardina (eds), *Qualitative Inquiry and the Politics of Advocacy*. Walnut Creek, CA: Left Coast Press, pp. 123–43.

Charmaz, K. (2014) *Constructing Grounded Theory: A Practical Guide through Qualitative Analysis* (2nd edn). London: Sage.

Chowns, G. (2006) '"No – you DON'T know how we feel": collaborative inquiry with children facing the life-threatening illness of a parent', unpublished doctoral thesis, University of Southampton.

Chowns, G. (2008) '"No – you DON'T know how we feel": collaborative inquiry using video with children facing the life-threatening illness of a parent', in P. Reason and H. Bradbury (eds), *Handbook of Action Research* (2nd edn). London: Sage.

Clare, L. (2003) 'Managing threats to self: awareness in early stage Alzheimer's disease', *Social Science & Medicine*, 57: 1017–29.

Clarke, A.E. (1998) *Disciplining Reproduction: Modernity, American Life Sciences and the Problems of Sex*. Berkeley, CA: University of California Press.

Clarke, A.E. (2003) 'Situational analysis: grounded theory mapping after the postmodern turn', *Symbolic Interaction*, 26(4): 533–76.

Clarke, A.E. (2005) *Situational Analysis: Grounded Theory after the Postmodern Turn*. Thousand Oaks, CA: Sage.

Clarke, A.E. (2007) 'Grounded theory: conflicts, debates and situational analysis', in W. Outhwaite and S.P. Turner (eds), *Handbook of Social Science Methodology*. Thousand Oaks, CA: Sage, pp. 838–85.

Clarke, V. and Braun, V. (2014) 'Thematic analysis', in T. Teo (ed.), *Encyclopedia of Critical Psychology*. New York: Springer, pp. 1947–52.

Clarke, V. and Spence, K. (2013) '"I am who I am": navigating norms and the importance of authenticity in lesbian and bisexual women's accounts of their appearance practices', *Psychology & Sexuality*, 4(1): 25–33.

Clarke, V. and Turner, K. (2007) 'Clothes maketh the queer? Dress, appearance and the construction of lesbian, gay and bisexual identities', *Feminism & Psychology*, 17(2): 267–76.

Clayman, S. and Heritage, J. (2002) *The News Interview: Journalists and Public Figures on the Air*. Cambridge: Cambridge University Press.

Clifford, J.L. and Marcus, G.E. (1986) *Writing Culture: Poetics and Politics of Ethnography*. Berkeley, CA: University of California Press.

Cohen, D.J. and Crabtree, B.F. (2008) 'Evaluative criteria for qualitative research in health care: controversies and recommendations', *Annals of Family Medicine*, 6: 331–9.

Colahan, M., Tunariu, A. and Dell, P. (2012) 'Lived experience and discursive context: a twin focus', *QMiP Bulletin*, 13: 48–57.

Conrad, P. (1987) 'The experience of illness: recent and new directions', *Research in the Sociology of Health Care*, 6: 1–31.

Corbin, J. and Strauss, A. (2008) *Basics of Qualitative Research* (3rd edn). Los Angeles, CA: Sage.

Couper-Kuhlen, E. (1996) 'The prosody of repetition: on quoting and mimicry', in E. Couper-Kuhlen and M. Selting (eds), *Prosody in Conversation*. Cambridge: Cambridge University Press, pp. 366–405.

Creswell, J.W. (1998) *Qualitative Inquiry and Research Design*. Thousand Oaks, CA: Sage.

Crossley, M.L. (1999) 'Making sense of HIV infection: discourse and adaptation to life with a long-term HIV positive diagnosis', *Health*, 3: 95–119.

Crossley, M.L. (2000) *Introducing Narrative Psychology: Self, Trauma and the Construction of Meaning*. Buckingham: Open University Press.

Curl, T. and Drew, P. (2008) 'Contingency and action: a comparison of two forms of requesting', *Research on Language and Social Interaction*, 41: 1–25.

Daly, J., Willis, K., Small, R., Green, J., Welch, N., Kealy, M. and Hughes, E. (2007) 'A hierarchy of evidence for assessing qualitative health research', *Journal of Clinical Epidemiology*, 60: 43–9.

Dapkus, M.A. (1985) 'A thematic analysis of the experience of time', *Personality Processes and Individual Differences*, 49(2): 408–19.

Davies, B. and Harré, R. (1999) 'Positioning and personhood', in R. Harré and L. Van Langenhove (eds), *Positioning Theory*. Oxford: Blackwell, pp. 32–52.

DeFina, A. and Georgakopoulou, A. (2012) *Analysing Narrative: Discourse and Sociolinguistic Perspectives*. Cambridge: Cambridge University Press.

Denborough, D. (2014) *Retelling the Stories of Our Lives: Everyday Narrative Therapy to Draw Inspiration and Transform Experience*. New York: W.W. Norton.

Denzin, N. (1995) 'Symbolic interactionism', in J.A. Smith, R. Harré and L. Van Langenhove (eds), *Rethinking Psychology*. London: Sage, pp. 43–58.

Derrida, J. (1976) *Of Grammatology*. Baltimore, MD: Johns Hopkins University Press.

Derrida, J. (1981) *Dissemination*. London: Athlone Press.

Dey, I. (1999) *Grounding Grounded Theory: Guidelines for Qualitative Inquiry*. San Diego, CA: Academic Press.

Dickson, A., Knussen, C. and Flowers, P. (2008) '"That was my old life; it's almost like a pastlife now": identity crisis, loss and adjustment amongst people living with chronic fatigue syndrome', *Psychology & Health*, 23: 459–76.

Douglas, C. (2002) 'Using co-operative inquiry with Black women managers: exploring possibilities for moving from surviving to thriving', *Systemic Practice and Action Research*, 14: 249–62.

Drew, P. (2003) 'Precision and exaggeration in interaction', *American Sociological Review*, 68: 917–38.

Drew, P. (2005a) 'Conversation analysis', in K.L. Fitch and R.E. Sanders (eds), *Handbook of Language and Social Interaction*. Mahwah, NJ: Lawrence Erlbaum, pp. 71–102.

Drew, P. (2005b) 'The interactional generation of exaggerated versions in conversations', in A. Hakulinen and M. Selting (eds), *Syntax and Lexis in Conversation*. Amsterdam: Benjamins, pp. 233–56.

Drew, P. (2012) 'Turn design', in T. Stivers and J. Sidnell (eds), *Handbook of Conversation Analysis*. Oxford: Blackwell, pp. 131–49.

Drew, P., Collins, S. and Chatwin, J. (2001) 'Conversation analysis: a method for research in health care professional–patient interaction', *Health Expectations*, 4: 58–71.

Drew, P. and Couper-Kuhlen, E. (2014a) *Requesting in Social Interaction*. Amsterdam: Benjamins.

Drew, P. and Couper-Kuhlen, E. (2014b) 'Requesting – from speech act to recruitment', in P. Drew and E. Couper-Kuhlen (eds), *Requesting in Social Interaction*. Amsterdam: Benjamins, pp. 1–34.

Drew, P. and Heritage, J. (eds) (1992) *Talk at Work*. Cambridge: Cambridge University Press.

Drew, P., Toerien, M., Irvine, A. and Sainsbury, R. (2014) 'Personal adviser interviews with benefits claimants in UK Jobcentres', *Research on Language and Social Interaction*. 47: 306–16. DOI: 10.1080/08351813.2014.925669

Dunn, J.L. (2002) *Courting Disaster: Intimate Stalking, Culture, and Criminal Justice*. New York: Aldine de Gruyter.

Dunn, J.L. (2010) *Judging Victims: Why We Stigmatize Survivors and How They Reclaim Respect.* Boulder, CO: Lynne Rienner.

Eastman, J. (2012) 'Rebel manhood: the hegemonic masculinity of the Southern rock music revival', *Journal of Contemporary Ethnography*, 41(2): 189–219.

Eatough, V. and Smith, J.A. (2006) '"I feel like a scrambled egg in my head": an idiographic case study of meaning making and anger using interpretative phenomenological analysis', *Psychology & Psychotherapy*, 79: 115–35.

Eatough, V. and Smith J.A. (2008) 'Interpretative phenomenological analysis', in C. Willig and W. Stainton Rogers (eds), *Handbook of Qualitative Psychology*. London: Sage.

Edley, N. and Wetherell, M. (2001) 'Jekyll and Hyde: men's constructions of feminism and feminists', *Feminism & Psychology*, 11(4): 439–57.

Edwards, D. (1995) 'Sacks and psychology', *Theory and Psychology*, 5(3): 579–97.

Edwards, D. (2000) 'Extreme case formulations: softeners, investment and doing non-literal', *Research on Language & Social Interaction*, 33(4): 347–73.

Edwards, D. and Potter, J. (1992) *Discursive Psychology*. London: Sage.

Edwards, D. and Potter, J. (2001) 'Discursive psychology', in A.W. McHoul and M. Rapley (eds), *How to Analyse Talk in Institutional Settings: A Casebook of Methods*. London: Continuum International.

Eikeland, O. (2001) 'Action research as the hidden curriculum of the Western tradition', in P. Reason and H. Bradbury (eds), *Handbook of Action Research: Participative Inquiry and Practice*. London: Sage, pp. 145–55.

Eisner, E.W. (2003) 'On the art and science of qualitative research in psychology', in P.M. Camic, J.E. Rhodes and L. Yardley (eds), *Qualitative Research in Psychology: Expanding Perspectives in Methodology and Design*. Washington, DC: American Psychological Association, pp. 17–30.

Eisner, S. (2013) *Bi: Notes for a Bisexual Revolution*. Berkeley, CA: Seal Press.

Elbow, P. (1981) *Writing with Power*. New York: Oxford University Press.

Elliott, R., Fischer, C.T. and Rennie, D.L. (1999) 'Evolving guidelines for publication of qualitative research studies in psychology and related fields', *British Journal of Clinical Psychology*, 38: 215–29.

Ellis, S.J. and Kitzinger, C. (2002) 'Denying equality: an analysis of arguments against lowering the age of consent for sex between men', *Journal of Community & Applied Social Psychology*, 12(3): 167–80.

Fahs, B. (2014) 'Perilous patches and pitstaches: imagined versus lived experiences of women's body hair growth', *Psychology of Women Quarterly*, 38(2): 167–80.

Fals Borda, O. and Rahman, M.A. (eds) (1991) *Action and Knowledge: Breaking the Monopoly with Participatory Action Research*. New York: Intermediate Technology Publications/Apex Press.

Farquhar, C. with Das, R. (1999) 'Are focus-groups suitable for sensitive topics?', in R.S. Barbour and J. Kitzinger (eds), *Developing Focus Group Research: Politics, Theory and Practice*. London: Sage, pp. 47–63.

Farvid, P. and Braun, V. (2006) '"Most of us guys are raring to go anytime, anyplace, anywhere": male and female sexuality in *Cleo* and *Cosmo*', *Sex Roles*, 55(5/6): 295–310.

Fechner, G.T. (1860; trans. partially 1966) *Elements of Psychophysics*. New York: Holt, Rinehart and Winston.

Fern, E.F. (2001) *Advanced Focus Group Research*. Thousand Oaks, CA: Sage.

Fine, G.A. (2010) *Authors of the Storm: Meteorology and the Culture of Prediction*. Chicago, IL: University of Chicago Press.

Fish, J. and Wilkinson, S. (2000a) 'Cervical screening', in J.M. Ussher (ed.), *Women's Health: Contemporary International Perspectives*. Leicester: BPS Books, pp. 224–30.

Fish, J. and Wilkinson, S. (2000b) 'Lesbians and cervical screening', *Psychology of Women Section Review*, 2(2): 5–15.

Flick, U. (1992) 'Triangulation revisited: strategy of validation or alternative?' *Journal for the Theory of Social Behaviour*, 22: 175–97.

Flick, U. (1998) *An Introduction to Qualitative Research*. London: Sage.

Flick, U. (2002) *An Introduction to Qualitative Research* (2nd edn). London: Sage

Foucault, M. (1971) *Madness and Civilization: A History of Insanity in the Age of Reason*. London: Tavistock.

Foucault, M. (1973a) *Birth of the Clinic: An Archaeology of Medical Perception*. New York: Vintage.

Foucault, M. (1973b) *The Order of Things: An Archaeology of the Human Sciences*. New York: Vintage.

Foucault, M. (1981) *The Will to Knowledge* (*The History of Sexuality*, Vol. 1). Harmondsworth: Penguin.

Fox, F.E., Morris, M. and Rumsey, N. (2007) 'Doing synchronous online focus groups with young people: methodological reflections', *Qualitative Health Research*, 17: 539–47.

Frank, A. (2013) *The Wounded Storyteller: Body, Illness and Ethics* (2nd edn). Chicago, IL: University of Chicago Press.

Freeman, M. (1993) *Rewriting the Self: History, Memory, Narrative*. New York: Routledge.

Freeman, M. (2010) *Hindsight: The Promise and Peril of Looking Backward*. New York: Oxford University Press.

Freire, P. (1970) *Pedagogy of the Oppressed*. New York: Herder and Herder.

French, D.P., Maissi, E. and Marteau, T.M. (2005) 'The purpose of attributing cause: beliefs about the causes of myocardial infarction', *Social Science & Medicine*, 60: 1411–21.

Frith, H. (2000) 'Focusing on sex: using focus-groups in sex research', *Sexualities*, 3(3): 275–97.

Frosh, S. (2010) *Psychoanalysis Outside the Clinic: Interventions in Psychosocial Studies*. Basingstoke: Palgrave Macmillan.

Frosh, S. and Saville Young, L. (2008) 'Psychoanalytic approaches to qualitative psychology', in C. Willig and W. Stainton-Rogers (eds), *The Sage Handbook of Qualitative Research in Psychology*. London: Sage.

Frost, N.A. (ed.) (2011) *Qualitative Research Methods in Psychology: Combining Core Approaches*. Buckingham: Open University Press.

Frye, N. (1957) *Anatomy of Criticism*. Princeton, NJ: Princeton University Press.

Fulford, R. (1999) *The Triumph of Narrative*. Toronto, ON: Anansi.

Furlong, M. and McGilloway, S. (2012) 'The *Incredible Years Parenting Program* in Ireland: a qualitative analysis of the experience of disadvantaged parent', *Clinical Child Psychology and Psychiatry*, 17(4): 616–30.

Garcia-Lorenzo, L. (2010) 'Framing uncertainty: narratives, change and digital technologies', *Social Science Information*, 49: 329–50.

Garfinkel, H. (1967) *Studies in Ethnomethodology*. Englewood Cliffs, NJ: Prentice-Hall.

Garfinkel, H. (2002) *Ethnomethodology's Program*. New York: Rowman and Littlefield.

Garrett-Peters, R. (2009) '"If I don't have to work anymore, who am I?": Job-loss and collaborative self-concept repair', *Journal of Contemporary Ethnography*, 38(5): 547–83.

Gaventa, J. and Cornwall, A. (2001) 'Power and knowledge', in P. Reason and H. Bradbury (eds), *Handbook of Action Research: Participative Inquiry and Practice*. London: Sage, pp. 70–80.

Gee, J.P. (1991) 'A linguistic approach to narrative', *Journal of Narrative & Life History*, 1: 15–39.

Geertz, C. (ed.) (1973) *The Interpretation of Culture*. New York: Basic Books.

Gergen, K.J. (1973) 'Social psychology as history', *Journal of Personality & Social Psychology*, 26(2): 309–20.

Gergen, K.J. (1989) 'Social psychology and the wrong revolution', *European Journal of Social Psychology*, 19: 463–84.

Gergen, K.J. (1994) 'Exploring the postmodern: perils or potentials?', *American Psychologist*, 49: 412–16.

Gergen, K.J. and Gergen, M.M. (1984) 'The social construction of narrative accounts', in K.J. Gergen and M.M. Gergen (eds), *Historical Social Psychology*. Hillsdale, NJ: Lawrence Erlbaum, pp. 173–90.

Gergen, K.J. and Gergen, M.M. (1986) 'Narrative form and the construction of psychological science', in T. Sarbin (ed.), *Narrative Psychology: The Storied Nature of Human Conduct*. New York: Praeger, pp. 22–44.

Gergen, M. and Davis, S. (eds) (1997) *Toward a New Psychology of Gender: A Reader*. New York: Routledge.

Gilfoyle, J., Wilson, J. and Brown (1992) 'Sex, organs and audiotape: a discourse analytic approach to talking about heterosexual sex and relationships', *Feminism & Psychology*, 2(2): 209–30.

Gilligan, C. (1993) *In a Different Voice: Psychological Theory and Women's Development*. Cambridge, MA: Harvard University Press.

Giorgi, A. (1970) *Psychology as a Human Science: A Phenomenologically-Based Approach*. New York: Harper & Row.

Giorgi, A. (1997) 'The theory, practice and evaluation of the phenomenological method as a qualitative research procedure', *Journal of Phenomenological Psychology*, 28: 235–60.

Glaser, B.G. (1978) *Theoretical Sensitivity*. Mill Valley, CA: Sociology Press.

Glaser, B.G. (1992) *Emergence vs. Forcing: Basics of Grounded Theory Analysis*. Mill Valley, CA: Sociology Press.

Glaser, B.G. (1998) *Doing Grounded Theory: Issues and Discussions*. Mill Valley, CA: Sociology Press.

Glaser, B.G. (2013) *No Preconceptions: The Grounded Theory Dictum*. Mill Valley, CA: Sociology Press.

Glaser, B.G. and Strauss, A.L. (1965) *Awareness of Dying*. Chicago, IL: Aldine.

Glaser, B.G. and Strauss, A.L. (1967) *The Discovery of Grounded Theory*. Chicago, IL: Aldine.

Glynos, J., Howarth, D., Norval, A. and Speed, E. (2009) *Discourse Analysis: Varieties and Methods*. ESRC National Centre for Research Methods review paper. August 2009, NCRM/01.

Goffman, E. (1959) *The Presentation of Self in Everyday Life*. Garden City, NY: Doubleday.

Goffman, E. (1983) 'The interaction order', *American Sociological Review*, 48: 1–17.

Golsworthy, R. and Coyle, A. (1999) 'Spiritual beliefs and the search for meaning among older adults following partner loss', *Mortality*, 4: 21–40.

Goodwin, C. (1993) 'Recording interaction in natural settings', *Pragmatics*, 3(2): 181–209.

Goodwin, C. (1995) 'Co-constructing meaning in conversations with an aphasic man', *Research on Language and Social Interaction*, 28(3): 233–60.

Gray, R.E., Fergus, K.D. and Fitch, M.I. (2005) 'Two Black men with prostate cancer: a narrative approach', *British Journal of Health Psychology*, 10: 71–84.

Gray, R.E., Fitch, M.I., Fergus, K.D., Mykhalovskiy, E. and Church, K. (2002) 'Hegemonic masculinity and the experience of prostate cancer: a narrative approach', *Journal of Aging & Identity*, 7: 43–62.

Greenbaum, T.L. (2000) *Moderating Focus Group Research*. Thousand Oaks, CA: Sage.

Greenwood, D.J. and Levin, M. (1998) *Introduction to Action Research: Social Research for Social Change*. Thousand Oaks, CA: Sage.

Greenwood, D.J. and Levin, M. (2006) *Introduction to Action Research: Social Research for Social Change* (2nd revised edn). Thousand Oaks, CA: Sage.

Guest, G., MacQueen, K.M. and Namey, E.E. (2012) *Applied Thematic Analysis*. Thousand Oaks, CA: Sage.

Gurwitsch, A. (1964) *The Field of Consciousness*. Pittsburgh, PA: Duquesne University Press.

Haaken, J. (2010) *Hard Knocks: Domestic Violence and the Psychology of Storytelling*. London: Routledge.

Hammack, P.L. (2008) *Narrative and the Politics of Identity: The Cultural Psychology of Israeli and Palestinian Youth*. New York: Oxford University Press.

Harré, R. and van Langenhove, L. (eds) (1999) *Positioning Theory*. Oxford: Blackwell.

Haworth-Hoeppner, S. and Maines, D. (2005) 'A sociological account of the persistence of invalidated anorexic identities', *Symbolic Interaction*, 28(1): 1–23.

Hayes, N. (1997) 'Introduction: qualitative research and research in psychology', in N. Hayes (ed.), *Doing Qualitative Analysis in Psychology*. Hove: Erlbaum.

Hayfield, N. and Clarke, V. (2012) '"I'd be just as happy with a cup of tea": women's accounts of sex and affection in long-term heterosexual relationships', *Women's Studies International Forum*, 35(2): 67–74.

Hayfield, N., Clarke, V. and Halliwell, E. (2014) 'Bisexual women's understandings of social marginalisation: "the heterosexuals don't understand us but nor do the lesbians"', *Feminism & Psychology*, 24(3): 352–72.

Hayfield, N., Clarke, V., Halliwell, E. and Malson, H. (2013) 'Visible lesbians and invisible bisexuals: appearance and visual identities among bisexual women', *Women's Studies International Forum*, 40(5): 172–82.

Heaven, V.M. (1999) 'Narrative, believed-in imaginings and psychology's methods: an interview with Theodore R. Sarbin', *Teaching of Psychology*, 26: 300–4.

Heidegger, M. (1927; trans. 1962) *Being and Time*. Trans. J. Macquarrie and E. Robinson. Oxford: Blackwell.

Heidegger, M. (1957; trans. 1993) 'The way to language', in D.F. Krell (ed.) (1993), *Basic Writings of Martin Heidegger* (2nd edn). London: Routledge.

Heider, F. and Simmel, M. (1944) 'An experimental study of apparent behavior', *American Journal of Psychology*, 57: 243–59.

Hennink, M.M. (2007) *International Focus Group Research: A Handbook for the Health and Social Sciences*. Cambridge: Cambridge University Press.

Hennink, M.M. (2014) *Focus Group Discussions*. New York: Oxford University Press.

Henriques, J., Hollway, W., Urwin, C., Venn, C. and Walkerdine, V. (1984) *Changing the Subject: Psychology, Social Regulation and Subjectivity* (re-issued 1998). London: Methuen.

Henwood, K. and Pidgeon, N. (1992) 'Qualitative research and psychological theorizing', *British Journal of Psychology*, 83: 97–111.

Hepburn, A. and Potter, J. (2011) 'Threat: power, family mealtimes, and social influence', *British Journal of Social Psychology*, 50: 99–120.

Hepburn, A. and Potter, J. (2013) 'Crying and crying responses', in A. Peräkylä and M.-L. Sorjonen (eds), *Emotion in Interaction*. Oxford: Oxford University Press, pp. 194–210.

Hepburn, A. and Wiggins, S. (2005) 'Size matters: constructing accountable bodies in NSPCC helpline interaction', *Discourse & Society*, 16: 625–45.

Hepburn, A. and Wiggins, S. (eds) (2007) *Discursive Research in Practice: New Approaches to Psychology and Interaction*. Cambridge: Cambridge University Press.

Heritage, J. (1984) *Garfinkel and Ethnomethodology*. Cambridge: Polity Press.

Heritage, J. and Clayman, S. (2010) *Talk in Action: Interactions, Identities, and Institutions*. Chichester: Wiley-Blackwell.

Heritage, J., Elliott, M., Stivers, T., Richardson, A. and Mangione-Smith, R. (2010) 'Reducing inappropriate antibiotics prescribing: the role of online commentary on physical examination findings', *Patient Education and Counseling*, 81: 119–25.

Heritage, J. and Maynard, D. (eds) (2006) *Communication in Medical Care: Interaction between Primary Care Physicians and Patients*. Cambridge: Cambridge University Press.

Heritage, J., Robinson, J.D., Elliott, M., Beckett, M. and Wilkes, M. (2007) 'Reducing patients' unmet concerns: the difference one word can make', *Journal of General Internal Medicine*, 22: 1429–33.

Heron, J. (1971) *Experience and Method: An Inquiry into the Concept of Experiential Research*. Human Potential Research Project, University of Surrey.

Heron, J. (1996a) *Co-operative Inquiry: Research into the Human Condition*. London: Sage.

Heron, J. (1996b) 'Quality as primacy of the practical', *Qualitative Inquiry*, 2(1): 41–56.

Heron, J. (1999) *The Complete Facilitator's Handbook*. London: Kogan Page.

Heron, J. and Reason, P. (2001) 'The practice of co-operative inquiry: research "with" rather than "on" people', in P. Reason and H. Bradbury (eds), *Handbook of Action Research: Participative Inquiry and Practice*. London: Sage, pp. 179–88.

Heron, J. and Reason, P. (2008) 'Co-operative inquiry and ways of knowing', in P. Reason and H. Bradbury (eds), *Handbook of Action Research* (2nd edn). London: Sage.

Hollway, W. (1984) 'Gender difference and the production of subjectivity', in J. Henriques, W. Hollway, C. Urwin, C. Venn and V. Walkerdine (eds), *Changing the Subject: Psychology, Social Regulation and Subjectivity*. London: Methuen, pp. 227–63.

Hollway, W. and Jefferson, T. (2000) *Doing Qualitative Research Differently: Free Association, Narrative and the Interview Method*. London: Sage.

Holton, G.J. (1973) *Thematic Origins of Scientific Thought: Kepler to Einstein*. Cambridge, MA: Harvard University Press.

Hood, J. (2007) 'Orthodoxy versus power: the defining traits of grounded theory', in A. Bryant and K. Charmaz (eds), *Handbook of Grounded Theory*. London: Sage, pp. 151–64.

Horne, G., Seymour, J. and Payne, S. (2012) 'Maintaining integrity in the face of death: a grounded theory to explain the perspectives of people affected by lung cancer about the expression of wishes for end of life care', *International Journal of Nursing Studies*, 49(6): 718–26.

Howitt, D. (2010) *Introduction to Qualitative Methods in Psychology*. Harlow, UK: Prentice Hall.

Husserl, E. (1900; trans. 2001) *Logical Investigations* (Vol. I) (2nd edn). Ed. Dermot Moran. London: Routledge.

Husserl, E. (1913; trans. 1983) *Ideas Pertaining to a Pure Phenomenology and to a Phenomenological Philosophy* (Vol. I). The Hague: Martinus Nijhoff.

Husserl, E. (1925; trans. 1977) *Phenomenological Psychology*. The Hague: Martinus Nijhoff.

Husserl, E. (1931; trans. 1960) *Cartesian Meditations: An Introduction to Phenomenology*. The Hague: Martinus Nijhoff.

Husserl, E. (1936; trans. 1970) *The Crisis of European Sciences and Transcendental Phenomenology*. Evanston, IL: Northwestern University Press.

Huxley, C., Clarke, V. and Halliwell, E. (2014) 'Resisting and conforming to the "lesbian look": the importance of appearance norms for lesbian and bisexual women', *Journal of Community and Applied Social Psychology*, 24(3): 205–19.

James, W. (1890) *Principles of Psychology* (2 vols). London: Macmillan.

James, W. (1902) *The Varieties of Religious Experience: A Study in Human Nature. Being the Gifford Lectures on Natural Religion*. London: Longmans, Green and Company.

Jefferson, G. (1984) 'On the organization of laughter in talk about troubles', in J.M. Atkinson and J.C. Heritage (eds), *Structures of Social Action: Studies in Conversation Analysis*. Cambridge: Cambridge University Press, pp. 346–69.

Jefferson, G. (1985) 'An exercise in the transcription and analysis of laughter', in T.A. Dijk (ed.), *Handbook of Discourse Analysis* (Vol. 3). New York: Academic Press, pp. 25–34.

Jefferson, G. (2004) 'Glossary of transcript symbols with an introduction', in G.H. Lerner (ed.), *Conversation Analysis: Studies from the First Generation*. Amsterdam: John Benjamins.

Jefferson, G. (2015) *Talking About Troubles in Conversation* (edited by P. Drew, J. Heritage, G. Lerner and A. Pomerantz). Oxford: Oxford University Press.

Joffe, H. (2011) 'Thematic analysis', in D. Harper and A.R. Thompson (eds), *Qualitative Methods in Mental Health and Psychotherapy: A Guide for Students and Practitioners*. Chichester: Wiley, pp. 209–23.

Johnson, J.M. (1997) 'Generalizability in qualitative research: excavating the discourse', in J.M. Morse (ed.), *Completing a Qualitative Project: Details and Dialogue*. London: Sage, pp. 191–208.

Johnson, R.B., McGowan, M.W. and Turner, L.A. (2010) 'Grounded theory in practice: is it inherently a mixed method?', *Research in the Schools*, 17(2): 65–78.

Jones, D. (2013) 'A family living with Alzheimer's disease: the communicative challenges', *Dementia* [online], 18 September. DOI: 10.1177/1471301213502213.

Josselson, R. (2013) *Interviewing for Qualitative Inquiry: A Relational Approach*. New York: Guilford Press.

Jovchelovitch, S. and Bauer, M.W. (2000) 'Narrative interviewing', in M.W. Bauer and G. Gaskell (eds), *Qualitative Researching with Text, Image and Sound*. London: Sage, pp. 57–74.

Joy, M. (ed.) (1997) *Paul Ricoeur and Narrative: Context and Contestation*. Calgary, AB: University of Calgary Press.

Kamberelis, G. and Dimitriadis, G. (2013) *Focus Groups: From Structured Interviews to Collective Conversations*. Abingdon: Routledge.

Karabanow, J. (2008) 'Getting off the street: exploring the processes of young people's street exits', *American Behavioral Scientist*, 51(6): 772–88.

Keane, E. (2011) 'Dependence-deconstruction: widening participation and traditional-entry students transitioning from school to higher education in Ireland', *Teaching in Higher Education*, 16(6): 707–18.

Keane, E. (2012) 'Differential prioritising: orientations to higher education and widening participation', *International Journal of Educational Research*, 53(1): 150–9.

Kearney, A.J. (2006) 'Increasing our understanding of breast self-examination: women talk about cancer, the health care system, and being women', *Qualitative Health Research*, 16: 802–20.

Kelly, G.A. (1955) *The Psychology of Personal Constructs* (2 volumes). New York: Norton. (Reprinted 1991, London: Routledge.)

Kendall, G. and Wickham, G. (1999) *Using Foucault's Methods*. London: Sage.

Kidder, L.H. and Fine, M. (1987a) 'Qualitative and quantitative methods: when stories converge', in M.M. Mark and L. Shotland (eds), *New Directions in Program Evaluation*. San Francisco, CA: Jossey-Bass, pp. 57–75.

Kidder, M. and Fine, M. (1987b) 'Qualitative inquiry in psychology: a radical tradition', in D. Fox and I. Prilleltensky (eds), *Critical Psychology*. London: Sage.

Kitzinger, C. (2005a) 'Heteronormativity in action: reproducing the heterosexual nuclear family in after-hours medical calls', *Social Problems*, 52: 477–98.

Kitzinger, C. (2005b) '"Speaking as a heterosexual": (how) does sexuality matter for talk-in-interaction?', *Research on Language and Social Interaction*, 38: 221–65.

Kitzinger, C. and Willmott, J. (2002) '"The thief of womanhood": women's experience of polycystic ovarian syndrome', *Social Science & Medicine*, 54(3): 349–61.

Kitzinger, J. (1990) 'Audience understanding of AIDS media messages: a discussion of methods', *Sociology of Health & Illness*, 12(3): 319–55.

Kleinfeld, J. (2012) *The Frontier Romance: Environment, Culture, and Alaska Identity*. Fairbanks, AK: University of Alaska Press.

Krueger, R.A. and Casey, M.A. (2009) *Focus Groups: A Practical Guide for Applied Research* (4th edn). Thousand Oaks, CA: Sage.

Kvale, S. (ed.) 1992 *Psychology and Postmodernism*. London: Sage.

Laing, R.D. (1965) *The Divided Self: An Existential Study in Sanity and Madness*. Harmondsworth: Penguin.

Langdridge, D. (2004) *Introduction to Research Methods and Data Analysis in Psychology*. Harlow: Pearson Education.

Leydon, G., Ekberg, K. and Drew, P. (2013) '"How can I help?" Nurse call openings on a cancer helpline and implications for call progressivity', *Patient Education and Counseling*, 92: 23–30.

Livingston, J.A., Bay-Cheng, L.Y., Hequembourg, A.L., Testa, M. and Downs, J.S. (2013) 'Mixed drinks and mixed messages: adolescent girls' perspectives on alcohol and sexuality', *Psychology of Women Quarterly*, 37(1): 38–50.

Lofland, J. and Lofland, L.H. (1995) *Analyzing Social Settings*. Belmont, CA: Wadsworth.

Lois, J. (2010) 'The temporal emotion work of motherhood: homeschoolers' strategies for managing time shortage', *Gender & Society*, 24(4): 421–46.

Lunch, N. and Lunch, C. (2006) *Insights in Participatory Video*. Oxford: InsightShare.

Lykes, M.B. (1997) 'Activist participatory research among the Maya of Guatemala: constructing meanings from situated knowledge', *Journal of Social Issues*, 53: 725–46.

Lyons, A.C., Emslie, C. and Hunt, K. (2014) 'Staying "in the zone" but not passing the "point of no return": embodiment, gender and drinking in mid-life', *Sociology of Health & Illness*, 36(2): 264–77.

MacMurray, J. (1957) *The Self as Agent*. London: Faber & Faber.

MacNaghten, P. (1993) 'Discourses of nature: argumentation and power', in E. Burman and I. Parker (eds), *Discourse Analytic Research*. London: Routledge, pp. 52–72.

Madill, A., Jordan, A. and Shirley, C. (2000) 'Objectivity and reliability in qualitative analysis: realist, contextualist and radical constructionist epistemologies', *British Journal of Psychology*, 91(1): 1–20.

Maines, D.R. (1993) 'Narrative's moment and sociology's phenomena: toward a narrative sociology', *Sociological Quarterly*, 34: 17–38.

Malik, S.H. and Coulson, N. (2008) 'The male experience of infertility: a thematic analysis of an online fertility support group bulletin board', *Journal of Reproductive and Infant Psychology*, 26: 18–30.

Malinen, K., Rönkä, A. and Sevón, E. (2010) 'Good moments in parents' spousal relationships: a daily relational maintenance perspective', *Family Science*, 1(3–4): 230–41.

Malterud, K. (2001) 'Qualitative research: standards, challenges, and guidelines', *Lancet*, 358: 483–8.

Mandelbaum, J. (2014) 'How to do things with requests: request sequences at the family dinner table', in P. Drew and E. Couper-Kuhlen (eds), *Requesting in Social Interaction*. Amsterdam: Benjamins. pp. 215–41.

Maslow, A.H. (1968) *Toward a Psychology of Being* (2nd edn). Princeton, NJ: Van Nostrand.

Maughan, E. and Reason, P. (2001) 'A co-operative inquiry into deep ecology', *ReVision*, 23: 18–24.

McAdams, D. (1985) *Power, Intimacy, and the Life Story: Personological Inquiries into Identity*. New York: Guilford Press.

McAdams, D. (1993) *The Stories We Live By: Personal Myths and the Making of the Self*. New York: Morrow.

McArdle, K.L. (2002) 'Establishing a co-operative inquiry group: the perspective of a "first-time" inquirer', *Systemic Practice & Action Research*, 14: 177–90.

Mcintyre, A. (2002) 'Women researching their lives: exploring violence and identity in Belfast, the North of Ireland', *Qualitative Research*, 2(3): 387–409.

McLean, K. (2008) 'Silences and stereotypes: the impact of misconstructions of bisexuality on Australian bisexual men and women', *Gay and Lesbian Issues and Psychology Review*, 4(3): 158–65.

Mead, G. (2002) 'Developing ourselves as leaders: how can we inquire collaboratively in a hierarchical organization?', *Systemic Practice and Action Research*, 14: 191–206.

Mead, G.H. (1934) *Mind, Self and Society*. Chicago, IL: University of Chicago Press.

Merleau-Ponty, M. (1962) *Phenomenology of Perception*. London: Routledge and Kegan Paul.

Meyrick, J. (2006) 'What is good qualitative research? A first step towards a comprehensive approach to judging rigour/quality', *Journal of Health Psychology*, 11: 799–808.

Miller, G.A., Gallanter, E. and Pribram, K.H. (1960) *Plans and the Structure of Behavior*. New York: Holt, Rinehart and Winston.

Mills, J., Bonner, A. and Francis, K. (2006) 'The development of constructivist grounded theory', *International Journal of Qualitative Methods*, 5(1): 25–35.

Mischel, W. (1971) *Introduction to Personality* (5th edn). Fort Worth, TX: Harcourt, Brace, Jovanovich.

Mishler, E.G. (1986) *Research Interviewing: Context and Narrative*. Cambridge, MA: Harvard University Press.

Misiak, H. and Sexton, V.S. (1973) *Phenomenological, Existential and Humanistic Psychologies: A Historical Survey*. New York: Grune and Stratton.

Mitchell, R.C. and McCusker, S. (2008) 'Theorising the UN Convention on the Rights of the Child within Canadian post-secondary education: a grounded theory approach', *International Journal of Children's Rights*, 16(2): 159–76.

Moller, N.P., Timms, J. and Alilovic, K. (2009) 'Risky business or safety net? Trainee perceptions of personal therapy: a qualitative thematic analysis', *European Journal of Psychotherapy & Counselling*, 11(4): 369–84.

Moran, D. (2000) *Introduction to Phenomenology*. London: Routledge.

Moran, D. (2005) *Edmund Husserl: Founder of Phenomenology*. Cambridge: Polity Press.

Morgan, D.L. (1988) *Focus Groups as Qualitative Research*. Newbury Park, CA: Sage.

Morgan, D.L. (ed.) (1993) *Successful Focus Groups: Advancing the State of the Art*. Newbury Park, CA: Sage.

Morgan, D.L. (1996) 'Focus groups', *Annual Review of Sociology*, 22: 129–52.

Morgan, D.L. (1997) *Focus Groups as Qualitative Research* (2nd edn). Newbury Park, CA: Sage.

Morgan, D.L. and Krueger, R.A. (1998) *The Focus Group Kit* (6 vols). Newbury Park, CA: Sage.

Morrison, T.G., Harrington, R. and McDermott, D.T. (2010) 'Bi now, gay later: implicit and explicit binegativity among Irish university students', *Journal of Bisexuality*, 10(3): 211–32.

Morse, J.M. (1995) 'The significance of saturation', *Qualitative Health Research*, 5: 147–9.

Murphy, R. and Jackson, S. (2011) 'Bodies-as-image? The body made visible in magazine *love your body* content', *Women's Studies Journal*, 25(1): 17–30.

Murray, M. (1997a) 'A narrative approach to health psychology: background and potential', *Journal of Health Psychology*, 2: 9–20.

Murray, M. (1997b) *Narrative Health Psychology*. Visiting Scholar Series No. 7, Massey University, New Zealand.

Murray, M. (1999) 'The storied nature of health and illness', in M. Murray and K. Chamberlain (eds), *Qualitative Health Psychology: Theories and Methods*. London: Sage, pp. 47–63.

Murray, M. (2000) 'Levels of narrative analysis in health psychology', *Journal of Health Psychology*, 5: 337–48.

Murray, M. (2002) 'Narrative accounts of breast cancer'. [Interviews with women who had undergone surgery for breast cancer.] Unpublished raw data.

Murray, M. and Sools, A. (2014) 'Narrative research in clinical and health psychology', in P. Rohleder and A. Lyons (eds), *Qualitative Research in Clinical and Health Psychology*. London: Palgrave Macmillan.

Natanson, M. (1973) *The Social Dynamics of George H. Mead*. The Hague: Martinus Nijhoff.

Neisser, U. (1967) *Cognitive Psychology*. New York: Appleton-Century-Crofts.

Nelson, G. and Prilleltensky, I. (eds) (2005) *Community Psychology: In Pursuit of Liberation and Well-being*. Basingstoke: Palgrave.

Nicolson, P. and Burr, J. (2003) 'What is "normal" about women's (hetero)sexual desire and orgasm? A report of an in-depth interview study', *Social Science & Medicine*, 57(9): 1735–45.

O'Byrne, R., Rapley, M. and Hansen, S. (2006) '"You couldn't say 'No', could you?": young men's understandings of sexual refusal', *Feminism & Psychology*, 16(2): 133–54.

O'Connell, D.C. and Kowal, S. (1995) 'Basic principles of transcription', in J.A. Smith, R. Harré and L. Van Langenhove (eds), *Rethinking Methods in Psychology*. London: Sage, pp. 93–105.

Olson, K. (2011) *Essentials of Qualitative Interviewing*. Walnut Creek, CA: Left Coast Press.

Opperman, E., Braun, V., Clarke, V. and Rogers, C. (2014) '"It feels so good it almost hurts": young adults' experiences of orgasm and sexual pleasure', *Journal of Sex Research*, 51(5): 503–15.

Packer, M. and Addison, R. (eds) (1989) *Entering the Circle: Hermeneutic Investigations in Psychology*. Albany, NY: State University of New York.

Palmer, R.E. (1969) *Hermeneutics: Interpretation Theory in Schleiermacher, Dilthey, Heidegger, and Gadamer*. Evanston, IL: Northwestern University Press.

Parker, I. (1992) *Discourse Dynamics: Critical Analysis for Social and Individual Psychology*. London: Routledge.

Parker, I. (1994a) 'Reflexive research and the grounding of analysis: social psychology and the psy-complex', *Journal of Community & Applied Social Psychology*, 4(4): 239–52.

Parker, I. (1994b) 'Qualitative research', in P. Banister, E. Burman, I. Parker, M. Taylor and C. Tindall (eds), *Qualitative Methods in Psychology: A Research Guide*. Buckingham: Open University Press.

Parker, I. (1997) 'Discursive psychology', in D. Fox and I. Prilleltensky (eds), *Critical Psychology: An Introduction*. London: Sage, pp. 284–98.

Parker, I. (1999) 'Critical reflexive humanism and critical constructionist psychology', in *Social Constructionist Psychology: A Critical Analysis of Theory and Practice*. Buckingham: Open University Press.

Peräkylä, A. (1995) *AIDS Counselling: Institutional Interaction and Clinical Practice*. Cambridge: Cambridge University Press.

Piran, N. (2001) 'Re-inhabiting the body from the inside out: girls transform their school environment', in D.L. Tolman and M. Brydon-Miller (eds), *From Subjects to Subjectivities: A Handbook of Interpretive and Participatory Methods*. New York: New York University Press, pp. 218–38.

Plummer, K. (2000) *Documents of Life* (2nd edn). London: Sage.

Polanyi, M. (1962) *Personal Knowledge: Towards a Postcritical Philosophy* (2nd edn). Chicago, IL: University of Chicago Press.

Polkinghorne, D. (1988) *Narrative Knowing and the Human Sciences*. Albany, NY: State University of New York.

Polkinghorne, D. (1996) 'Narrative knowing and the study of human lives', in J.C. Birren, G.M. Kenyon, J.-E. Ruth, J.J.F. Schroots and T. Svensson (eds), *Aging and Biography*. New York: Springer, pp. 77–99.

Pomerantz, A. (1986) 'Extreme case formulations: a new way of legitimating claims', in G. Button, P. Drew and J. Heritage (eds), *Human Studies (Interaction and Language Use Special Issue)*, 9: 219–30.

Pomerantz, A. and Fehr, B.J. (1996) 'Conversation analysis: an approach to the study of social action as sense-making practices', in T. Van Dijk (ed.), *Discourse as Social Interaction* (Vol. 2). London: Sage, pp. 64–91.

Pope, C. and Mays, N. (1995) 'Rigour and qualitative research', *British Medical Journal*, 311: 42–5.

Potter, J. (1996) *Representing Reality: Discourse, Rhetoric and Social Construction*. London: Sage.

Potter, J. and Hepburn, A. (2005) 'Qualitative interviews in psychology: problems and possibilities', *Qualitative Research in Psychology*, 2: 38–55.

Potter, J. and Wetherell, M. (1987) *Discourse and Social Psychology: Beyond Attitudes and Behaviour*. London: Sage.

Potter, J. and Wetherell, M. (1995) 'Discourse analysis', in J.A. Smith, R. Harré and L. Van Langenhove (eds), *Rethinking Methods in Psychology*. London: Sage, pp. 80–92.

Prus, R.A. (1987) 'Generic social processes: maximizing conceptual development in ethnographic research', *Journal of Contemporary Ethnography*, 16: 250–93.

Rance, N.M., Clarke, V. and Moller, N.P. (2014) '"If I see somebody… I'll immediately scope them out": anorexia nervosa clients' perceptions of their therapists' body', *Eating Disorders*, 22(2): 111–20.

Randall, R. and Southgate, J. (1980) *Co-operative and Community Group Dynamics … Or Your Meetings Needn't Be So Appalling*. London: Barefoot Books.

Reason, P. (1988) 'Whole person medical practice', in P. Reason (ed.), *Human Inquiry in Action*. London: Sage, pp. 102–26.

Reason, P. (2002) *The Practice of Co-operative Inquiry*. Special issue of *Systemic Practice & Action Research*, 15(3): 169–270.

Reason, P. (2006) 'Choice and quality in action research practice', *Journal of Management Inquiry*, 15(2): 187–203.

Reason, P. and Bradbury, H. (2001a) 'Inquiry and participation in search of a world worthy of human aspiration', in P. Reason and H. Bradbury (eds), *Handbook of Action Research: Participative Inquiry and Practice*. London: Sage, pp. 1–14.

Reason, P. and Bradbury, H. (2001b) 'Preface', in P. Reason and H. Bradbury (eds), *Handbook of Action Research: Participative Inquiry and Practice*. London: Sage, pp. xiii–xxxi.

Reason, P. and Bradbury, H. (eds) (2006) *Handbook of Action Research* (concise paperback edn). London: Sage.

Reason, P. and Bradbury, H. (eds) (2008) *Handbook of Action Research* (2nd edn). London: Sage.

Reavey, P. (ed.) (2011) *Visual Methods in Psychology: Using and Interpreting Images in Qualitative Research*. Hove: Psychology Press.

Reuber, M., Monzoni, C., Sharrack, B. and Plug L. (2009) 'Using interactional and linguistic analysis to distinguish between epileptic and psychogenic nonepileptic seizures: a prospective, blinded multirater study', *Epilepsy and Behavior*, 16: 139–44.

Ricoeur, P. (1970) *Freud and Philosophy: An Essay on Interpretation*. New Haven, CT: Yale University Press.

Ricoeur, P. (1972) 'Appropriation', in M.J. Valdes (ed.) (1991) *A Ricoeur Reader: Reflection and Imagination*. Toronto, ON: University of Toronto Press, pp. 86–98.

Ricoeur, P. (1984) *Time and Narrative* (Vol. I). Trans. K. McLaughlin and D. Pellauer. Chicago, IL: University of Chicago Press.

Ricoeur, P. (1987) 'Life: a story in search of a narrator'. In M.J. Valdes (ed.) (1991) *A Ricoeur Reader: Reflection and Imagination*. Toronto, ON: University of Toronto Press, pp. 423–37.

Ricoeur, P. (1988) *Time and Narrative* (Vol. III). Chicago, IL: University of Chicago Press.

Riessman, C.K. (2008) *Narrative Methods for the Human Sciences*. Thousand Oaks, CA: Sage.

Riley, S. and Scharff, C. (2013) 'Feminism vs femininity? Exploring feminist dilemmas through cooperative inquiry research', *Feminism & Psychology*, 23(2): 207–23. DOI: 10.1177/0959353512454615.

Robinson, I. (1990) 'Personal narratives, social careers and medical courses: analysing life trajectories in autobiographies of people with multiple sclerosis', *Social Science and Medicine*, 30: 1173–86.

Robrecht, L.C. (1995) 'Grounded theory – evolving methods', *Qualitative Health Research*, 5: 169–77.

Robson, C., Drew, P. and Reuber, M. (2012) 'Catastrophising and normalising in conversations between doctors and patients with epileptic and psychogenic nonepileptic seizures', *Seizure: European Journal of Epilepsy*, 21: 795–801.

Rock, P. (1979) *The Making of Symbolic Interactionism*. London: Macmillan.

Rogers, C.R. (1967) *On Becoming a Person: A Therapist's View of Psychotherapy*. London: Constable.

Rolfe, A., Orford, J. and Dalton, S. (2009) 'Women, alcohol and femininity: a discourse analysis of women heavy drinkers' accounts', *Journal of Health Psychology*, 14(2): 326–35.

Rose, N. (1999) *Governing the Soul: The Shaping of the Private Self* (2nd edn). London: Free Association Books.

Rudolph, J.W., Taylor, S.S. and Foldy, E.G. (2001) 'Collaborative off-line reflection: a way to develop skill in action science and action inquiry', in P. Reason and H. Bradbury (eds), *Handbook of Action Research: Participative Inquiry and Practice*. London: Sage.

Sacks, H. (1992) *Lectures on Conversation* (Vols I and II). Ed. G. Jefferson. Oxford: Blackwell.

Sarbin, T. (ed.) (1986) *Narrative Psychology: The Storied Nature of Human Conduct*. New York: Praeger.

Sarbin, T.R. (1997) 'The poetics of identity', *Theory & Psychology*, 7: 67–82.

Sartre, J.-P. (1958) *Being and Nothingness*. New York: Philosophical Library.

Schegloff, E.A. (1992a) 'Introduction', in H. Sacks, *Lectures on Conversation*, Vol. 1: *Fall 1964– Spring 1968*. Ed. G. Jefferson. Oxford: Blackwell, pp. ix–lxii.

Schegloff, E.A. (1992b) 'Repair after next turn: the last structurally provided-for place for the defense of intersubjectivity in conversation', *American Journal of Sociology*, 95(5): 1295–345.

Schegloff, E.A. (1993) 'Reflections on quantification in the study of conversation', *Research on Language & Social Interaction*, 26: 99–128.

Schegloff, E.A. (1996) 'Confirming allusions: toward an empirical account of action', *American Journal of Sociology*, 104(1): 161–216.

Schegloff, E.A. (2007) *Sequence Organisation in Interaction: A Primer in Conversation Analysis*. New York: Cambridge University Press.

Schutz, A. (1972) *The Phenomenology of the Social World*. London: Heinemann.

Scott, J.S. (1997) 'Dietrich Bonhoeffer, *Letters and Papers from Prison* and Paul Ricoeur's "Hermeneutics of testimony"', in M. Joy (ed.), *Paul Ricoeur and Narrative: Context and Contestation*. Calgary, AB: University of Calgary Press, pp. 13–24.

Seidman, I.E. (2006) *Interviewing as Qualitative Research: A Guide for Researchers in Education and the Social Sciences* (2nd edn). New York: Teachers College Press.

Selener, D. (1997) *Participatory Action Research and Social Change: Cornell Participatory Action Research Network*. Ithaca, NY: Cornell University Press.

Seymour-Smith, S., Wetherell, M. and Phoenix, A. (2002) '"My wife ordered me to come!": a discursive analysis of doctors' and nurses' accounts of men's use of general practitioners', *Journal of Health Psychology*, 7(3): 253–67.

Shaw, R.L., Larkin, M. and Flowers, P. (2014) 'Expanding the evidence base within evidence-based healthcare: thinking differently about evidence', *Evidence-Based Medicine* [Online], 10.1136/eb-2014-101791.

Shotter, J. (1993) *Cultural Politics of Everyday Life: Social Construction and Knowing of the Third Kind*. Buckingham: Open University Press.

Sidnell, J. (2010) *Conversation Analysis*. Chichester: Wiley-Blackwell.

Sidnell, J. and Stivers, T. (2013) *The Handbook of Conversation Analysis*. Chichester: Wiley-Blackwell.

Silver, C. and Fielding, N. (2008) 'Using computer packages in qualitative research', in C. Willig and W. Stainton Rogers (eds), *The Sage Handbook of Qualitative Research in Psychology*. Los Angeles, CA: Sage, pp. 334–51.

Silverman, D. (1993) *Interpreting Qualitative Data*. London: Sage.

Silverman, D. (1997) *Discourses of Counselling: HIV Counselling as Social Interaction*. London: Sage.

Smith, B. (2010) 'Narrative inquiry: ongoing conversations and questions for sport psychology research', *International Review of Sport Psychology*, 3(1): 87–107.

Smith, J.A. (1996) 'Beyond the divide between cognition and discourse: using interpretative phenomenological analysis in health psychology', *Psychology & Health*, 11: 261–71.

Smith, J.A. (1999) 'Towards a relational self: social engagement during pregnancy and psychological preparation for motherhood', *British Journal of Social Psychology*, 38: 409–26.

Smith, J.A. (2007) 'Hermeneutics, human sciences and health: linking theory and practice', *International Journal of Qualitative Studies on Health & Well-being*, 2: 3–11.

Smith, J.A. (2011) '"We could be diving for pearls": the value of the gem in experiential qualitative psychology', *Qualitative Methods in Psychology Bulletin*, 12: 6–15.

Smith, J.A., Flowers, P. and Larkin, M. (2009) *Interpretative Phenomenological Analysis: Theory, Method and Research*. London: Sage.

Smith, J.A., Harré, R. and Van Langenhove, L. (1995) 'Idiography', in J.A. Smith, R. Harré and L. Van Langenhove (eds), *Rethinking Psychology*. London: Sage, pp. 59–69.

Smith, J.A. and Osborn, M. (2007) 'Pain as an assault on the self: an interpretative phenomenological analysis', *Psychology and Health*, 22: 517–34.

Smith, J.A. and Rhodes, J. (2014) 'Being depleted and being shaken: an interpretative phenomenological analysis of the experiential features of a first episode of depression', *Psycholology and Psychotherapy*. DOI: 10.1111/papt.12034

Speer, S. and McPhillips, R. (2013) 'Patients' perspectives on psychiatric consultations in the Gender Identity Clinic: implications for patient-centred communication', *Patient Education & Counseling*, 91: 385–91.

Spencer, L., Ritchie, J., Lewis, J. and Dillon, L. (2003) *Quality in Qualitative Evaluation: A Framework for Assessing Research Evidence*. Government Chief Social Researcher's Office. Available at: www.civilservice.gov.uk/wp-content/uploads/2011/09/a_quality_framework_tcm6-38740.pdf (accessed 27/04/2014).

Squire, C. (2013) *Living with HIV and ARVs: Three-letter Lives*. London: Palgrave Macmillan.

Srivastva, S., Obert, S.L. and Neilson, E. (1977) 'Organizational analysis through group processes: a theoretical perspective', in C.L. Cooper (ed.), *Organizational Development in the UK and USA*. London: Macmillan, pp. 83–111.

Stafford Smith, S. (2010) 'Fixed, weighted and misrecognised in space: young women's body conscious experiences in a co-operative inquiry', Masters in Research dissertation, University of Bath.

Stainton Rogers, R., Stenner, P., Gleeson, K. and Stainton Rogers W. (1995) *Social Psychology: A Critical Agenda*. Cambridge: Polity Press.

Star, S.L. (1989) *Regions of the Mind: Brain Research and the Quest for Scientific Certainty*. Stanford, CA: Stanford University Press.

Stephens, C. (2010) 'Narrative analysis in health psychology research: personal, dialogical and social stories of health', *Health Psychology Review*, 5: 62–78.

Stephens, C. and Breheny, M. (2013) 'Narrative analysis in psychological research: an integrated approach to interpreting stories', *Qualitative Research in Psychology*, 10: 14–27.

Stewart, D.W. and Shamdasani, P.N. (2014) *Focus Groups: Theory and Practice* (3rd edn). Thousand Oaks, CA: Sage.

Stewart, K. and Williams, M. (2005) 'Researching online populations: the use of focus groups for social research', *Qualitative Research*, 5(4): 395–416.

Stiles, W. (1993) 'Quality control in qualitative research', *Clinical Psychology Review*, 13: 593–618.

Stivers, T. (2007) *Prescribing under Pressure: Parent–Physician Conversations and Antibiotics*. New York: Oxford University Press.

Stokoe, E. (2014) 'The conversation-analytic role-play method (CARM): a method for training communication skills as an alternative to simulated role-play', *Research on Language & Social Interaction*, 47(3): 255–65.

Strauss, A.L. (1987) *Qualitative Analysis for Social Scientists*. New York: Cambridge University Press.

Strauss, A.L. (1993) *Continual Permutations of Action*. New York, NY: Aldine de Gruyter.

Strauss, A.L. and Corbin, J.A. (1990) *Basics of Qualitative Research: Grounded Theory Procedures and Techniques*. Newbury Park, CA: Sage.

Strauss, A.L. and Corbin, J.A. (1998) *Basics of Qualitative Research: Grounded Theory Procedures and Techniques* (2nd edn). Newbury Park, CA: Sage.

Strauss, A.L. and Glaser, B.G. (1970) *Anguish*. Mill Valley, CA: Sociology Press.

Taylor, G.W. and Ussher, J.M. (2001) 'Making sense of S&M: a discourse analytic account', *Sexualities*, 4(3): 293–314.

ten Have, P. (1999) *Doing Conversation Analysis: A Practical Guide*. London: Sage.

Thomas, J. (1993) *Doing Critical Ethnography*. Newbury Park, CA: Sage.

Thomas, W.I. and Znaniecki, F. (1918) *The Polish Peasant in Europe and America*. Chicago, IL: University of Chicago Press.

Thornberg, R. (2007) 'A classmate in distress: schoolchildren as bystanders and their reasons for how they act', *Social Psychology of Education*, 10(1): 5–28.

Thornberg, R. (2009) 'The moral construction of the good pupil embedded in school rules', *Education, Citizenship and Social Justice*, 4(3): 245–61.

Thornberg, R. (2010) 'A student in distress: moral frames and bystander behavior in school', *The Elementary School Journal*, 110(4): 585–608.

Thornberg, R. (2012) 'Informed grounded theory', *Scandinavian Journal of Educational Research*, 55(1): 1–17.

Thornberg, R. and Charmaz, K. (2014) 'Grounded theory and theoretical coding', in U. Flick (ed.), *Handbook of Qualitative Data Analysis*. London: Sage, pp. 153–69.

Thornberg, R. and Jungert, T. (2014) 'School bullying and the mechanisms of moral disengagement', *Aggressive Behavior*, 40(1): 99–108.

Timotijevic, L. and Breakwell, G.M. (2000) 'Migration and threat to identity', *Journal of Community & Applied Social Psychology*, 10: 355–72.

Todd, Z., Nerlich, B., McKeown, S. and Clarke, D.D. (2004) *Mixing Methods in Psychology: The Integration of Qualitative and Quantitative Methods in Theory and Practice*. Hove: Psychology Press.

Tong, A., Sainsbury, P. and Craig, J. (2007) 'Consolidated criteria for reporting qualitative research (COREQ): a 32-item checklist for interviews and focus groups', *International Journal of Quality in Health Care*, 19(6): 349–57.

Tong, R. (1991) *Feminist Thought: A Comprehensive Introduction*. London: Routledge.

Torre, M.E., Fine, M., Boudin, K., Bowen, I., Clark, J., Hylton, D., Martinez, M., Roberts, M.R.A., Smart, P. and Upegui, D. (2001) 'A space for co-constructing counter stories under surveillance', *Under the Covers: Theorising the Politics of Counter Stories*. Special issue of *The International Journal of Critical Psychology*, 4: 149–66.

Toulmin, S. (1990) *Cosmopolis: The Hidden Agenda of Modernity*. New York: Free Press.

Tuckman, B. (1965) 'Development sequences in small groups', *Psychological Bulletin*, 63: 419–27.

Ussher, J. (ed.) (1997) *Body Talk: The Material and Discursive Regulation of Sexuality, Madness and Reproduction*. London: Routledge.

Ussher, J.M. (1999) 'Eclecticism and methodological pluralism: the way forward for feminist research', *Psychology of Women Quarterly*, 23(1): 41–6.

van Manen, M. (1990) *Researching Lived Experience: Human Science for an Action Sensitive Pedagogy*. London, ON: Althouse Press.

Vaughn, S., Schumm, J.S. and Sinagub, J. (1996) *Focus Group Interviews in Education and Psychology*. Thousand Oaks, CA: Sage.

Veale, A. and Stavrou, A. (2007) 'Former Lord's Resistance Army child soldier abductees: explorations of identity in reintegration and reconciliation', *Peace and Conflict: Journal of Peace Psychology*, 13(3): 273–92.

Wasserman, J.A. and Clair, J.M. (2010) *At Home on the Street: People, Poverty, and a Hidden Culture of Homelessness*. Boulder, CO: Lynne Rienner.

Watson, J.B. (1913) 'Psychology as a behaviorist views it', *Psychological Review*, 20: 158–77.

Weingarten, K. (2001) 'Making sense of illness narratives: braiding theory, practice and the embodied life', in Dulwich Centre Publications (ed.), *Working with the Stories of Women's Lives*. Adelaide, SA: Dulwich Centre Publications. Available at: www.dulwichcentre.com.au/illness-narratives.html (accessed 15/05/2014).

Welford, A.T. (1968) *Fundamentals of Skill*. London: Methuen.

Welsh, S., Carr, J., Macquarie, B. and Huntley, A. (2006) '"I'm not thinking of it as sexual harassment": understanding harassment across race and citizenship', *Gender & Society*, 20(1): 87–107.

Wertz, F.J., Charmaz, K., McMullen, L.J., Josselson, R., Anderson, R. and McSpadden, E. (2011) *Five Ways of Doing Qualitative Analysis: Phenomenological Psychology, Grounded Theory, Discourse Analysis, Narrative Research, and Intuitive Inquiry*. New York: Guilford Press.

Wetherell, M. (1998) 'Positioning and interpretative repertoires: conversation analysis and post-structuralism in dialogue', *Discourse & Society*, 9(3): 387–413.

Wetherell, M. (2001) 'Debates in discourse research', in M. Wetherell, S. Taylor and S.J. Yates (eds), *Discourse Theory and Practice: A Reader*. London: Sage.

Wetherell, M. and Potter, J. (1992) *Mapping the Language of Racism: Discourse and the Legitimation of Exploitation*. Hemel Hempstead: Harvester Wheatsheaf.

White, M. and Epston, D. (1990) *Narrative Means to Therapeutic Ends*. New York: W.W. Norton.

Whitty, M.T. (2005) 'The realness of cybercheating: men's and women's representations of unfaithful internet relationships', *Social Science Computer Review*, 23(1): 57–67.

Whyte, W.F. (1943/1955) *Street Corner Society*. Chicago, IL: University of Chicago Press.

Wiggins, S. and Potter, J. (2008) 'Discursive psychology', in C. Willig and W. Stainton Rogers (eds), *The Sage Handbook of Qualitative Research in Psychology*. London: Sage, pp. 73–90.

Wiggins, S., Potter, J. and Wildsmith, A. (2001) 'Eating your words: discursive psychology and the reconstruction of eating practices', *Journal of Health Psychology*, 6(1): 5–15.

Wilkinson, S. (1998a) 'Focus groups in health research: exploring the meanings of health and illness', *Journal of Health Psychology*, 3: 329–48.

Wilkinson, S. (1998b) 'Focus group methodology: a review', *International Journal of Social Research Methodology*, 1: 181–203.

Wilkinson, S. (1999) 'Focus groups: a feminist method', *Psychology of Women Quarterly*, 23: 221–44.

Wilkinson, S. (2000a) 'Breast cancer: a feminist perspective', in J.M. Ussher (ed.), *Women's Health: Contemporary International Perspectives*. Leicester: BPS Books, pp. 230–7.

Wilkinson, S. (2000b) 'Women with breast cancer talking causes: comparing content, biographical and discursive analyses', *Feminism and Psychology*, 10: 431–60.

Wilkinson, S. (2006) 'Analysing interaction in focus groups,' in P. Drew, G. Raymond and D. Weinberg (eds), *Talk and Interaction in Social Research Methods*. London: Sage, pp. 50–62.

Wilkinson, S. (2007) 'Breast cancer: lived experience and feminist action', in M. Morrow, O. Hankivsky and C. Varcoe (eds), *Women's Health in Canada: Critical Theory, Policy and Practice*. Toronto, ON: University of Toronto Press, pp. 408–33.

Wilkinson, S. (2011) 'Analysing focus group data', in D. Silverman (ed.), *Qualitative Research: Issues of Theory, Method and Practice* (3rd edn). London: Sage, pp. 168–84.

Wilkinson, S., Joffe, H. and Yardley, L. (2004) 'Qualitative data collection', in D. Marks and L. Yardley (eds), *Research Methods for Clinical and Health Psychology*. London: Sage, pp. 39–55.

Wilkinson, S. and Kitzinger, C. (eds) (1995) *Feminism and Discourse*. London: Sage.

Williams, L., Labonte, R. and O'Brien, M. (2003) 'Empowering social action through narratives of identity and culture', *Health Promotion International*, 18: 33–40.

Willig, C. (1995) '"I wouldn't have married the guy if I'd have to do that": heterosexual adults' accounts of condom use and their implications for sexual practice', *Journal of Community & Applied Social Psychology*, 5: 75–87.

Willig, C. (1998) 'Constructions of sexual activity and their implications for sexual practice: lessons for sex education', *Journal of health Psychology*, 3(3): 383–92.

Willig, C. (ed.) (1999) *Applied Discourse Analysis: Social and Psychological Interventions*. Buckingham: Open University Press.

Willig, C. (2001) *Introducing Qualitative Research in Psychology: Adventures in Theory and Method*. Buckingham: Open University Press.

Willig, C. (2013) *Introducing Qualitative Research in Psychology* (3rd edn). Buckingham: Open University Press.

Willig, C. and dew Valour, K. (1999) 'Love and the work ethic: constructions of intimate relationships as achievement', paper presented at the London Conference of British Psychological Society, London, 20–21 December.

Willig, C. and dew Valour, K. (2000) '"Changed circumstances", "a way out" or "to the bitter end"? A narrative analysis of 16 relationship break-ups', paper presented at the Annual Conference of Social Psychology Section of British Psychological Society, Nottingham, 6–8 September.

Winter, D.G. and McClelland, D.C. (1978) 'Thematic analysis: an empirically derived measure of the effects of liberal arts education', *Journal of Educational Psychology*, 70(1): 8–16.

Wittgenstein, L. (1953) *Philosophical Investigations*. Oxford: Blackwell.

Wodak, R. (1996) *Disorders of Discourse*. Harlow: Addison-Wesley Longman.

Woodrum, E. (1984) 'Mainstreaming "content analysis" in social science: methodological advantages, obstacles, and solutions', *Social Science Research*, 13(1): 1–19.

Wooffitt, R. (2005) *Conversation Analysis and Discourse Analysis: A Comparative and Critical Introduction*. London: Sage.

Wootton, A. (1997) *Interaction and the Development of Mind*. Cambridge: Cambridge University Press.

Wundt, W. (1874; trans. 1904) *Principles of Physiological Psychology*. New York: Macmillan.

Yardley, L. (ed.) (1997a) *Material Discourses of Health and Illness*. London: Routledge.

Yardley, L. (1997b) 'Introducing discursive methods', in L. Yardley (ed.), *Material Discourses of Health and Illness*. London: Routledge, pp. 25–49.

Yardley, L. (2000) 'Dilemmas in qualitative health research', *Psychology & Health*, 15: 215–28.

Yardley, L. and Bishop, F.L. (2007) 'Mixing qualitative and quantitative methods', in C. Willig and W. Stainton Rogers (eds), *Handbook of Qualitative Methods in Psychology*. London: Sage.

Yardley, L., Bishop, F.L., Beyer, N., Hauer, K., Kempen, G.I.J.M., Piot-Ziegler, C., Todd, C., Cuttelod, T., Horne, M., Lanta, K. and Rosell, A. (2006) 'Older people's views of falls prevention interventions in six European countries', *The Gerontologist*, 46(5): 650–60.

Yardley, L., Donovan-Hall, M., Francis, K. and Todd, C. (2006) 'Older people's views about falls prevention: a qualitative study', *Health Education Research*, 21: 508–17.

Yardley, L., Donovan-Hall, M., Francis, K. and Todd, C.J. (2007) 'Attitudes and beliefs that predict older people's intention to undertake strength and balance training', *Journal of Gerontology*, 62B: 119–25.

Yaskowich, K.M. and Stam, H.J. (2003) 'Cancer narratives and the cancer support group', *Journal of Health Psychology*, 8: 720–37.

Index